DØ7Ø7122

Acknowledgments

I wish to express thanks to my wife, Elizabeth, who is a writer of diaries and a taker of notes at family gatherings. It was she who gathered, organized and filed a large number of bits and pieces written by Mother and found among her effects at the time of her death. I am indebted to my older sister Grace for many memories shared and for her delightful unpublished story, "Santa is Pure Magic," based on her Christmas experience as a small child in Goshen, Utah, in 1916. I wish to thank her son Robert Jenkins for sharing the story.

My thanks to sister Connie, who has shared many of her memories, and to my younger brother David and his wife Alice, who have shared their memories as well as their transcribed copies of many of Mother's handwritten reflections. I am indebted to Amy Moser for her research on roads, trains, and small towns in Salt Lake County; Irma Penrod, senior citizen of Goshen, who grew up there and kindly shared her memories; the pastor of the Community Presbyterian Church of Brigham City, who provided a history of his church; the secretary of First Presbyterian Church of Salt Lake City who sent copies of church records. I am grateful to the Boise Public Library for providing me with microfilm of the Salt Lake Tribune and The Deseret News for 1923. I appreciate the library research of Mrs. Frances Brass of the Perth Tourist Board in Scotland and her mapping of the places of importance to my mother.

My special thanks go to Naida West, excellent writer of history novels. She is my niece as well as my chief editor and publisher. Thanks also to her assistant editor and sister, Marguerite Flower.

Don Ian Smith
Salmon, Idaho

Photographs and Maps

Symon's Daughter

A Memoir of Elizabeth Symon Smith

by Don Ian Smith

Naida Smith West
July 19, 2012

Bridge House Books

Library of Congress Catalog Card No. 2001-131221
ISBN 0-9653487-8-4
Cover design by Allen Takeshita, allent@neodesigninc.com
Background cover photo by Christine M. Miller, MilChristine@aol.com
Printed by Hignell Book Printing, Canada

Table of Contents

"From everlasting to everlasting. . ."

Prologue

The funeral service for my mother was a statement of hope and comfort, just as her life had been. A choir of her grandchildren sang two of her favorite hymns: *Rock of Ages* and *Abide With Me.* They sang well and I was wishing she could have heard them when I felt her presence so near that I was certain she could hear their voices.

My two sisters and three brothers were there with me in the front of the church. A minister who had been her pastor many years earlier led the service. He had known her at the peak of her vigor and knew well her intense interest in religion and politics. They had been good friends who could speak their minds freely to each other. He recalled for us a conversation he had shared with Elizabeth. She expressed her opinion on a political matter in a way that reflected her passionate concern for the poor. He responded: "Elizabeth, you know that is just mush!"

As squarely as a woman five feet tall can look into the eyes of a man who stands six feet and four inches, she stated emphatically, "George, the world is dying for mush!" He told the assembled mourners, "I always admired her spunk."

That conversation had occurred many years earlier. Now her flight for the one way trip into eternity had been called. With her boarding pass of faith she had walked with confidence through the gate and was happily "flying the friendly skies." The minister read the wonderful words from Psalm 23, which Elizabeth believed with all her heart:

Though I walk through the valley of the shadow of death, I will fear no evil, for Thou art with me ...

He read from Psalm 90:

Lord, thou hast been our dwelling place in all generations.

I felt Mother's presence by my side assuring me that God was with me now. He was with me as he had been with her when he guided her childhood in Scotland. He was with me as he had been with her when, an orphan girl of 18, she had traveled alone to America to take a teaching job in Utah; as he had been with her through the lonely year she spent in a small community where she was the only non-Mormon. He had been beside her during the Great Depression as she struggled to raise her children under primitive conditions on a farm in Idaho.

God was with me as he had been with her when she stood beside the grave of my father and committed her companion of fifty years into God's care. Now, I knew God was with me and would be with my children and their children. The words: "*From everlasting to everlasting thou art God*" took on a new and very personal meaning.

So my children will know something about my early life and background, I was born in Perth, Scotland, March, 20, 1887. . .

1 The Manse

The frustrated little girl grabbed the iron bars of the gate and angrily yanked on them, wishing she could rip them apart. They stood for all the things that limited her life. Longingly she watched the rowdy children playing in the street and listened with envy to their laughter and shouting. She yearned to be one of them. They were playing a running and dodging game, and she loved to run and dodge. She was small for her eight years, having recovered from the serious bone infection. It had started when she was a little past three and lasted for almost a year. Her right foot and lower leg had given her weeks and months of pain. The best available doctors from Perth and Edinburgh had studied it. In an effort to stop the infection they had, from time to time, scraped the bone. For several days after each of these treatments the pain had been intense. But now this nightmare of misery lay behind her. She had made a remarkable recovery—some members of her father's congregation called it "miraculous." Now she had only a slight limp, one that didn't show at all when she was running, a limp she was determined to overcome.

Though it had been a long time ago she would never forget the night she heard her parents talking. Her mother had been sitting at her bedside reading to her. Liz, as she was affectionately called by the family, was tired and had closed her eyes. It was well past her regular bedtime. Assuming she was asleep, Mother gently tucked the blanket around her shoulders, quietly turned off the light, and left the room. Liz found it easier to continue as though she were asleep than to open her eyes and bid Mother good night.

She was almost asleep when the sound of Father's footsteps in the hall just outside her room roused her a bit. The door was slightly ajar, the way she liked them to keep it while she slept. She heard their quiet greeting and Mother's soft words. "She's sleepin' now, John. She loves it when you're home in time to kiss her good night and have a wee prayer together, but it's late. We'd best let her sleep. She surely needs all the rest she can get."

"You're right," he said.

Liz was quite sure her parents had embraced and kissed each other, something they did only when confident that they were completely alone.

"I'm sorry to be so late, Libby. My last call was at the McMurray home and I spent a good deal of time there. You'll remember they just lost their precious little Jamie. Only three years old he was. We prayed and read scriptures. I tried to bring a bit of comfort."

Liz could hear the fatigue and sorrow in Father's voice. She remembered little Jamie and pictured him sitting in church with his father, mother, brothers and sisters.

Father continued speaking softly to Mother. "After leaving the McMurray's house, I was thinking of our own precious little Liz and stopped to see Dr. Foster." He paused, and when he spoke his voice had roughened. "He's had another consultation with the specialist from Edinburgh. They say she will never run and play like a normal child. We'll have to let the doctors remove the lower leg."

This jerked Liz wide awake. "He assured me it is the only way we can keep the infection from spreading. It's our only hope of saving her life."

Terrified, Liz shivered. Then, with a thrill of hope she heard the defiant tone in Mother's voice, the anger and determination of a mother cat standing between her kitten and a mean dog. "John, we will *not* permit those incompetent doctors to take our daughter's foot! And she will live! She must live! But I did not birth her to be a cripple!"

All her life Liz would remember those exact words. She would tell them to her children. She would reflect that stubbornness and lack of trust in the competence of doctors when she was raising her own children. At times in the years that lay ahead she would find herself facing what seemed like impossible odds, and she would fit exactly that image of a determined mother.

As soon as Mother could make the necessary arrangements, she took Liz to the home of Uncle William, Father's youngest brother, a crofter in the Highlands. The home was humble, the family poor, but the farm they worked provided an abundance of wholesome food—butter, eggs, meat, and fresh vegetables from the garden. Though fruit was scarce, Uncle William added some oranges to the diet with the money Mother provided to help pay for Liz's care. The only unpleasant part was that a visiting parish nurse stopped at the house each morning. Mother would hold Liz down while they soaked her foot and lower leg for long periods in a crock of water so hot that Liz screamed with pain. The nurse said the heat and blood circulation might heal the bone and save the leg from the doctor's knife. Liz tried to keep that in mind as the nurse dipped out water that had cooled and poured in more boiling water from the kettle, but she couldn't help but cry. After about three weeks Mother returned to Perth, leaving the treatments to Aunt Mary and the nurse.

The little farm lay in a beautiful setting far from the smoke-filled air and crowded industrial area around Perth. Not far distant from the farm the green slopes of Ben Macdui could be seen, the second highest point in Scotland. Here was all the lore and legend of the Highlands. Here Liz had the joy of riding in the pony cart with Uncle William and his family as they traveled on Sunday mornings to the historic old church of Crathie Parish. Here she discovered a joy in living, an enthusiasm for life that would never leave her.

Uncle William and Aunt Mary were hard-working people. It took all their daylight hours to care for the little farm and keep the house neat and clean, but they always seemed to have time for a pleasant word, a joke and good laughter. The invigorating air of the country, the varied diet, and the happy atmosphere of the home—along with the hours spent soaking her leg—worked wonders of healing that the doctors in Perth and the specialist from Edinburgh could not. The debilitating infection, which Liz would later learn was called osteo-myelitis, was arrested and began to recede. She began to walk and play with her cousins, the crofter's young children. Years later she decided that the exercise must have contributed to her improving health.

During that summer Liz heard the sharp descriptive tongue of the Gaelic dialect, the common language in that Highland home, and later she continued to hear that dialect spoken at church by some of Father's parishioners in Perth. Throughout her life it was easy for her to slip into using the beautiful Gaelic speech. This, along with her returning health, was a lifelong gift she would enjoy and cherish.

All her life Liz would remember with gratitude that summer of healing and a mother's courage that made it possible. Had she lost her lower leg, she could never have emigrated to America. The United States immigration service excluded people with disabilities that they thought would interfere with the ability to be self supporting.

Back in the manse in Perth, with the infection gone, Liz pushed herself to keep up with her brother Laurence. At age eight, despite a slight lingering limp, she was able to outrun many children her age. She was anxious to mix with them, play their games, and demonstrate her athletic ability. She knew it was not any physical weakness that kept her confined to the yard. It was Father's absolute rule that she was not to play with the common children of the street. She was not to have her speech and behavior corrupted by the vulgar ways of working class children.

On Sunday, when she walked the mile to church with her mother and older siblings, she enjoyed setting a rapid pace, sometimes skipping ahead. It gave her special pleasure to see her eldest brother David smiling and watching her. She loved this brother. He was now a man of twenty-four, still single and living at home though he'd been working full time for the railroad since the age of seventeen. A very special bond had developed between him and little Liz, the youngest of seven. He was a kind, strong, athletic man, and her earliest and fondest memories were of the security she felt in his arms as he carried her, a frail little crippled girl, on the long walk to church. Now it was a joy to show him how very well she could manage by herself.

She respected her father and perhaps feared him a little. As pastor of the Presbyterian Scottish Free Church he was one of the best known and most respected men in the city of Perth. But deep inside, a stubborn and rebellious disposition told her there was something unfair about his rule that kept her segregated from the children of the streets, many of them from families in his church. He was known throughout the city for his dedication to the working class poor. St. Paul's Free Church, where he was pastor, was called a working man's church. It was located in a poor section of the city, and he gave most of his waking hours to his ministry in this parish. The manse where Liz peered through the iron-barred gate stood on a street that served as a playground for children from the poor homes.

A naturally sociable child, Liz yearned to share their laughter. She was certain that the words she heard spoken by those children—some never uttered in her home or church—would not hurt her or change her way of speaking. So why couldn't she join the fun in the street? She could not understand it. It made her angry, yet she knew she wouldn't dare mention it to Father.

He seemed stern and somewhat distant. Although his sermons were long, she didn't mind going to church. She felt proud that it was her father in the pulpit. People spoke of him as a powerful preacher, truly a man of God. She never questioned her own faith, and enjoyed memorizing Bible verses. Faithfully she said her prayers. The fact that her mind sometimes wandered during her father's sermons gave her feelings of guilt, but at times Mother would open her purse and fish out a piece of hard candy for her. Putting the sweet in her mouth, Liz loved the secret smile they shared.

In the front of the church two tall pillars supported the building. Sometimes during a sermon she would slip into a fantasy in which the pillars became great striped sticks of peppermint candy, or Father in his flowing black robe became a great glob of chocolate. She hoped God would not look on her too harshly for her inattention. She loved God and sometimes felt that He was not as stern in some matters as Father.

A feature of the church services that Liz truly enjoyed involved babies. Later Liz wrote about the very large families that made up the congregation, all poor people:

> There were always babies being presented for Christian baptism. I was very fond of these teeny babies that were brought to the altar. I had a tremendous love for them, being the last of a large family. My mother always took me up at the end of the service and I would gaze on their faces like they were little angels, these beautiful little faces, because I didn't have one at home. There was a great mystery to me in my life: In Scotland you always knew if it was a baby boy or a baby girl according to what it wore. Boys wore little hats; girls wore little bonnets. But the thing that worried me terribly as a child was: How in the world did people know what they were when they didn't have their hats or bonnets on? Mother never told me about the birds and the bees. It was my sister Marjorie who told me about the bad stuff. (Here the reader might imagine Liz's wry smile.)

In the pastor's family it was unthinkable to stay home from church unless one was ill. And one was never late. When the worship service began, the church doors would be closed and locked. Decreed not by

Father but the elders of the church session, this was based on the biblical parable of the foolish bridesmaids—Matthew 25, Verse 10. For lack of planning, the foolish bridesmaids had to go at the last minute to buy oil for their lamps. When they returned to enter into the marriage feast "the door was shut." This meant that church services were not to be interrupted by latecomers. Liz never forgot the Sunday morning when she was late for church and the door was shut.

This happened soon after her leg recovered, when she was about five years old. Older sister Alice had been excused from attending due to illness. Sister Marjorie waited for Liz, but Liz wanted to stay home with Alice. After all, Alice had often stayed with her during her illness. She was stubborn about it and argued with Marjorie, who finally left without her. A while later Liz decided she could not risk being absent from divine worship. By now it was late. She ran almost all the way, becoming terribly out of breath, but the great front door of the church was shut. She dared not pound on it to attract an usher and gain admittance. She knew she had sinned against Father, the Church, and God. Burdened with guilt, she trudged home, much fearing her later confrontation with Father. Alice couldn't offer much consolation.

When Father returned home, looking very tired, he said in a voice that cut her to the quick, "I'm disappointed in you, Liz. You know very well that you are not to miss church unless you are ill. And you are not to be late! Go to your room now and stay there for the rest of the day."

Spanking was not often used for discipline in the Symon family, but it was Mother who climbed the stairs after Liz, repeating what a disappointment she had been to Father. She removed Liz's Sunday frock, turned her over her knees and spanked her. It hurt, and injured Liz's pride. She lay crying on her bed and feeling very sorry for herself.

Missing Sunday dinner hurt almost as much. Sunday dinners were special at the manse, the finest meal of the week. Liz could smell the roasting beef and knew there would be sweet trifle for dessert. She felt hungry and terribly ashamed. Sobbing, she lay in her petticoat imagining the family gathered at the table sharing the happenings of the morning. She always looked forward to Sunday dinner, when the family was relaxed, and since she had become active after her lameness, she was always hungry at mealtime. Several hours later she knew the family had gathered again to share their light Sunday supper. Now she feared that she would starve to death and no one cared.

There came a soft knock on her door. The door opened and Agnes, the servant girl, entered with a sandwich and a glass of milk on a tray. No words passed between them, but Liz felt comforted by the knowing look of Agnes, who seemed to be saying, "Don't fret it, dearie. Believe me, I know. There's much worse things in this life than missin' your dinner."

Sitting up and accepting the tray, Liz pondered her situation. Mother must have sent up the sandwich and milk after Father had gone to bed early, his "Sunday after church rest," which he always needed these days. Mother had spanked her but did not want her to starve for her wickedness. Mother loved her after all.

Nevertheless, the image of those large oak doors would stay with her to the end of her life. When discussing eternal life or listening to sermons on sin and judgement, she would picture those great doors—shut and locked against a naughty little girl—and imagine that as the fate of the unrepentant sinner. She would outgrow much of her childish religion, but always the gates of heaven would resemble the oak doors of her father's church, doors that were warmly inviting when open, but could also be locked against a sinner.

The twice-yearly celebration of communion was a very important time in the life of the church. Children did not participate in the communion service, but were allowed to watch. Liz was deeply impressed by the serious attention the faithful worshippers gave to this observance. But the words, "O joyful communion, what a wonderful season" had a somewhat more festive meaning for her. Father was paid twice a year, coinciding with the communion. So this was also

the time for the family to buy many needed items and new clothes—
dresses, shoes and sundries like ribbons.

For adult members of the congregation, communion was truly a
soul-searching experience. Elders visited the members to make sure
they were among the "faithful." Each member was given a card that
carried the warning: "He that eateth or drinketh unworthily, eateth
and drinketh damnation." Preparatory meetings were held—prayer
meetings for all to examine their hearts. On the Sabbath the bookboards
were draped in white throughout the church. Everyone shared a common communion cup. "That was before the health authorities lost
their faith," Liz later wrote with characteristic humor.

These very strict and restrictive communion customs left a lasting
impression on her. In later years, after a communion service conducted
with much less formality, she wrote:

> Often I long for a greater sense of dedication
> for these moments of solemnity.

The manse was a fine home for the family. The large kitchen had
a cement floor, sink with running water, and a half stove and open fire
combination for heating and cooking. Adjoining this, the scullery
served for cleaning and washing vegetables, storing pots and pans and
doing other food preparation such as plucking chickens. Above this, a
lonely "servant's bedroom" connected to the kitchen by means of a
wooden stairway, making it possible for the servant girl to live completely separated from the family. Here she slept alone, her room off
limits to all the family except Mother. The stairway gave her direct
access to much of her work—helping Mother with the cooking, serving meals, and doing all the cleanup work. She also cleaned and dusted
the rest of the house. Liz always remembered that house:

> Upstairs there were five rooms, one of which was Father's
> study where children never entered without special con-

sent from Father. There was also a makeshift bathroom. It was cold of course—no central heating—but the downstairs rooms and some upstairs rooms had fireplaces that we used. We dressed warmly. I was a sickly child and invariably wore a Shetland shawl around my shoulders, crossed and tied under the arms in the back. Sweaters were not yet in vogue—still, as the climate was not severe, I don't remember being so cold or else we had learned "In whatsoever state we were, therein to be content."

There was a large dining-living room combination where visiting ministers and church officials could be entertained, and where the family ate on special occasions. The children slept, played and ate in a large room called the nursery. Here the parents came to eat with the children if there were no special guests. When other adults were present, parents and guests ate in the dining room and children ate alone in the nursery. It was felt that children should not be present for adult conversation. On one occasion, in the presence of the older girls, a visiting minister referred in some detail to a woman who had recently had a baby. Liz's mother was annoyed with him for crossing the line of decency. Liz later wrote:

> My parents were very strict in regard to the relationship between the sexes. They watched David very closely. They were especially on their guard about the servant girls, and my brother often chatted with them and seemed to enjoy their company. This made my parents very uneasy… In a minister's family if any irregularity in conduct had been manifest, it would have been the end of the minister's influence for all time…
>
> Nellie and Marjorie were both learning to be teachers, and when they went to their teachers' classes at night

Father would always walk up to the corner and watch for them when they would be coming home with some boys. He was always very much against this. He would wait until the boys said good night, then he would accompany his daughters home. They never had the last word.

The seven children tended to divide themselves into pairs, based on temperament and interests. David and Alice, the eldest, had experienced much more of the family's struggle with poverty during the years when Father was preparing for the ministry and beginning his early preaching assignments. They knew more of the practical matters of survival and were less given to dreams of adventure. David was a very kind person, devoted to the family. By age seventeen he was working for the railroad to help support the family. He was not interested in following his father into the ministry. Alice also looked at the practical matters of life and devoted herself to helping with the management of the household. She was a kind and helpful person who never sought favor or reward for herself. If she had dreams, she loyally sublimated them to the family.

Nellie and Marjorie had much in common, and Nellie was something of a role model for Marjorie. Eager to be independent, she took her teacher's training by the time she was seventeen. Marjorie followed, knowing that a teaching career would give her independence. Marjorie resisted the restraints and strictness of their parents. Often moody, she frequently went her own way in solitude, saying she was "thinking over her own thoughts." She adored Nellie, who somehow seemed better able to shrug off the strict discipline without causing any upset. Later the two would be student teachers together.

Laurence and John were a pair, leaving me much by myself and they resented the feeling that I was very much Father's favorite. I did get much special treatment,

Front l–r: Marjorie 16, Elizabeth Crawford Symon 53, "Liz," 8, Reverend John Symon 52, Laurence 10
Perth, 1895
Back row: Alice 21, David 23, Nellie 19, John 13.

perhaps because of my early illness. John was strong willed, resentful of Father, and he often complied with Father's rules only because of authority, not out of respect. Laurence was more mild and easier to live with. Sometimes John would strike me.

My parents were too strict and never understood that a child could resent the parents, and when "all was quiet" took it for a sign that all was well and the family was loving each other and them. I longed for companionship. Sometimes my brothers would play with me. But they objected to little girl games. The wide fireplaces gave my brothers an idea. On one occasion they said they would play with me if I would consent to put up my doll as a Christian martyr. I consented to the utter destruction of the doll. They told me stories of Christian martyrs burned at the stake, and finally talked me into allowing my doll to testify to its faith. That was really difficult. My doll was totally consumed in an open fireplace. It was made with something like sawdust filling in its body and the boys thought it made a good martyr. Whether I consented or not, its martyrdom was of short duration. My parents never knew about this. I think I was coerced into secrecy.

All our rooms had fireplaces. One morning on awakening I realized that something was flying around in the room. A beautiful bird had come down the chimney. We easily could have believed in Santa coming down the chimney, but because of my parent's theological beliefs Santa was a forbidden saint in our family. My parents did not celebrate Christmas lest it smack of Catholicism. We knew of the birth of Christ, but no trees, candles, gifts, nor any frivolity. At New Year we hung up our stockings and received a "threepenny bit," some cake, and oranges; we never felt slighted.

In school our teachers were strict. I remember one sweet teacher but she was there only a short time. The headmistress ruled mercilessly. She always said she had an eye in the back of her head and I thought of a fearful eye under the bun she wore. How we feared and disliked her!

At home Father was so afraid of his family reading trashy books. My older sister said they had a book under the mattress. It had one "damn" in it and they thought that was the objection. In later years they realized it was far from being suitable reading, but at that time they were too young to understand its contents.

When I was eight Father took away from me an Annie Swan production [a book]. I could read, but its love story meant absolutely nothing to me. I really was quite pure.

My parents were very afraid I would play with children who might be undesirable companions. However they approved a friend's child who came visiting with her mother, bringing another "superior" child with her. Even yet I recall some of the very doubtful little jokes and songs, but I never told Mother. Forever the friendship would have been broken had my parents suspected. I'm quite sure there were "safer children" living in the old houses around the corner, but they were debarred— or I from them.

I guess we children harbored some doubts about biblical stories. My older sisters used to discuss Adam and Eve and how we all had to die because Eve ate an apple. Now, we knew that an apple must have been a temptation because sometimes Father bought a barrel of wonderful American apples and we loved them. Even so it seemed a bit unjust, and I remember feeling a great aversion to our first parents, who so selfishly brought death to all.

The Symon family always kept a live-in servant girl—the girls being replaced quite often. They came from a special boarding school for girls who were orphans or whose homes were considered unfit, perhaps because of a drunken father or mother, or both.

In addition to doing housework the girls took care of Liz and Laurence when other members of the family were not at home. Liz would later tell her own children that she had liked those girls and felt that it was unfair that they had to live such lonely lives apart from the family. If she was at home with them, they would talk to her for company. One night when only Liz and the servant girl were in the house, a man came through the gate and knocked on the door. The girl was terrified. When he knocked a second time she seized Liz's hand, ran upstairs and looked out the window. To be faithful to her duties, the girl needed to ask who came, so she opened the window a crack and called out: "Who is there?"

A voice replied, "I am Mr. Herschel from the cemetery." With this information the girl nearly fainted, but was able to ask what he wanted. He told her he wanted to see the Reverend on business and would come back at another time.

There was much that young Liz did not know about her father. Later she would learn that he was not only respected as a fine preacher, he was in demand for all sorts of speaking engagements. His opinions were sought by the leading men of the city. All Liz knew at the time was that when he arrived home from church, always later than the rest of the family, the pride in Mother's voice resonated when she said, "Aye, John, that was a powerful sermon you preached today."

Liz could not understand a life so fully dedicated to serving the parish. Father walked to his appointments and spent many hours, day or night, in homes where people were dying, homes where there was hunger, disease and despair, homes where his spiritual support was all they had to cling to. From her window Liz often saw him hanging his black outer garments on the clothesline. There they would dance in the breeze like scarecrows in a puppet show. She hesitated to ask him about it. After he died, Mother explained:

"Your father had a great love for his people. When they were suffering and in need of his prayers he went into many homes where there was deathly sickness. He never feared for himself, but feared he might bring the sickness to his family. So he hung his outer garments on the line where the fresh air would purify them."

At the time Liz didn't know how much he suffered from his own failing health, a stomach problem that gave him much pain. If he ever complained it was to his God, or his wife in the privacy of their room. The specter of his own death plagued him—the fear of leaving the family he loved without support. The little time he could find to be at home was time Liz would have liked spent with her. Instead he had to rest. Feeling that he neglected her, she took her sorrows to big brother David and appreciated the way he listened. Only after his death did Liz begin to understand how much her father had suffered, how much he had loved her, what a truly kind and loving father he had been, and how much she missed him.

While he was "visiting his flock" or resting, she found delight in the spacious yard. Ivy grew up one wall of the house and flourished on the stone fence between the manse and the street. Birds nested in the ivy. In their season many different flowers blossomed in well kept flower beds. Duff, the skilled and devoted gardener, spent his full time caring for the large yard surrounding the manse. If he had a first name she never knew it. She called him Old Duff. He was old, but by working slowly and steadily for a great many hours, he finished all the work and kept a beautiful yard that was a playground for a lonely little girl. The parishioners made his service possible as a luxury for the Rev. John Symon, who in that working class parish never received a large salary. It was part of the same class system that provided the servant girl—a system that made it necessary for daughters of very poor families to work as house maids for nothing more than a respectable place to live and the hope of learning skills and earning a recommendation for work in the home of a wealthy family, where a maid could earn a salary in addition to room and board. It was a system that required an old man who had no other means of support to work as long as he possibly could just for food and lodging. The parish may have provided some sort of allowance for Old Duff. Whatever the arrangement, John Symon never discussed such things with his family, but was grateful for the service of the fine old man.

Duff was a friend and confidant to Liz. The long hours he willingly spent working at the manse suggested that he had no family of his own. Perhaps the bright, inquisitive little girl filled the role of an affectionate granddaughter. For hours, while continuing his work, he would listen to her childish thoughts. He never scoffed at her ideas, but helped find her ball in the deep growth of ivy. He never frowned when she got in his way. Unlike her relationship with the servant girls, Liz was not restricted in her friendship with Old Duff. Perhaps her parents trusted that he would not give her notions inappropriate for a proper young lady.

Duff explained to Liz that her father served God in his ministry at the church, and he served God by making a beautiful place for the minister's family. He smiled when she admired his gardening skill. When she was of a mind to help, he patiently let her assist with the planting of seeds or the gathering of vegetables. Each day, in season, he helped her choose the flowers that would grace the living room of the manse, letting her feel that it was her good taste that provided such lovely arrangements. Though he was a commoner, he and little Liz met on a level of something like equality, and when not in school or doing homework she spent many happy hours with him.

Looking back, Liz realized that she had enjoyed her childhood and had been truly blessed by parents who guided her in the direction of a fine education, an appreciation of the world around her, and an interest in and concern for other people. She would remember with great affection her Scottish roots and the fine old city of Perth where she was raised:

> So my children will know something about my early life and background, I was born in Perth, Scotland, March, 20, 1887. Beautiful Perth stands on the river Tay at a point where the river in its wanderings and picturesque journey from the far northwest is nearing its firth which eventually empties into the North Sea 20 miles away. To the north and south of the city lie the two "Inches," famous beauty spots like great parks, always open to everyone. These are vast meadows given, according to old bylaws, "for the honest recreation of the citizens."
>
> On the North Inch the famous battle of the Clans was fought in the late 14th century. Near the Tay River, and easily accessible from both High Street and South Street, stands the Kirk of St. Johns. The original church was said to have been founded in the 5th century, and the name and transept of the existing church in the 13th century. Here John Knox preached one of his most famous and fiery sermons in 1559.
>
> A replica of the ancient Mercat Cross stands opposite the city hall in King Edward Street. The original cross was destroyed by Cromwell. The history of Perth dates back to a Roman settlement, which gave it the name of Bertha—thus later Perth. Much early Scottish history revolved around Perth and its environs. Its strategic location is at the center of exploration of some of Britain's most magnificent scenery. Immortalized in *The Fair Maid of Perth,* Sir Walter Scott says, "It forms the fairest portion of the Northern Kingdom." Across its

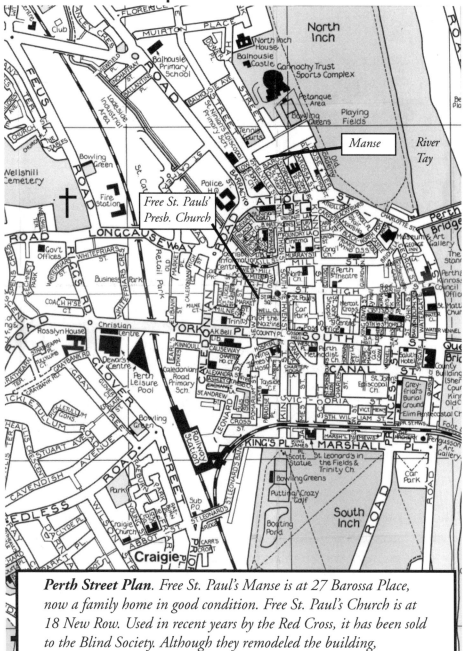

Manse

River Tay

Free St. Pauls' Presb. Church

Perth Street Plan. *Free St. Paul's Manse is at 27 Barossa Place, now a family home in good condition. Free St. Paul's Church is at 18 New Row. Used in recent years by the Red Cross, it has been sold to the Blind Society. Although they remodeled the building, the stained glass window dedicated in memory of the Reverend John Symon remains intact. Another St. Paul's church stands 100 yards away. The River Tay runs N-S along the eastern side.*

Courtesy of the Perth Tourist Board

expanse lie roads between North and South, used by the Romans in the 1st century, and by travelers and tourists in the 20th. [Perth is on the rail line from Dumbarton to Stonehaven, which is considered the dividing line between Highlands and Lowlands.] Scone, just across the river, was the crowning place of kings. They were crowned on the famous Stone of Destiny, which, according to old tradition, was the same stone used by Biblical Jacob to pillow his head at Bethel.

I am proud to know Perth as my native city. How little did I know it or appreciate its grandeur when I was a child! But that is the way with children. They are engrossed, not with the past—but with the present...

Father, in his prayers often said, "We thank Thee for an unbroken family circle." Why should he say that? The family circle, I thought, could never be broken... Nothing could happen to the family or our little world. Now that unbroken family circle sleeps in far flung corners of the earth, Scotland, Canada, France, the United States. How trusting is childhood!

Grand old Perth in the 1890s—a city of contrasts: the very wealthy and the extremely poor; a city of dignity and morality plagued with drunkenness and brutality; a city literally at the crossroads, where the Gaelic tongue of the Highlands met and mingled with the common English of the Lowlands; a center of culture and education in the midst of gross ignorance and illiteracy. It was there, in search of jobs in the industrial sectors, that hungry Highland crofters, dispossessed by the wholesale Highland "Clearances" of the 19th century, came in great numbers. Among them was Liz's grandfather, John Symon, Sr., who found work in the railroad shops at Arbroath, on the coast not far from Perth.

"Rising himself from humbler classes, Mr. Symon possessed a uniqueness of character and force of personality that only occasionally is to be met with."

Perthshire Courier, August 25, 1896

2   The Reverend John Symon

Liz's father was a man of strong character, great determination, and an intense Christian faith. He was born in Dunbar, Scotland, in 1843, the eldest son of John Symon, Sr., originally a farmer. His mother was Elizabeth Lindsay. Not long after young John was born, John Sr. moved the family from the Highlands to the coastal town of Arbroath, where he was employed as an "iron turner" in the locomotive works of the "Aberdeen and Arbroath" railway. Five more children would be born to the family, giving young John two sisters and three brothers. At an early age John Jr. was apprenticed in the same employment as his father. When he had served his apprenticeship, he was moved to the locomotive works at Perth, the company headquarters.

While still living in Arbroath young John came under the influence of a religious "revival" that had a profound influence on him. He committed himself to a life of preaching the gospel to the poor of the working class, his own station in life at that time. This became the all-consuming passion of his life. Till the time of his death he never wavered from this work. He never became involved in political activity in an attempt to change or improve the economic system, the "oppressive capitalism" that Karl Marx and Friedrich Engels had been writing about in London. His concern was to give comfort and encouragement to those who lived in poverty and to help the believer deal with the hardships that John saw as part of the inevitable circumstances of life. He preached Christian faith, personal morality, and self discipline. Faith, prayer, sobriety, hard work and thrift defined his life, and these values served him well.

Not yet twenty years old, he began preaching at open air meetings in addition to his daily work as a "turner" for the locomotive works. He discovered he had a gift for preaching, for communicating the gospel to the uneducated working class poor. One observer noted: "His fervent, zealous manner and rough eloquence entered the heart where many polished tongues would fail to find entrance."

He shared in the toil and knew the discipline of the factory whistle. He knew the heat, grime, soot and long hours of the six day work week. Despite enormous obstacles, he decided to get an education and become a clergyman in the Presbyterian Free Church, the church of his devout parents. By dint of sheer determination, self discipline and natural talent as a public speaker, he achieved his goal. But though he lifted himself, he never separated himself from the cares, concerns and struggles of the poor. He never forgot their need for spiritual guidance and faith to help them cope with their ever-present sorrows, illnesses, poverty and bereavements.

The year John was born, 1843, the Free Church had declared independence from the Established Church of Scotland—both of them Presbyterian. The so-called Disruption was caused by the independent spirit of the Free Church leaders, who insisted on the right of congregations to refuse the appointment of pastors not of their choosing. The Nonintrusion Party, as they called themselves, was led by the great preacher, teacher and theologian Thomas Chalmers, who was so admired by the young John Symon that he later named a daughter Helen Chalmers Symon—"Nellie."

In those days religious convictions were held with great intensity. The 19th century was not far removed from the period in English and Scottish history when great persecutions and religious wars wracked Britain, indeed much of Europe. Family tradition has it that the fiercely independent Protestant faith of the Symons originated in part with the Huguenots of France—Protestants who were a French outgrowth of the Reformation, an early leader being John Calvin. The intense resistance to Catholicism, which was so much a part of the faith of the French Huguenots, joined the independent thinking of the followers of John Knox in Scotland when the Frenchman Jacques "James" Symon, grandfather of the Reverend John Symon, married the daughter of Presbyterian Highlander, Angus McIntosh.

According to family accounts, Jacques was a sturdy French Huguenot farm boy who had been impressed into the service of France in Napoleon's army. Britain was at war with France between 1793 and 1815. Sometime during this period Jacques was captured by the British in a battle in France and shipped as a prisoner of war to a prison camp near Balmoral Castle on the river Dee in Aberdeenshire. Liz recalled hearing of the ruins of an old prison in that area. Jacques was fortunate to have his life spared. Whether he was released during a lull in the hostilities, or escaped because the local Scottish population had no more love for the British than the French, is not known. At any rate, he found himself an impoverished French-speaking soldier in the Scottish Highlands.

A strong young man willing to work hard, he picked up a little of the Gaelic tongue and found a job with a crofter named Angus McIntosh, who needed help on his farm. Now "James" had food to eat and a place to sleep in the barn loft. He had no desire to return to France and serve again in Napoleon's army. He and the Scottish crofter became fast friends. Soon James was taking his meals at the family table and enjoying the fellowship of the family. He shared in their Bible readings and prayers, and together they worshipped in the great old Presbyterian Church of Crathie Parish.

A devout and naturally sociable man, James was well received by the congregation and became an active member of the church. He adapted well to his new home, loving the beauty and freedom of the Highlands. Becoming fluent in Gaelic, the handsome, well mannered and hard working young man caught the eye of the strong-willed Highland lass, Elizabeth, eldest daughter of McIntosh. She was pleased to find that he shared her affection and was well approved by her father. After duly posting their banns and declaring their intentions to the congregation, they were married in the church, to which he remained fiercely loyal throughout his life.

In due time Elizabeth gave birth to son John, who would share the family faith and devotion to the church. At that time many crofters who worked the land but did not own it were pushed off their farms by wealthy landowners, and there was no opportunity for a young farmer to get a start, except in cases where the father died and the young man stepped into his place. With no prospect of that, young John left the farm along with hundreds of other young Highlanders. He become a railroad worker in Dunbar, just south of the Firth of Forth. There he married Elizabeth Lindsay, a working girl employed in the textile mills. They named their first born son John.

John the father was an excellent worker and got on well with the railroad company. A promotion took him to the railroad shops of Arbroath on the coast just north of the Firth of Tay. There he raised his family: John Jr., Jean, Alexander, Margaret, James and William. John Jr. became a minister and father of seven children, including Liz. As a young man, William reversed his father's travels and returned to Crathie Parish to become the crofter whose home proved such a blessing in the healing of little Liz. It may be that by this time he was able to take over the farm from his father "James." Later, around 1900, William emigrated to the United States and became involved in ship building in California.

The untimely death of John Sr., Liz's grandfather, at age forty-three, left young John the head of the house with the responsibility for his mother and the younger children. He was seventeen, working in the railroad shop as an apprentice iron turner. The hardship and long hours of the work intensified his zeal for the church. Drawing large crowds, he continued preaching in the open air. The Home Mission Committee of the Free Church of Edinburgh recommended him, and he was engaged as a missionary to lead Fountainhead Free Church, a mission in Edinburgh. Such missions were established in extremely poor urban areas, receiving support, albeit minimal, from the main church.

While in Edinburgh John attended the University, continued preaching in the mission church, and drew the interest of several influential people who helped his career. Among them was a Miss Chalmers, daughter of the late Thomas Chalmers. John received much encouragement to continue his efforts to become a fully ordained minister. In two years he finished his work in the University, in the Divinity Hall, New College, which had been established by the Free Church for training its ministers.

During this period of gaining his education he married Elizabeth Crawford, an intelligent young woman from Aberdeen. Meanwhile he continued to preach and worked hard to support a growing family. Three children were born during these years, David, Alice and Helen, who was always called Nellie. These were years of extreme sacrifice for both John and Elizabeth, as they pursued their dream of the ministry. They struggled to live on a bare subsistence support. The housing they could afford was in a tenement with the poor. In later years David recalled entertaining himself, as a very a small child, by making friends with a rat, one of many that infested the tenements and posed a constant worry and challenge for his mother. It was only her strong character, determination, and her abiding faith in the calling of her husband that Elizabeth, whom he called Libby, survived those austere years and provided the family with a home. John received his full ordination "by leave of the Assembly" in 1881, ten years after the birth of his first child and six years before Liz's birth.

Free St. Stevens congregation in Perth, having obtained a new building, sold their old building, and it became the start of a mission church under the name of Free St. Paul's. The newly ordained John Symon was chosen as its first minister. The congregation was small at first, but his eloquent preaching and faithful, full-time work as a pastor quickly attracted a large congregation. Very soon the church was able to pay off the debt on their building and buy both the manse and a hall for additional church activities. In the next few years the church grew to a membership of 650, with an additional 350 who attended regularly without becoming full members.

The move into the manse of Free St. Paul's was more than an escape from poverty. It was to the Symons and their three children the sudden onset of pure luxury—a roomy house with a servant girl and gardener, a beautiful yard and gardens, and a position of honor and respect in the community. In the social structure of the times, being an ordained a minister called to serve a church amounted to being in the upper class. The peers of the Symons were landed gentry with titles, men in the law and government, military leaders and other churchmen. Such a rising from the lower working class to the upper class was a very rare accomplishment.

In due time children David Lindsay, Alice Mary and Nellie Chalmers were joined by Marjorie Stewart, John Crawford, Laurence Chapman, and Elizabeth, called Liz to distinguish her from her mother. Three other children had died soon after birth. One of these had been given the name of Elizabeth, but since she did not live to use it, the name was given to Liz. Her middle name, Dewar, was in honor of a much loved and respected parishioner.

John Symon had achieved his goal by extremely hard work and sacrifice, a great faith, and remarkable natural talent. He had been greatly aided by a determined and committed wife who worked tire-lessly to nurture her family, accepted hardship with good spirit, and faced adversity with courage. And thus it transpired that the first nine years of little Liz's life were lived as an upper class girl. She knew nothing of cooking or the daily tasks of house keeping. Instead she devoted herself to her studies, music lessons, good manners and all that was involved in becoming a lady. With a servant girl to care for housekeeping duties and much of the cooking, mother could devote her time to her children, giving them extra instruction in addition to their school work. Liz became an avid reader and by age nine was already developing her lifelong passion for English and Scottish literature and history.

After the arduous years of constant work in Edinburgh, John Symon made a concession to his need, and the need of his family, for recreation. As pastor of St. Paul's he could determine his own schedule. He initiated the custom of a regular two-week vacation each summer at Carnoustie, a little resort town between Dundee and Arbroath, with miles of beautiful beach. He would take lodging for the two-week holiday. As the children grew older he rented a house for the family for a month, though he would stay only two weeks, then return to his duties in Perth.

Carnoustie, with its golden strand and golf links, where the children learned to play golf, was the brightest spot in the year for the family. Very little could be purchased at the resort, so, using her credit with the local grocer in Perth, Mother took vast amounts of groceries, with more treats than were common the rest of the year.

The swimming area of the beach was strictly divided, one side for men and boys, the other for women and girls. Mother and the girls never swam, only bathed. An odd little bathhouse on wheels was available and, for a penny, a man with a horse would pull the bathhouse out to the desired depth, where people would change clothes. The swimming costumes completely covered the body from ankles to chin. The few times that Liz made the trip to Carnoustie, before those happy times were cut short by Father's death, forged memories that she cherished for a lifetime.

Though the beach was divided by sex, when a swimmer on the men's side swam out from shore he could be seen from the women's side. Father was a powerful swimmer and enjoyed the water. Liz had a picture imprinted in her mind of Father's head above the water, moving out from the shore until it disappeared in the distance. She would watch eagerly for some time, until it returned to her vision and made its way back to shore. She also remembered the day her mother gave a thorough tongue lashing to a man who was seen walking a good way back from the beach, but within sight of the women's bathing area.

Fondly Liz recalled the religious services held on the beach for the children. She and Laurence, just two years older, attended faithfully. In preparation, all the children would make a would-be tabernacle in the sand, having to redo it each day since the tide would come in and ruin it. A group of young men who were preparing to be missionaries in the foreign mission field conducted the service. They urged the children to give their lives to Christ. Many, including Liz, made their commitment.

A cheerful little song was played on the portable organ, and she remembered it many years later to sing to her children.

> Quickly haste and come
> Where happy children meet.
> Hither come and sing
> The savior's praises sweet.
>
> When we heard this music we dropped our
> buckets and spades and ran to our tabernacle.
> It was Presbyterian—no overdoing the emotions
> of children—but telling them stories and urg-
> ing them to direct their lives Godward.

At these pleasant meetings Liz met the Baillie Brothers, two of the young men preparing themselves as missionaries. They were only a few years older than Liz. Later, as they achieved world recognition in theological circles as preachers, writers and educators, she followed the news of them but was never again to meet them. John Baillie became Principal of New College in Edinburgh and Dean of the Faculty. He was elected one of the Presidents of the World Council of Churches and was named Chaplain to the Queen in Scotland. His books gained a worldwide audience.

Soon after her ninth birthday, Liz began to realize that something was very wrong with Father. The family shielded her from the details about his health, but days came when he didn't leave his room, though the garden burgeoned with spring daffodils. She saw the doctor come daily. Inside, the house was much too quiet. Then came Sundays when he did not go to the church to preach. Life at the manse had changed. Mother spent most of her time with Father in their room, the door shut. Later Liz would learn that during his last weeks her father's suffering was intense. All the doctor could do for him was give him laudanum in ever increasing amounts to dull the pain in his stomach. But the worst of his suffering was his inability to go to his pulpit on Sunday and to make his rounds among "his people." Additionally, there was the pain he expressed to his wife: "Libby, I'll never see our Liz up."

On August 20, 1896, at age fifty-three, John Symon died at his beloved home. His life ended at the very peak of his career.

At the funeral service Liz sat beside her mother, surrounded by Marjorie, Nellie and Alice. Brothers, David, John, and Laurence sat with the other pall bearers in the front row. The church was overflowing with mourners, many standing along the walls, others sitting on chairs placed in the aisles. She tried to concentrate on what the man at the pulpit was saying, but couldn't stop staring at the coffin. A single thought overwhelmed all else: Father's spirit was in heaven now and he would never again speak from that pulpit. When the service was over, David, John and Laurence rose with the other pall bearers and carried the coffin to a hack pulled by a pair of black horses. Along the mile route to the cemetery Liz and the family walked slowly behind. People watched from both sides of the street, many wiping tears. Liz felt the pity in those glances, and the love they all had for her father.

Five days later, August 25, 1896, Mother asked the children to join her in the living room, a place normally reserved for adult guests. As they all took seats on the davenport and chairs, Mother sat in her upholstered chair and unfolded that day's copy of *The Perthshire Courier.* "Here is what the town is reading today," she told them, then read aloud:

DEATH OF REV. JOHN SYMON, PERTH.
ENGINEER, EVANGELIST, AND MINISTER

It is with deep regret we have to announce that the Rev. John Symon, minister of Free St. Paul's Church, died at his residence, The Manse, Barossa Place, early on Thursday morning... Rising himself from humbler classes, Mr. Symon possessed a uniqueness of character and force of personality that only occasionally is to be met with. He was a friend of all and his kind and genial countenance, accompanied by some suitable word of encouragement, will be missed by every one to whom he was known.

Liz saw a quiver in her mother's chin and moisture welling in her eyes as she struggled to contain her emotions. In all Liz's nine years Mother had been a stern and unemotional disciplinarian. Now her heart was breaking. Liz rose from the davenport to stand at her mother's knee where she could see the headline of the story and be nearer to her mother. Mother continued, enunciating each word as though she were reading the Bible.

Under the pastoral care of Mr. Symon, Free St. Paul's congregation has grown and flourished. It was a mere handful when the deceased came to the church, and the accommodation now is of such a nature that a new church is to be built. . . The funeral sermon was preached on Sabbath forenoon by Rev. A.K. McMurchy, Scone. The building was crowded in every part, and additional seats had to be placed in the passage ways. . . Among those present was the Very Rev. Dean of St. Andrews [Episcopalian]. . . The Dean, preaching on the Sabbath in Perth Cathedral, thus alluded to the Rev. John Symon:

"There are occasions when the unbought, perfectly spontaneous manifestation of feeling around the grave of a departed Christian shows unmistakably what the character of his life has been. It has been my privilege during a ministry of over 20 years to witness many such scenes, but seldom have I seen more eloquent testimony borne to the value of a simple but true Christian life in any community than on Saturday when I followed the remains of my friend and neighbor the Rev. John Symon to Wellshill Cemetery.

Mother's voice had grown thin and scratchy. She shut her eyes as though in silent prayer, took a long breath, and continued reading the Dean's words:

"Here was a man who had no extraordinary gifts of this world's giving; neither wealth nor station, nor enticing words of this world's wisdom. He was simply a hard-working loving minister among Christ's poor, but as he was carried to the grave the people lined the streets with faces of real sorrow; many of the sons and daughters of toil, and even little children, were shedding tears. What pomp and circumstance of long drawn funeral array, what melting music, or accumulation of touching ritual observance, or cartloads of wreaths can match or rival the spontaneous tribute of a population in sorrow for one whose face they should see no more.

"What an influence—unsuspected up to that day—

he has been exercising; how by deeds of kindness and words spoken in due season has he been winning all hearts to Christ; how much, therefore, his death is felt to be a real loss.

"In many of what are called Church principles, he and I were, I suppose, as poles asunder. But he was a true servant of our common Lord and Master, Jesus Christ. He preached Jesus Christ and Him crucified as the sole hope of sinners. Better still, he lived that faith. He bore excruciating sufferings for many months without a murmur and died in a hope of—"

The obituary continued, but Mother could read no more. She dropped her head and covered her face. Her shoulders moved as she silently sobbed. For days she had shown a proper, dry-eyed Scottish stoicism as people came with food and condolences—her sisters, Aunt Grace, whose husband had been lost at sea, Aunt Jessie with Liz's grown-up nephews and nieces, Father's relatives from Dunbar and Crathie, parishioners and family friends, but now she could no longer stop the tears.

"This tribute," Mother managed at last to say, "was delivered at the Cathedral before it was given to the newspaper. Ye must know, then, that your father was held in high esteem by the leaders of many churches." Swallowing hard, she folded the paper.

David and Alice exchanged a glance, as did Marjorie and Nellie. John and Laurence stared at Mother, no doubt in wonder at the sight of moisture streaking her face. Liz felt tears pricking her own eyes to see her mother weep.

Mother pushed up from the chair, and Liz guessed that she would go to her room and weep in private. At the doorway she looked back at them. "You should all be very proud to hail from a father such as that."

"Laurence and I were the aristocrats of the gang..."

3   The Common Herd

The death of John Symon brought a profound change to the family. Not only did they lose a father who loved them but they lost the man who defined their position in society. Social class was a very real and powerful force in 19th century Britain, though it was somewhat declining by the 1890s. The class system was nurtured by the deference of those who were lower on the social ladder toward their social betters—whether royalty, people with inherited titles conferred by royalty, or those duly ordained to positions of power and leadership in the church. For the Symon children growing up in the manse, this sense of belonging to the upper class was made obvious by the deference shown to the Reverend John Symon and transferred to his family. It was reinforced by the presence in the home of a servant girl and gardener, who relieved the family of "common labor." The sense of "upper class" was more ingrained in Liz than in her parents and eldest siblings. She had been born in the best of times and had never experienced hunger, inadequate clothing, freezing cold with no money for coal, or fear for what tomorrow might bring.

Since there was no inherited wealth or title, the death of the father meant the loss of any claim the family had to a superior social status. Nevertheless, a sense of class becomes a part of one's personality. Having lived her most impressionable years as an upper class person, Liz would never think of herself as anything else, even when in later years she would live in near poverty in America's supposedly classless society. She would come to define her class by education, morality, a disdain for menial work, and the ability to keep well informed in matters of theology, politics, and great literature. A time would come when she would of necessity do a great deal of menial work, but it would never define her. She would put nourishing meals on the table and keep a reasonably clean house, but take no pride in her cooking or housekeeping. She would never articulate it, but those who knew her well had the impression that she thought such work was beneath her. She would take pride in the achievements of her children and her part in rearing them properly. She would take pride in a well taught Sunday school class, organizing an excellent program for the Grange or representing her local church as a delegate to the annual conference. She would give hours to visiting the sick, helping refugees from the "dust bowl" find temporary housing, but could not enjoy helping the ladies of the church put on a dinner or bake sale.

In years to come she would serve large midday meals to the neighboring men who went from farm to farm helping thresh the grain and stack the hay. The "host" women vied with each other to be the best cooks. She would privately speak of those good women with a tone of pity, as though to say "the poor thing has nothing better to occupy her mind." When the crews came to her house, she put the meal on the table, but not her mind. The upper class feeling had been so deeply ingrained in the first nine years of her life that it stayed with her as long as she lived.

Wordlessly she conveyed this sense of class to her children. A half century later one of them joked at a family reunion that as a child he rode the school bus in frayed clothing and down-in-the-heels shoes reeking of manure, having milked the cow, but as he watched the well-dressed kids from the big white house on the hill take their seats, he felt genuine pity, for they were deprived of a finer life. Liz would never have been comfortable with any of her children accepting common labor as their life's work.

After her father's death the manse had to be vacated for a new minister. The church session considerately allowed a reasonable time for the family to move out. Mrs. Symon moved the family to a modest rented house in southern Perth. Unable to bear seeing another man in what she felt was her husband's pulpit, she joined a different church. David, now twenty-seven and employed by the railroad, still lived at home. His wages largely supported the family. As the widow of a minister, Mother received a small pension, and with David's wages the family managed, but on a much more limited scale than they had known in the manse. Now they paid rent for a much smaller house and had no servant or gardener.

Mother never entirely recovered from the blow. The day and night care required by Father the last few months of his life, the concern and worry as she saw his suffering, the stress of his death, and the uprooting of the family took a tremendous toll. Her health declined rapidly and, among other problems, she was diagnosed with a kidney disorder.

Alice, now twenty-four, found herself more and more responsible for the marketing, cooking, cleaning, and mothering of Liz and Laurence. A kind and gentle person, she sublimated her life to become "mother," care-giver and homemaker for the family. Liz had just turned eleven. Just prior to Father's death, Nellie had completed her education and teacher training. Now, at age twenty-one, she was teaching school in an outlying town. Marjorie, eighteen, was completing her academic work and starting her teacher training in England.

Once again the household turned strangely quiet. Alice spent too much time in Mother's room with the door shut. Liz felt lonely and worried. One mid morning during summer recess she and Laurence sat in the kitchen peeling their hard-boiled eggs. As Liz told the story years later, Alice poured their tea and, as she did each day, readied a tray and took it to Mother in her room.

Suddenly a scream. Alice cried out sharply, "Laurence, run. Fetch the doctor!"

Laurence accidentally inhaled his egg whole. He gagged violently and turned red. At last he expelled the mangled egg and, gasping, took off running. In the meantime Liz hurried to Mother's room, but

Alice kept her in the hall.

"I want to see her," Liz called through the door, fearing what might be happening inside. But Alice would not allow it.

The doctor arrived behind Laurence, both out of breath. Alice let the doctor into the room and again shut the door, not admitting Liz and Laurence. After about five minutes the doctor emerged. Looking at each of them— Laurence, Alice, and Liz—he said, "I'm sorry," then left.

Still Alice kept Liz and Laurence out of the room, going back in herself and shutting the door.

To the end of her life Liz would tell a strange story of sitting on her bed after the doctor left the house. Very troubled, she had no idea what had happened. Mother entered the room in her nightgown and spoke to her, telling her to be a good girl and do as Alice and David said she should. Liz noticed her peaceful expression. Then Mother turned around and left. Because of that appearance Liz found it impossible, at first, to believe Alice when she insisted that Mother had been dead on the floor beside her chair when the doctor arrived, and that she had probably died of a stroke. Alice said they picked her up and laid her body on the bed, and that most certainly she was dead. The appearance of "shades" were thought to be common and were believed in by many at the turn of the century, but Liz told of no other such ghostly apparitions during her long life.

David was summoned. He contacted the new pastor at St. Paul's Church and made arrangements. Nellie and Marjorie came home. With David acting as head of the family, Mother was sadly and lovingly taken to Wellshill cemetery and laid to rest above her husband and beside the three tiny children they had lost.

David worked long hours six days a week at the railroad shop. As the primary breadwinner he was recognized as the head of the household and the guardian of Liz and Laurence. With what free time he had, he did his best to be a father to the two younger children. The bond between him and Liz strengthened. She could tell him her troubles and he listened with affection and understanding. He was not as strict as Father had been but did maintain sound discipline, which Liz respected.

John grew surly. He felt that the two younger children received favored treatment. He had been strictly disciplined by Father on many occasions and had resented the discipline. A sixteen-year-old with both parents gone, he was not about to be told what to do by an older brother or sister. He had grown as tall and almost as strong as David. Tension crackled between them. Good natured David never lost his temper, but arranged an apprenticeship with a local businessman. John accepted it willingly, went his own way and declared his independence from the family.

The Caledonian Railroad liked David's work and gave consideration to the fact that he had a family to support. They promoted him to assistant superintendent of a section of the railroad. He gave up the small house in Perth and moved with Alice, Laurence and Liz to the industrial city of Glasgow, headquarters for his new job. With a population of nearly a million, Glasgow presented a kind of life the family had never known before. Thousands of working people with wages that barely sustained them were crowded into tenement houses. David and Alice found an apartment with two small bedrooms, a living room, kitchen and a "water closet" shared by all the other families on their floor. John didn't make the move with the family and soon grew quite out of touch.

David and Laurence shared a bedroom. Liz slept with Alice. To provide even this much living space, the rent was high in relation to David's income. The small widow's pension was now paid to David to help support the two children, but, even so, Alice found it difficult to serve adequate meals and meet the other expenses.

The greatest change came in the life of the two children. Liz and Laurence now joined the street children. Alice, wanting to be proper, was terribly troubled by this, but could do nothing about it because there was no other place for them to play. Liz rather relished it. She had broken through the iron bars of the manse and was now one of about twelve boys and girls who laughed and ran up and down the narrow streets, dodging vendor carts and horse-drawn conveyances. In unsightly alleys and around construction jobs they played knights and ladies. Liz reflected on this in later life:

> There were some really fine kids in the group and I got
> to know them as friends. Laurence and I were the aris-
> tocrats of the gang and were soon leaders, suggesting
> the games and leading the gang on adventures.

Liz was now among the poor and the lowly, but not as poor as most of them. Her natural charisma and dominating personality began to surface. No doubt the gang appreciated her humor, as people would for the rest of her life.

Troubled by the ease with which Liz adapted to the "common herd," Alice determined that in spite of the cost, Liz must attend a private school and not mingle with the students at the nonpaying school for the poor, though it was much closer to the tenement where they lived. Liz was enrolled at Hillhead, a long walk for her.

She fit in well with the upper class kids, but missed the easy camaraderie of her tenement friends. Then came a flare up of infection in her knee, a return of the infection from her early childhood. It became impossible to walk to Hillhead each day. She found herself, with no regrets, back in the nonpaying school with the poor children.

She did, however, fear the punishment meted out for the least infraction of the rules. The guilty child was ordered to hold out his or her hand, palm up. The teacher would strike the palm a very sharp blow with a stick that was large enough to deliver stinging pain. It happened only once to Liz, and she determined it would never happen again on account of anything she would do.

The incident that led to the punishment was not of her doing, though it amused her as much as the rest of the class. A teacher who was disliked by the students because of his gruff and unfriendly manner happened to have a wooden leg. The class gathered around a table, the teacher with his wooden leg next to a table leg. Liz sat at an angle where she saw a boy beside the teacher, with all the skill of a promising young pickpocket, use his book strap to strap the wooden leg to the table leg. Wisely and quietly he left his seat. Other children changed seats from time to time as they worked on their projects. Later, the surprised teacher tried to rise from the bench and found himself trapped. His face turned red with anger.

"Who did this?" he bellowed

Though many in the class knew who had done it, no one would identify the guilty party. The teacher required every member of the class to file past him and hold out a hand for the dreaded blow. Liz, with her keen sense of justice, felt outraged. At the same time she respected the code of silence and privately admired the courage and skill of the boy with the book strap.

A few months later, having recovered the full use of her knee, Liz found herself back at Hillhead. There she finished the eighth grade and received her certificate of graduation. In spite of all the changing of schools, a notation on her certificate stated that she had graduated with an outstanding academic record. She was bright, a natural-born student and had learned the very best English at home. She enjoyed school, liked to study, and constantly read English and Scottish literature. Accounts of kings and queens fascinated her, as did the Scottish struggles for independence and the legends of Robert the Bruce. She relished the work of Robert Burns. Her knowledge of Gaelic gave her an edge in understanding the deeper meaning of his poetry, its subtle commentary on the living conditions of the poor. She greatly enjoyed the way Burns ridiculed those who made a show of their wealth and status, and she admired the way he found virtue in the simple life and faith of the hard-working, poor farmers among whom he had grown up nearly a hundred years earlier.

Eventually David found it necessary to move the family to less expensive rooms in a worse tenement. Nevertheless, Alice insisted Liz stay at Hillhead. Shifting back and forth between the school for the poor and Hillhead, Liz found she could fit in and enjoy the company of both, yet always she held herself to a high standard of morals and language, the marks of class in Britain.

One early morning as she hurried out of the building clutching her schoolbooks, she stumbled over a man who was curled up and sleeping in the shelter of the doorway. Shock raced through her. Was he dead?

He groaned, moved a little and half opened his eyes—bleary within his lumpy, unshorn face. The stench of alcohol and urine rose around him. A small stream of yellow ice meandered from a puddle near his head down into the rutted street. She felt nothing but revulsion for this man, who of his own free will had chosen the life of a drunk. Feeling sullied, she hurried away. Father had preached strong words on the subject of liquor. He had lectured to groups in and out of the church on the evils of profiteering from liquor—seriously antagonizing the local distillers and pub owners. Now this disreputable drunk had brought her father's words to life inside her. In future years she would work hard to make liquor illegal.

Having developed deep and lasting religious convictions, Liz always tried to remain active in the church, as did David, Alice, and Laurence. It stunned her when the minister of the church in the poor section of Glasgow did not befriend them, something she just naturally supposed he would do. She felt that, to him, she was just one of the poor people and as such did not rate the attention of this minister. This hurt her pride.

Nevertheless, that church with the unfriendly minister gave Liz, with her fine sense of humor, a cherished memory. Years later she enjoyed sharing it with her children. In Scotland at the time it was considered improper to sing songs not directly from the Bible. The congregation did not read as they sang. An appointed song leader stood before them and led the singing from Psalms. She liked this rather plump song leader. It was his task to "line out" the words, quickly singing the next line to be sung. This kept the congregation's attention directed toward him. To make the Psalms more singable, he often adjusted the words to fit the beat of the music. On this particular Sunday he chose an unfortunate meter for Verse 29 of Psalm 22. The line should have been sung: "Before the Lord we bow." To make the beat come out right he lustily sang out: "Before the Lord we bow wow wow."

Picturing a joyous group of singing dogs, Liz could not refrain from laughing, though laughter in church was frowned upon.

It was only as she grew older and gained experience that she came to realize that her father's genuine love and concern for the poor was not typical of all ministers, and many served among the poor only because they had never been called to a wealthier parish, something they earnestly hoped for. As she grew in wisdom and knowledge, she appreciated ever more that she had been raised by very gifted, sincere and dedicated parents, and she did her best to be true to their teaching and example. Like her father, she would always have affection and concern for the unfortunate of the world.

A change came when David received another promotion, becoming superintendent of a branch line in Dumbarton. The family moved with him in the summer of 1899. The railroad provided a better salary and a rather nice house in Dumbarton, in better surroundings than what the family had known in Glasgow. The rent was very modest, a benefit available to workers who made it to the level of branch-line superintendent. The move came at a wonderful time for Liz, for it put her within easy walking distance of Dumbarton Academy, a fine secondary school. She was now thirteen and about to receive an excellent education and make a host of new friends.

That autumn all of Scotland was talking about the turn of the century. Many people thought Armageddon was near and the world would end. Signs in windows advertised seers, palm readers and astrologists. Itinerant evangelists set up tents on the outskirts of the city and held week-long services. Every sort of spiritual help was sought by the worried populace.

For Liz, the only noticeable difficulty brought by the new century was that she had to train her hand to write 1900 on school papers. It felt even stranger to be living in the "twentieth" century. Her tongue rebelled against the sound of it. Nevertheless, holding tight to her faith, she didn't feel the general anxiety. Like her siblings she looked askance at the proliferation of "superstitions."

A more personal problem was becoming evident. As she listened carefully to what was being said in her new school, she realized that women couldn't climb the social ladder by virtue of hard work and achievement as her father had done. Young women of lesser social standing dreamily discussed how they might attract an upper class man. The assumption was that the worth of a woman was judged solely by the status of the man she married. Yet the social rules precluded upper class men from meeting and courting girls from lower classes, thus only girls of great wealth and beauty had the remotest possibility of success. It offended Liz's sense of justice to imagine competing in that game. Instead, she decided to become an excellent teacher and be judged by her merits. Her natural affection for little children would help. Marjorie and Nellie were already teaching, and Liz determined to follow their example.

It seems a long time ago, but memories came flooding back through the tears...

4 Sisters

Marjorie had just returned from Africa. She wrote that Liz should join her in Manchester, England, where two years ago Marjorie had finished her teacher training and now had been hired to teach school in a nearby town. She recommended the teacher training to Liz.

Eager for an adventure of her own, Liz packed her bags and boarded the train. Besides attending a good school she looked forward to hearing about Marjorie's African adventure. Marjorie met the train, looked her straight in the eyes and gave her the jokingly stern look that meant she was glad to see her. She settled Liz in the apartment, having added a cot to the bedroom. The next day she helped Liz enroll in the school.

Marjorie obviously liked having Liz's company. She was filled with good humor while getting ready for work in the mornings, and in the evenings told more and more of her story. After getting her teaching credential, she had taught near Manchester for one year when the church in which she was active put out a call on behalf of the Free Church Mission Board. They needed teachers for a mission in Africa. She applied immediately. The idea of teaching young African children who were just then hearing the Christian message excited her.

"Were there many applicants?" Liz asked as they sat in the kitchen nook having tea on Saturday afternoon.

"Yes, there were quite a number, but I think winning that scripture contest helped." Outside, the streetcar clanged.

"We were all so very proud of you!" Liz and the family had followed the contest closely. Not only the Free Church, but the entire

Presbyterian Church of Britain had sponsored the contest through the adult Sunday School Division. It had been conducted all over Scotland and England, and Marjorie had won first prize.

"Well, that gave me a good deal of recognition," Marjorie admitted. "It was publicized in every church handbill." She lifted the cup and sipped. "They accepted me and I sailed for Africa." She had a faraway look as she replaced the cup in its saucer.

Liz was still in awe of Marjorie's ability to learn that difficult tongue. "Say 'Jesus loves me' in that African language."

Marjorie uttered a string of unworldly sounds, including clicks that seemed to come from her throat—sounds Liz couldn't begin to imitate. The head missionary had been extremely pleased with her work. Marjorie sighed. "I loved teaching those bright-eyed children. You should have seen them leaning forward on their benches to hear Bible stories for the first time."

But the climate and food had not agreed with her, and for much of the year she had suffered terribly with dysentery. Disheartened, she returned to England at the end of the year and found the teaching position she now held on the outskirts of Manchester.

Marjorie suddenly changed the subject. "We'll manage all right on what we have, Liz. David wrote that he'll send the pension check for you, but it will stop when you turn sixteen."

The small monthly pension Liz received as the child of a deceased minister hardly covered her food, but every little bit counted. David, her legal guardian, received the check from the Church. In March it would be halved, and after that they would both live on Marjorie's salary. "Marj, I've done some thinking," Liz said. "Next term I shall sign up for extra classes. Next year too, so I can finish my training in two years instead of three. Then I will be less a burden to you."

Marjorie raised her eyebrows. "I don't know if that can be done. You're a bright girl but this is a demanding curriculum."

"I'll do it." Liz had noticed that she was one of the top students—as she had been in Dumbarton Academy.

The plan worked. Despite the heavy load, Liz kept up with and enjoyed her studies. At mid term Alice arrived to keep house for them, sleeping on a third cot set up in the bedroom. Liz immersed herself totally in her studies and training, including learning to play the piano—a requirement for an elementary certificate. The piano instructor worked with her in one of many small rooms in a special wing of the campus, each just large enough for an old piano, then left her to practice. But her studies didn't stop her from thinking about Africa. It seemed to her that to spread the Gospel to the heathen was the highest calling, and, unlike the ministry, such teaching assignments were open to women. Should she test her faith and dedication on a mission? The specter of illness bothered her, however, and she kept her thoughts to herself. In later years she would speak to her children and grandchildren in great admiration of the work of Christian missionaries in China, India, and Africa.

During that year in Manchester Liz also grew close to Nellie, who had been teaching for several years in Scotland but had very bad teeth and began to suffer from generally poor health. Ultimately she found it difficult to live alone. Nellie gave up her teaching and went to live with David in Dumbarton. On holidays Marjorie, Alice and Liz took the train to visit Nellie and David, and the family vacationed together, except for John. During these holidays Liz shared a room with Nellie, who fascinated her in a different way than Marjorie. Despite their greater age disparity a bond of affection tightened between them. They talked long into the night discussing religion, the occult, the teaching profession, politics, and a certain charming man. Nellie confided that the previous Christmas she had gone with him on a visit to London, two days to the south. Liz hid her shock. Nellie spoke of this admirer in veiled tones as though they might be secretly married. However, Nellie wore no ring. Liz didn't feel free to question her.

Nellie's health failed to improve. Her teeth and her head ached. She felt weak and weary. Liz told her that when her own teeth ached she sometimes went into the chemistry room in Manchester when no

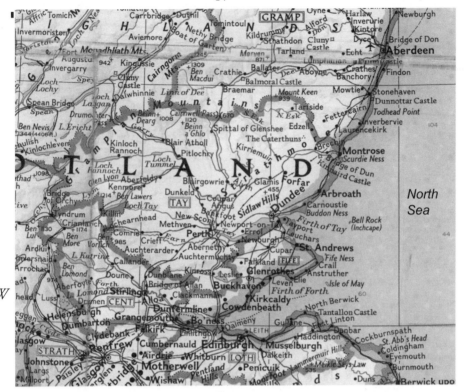

Scotland: Perth low center, Crathie north center. Edinburgh, Glasgow, Dumbarton south, Loch Lomond just north of Dumbarton. Atlantic Ocean just off map to the west. This space compresses about 112 miles southward to England. 1" = 26 miles

Irish Sea along west coast, Liverpool southwest, Manchester about 39 miles inland. Visible in northeast corner: North Sea. Directly south of it lies Lincolnshire, home of Sarah Pidd. 1" = 26 miles

one was there and took a wee bit of cocaine powder to rub on her gums. For a time it lessened the pain. Nellie purchased a vial of that powder at the apothecary and tried it, but it wore off quickly and didn't stop her health from deteriorating. Eventually Alice moved back to Dumbarton to care for Nellie. Train service was good between Dumbarton and Manchester, and thanks to David all the sisters had railroad passes. With or without Marjorie, Liz made the trip as often as she could, utilizing her time on the train to read her books and do her schoolwork.

Nellie's admirer came from time to time to see her. A handsome, charming man, he occasionally took her out to dinner or an evening of entertainment. One Saturday evening when Nellie was getting ready and the man was waiting, David questioned him about his work.

Curious, Liz listened intently to the response. "I made a bundle in South Africa," he said, "so don't need steady employment."

That night when she returned to the house, Nellie tiptoed into the bedroom, but Liz lay awake. They talked.

"I love him," Nellie confided. "I can't imagine life without him." She groaned. "I'm sure he would buy a house for us to settle in if I were well. Oh but my head hurts. I'm sure it's from these corrupted teeth!"

Liz tried to believe the man's stories and trust in Nellie's hopes. Hard working, sensible David, on the other hand, doubted and disapproved of the man.

Tooth decay was common around Perth. Some blamed the water. It seemed that Liz and Nellie were constantly seeing the dentist. Liz, who was then sixteen, gladly made an appointment to have several of her teeth removed and a partial plate of artificial teeth installed. "If your eye offends thee, pluck it out," she quipped to Nellie.

Nellie, at age twenty-seven, was advised by the dentist to have all her teeth removed and be fitted with a complete set of false teeth. She set a date for the extractions just after Liz's plate was installed. "When I'm well," Nellie confided to Liz, "I'll be getting married the proper way. You'll see."

Liz returned to school in Manchester and heard the story later. Nellie felt particularly unwell the day she went in to have her teeth pulled, but tried to smile as she told Alice, "Soon I'll be myself again."

The dentist gave her chloroform. Afterwards, while she was regaining consciousness in the dentist's chair, the nurse opened the windows wide to clear the air of the smell of the chloroform. It was a cold, raw April day and Nellie became thoroughly chilled. Alice took her home in a hired buggy, but with her best efforts could not make her warm and comfortable. Quickly she developed what seemed a bad cold. It worsened. David hired a nurse to help Alice, but a few days later, on April 23rd, Nellie died.

Liz was devastated. Nellie had filled an important place in her life, a close confidant during her time of growing into a young woman. Once again David made funeral arrangements. The service was held in St. Paul's Free Church in Perth, attended by many who fondly remembered the Symon family. With a great many tears Nellie was laid to rest in the family plot beside Father, Mother and the graves of the three infants. Nellie's supposedly ardent admirer made no appearance at the funeral. Liz privately concluded that he lacked the means of supporting a wife. David thought worse of him, that he'd never intended to support one. The man had visited after they hired a nurse for Nellie, but despite his supposed fortune, never offered to help with the expenses.

After Nellie was buried, her suitor came to the house while David was gone, claimed he had given Nellie a rather large sum of money and wanted most of it back. He insisted that either Alice, Liz or the nurse had taken the money and hidden it away. He insisted on searching the house. After causing a lot of trouble and confusion—finding no money—he angrily left and was never heard from again. David, when he returned, called the man an unscrupulous fraud. "He staged that entire scene," he declared, "to excuse himself for not offering to help pay any of the medical and burial costs."

Liz grieved not only for the loss of her beloved sister but for the way Nellie must have suffered as a result of her treatment by that faithless lover. A sentimental and romantic sixteen-year-old, Liz felt deeply troubled by the entire affair and would for years to come. It was a cautionary tale she would later tell her daughters and granddaughters. It also angered her, with her rigid morality, to be accused of taking the money. She simply could not understand how anyone could be such a villain.

Nellie's death devastated Marjorie. From earliest childhood they had shared their frustration over the strict discipline in the family, and for a long time shared plans to become teachers. Nellie had been a stabilizing influence for the younger, more impulsive Marjorie. Now Liz, though buried in her studies, couldn't help but notice Marjorie's growing restlessness.

One evening as the three sisters ate their light supper, Marjorie sighed, "Maybe I shouldn't have left Africa."

"But you were ill for so long!" Alice exclaimed. "You could have died."

"Maybe I was being tested and didn't endure long enough. Maybe I failed God."

"But Marj," Liz pointed out, "You are an excellent teacher. That must be God's purpose for you."

Marjorie toyed with the spoon on her saucer. "Maybe I just don't want to spend the rest of my life as an old maid teacher."

That stunned Liz, who had been eagerly anticipating receiving her teaching certificate so she could spend her days in a schoolroom and her evenings with Marjorie. "I thought you didn't want to marry."

Marjorie looked at her, then got up from the table and shrugged on her coat. "Come, let's go to town and see what's happening."

Rising to gather the plates, Alice told them she would tidy up. "Go on you two. Have a good time."

On the way to the corner streetcar-stop, Liz recalled several letters she'd seen in the mailbox addressed to Marjorie, posted from the United

States. Marjorie hadn't mentioned them and Liz's strong sense of privacy kept her from saying anything. Now she wondered if a man had sent them. As the streetcar wended its way to the old town center, Marjorie's remark about being an old maid lingered in Liz's mind. Stepping off the car, Liz looked around. Often they came upon public meetings of political or religious interest, and this appeared to be a promising evening. A large number of people strolled the streets in the spring air, the days having become long.

"This is none of my business," Liz said, "but are you writing to someone in the United States? I couldn't help but see the letter in he box yesterday."

Clearly not at all upset, Marjorie said, "Yes. James." Suddenly she became animated and her step quickened. "He knew Father in Edinburgh when he was finishing at the University and preaching at the mission church. Isn't that interesting? He wrote that Father was one of the best preachers he'd ever heard. James went to his services every Sunday and made a point of meeting Father. He remembers meeting Mother too, with David and Alice when they were wee. Oh Liz, he writes fine letters! His penmanship is elegant. I'll show you when we get home."

"When did you meet him?"

"I haven't met him. He's been in the United States for years. He wrote to the Free Church board asking about the Symon family. My minister heard of it and sent James my address. I wrote to him."

"How long have you corresponded?"

"I got the first letter in Africa."

Liz sensed that this was no small matter. "What is he doing in the United States?"

"He's an attorney. Quite prosperous. Very intelligent, very kind. She grabbed Liz's hand and pulled her swiftly toward a crowd that had gathered around the steps of a building. "This must be the Mormons! James wrote that they'd be here tonight. He told them about us, told them we're the daughters of John Symon and we should hear about the Mormons."

"Mormons?"

"It's a new religion." She lowered her voice to a whisper, for they were edging into the crowd and a man on the stairs was speaking. The slanting rays of the sun down the street colored the stone blocks of the building a golden hue.

This was no ordinary religious revival. The speaker said he was on a mission and had come to tell the people of England about a beautiful place called Utah. He told of a lake so filled with salt that people floated like corks when they went out for a recreational swim. Liz recalled the word "Utah" on the letters. Always curious to learn about new religions, she listened attentively. The speaker introduced a second "elder," who spoke about a latter-day prophet named Joseph Smith. He ended his talk with a glowing report of the happy community of love and good will in Utah, a land "flowing with milk and honey" where everyone had a good job, a good home and plenty of food. Then, with the help of the other elder, he circulated some literature.

People dispersed or stood talking. Marjorie pulled Liz toward the last speaker. "I am Marjorie Symon," she said, accepting a pamphlet. "And this is my sister Liz."

The man's middle-aged face stretched in a smile. "Well, how do you do! I was told to look for you when we were here. You have a friend who speaks highly of your father, God rest his soul."

The missionaries stayed in Manchester two weeks, speaking every evening. Marjorie and Liz attended several times, but the more Liz heard the preaching the less impressed she was. This faith seemed very odd, in no way similar to the one in which she had grown up. She found nothing attractive about it, except the beautiful country without poverty. With Marjorie it was different. Perhaps thinking more about James than the theology, she listened eagerly to the missionaries and pored over their literature. Liz learned that James wanted Marjorie to come to Utah. He had hinted at the possibility of marriage. He assured her there was a great need for school teachers in the developing new country.

The sisters were having tea and scones one morning when Marjorie announced, "I've decided to go see what might be in store for me in Utah."

Alice caught her breath. Liz wasn't surprised, but felt uneasy for Marjorie. Over the next two weeks she and Marjorie talked about the fact that Marjorie had never met James. They talked about the strangeness of a religion in which a man who called himself a prophet of God had witnessed religious beliefs written in an unknown language on golden tablets, then translated with the help of a special God-given instrument—the urim and thummim. They discussed whether the Latter Day Saints were Christian, and what it meant to be a Christian. As they lay in the dark one night, Marjorie promised Liz and Alice that she would not join "The Church" until she had met James and experienced the religion to be sure it was all that he and the missionaries said it was.

"I'm glad to hear that," Liz said truthfully.

"I think I'm a fair teacher," Marjorie said. "So I—"

"Excellent teacher," Liz corrected.

"So regardless of what happens between Jimmy and me, I can always support myself. Maybe better in America than in Scotland or England."

Relieved to hear that Marjorie would wait to join the church of the Latter Day Saints, Liz felt herself drifting into sleep, for it was very late.

"I can't believe the coming of the missionaries was a coincidence," Marjorie said, "I believe it was providential—God's guidance for my life just when I needed it."

After supper the next day Marjorie left to sign up with the group of converts who were making plans to emigrate. Liz stayed with Alice. They decided to talk to the minister of the Free Presbyterian Church, which they attended here in England, and see if he would reason with Marjorie.

Marjorie agreed to visit the minister. He tried his best to dissuade her from leaving with the Mormons. He mentioned stories about polygamy, a marital arrangement that Marjorie had seen in Africa among the "unwashed." But Marjorie felt completely confident that, through James, Utah offered Truth and Hope.

In May, 1904, as Liz completed the first year of her teacher training, Marjorie and the Mormon converts boarded a ship in Liverpool. With heavy hearts and a deep sense of loss, Liz and Alice accompanied Marjorie to the docks. They promised to write as soon as they had an address. For a long time they stood hand in hand watching the ship disappear in the west.

They returned to Manchester to close up Marjorie's apartment, Liz having decided to leave England. She told Alice, "I feel we are closing a chapter in our lives." The bonds that had bound the family together were coming apart. Father, Mother and Nellie were dead. Marjorie was gone, John made no attempt to keep in touch, and Laurence was busy with his own affairs, thinking of emigrating to Canada, where, he thought, a man could get ahead faster. Looking to the one dependable anchor in their lives, Liz and Alice returned to Dumbarton to live with David, who was always willing to provide them a home.

—

They didn't plan to stay long with David. Alice, ever anxious for Liz to have the best education, arranged for her to study at an excellent girls college in Edinburgh. At the end of a wonderful summer with her Dumbarton friends, Liz boarded the train with Alice, who would keep house for her in Edinburgh. But as the train sped toward the capital city of Scotland, Liz knew her country wasn't the same without Nellie and Marjorie. She felt very much alone. She loved Alice but saw her more as a mother than a sister in whom she could confide and share adventures. She and Alice had very different temperaments. Practical Alice was concerned with the details of daily living. Liz was more like Marjorie—idealistic, willing to take chances, always wondering about the world beyond.

In Edinburgh Liz threw herself into her studies at the college, becoming one of the top students, but her social life was in Dumbarton. On weekends and holidays she commuted back there to be with the many friends she had made at the Dumbarton Academy. The most important of these was Margaret MacKenzie, called Maggie by her friends.

Maggie was a serious, hard-working student, but like Liz she was full of fun and interested in many things. The two had been friends since they entered the Academy in the same class and worked together on study projects. Maggie, who lived with an aunt and had no brothers or sisters, was as eager for friendship as Liz. During the summer after Marjorie emigrated, the girls had done many things together—attending lectures on all sorts of subjects as well as street rallies and revivals. For fun they had visited mediums who claimed to call up spirits of the dead. They enjoyed each other's company very much. David and Alice had been concerned about Liz being out on the streets, but felt some comfort knowing the two girls were always together. Maggie's aunt had felt the same. This was a period of great independence for Liz and Maggie as they grew into self-reliant young women. So now, commuting on weekends back to Dumbarton, Liz relished the resumption of that fun and independence.

They were fortunate in sharing high ideals, and they supported each other in their personal standards. Both were active in their respective churches—Liz still loyal to the Free Church and Maggie active in the Presbyterian Church of Scotland. They had long discussions about their churches and often attended services with each other. They could see no reason the churches should not get back together. The reasons for the division were diminishing. Church leaders were debating the possibility of reunion, but it was not until 1929 that the two branches officially reunited, something that Liz and Maggie would have welcomed in 1904. They often discussed an incident that had taken place in Glasgow a few years earlier when Liz and her family had been attending church there:

> About the time I was in my early teens the Free Church united with a branch of the Presbyterian Church. However, a segment of the Free Church refused to go along. In an early court ruling the property was awarded to the "Wee Frees" as they were called. One Sunday the churches made quite a spectacular move. The "Wee Frees" (few in number) went to the building for their service. The United, now excluded from the building, gathered on the outside. Inside, the small congregation began singing rather weakly, "Oh God of Bethel by whose hand Thy people still are led." Outside our larger group sang simultaneously, "Behold, how good a thing it is, in unity to dwell." Then singing "Onward Christian Soldiers," we marched off to the town hall where we invoked God's Blessing... "God is our refuge and strength." The courts reversed the ruling later and we moved back [into the church building] and the "Wee Frees" had to move. Finally the separation was seen for what it was. They all joined together in the United Free Church."

During this second year of her college training, the serious side of Liz gave a great deal of thought and prayer to the matter of her own religious faith and commitment. She had been too young to join a church before Father died, and with all the moves and changes, had not felt sufficiently involved in a church to become a member. But in the fall of 1904, her seventeenth year, she had a remarkable spiritual experience. In a letter to her son many years later she described it vividly:

Yesterday while looking through some cards I found the card that was given to me when I joined the Church long ago in Scotland. It was dated October 16, 1904. Seems a long time ago, but memories came flooding back through the tears.

How well I remember that day. I notice it was on Don's birthday, fourteen years before he came. I had decided to be a Christian two months before joining the Church. In fact, I had been trying to "be saved" many times, but not understanding the Christian Gospel, I had felt that my salvation depended entirely on me, and always when my sense of humor got the best of me, I decided I was not a Christian, and that God did not want such as I. However, I could not be happy apart from Him, so after I had attended a six week preaching meeting held in a tent, I made the great decision on the last night of the meetings.

Scotch make no show of their emotions, but feelings are deep. I came out of that meeting feeling like a new person. The grass looked greener and the sky bluer—Oh yes, it is daylight till very late there in the summer.

The night before [joining the church in October] I had walked alone six miles in the country, wondering if I should take this decisive step. I can see again the old stone wall where I stood for a long time before starting home as yet undecided.

I remember the day I came into the church and had my first communion. As was the custom then in Scotland the bookboards were draped in white linen. We sang, "Here O my Lord I see Thee face to face" and every verse had a personal meaning for me.

But even then I had not learned that when sometimes our feelings grow cold and we seem to be out of touch with God, that God does not change and is always wanting us back, and waiting for us. It was only after coming to the U.S. that I learned and realized that when I failed and grew discouraged, that I could find no other satisfaction than in confession and renewal.

And I have failed so often and so terribly, for on that Communion Day my expectations were so high! But when I look at you wonderful six children, all strong in every way, all with keen minds, and above all else all good, then I know that all my religious longings, all my desires to be something I never seemed able to be, were the spiritual seeds that helped produce the kind of children you all came to be.

Maggie, who already belonged to her church, rejoiced with Liz in her conversion and attended with her when Liz made her first communion and was accepted into full membership. Not until this conversion experience in the fall of 1904 had Liz felt secure enough in her faith to join a church. Now, feeling fully adult, she attempted to get people to call her Lizbeth. She filled out her membership card with the name Lizbeth Symon. But Maggie and her other friends found it difficult to change their habit of calling her Liz.

The companionship of Maggie opened many activities that Liz would not have ventured by herself. A favorite pleasure was packing a picnic basket and hiking to the many parks and recreation areas in the beautiful country around Dumbarton.

Liz and Maggie would tighten their corsets, put on their petticoats and big-sleeved dresses, lace their sturdy high-topped shoes, and go for long, vigorous walks. Often they walked the wooded trails and beaches around Loch Lomond. Many people hiked its shores. They came in family groups, and many young people came in church groups. Often the girls were invited to join a group, and they walked with new friends. There was no dating as such, no pairing off in couples, but they made the acquaintance of young men and enjoyed talking to the ones who gave favorable impressions. Scottish society remained very Victorian and "proper" in regard to the relationships between the sexes, and both girls had been brought up to be proper. Maggie's eyes began to twinkle whenever she walked with a particular young man from a nearby hamlet. He began arranging for her and Liz to picnic with his church group on the banks of the lake.

In later years Liz would recall the last year of her schooling in Edinburgh as one of the best years of her life—commuting by train to Dumbarton every weekend and holiday. She would fondly remember the good times and her friendships with Maggie and many others.

Meanwhile Marjorie wrote unenthusiastic letters from Salt Lake City—descriptions of the country and comments on her work as a teacher. She never mentioned James. Liz sensed that they were no longer seeing each other, but something about the mood of the letters prevented her from asking about him.

Then in May of 1905, one year after Marjorie sailed from Liverpool, Liz received the letter that totally changed her life.

"Weeping may endure for a night, but joy cometh in the morning."

5 America

"Do come and accept the job," Marjorie wrote. Only briefly did she mention what Liz had suspected. She was not married, was not involved in "The Church," but was finding enjoyment in her teaching. She said the school salaries were better than in England and Scotland. She had found an opening in her district and, simply on her recommendation, the position would be given to Liz if she would accept it. "I told the school board that the credentials you have received in Edinburgh are the same as mine. They are quite ready to accept them. Dear Liz, I know you will make a wonderful teacher. And good teachers are in great demand here."

Liz sensed an urgency and a wistfulness in the letter. Marjorie was lonely. This would solve the immediate problem of looking for a job. In the past year, with her heavy schedule at school and her active social life, Liz had given little time to thinking about a job. And she did long to be with Marjorie again, particularly now that Marjorie needed her. And oh, the great adventure of going to America!

Still, it was a difficult decision. She discussed it with David and Alice. They said they would miss her very much but with Marjorie there, it might be a way to improve her circumstances. Laurence was planning to go to Canada. David said he had thought about going too. Only his good position with the railroad kept him from emigrating. His friends who had gone to the United States were all doing well and it really did seem to be a land of opportunity.

It hurt to think of leaving Maggie, but Maggie's young man was interested in her and it was likely they would soon be posting their banns. She would become involved with a family, and Liz's precious friendship with her would not be the same. She prayed earnestly about the decision, and ultimately felt that she had God's approval to seek her fortune in the United States. She wrote Marjorie saying she would come and accept the teaching position. She would sail in July and be ready for work in September.

When her schoolwork finished in May, Liz put all her time and effort into preparations for the journey to the New World. Maggie helped her decide what to take and what to leave. The likelihood of never seeing each other again pained them both, but the future was calling them in different directions.

David procured two trunks into which Liz put her goods. Alice also helped her decide what clothes to wear on the ship and what to carry in her valise. Unsure of what might be available in Utah, Liz wanted an adequate wardrobe that would last for awhile. She had many treasured books but had to choose only a few to go. Finally the trunks were packed. Friends gave her a final farewell party, then the day of departure arrived. The trunks were locked and sent to the docks in Glasgow the day before she was to sail. To be sure she would not forget her trunk keys, David hung them on the chandelier in the living room of his Dumbarton home, the place they would still be hanging when she remembered them the day her ship docked in New York. She would be grateful to a good natured customs official who managed to open and re-shut the trunks without her keys. He had done that many times for other travelers.

David arranged her passage on the ocean liner *Columbia* of the Anchor Line, a modern steamer. The day of her departure in early July of 1905 bonnie Scotland was at her bonnie best. The sun was bright, but the breeze over the water made the people standing on the deck button their coats and hug their knit shawls. As the ship slipped away from the Glasgow dock for its passage down the River Clyde toward the ocean, the air was so clear she could see the green hills for miles and miles beyond the city.

The ship would be visible as it passed Dumbarton Castle, "the Rock." By prearrangement Maggie and some other friends would be there to wave a farewell with a large white sheet. Liz strained her eyes to catch sight of it, and when she did the distance was such that it appeared to be the size of a white handkerchief. She could not distinguish the people who waved it. This would be Liz's last sight of anything in Scotland.

A great sadness welled up within her as she realized she was leaving everything she had cherished and loved—David and Alice who had given so much of themselves to help her through the loss of her parents, Father in the pulpit of the fine old church in Perth, Nellie who rested beside her parents in the graveyard, the wonderful group of friends connected to the white dot on the old castle, Scotland herself. All disappeared as the ship moved down the firth to the sea.

Was it the distance or the tears that finally shut Dumbarton Castle and the tiny white flag of friendship from her eyes? She found herself engulfed by acute grief, accented by a deep weariness from her last few days of preparation. She made her way to the little room that she would share with another young lady passenger and threw herself on her bunk. There she wept like a little girl sent to her room, isolated from family and friends, afraid she had lost everything of value to her, adrift from the anchors of her life. Meanwhile the ship plowed through the Firth of Clyde into the North Channel, past the coast of Northern Ireland and into a beautiful sunset on the Atlantic Ocean.

"Weeping may endure for a night, but joy cometh in the morning," Liz later wrote of the experience. Fortune had smiled on her in the selection of a roommate. They had been introduced when they agreed to share the little room for the voyage, but had gone their separate ways. Mary Jane did not disturb her when she found her roommate asleep. In her weariness and sorrow Liz slept straight through supper and the night. It was not until they were dressing the next morning that they actually became acquainted.

"As I recall, your name is Elizabeth," Mary Jane said with a big smile.

"Lizbeth," she told Mary Jane, who was enthusiastic about the trip and clearly eager to visit. Liz, being naturally very sociable, could not continue to grieve in the presence of this chatty outgoing girl. At once they became fast friends.

Smooth seas and fair weather made for a pleasant crossing. Liz and Mary Jane spent many hours walking the decks and talking about their lives in Scotland and their hopes and dreams for the future. They shared daily Bible readings and afternoon tea. They had much in common and many differences to share. Like Marjorie, Mary Jane was on her way to meet a man she hoped to marry. This bothered Liz but she held her tongue. Like Maggie, Mary Jane had been a faithful member and worker in the Presbyterian Church of Scotland, teaching in the Sunday school. Liz, who since her summers in Carnoustie had loved the sea, enjoyed the cool air on the deck. Mary Jane did too. They discussed their religious views. Mary Jane's commitment was less intense but she too had been raised by a close-knit family with strict morals.

Her older brother had emigrated to New York a few years before and was a successful businessman. Liz, who was concerned about getting through customs and finding the right train connections to Utah, was glad to hear that brother Robert would meet them at the docks in New York. "I might need to find lodging and stay over a day or two," she told Mary Jane. "Do you suppose Robert could advise me where to stay?"

"Oh, don't worry about a thing," Mary Jane said. "Robert will take care of everything. He's a wonderful brother. I'm going west as far as Chicago. He'll take care of both of us for the stopover. I'm so much looking forward to seeing him again! And meeting his wife! He married since he went to New York. She's a real American but her parents came from Sweden. Robert says everyone in America came from somewhere else."

Mary Jane's friendship proved a blessing for Liz and lifted a big concern from her. In Scotland, brother David had made all the arrangements for her trip to New York, but on landing in New York she would have been totally on her own in a strange country. "How wonderful to have him guide us through the American wilderness." She quipped to Mary Jane.

And it was wonderful. Robert saw to their luggage and helped them through customs. Before she boarded the *Columbia*, Liz had already passed all the requirements for entering the United States. In those days the shipping lines made sure all immigrants would be accepted by the U.S. authorities; the law required that rejected passengers be returned to their home country at the expense of the shipping company. This was a time of very heavy immigration, and the rules were strictly enforced. Long lines of tired people waited at Ellis Island, many who spoke only a foreign language, some needing health exams if it was deemed that they hadn't been adequately checked before leaving their home ports or if illness had arisen during the passage. Having an American meet the boat and vouch for a passenger saved a great deal of time in clearing customs. Except for the brief problem of locked trunks and no keys, Liz and Mary Jane avoided the delays that were such a burden to many who passed through the crowded and frightening "Ellis Island experience." The customs official spelled Liz's name "Symons," but Liz didn't bother to correct it.

They landed in New York on Saturday after a ten-day crossing. "Brother Robert" made reservations for them to board the train for Chicago on Monday. This gave them a rest on Sunday and the opportunity to see New York. Relieved to be safely through customs and no longer worried about lodging and train connections, Liz relaxed and thoroughly enjoyed her day in New York.

But how different was this Sunday with her new friends! Robert and his wife said the girls simply had to visit Coney Island. That place was like nothing Liz had ever experienced before. It amazed and shocked her. She had a guilty feeling about spending the Sabbath in such a place. Yet another part of her eagerly joined the large crowds of happy people. Coney Island epitomized the "Gay Nineties" and the American love of glitter and entertainment. The very size of it astounded her. It was world famous, but though she had heard of it, she had given it no thought. Thousands and thousands of people in a holiday mood were enjoying the more than two miles of public beaches, a broad board walk, public bathhouses, carousels, exhibitions, dancing, concerts, freak shows, a gigantic roller coaster, penny arcades, assorted game booths, ferris wheels, shooting galleries, souvenir shops, and hundreds of eating places. So this was America! Liz never forgot that day, mentioning it whenever people asked her to reminisce about her first impression of America.

As Liz and Mary Jane settled into their comfortable seats for the long journey to Chicago, they continued to share their astonishment about the sideshows on Coney Island. But soon the subject returned to Mary Jane's reason for coming to America, for it continued to bother Liz. She ventured, "Are you sure you'll be happy marrying a man you haven't met face to face?"

On shipboard Mary Jane had bubbled with excitement and anticipation about getting married. She had shown Liz a picture of Danny. Liz hadn't allowed her disapproval to show, having been taught to keep criticism about other people to herself. She had been only a little less circumspect with Marjorie, though they were sisters.

In her optimistic and enthusiastic way Mary Jane assured Liz that it would all turn out wonderfully. She just knew Danny was marvelous. With a confidential smile she added, "He comes highly recommended by friends. And you know, Liz, this is what people all over America are doin'. The men come from every country. They get settled with jobs then send back home for a girl to come and marry them."

"But I expect this would normally be a girl they knew and loved. Someone known to the family." To Liz the idea of marriage to a total stranger seemed barbaric, bordering on immoral. "My sister's intended knew our father and there were family friends in common, but even then something seems to have gone wrong."

With a reassuring smile Mary Jane reached over and patted Liz's hand. "Dinna' worry, dear friend. Danny is the answer to my dreams."

The train passed through more farmland than Liz had ever seen before. New passengers boarded at the stops. Liz and Mary Jane visited all day, eating in the dining car. They exchanged covertly elevated eyebrows at some of the more interesting passengers. Gradually daylight faded and darkness enveloped the train. Even the people in the seats in front and behind were obscured, until the conductor came by to light small oil lamps ensconced above some of the seats, politely asking nearby passengers whether they wished to be left in darkness. Many did, having curled up on their seats to sleep. Liz and Mary Jane continued to talk and needed no light. But it had been a long day and the padded seatback and armrest became ever more comfortable. Their talk slowed down. Then it seemed to Liz she was on the evening train from Dumbarton to Edinburgh. She slept to the lulling sway of the car and the click of the rails. Several times in the night she became momentarily aware of Mary Jane's head on her shoulder, or that her head had been on Mary Jane's shoulder.

Morning arrived to the tune of shrill whistles, jerky stops, and the clang of bells as vendors boarded the train selling breakfast rolls, fruit and coffee. Liz barely had time to comb out her long, curly hair, pin it up, and put on her hat when the conductor announced "Chicago." Here she would change trains and leave Mary Jane.

Brushing wrinkles out of her frock, Mary Jane grinned at Liz with excited anticipation. They took their bags and stepped off the train under the high vaulted structure of a large station. Mary Jane waved happily at a man holding a handpainted sign that read: MARY JANE. He strode toward them, tossing away the sign. "Why you're as pretty as your picture," he said, taking Mary Jane by the shoulders and kissing her—a public demonstration of affection that embarrassed Liz.

Blushing, Mary Jane introduced Danny and Liz. Handsome in a rugged sort of way, Danny handled the luggage in a manner that indicated he was used to being in charge. He loaded Mary Jane's trunks on a push wagon, and they accompanied Liz as she checked her trunks through to Salt Lake.

Danny remarked, "I hope you like them damned Mormons." His accent was strange to Liz, as was the crude remark directed at a young lady.

Liz instinctively disliked the man and felt a twinge of concern for her friend. Danny was clearly anxious to leave. Mary Jane looked at Liz with an expression that made her seem a little lost. Liz hugged her. They clung to each other for a desperate moment, Liz aware that they had shared every mile of a very critical transition in their lives. They promised to keep in touch. As Mary Jane and Danny disappeared into the noisy crowd, Liz once again felt a deep sense of loneliness and a concern for the future. In all the vast Chicago station she saw not one friendly face, not one smile.

She sat on the bench, bowed her head and prayed earnestly for God's guidance for her new friend and for herself in the days ahead. She prided herself on her ability to judge character and feared for Mary Jane's happiness. She was not surprised when, just two weeks later at Marjorie's address in Salt Lake, she received a letter telling her that Mary Jane was en route back to bonnie Scotland. The letter had been posted from New York, where Mary Jane was enjoying a visit with Robert and his wife. The letter was short on details concerning the Chicago adventure, but, in Mary Jane's enthusiastic manner, was filled with accounts of the wonderful sights of New York.

Liz could think of no kind way to respond to the letter. As it turned out, she needn't have worried. She had no address in Scotland for Mary Jane nor did she remember an address for Robert in New York. She waited for a letter from Scotland that never came. Among her memories, Mary Jane would be cherished all her life under the label: "Ships that pass in the night." If a child or grandchild asked what she meant by that, she would quote a bit of Longfellow's poem and explain that people "sailed" past each other on the differing courses of their lives. She would describe the vast dark of the sea at night and the surprise and happiness of the passengers upon seeing the lights of an approching vessel and hearing the voices of the passengers calling. But soon again there was only darkness and silence.

Liz would pass a couple more "ships" on her journey to Salt Lake. But now, in the Chicago train station, she felt crushed by the sounds of unfamiliar languages, or English spoken with such strange accents that it sounded alien. Never before had she felt so alone. Even among strangers there had always been the pleasant sound of familiar words and a comfortable knowledge that within an easy train ride she could return to a home cared for by David and Alice. The fearful distance from Scotland hurt like a knife in her breast.

Seeing a news stand, she thought something to read might ease the pain. She browsed and found an inspirational religious book that caught her fancy, *Pearls From Many Seas.* Hoping it would provide some useful guidance, she bought the book and read a few pages before her train was announced on the loudspeaker.

She closed the book on her finger and lugged her valise toward the platform. A older, uniformed conductor smiled in a friendly way as he relieved her of her bag and gave her a hand up the stairs. She thanked him.

"The pleasure is mine, Miss Symon," he said reading the tag on her luggage. Scotland resonated in his voice.

Smiling her further thanks, she found a seat. As the friendly conductor made his rounds, checking the tickets and making sure all the passengers in his care were settled, she continued to read her book. Then he was lowering himself into the vacant seat next to her. "Have ye done much traveling then?" he inquired with a warm smile.

"Only in Scotland and England. I had a rail pass. My older brother is superintendent of the Dumbarton Line."

"I once knew that line well."

This made her feel almost at home. She told him about all the traveling she had done between Manchester and Dumbarton, then between Manchester and Edinburgh. But everything in America is so very strange, and so big."

"Ay, but ye'll get the drift of it before you know, and you'll like America." Noting the book she was reading he asked, "Are you a church girl?"

"Oh yes, yes." She told him about her background in the Free Church.

They visited while watching the remnants of Chicago blend into the countryside—vast farms stretching farther than she could see. He said he also came from a religious background in the Presbyterian Church. Later when the conversation got around to her short stay in New York, she told him of her visit to Coney Island.

He looked shocked. "Little girl," he said sternly, "ye'll find it much harder to be a Christian in America than in Scotland. Always be true to your faith. With the fine background that ye have I'm sure you won't neglect it."

"No sir, I won't." She and the old conductor enjoyed each other's company, and had time for much conversation in the long stretches between stops. After seeing to his duties, he always reclaimed his seat beside her. Some of the stops were nothing more than a slowing down at a forlorn station in the vast prairie while the assistant engineer hooked the waiting mail bag. At one such station she saw two women sitting on the sidetrack, tugging blankets over their shoulders. Long black braids hung down their backs.

Alarmed, she asked the conductor if the train would be in any danger as they penetrated deeper into Indian country.

He smiled indulgently and shook his head. "The last Indians were subdued several years ago, just before the turn of the century. All the troublemakers are on reservations, so I've heard. We've never had the slightest problem."

Relieved, she appreciated his friendship. She asked his advice in setting up her Pullman bed. As he provided details of American train travel, she was increasingly awed by the vastness that stretched far and wide out the window, where night was beginning to shadow the scenery again. Though it traveled at a high speed, the train seemed to be making little progress crossing the plain. In the twilight the little farmhouses stood farther and farther apart. In between were enormous stretches of land with nothing except occasional herds of cattle and an occasional windmill. The conductor accompanied her to the dining car, though he ate in the employee's car.

At the supper table she met a family with older children, laughed at their jokes, and told them where she came from. They planned to go to Oregon and make their fortune.

The next morning, to her surprise, the plains hadn't changed at all. Returning to his seat beside her, the friendly conductor told her about the homestead laws and explained that many of the travelers on the train, including families with small children, were going west to find land and start new homes. "It's an entirely new country out here," he said with obvious pleasure. "It's got some rough edges and a number of rough people, but also some very cultured people. There are wonderful opportunities for young people." Flipping his *r*'s for emphasis, he concluded, "A verra great future here."

By the end of the day she was beginning to see a formidable looking range of mountains in the west, behind the setting sun. The train stopped for longer than usual in Colorado, adding an additional engine for the steep grades ahead. The friendly conductor came to say good-bye, for this ended his run. He introduced her to the new conductor. Later she would remember it as "entrusting her to the new conductor," who also proved to be kind and helpful, though he was not Scottish. The friendship and care of the conductors, the chance to visit with other travelers and learn something about them, and the simple pleasure of her upper Pullman bunk where she slept soundly to the rhythmic clicking of the rails made her journey a generally pleasant experience.

Not least among the pleasures of the trip was a fine looking young man who took to sitting beside her. He had an open smile, a keen sense of humor, and a definite interest in visiting with her. Dressed in worn but well washed work clothes, he exuded a natural confidence without seeming the least bit arrogant. He was enthusiastic about the West. Growing up on a farm in Illinois, he had always dreamed of going west. Now, having finished high school and two years of working on neighboring farms, he had saved money enough for his trip. He planned to find work on a cattle ranch, learn all about the business then get a ranch of his own. He was so sure, so confident— typical, she would later learn, of the people heading west for a new start in "the promised land"—that she didn't want to tell him of her fears. Clearly he felt none of the uncertainties that bothered her.

He would get a twinkle in his eye and tell her one of his many little jokes, such as, "A stranger rode up to a cowhand sitting on a fence and said, 'Howdy, I'd like to talk to your boss. Would you mind getting him for me?' The cowhand replied, "The SOB hasn't been born yet!"

She didn't understand SOB, but the rest made her laugh. His enthusiasm for the West was contagious. His way of describing western ways had her laughing more than she had laughed since leaving Dumbarton. As the train chugged slowly up a mountain through spectacular scenery she told him she had a teaching position waiting for her.

His eyes opened wider and his smile filled with something she didn't understand. "Why, that's wonderful!" Then he began to laugh. "Maybe you'd oughta know, school marms in the West don't teach for very long."

"And why would that be?"

He glanced out the window where the black smoke streamed past, perhaps looking beyond it to the evergreen forests and endless mountains with blue peaks in the distance.. Then he turned to her with both eyes crinkled in a smile. "Well, there aren't enough ladies out there. Ranchers and cowboys look to the schoolhouses to find the best wives. Yes siree, one of the finest things about the West is all them fine-talkin' ranch wives who came out to teach school. They sure do raise up bright kids and good citizens." He gave her smile. "Not many as pretty as you are, Lizbeth. Nor as fine talkin'."

His irrepressible humor returned. "Why, I'd think you hadn't read any dime novels! Don't you know the rancher always gets the schoolmarm? So's they can populate the country with smart people?"

Liz laughed along with him. "Be assured," she told him with mock archness, "that was hardly foremost on my mind while I studied all those books in Scotland. I guess I'll have to start reading dime novels."

He laughed good naturedly, then asked in a more subdued tone, "Are you a Mormon?"

She assured him she was not. Under his breath he said something disparaging about Mormons that she didn't catch. "Then why go to Utah? I'm sure you'd find Wyoming more to your liking. Wyoming's prime territory. A man can start at the bottom and work his way to the top. Why, before he's through he could own one of the biggest outfits."

"Why don't you go to Utah and become a rancher there?"

"I wouldn't want to try for a ranch there. The Mormons have everything all wrapped up."

That remark bothered her some, but she was enjoying herself. This conversation was more open and easygoing than any she remembered with young men in Scotland. He was obviously a decent fellow but his personal remark about her looks and his implication that he would be pleased if she would teach school near where he would be ranching just wouldn't have been made in Scotland, not by any man she'd just met. Nevertheless she liked this relaxed manner and found herself sharing more about herself than she would have on a train back home. America was different, and the difference interested her.

They were in Colorado near the Wyoming border when he gathered his things and prepared to leave the train. As the train slowed he said he had corresponded with the owner of a large ranch. "I'll probably spend my time diggin' postholes before they let me work the cattle." With a grin he quipped, "Leastwise that's one job where a man can start at the top."

He obviously thought he'd said something funny and Liz laughed with him, though, knowing nothing about postholes, she feared she'd missed some of the point of his joke. As he stood up in the aisle, napsack over his shoulder, he gave her hand more of a squeeze than a hand shake. Still holding it he looked into her eyes and said, "When you get tired of Utah, come to Wyoming. I'm sure you'll find a school there."

She liked the feel of her hand in his big strong calloused hand. She had never had a handshake quite like it. She found herself wondering what life would be like on a ranch in this country where towns were so far apart. It had been a very long time since she'd seen one. She found it impossible to imagine living so far from other people. She had never known anything but city life, with family and friends always nearby. It would be frightening, she realized, to be cut off from civilization.

The next day, her last on the train, Liz realized that she had been putting aside her fears by showing a cheerful face and joking with people. Now she sat alone. By the time darkness snuffed out the mountain scenery there were a few hours before the train was due to arrive in Salt Lake City. Her thoughts had turned inward, where serious doubts and fears haunted her.

The remarks of the young man about the Mormons niggled at her. She worried about polygamy. Would Utah be the right place for a young lady? What if the worst stories were true? And what if Marjorie had become cynical and unkind? Her letters had seemed a little terse. What would it be like to teach Mormon children? Maybe their parents would hate her for not being Mormon. What if— what if? The cold hand of unreasoning fear gripped her ever more tightly. She found it difficult to breath as the train sped through a deep gorge, then over a high trestle above a yawning, shadowy canyon—a place she'd never dreamed a train ought to go. The shadowy unknown that awaited her gave her that same feeling of hurling herself into grave danger. She bowed her head and prayed to Him to whom she had entrusted her life.

It was midnight when the Denver and Rio Grande finally rolled into the depot. Later she would write:

> I picked up my bag and stepped off—and to reassurance. There was Marjorie rushing down the platform to meet me. I felt fearless again.

"And how shall I sing the Lord's song in a strange land?"

6 Teaching

The sisters hugged, though that had been unusual behavior in Scotland. Marjorie smelled of home and wore her old plaid shawl crossed and tied behind. When they finally pulled apart under the electric streetlight she had tears on her cheeks, as did Liz. They laughed as they wiped their faces. The bond between them carried a lifetime of shared memories, all that was involved in their family's unique traditions. They found in each other an attachment to a reality that defined who they were, the more poignant in this foreign land.

It was nearly midnight and no cab could be seen to haul the trunks. They decided to fetch them in the morning. As they waited for the late streetcar Liz tried to find the right words to describe her journey. They boarded, but she had only begun her tale when the streetcar stopped at Marjorie's corner. From there it was a short walk to 30 North Temple Street. The two-room apartment was just as Marjorie had described it, "right under the shadow of the Temple."

Marjorie served a supper that she had prepared. Liz later wrote that for the first time in her life "I found myself eating raw raspberries." They tasted delicious.

By now the serious visiting was underway. Liz wanted to know what had happened with Jimmy. Marjorie explained her disappointments. He had met her at the train. He was indeed intelligent, well educated and his speech, like his letters, was interesting and cultured. But he was much older than she had expected, and though he had mentioned being somewhat crippled, she was surprised to find him more limited physically than she had imagined from his letters. These problems she could have managed. The crowning disappointment came when she learned that he had a wife and had hoped that Marjorie would become his plural wife under the "Divine Principle," which he still believed in. He hadn't bothered to explain this in his letters. She was horrified and angry. He professed his great love for her and promised to divorce his first wife if Marjorie couldn't accept the principle of plural marriage. The more he talked the angrier Marjorie felt. Polygamy had been outlawed in Utah for fifteen years, but that wasn't the point. Marjorie had expected that, knowing Reverend Symon, he could never have proposed such a thing. "And to think he brought me all the way to Salt Lake to say it!"

Liz commiserated, agreeing that the situation was so distasteful, so contrary to everything they had been taught to believe about marriage, that of course Marjorie could have no respect for him or for his religion, which had been so beautifully described. Her trust in him had been completely misplaced.

Liz didn't know then that Marjorie had joined the Mormon church, but had left it. Or that she would never fully recover, never again trust any form of organized religion. Ultimately she returned to the Presbyterian Church but not with the enthusiasm she had known as a younger woman.

Now Marjorie confessed that at the time she wrote the letter asking Liz to come to Utah, she had been engulfed in a great loneliness. "I still can't put it into words, a nameless longing, akin to drowning and needing air. Sometimes it seemed to paralyze me. I felt I couldn't get up and go to school. When your letter came saying you would come, it lifted. I knew I could go on again. I am very grateful to you for coming."

Liz could well imagine such despair in the vastness of this foreign land. Marjorie had needed someone who could link her again with her earlier life of faith and confidence. Liz knew she needed Marjorie just as much, and for the same reason.

They talked about the school that awaited Liz. At three in the morning their visiting finally slowed down and they prepared for bed. Anticipating Liz's arrival, Marjorie had purchased what was then called a sanitary couch—an all-metal bed made of wire mesh attached to an iron frame by springs that gave a degree of softness. On each side there was a drop-leaf operated much like the leaf on a dining table. These drop-leaves could be raised to make a one person cot into a double bed. The name "sanitary" in Victorian times came from the fact that insects were a problem in wood and mattresses, and were thought to spread disease. Being all metal, the bedframe could easily be disinfected and didn't need a mattress. During her life Liz often told the story of that bed, and later wrote:

> Even though I was a guest, Marjorie serenely got into bed first. In my ignorance I got in on the same leaf side, tipping the whole thing, and in a moment we were both hurled to the floor where we were both lying— but convulsed by laughter. Apart from the inconvenience it was a minor affair. I thought Americans certainly had strangely constructed beds—ready to catapult the occupants out with no warning.

For breakfast Marjorie served scones from the corner bakery. They tasted like they could have been made in Perth. As Marjorie poured tea into their matching cups painted with little purple flowers, Liz realized how well she had slept beside Marjorie. She was fully rested. Now she couldn't help but stare out the window at the high walls of the Mormon Temple.

"Do you still use two lumps of sugar, Liz?"

"Three." She watched Marjorie drop the little cubes into her cup. Stirring the cream into the good-smelling tea was itself like a joyful homecoming. She savored the taste, not having had a good cup of tea since she and Mary Jane sat in the tearoom on the *Columbia*.

"I have changed my name now," Liz said, "and would like you to call me Lizbeth." She put the cup into its saucer. "Everybody called me that on the passage and I've become quite used to it."

Marjorie gave her a skeptical look. "Lizbeth?"

"That's the name I recorded when I joined the church in Dumbarton and took my first communion. My life was changed then. I wanted a changed name to go with it."

Marjorie made a scoffing sound. "To me you'll always be Liz. And I've already told the other teachers and the principal that your name is Liz."

Liz decided not to force it. A piece of her old life had preceded her to Utah. They went out to fetch the trunks from the station, but first she marveled at the great buildings in all their full daylight splendor: the Mormon temple and tabernacle. Enclosed by an attractive fence, the buildings stood on beautifully landscaped grounds. Old Duff would have been proud. The temple dominated the city like a great cathedral in a Roman Catholic city. But Marjorie assured her there were other churches.

After they rented a cab and the horse plodded back to the apartment with Liz's belongings, Marjorie gave her a walking tour of the city. The summer day was bright and warm, and she appreciated the fresh air that came off the Wasatch Front—the spectacular mountain the rose straight up from the city. She was pleased to find that Salt Lake City had wide clean streets, large parks, and houses such as might have stood in Dumbarton. This was a gracious and beautiful city, though located in the middle of a vast wilderness of a continent. If this city was the influence of Mormonism it spoke volumes for the faith of the people.

On her first Sunday she asked Marjorie for directions to the Presbyterian Church. Marjorie gave her directions but refused to go with her.

Disturbed by that but homesick for the fellowship of church, Liz went alone. She found the church, but even inside felt quite lost. It was so different from the Free Church, or even the Church of Scotland! She had expected to be welcomed into a warm, comforting fellowship of like-minded Christians. Here, however, the people acted friendly with each other but seemed to have no interest in a stranger with a definite Scottish accent. Later Liz would write:

> I often think about immigrants who don't know the language. I knew the language, but oh the coldness, oh the loneliness. I found them very modern in a Sunday School class, reviewing a recent novel. To me, then, this seemed sacrilege—I couldn't go to this church—I felt no one cared. I had a feeling, not that God was dead— but surely He had missed the boat and hadn't emigrated.
>
> Marjorie suggested another [church] on the other side of town. Next Sunday I tried, but like the old story, I couldn't find the place. Then I came upon a church. By then I was late, but they were singing a familiar hymn, so I quietly entered and sat in the back. It was a different denomination [Baptist], but there I attended for that school term. I was immersed there on Christmas Eve [and enrolled as a member]. The minister tried to tell me and the other girl being immersed that we had better postpone the baptism as the heating system had broken down, but I urged we go ahead. We did.
>
> These people were friendly and kind. I had so many warm friends at home that I was desperately homesick, but I had to carry on. Who else would? I knew that I had a glimpse of the Gospel. I *believed* that, and I will never lose this testimony.

Much of the summer had passed, and Liz had to get busy studying for her Utah teaching certificate. She must pass a test in thirteen subjects. The twelve subjects on general knowledge were easy. But American history was unknown to her. She had to concentrate all her effort on that. She read several books and found it a "fascinating story" but very different from British history with all its "Perpetual Dates." Everything in America had happened so recently! Nothing like the coming of the Romans A. D. 45, the arrival of Christianity in Scotland with the mission of St. Columbia in 563, the uniting of the four tribes into the Kingdom of Scotland in 843. Then there was the story of the American Revolution, a completely different account of that conflict than any she had read at home. But she studied hard and before school started passed her exams in good order.

In an early meeting with the principal, he asked if she belonged to "The Church." That, of course, meant only one thing, the Mormon Church.

> "Yes," I replied. "I belong to the church but not the Mormon Church."
>
> He responded very bluntly. "I know that God lives, I believe Joseph Smith was a prophet of God. Someday I will meet you at the Judgement Bar of Christ and condemn you on this testimony."
>
> That was all. I guess I slunk out—but I was not intimidated. [In retrospect] I really believe he liked my spunk.

From the first day she truly loved the first and second graders and found a great joy in teaching. She had a way with little children. They enjoyed the rhymes and songs from Scotland. Sensing how much she loved them, they wanted to please her by reading and singing well. On the rare occasions when a child was disobedient, a stern look from Miss Symon would make them burst into tears and go to her for a hug. For her, the warmth and affection of the children helped ease the estrangement she felt from the rest of society.

Sometimes the other teachers, particularly as they grew closer to Liz and learned that she was not Mormon, would say in all kindness,

"I need to tell you that the Mormon church is the only true church." If she told them of her father's church or her religious commitment, they would say, "But that is a false church. You cannot go to heaven unless you join the Mormon Church."

Regarding the principal, she later wrote that he was "not only a staunch Mormon, but believe it or not, he had two wives." However he had an appreciation for good teaching and was very fair. He complemented her work and at the end of the year recommended a raise in pay.

After Liz's first year of teaching, Marjorie was very anxious to leave Utah. They had not signed contracts for the following year. Liz had loved her school children and enjoyed her teaching, but found nothing else about Utah that was important to her. She quite willingly followed Marjorie's lead to look elsewhere. They decided things might be better in Idaho, less Mormon influence. Boise seemed a likely place. Liz thought Wyoming might be interesting but didn't know any particular city to suggest and never mentioned it to Marjorie.

They took a train north to Pocatello and another westbound to Boise. There they spent a pleasant week in a nice hotel visiting Idaho's capital city, a supply center for the mining and timber industries and the center of a growing agricultural area. As hoped, they met few Mormons and saw churches of other denominations. But when they looked into the opportunities for teaching, they were disappointed. Utah did not require a teacher to be a citizen of the United States. Idaho did. In 1906 there were only two ways for a woman to become a citizen: to be born in the States or to marry a man who was a citizen. The disappointed sisters sadly returned to Salt Lake City.

It was late in the summer to be searching for work. However because of their good records as teachers, they both found positions. Liz felt a particular satisfaction in the glowing recommendation given by the principal who planned to "meet her at the Judgement Bar of Christ and condemn her on her testimony." Later she would often relate that story, always with pleased laughter.

Her new school was in the little town of Granite. Marjorie was hired in Draper, about seven or eight miles south of Granite and a little west. Now they would be separated and well away from the city, not even on the interurban railroad. Both towns were solidly Mormon with no other churches, a situation that troubled Liz much more than Marjorie.

The Mormon bishop of Granite, Parley Muir, and his wife Emma were waiting for Liz at the train station. The bishop put her trunks in the wagonbed, and she climbed up to join them on the buckboard. She noticed with relief that they were both cordial and polite, noticeably kind. As the team trotted up the bumpy road, Bishop Muir explained that his wife had been named Emma for the first wife of Joseph Smith.

He also explained that his household was the only one in Granite that took in boarders, so Liz would be living with Parley and Emma. As they bounced along the road a number of long miles, she felt increasingly confined between the bishop and his wife. She would not only be living in a Mormon household, but with the head Mormon. They arrived at a number of small frame houses and big barns clustered around a Mormon church. She saw the little schoolhouse. Farm animals could be seen here and there and she could smell their dung. Everything about the place seemed distasteful. The tiny town lay in complete isolation near the mouth of Little Cottonwood Canyon at the base of the brooding Wasatch Mountains.

Parley Muir took down the trunks and a man came over to help. Emma introduced Liz to the two other boarders, who had come to meet her. One was the teacher of the upper grades, the other Emma's niece, with her young son holding her hand.

Liz followed Emma up a narrow flight of stairs and down an equally narrow hallway past two shut doors—those of the other boarders—and into a narrow room. She felt trapped and desperate. Years later she would write that her first thought in Granite was: "I can't stand it; what shall I do?" She was a city girl who would now live in this stark wilderness, separated from her church, her sister and the new friends she had met in Salt Lake. She would be seen as a stranger, a perpetual outsider. Mormons believed anyone who belonged to a different faith was barred from an everlasting life. The theology here seemed as narrow as her room. She had seen forlorn hamlets like this from the train and wondered how human beings could tolerate such isolation. Pushing her trunks flush against the wall, she decided she needed to walk. She told the curious people gathered at the foot of the stairs that she needed exercise. She walked for hours, alone in the hills, pondering her situation.

In times of emotional stress Liz had always found that a brisk walk helped her regain perspective. Once again in this new crisis, walking helped her face the reality of her situation. What alternative did she have but to stay here and do her best? She had to support herself. No one else would do it. School would soon start and the little children, she felt confident, would be delightful. They always were. As she accepted this reality and settled in, she found that the Bishop's house was a good home.

There was no tea, but the farm produce was fresh and skillfully cooked. Liz found that her natural humor and personal charisma led to a happy year. She and the teacher of the upper grades had a similar outlook, always seeking to improve the minds of the children. Liz shared her belief that the Catholics knew the truth when they said they wanted "the first seven years of a child's life," because those years did indeed determine all that followed. The two teachers and Emma's niece visited many long hours. They shared songs to play on their classroom pianos. They argued religion, but the three respected each other and became fast friends.

On her twentieth birthday in March, Liz was given a party. By then she had been teaching in Granite for seven months, and her custom of visiting the homes of her pupils had made her many friends. Emma invited them all to the house for the birthday party.

The Bishop and his wife acted like a father and mother to her, and she had become fond of them. She noticed that they took their responsibilities seriously. Time and time again she saw them going into the homes of the community where there was illness or other problems, seeking to help. When Liz was ill, Emma watched over her tenderly and gave her the best of care. Both the Bishop and his wife had a natural kindness that overshadowed religious differences, and they never pressed Liz about the matter of religion, other than a perfunctory remark about the Mormon Church being the only true church.

Liz loved the school children. She discussed with their parents any problems the children had with the work. It intrigued her that so many children in her classroom shared definite physical features that would indicate that they were closely related—perhaps half brothers or sisters—though they were the same age and in the same grade. Sometimes on her home visits she became very suspicious, seeing who lived with whom and hearing comments from her pupils about members of the household. By now it had been sixteen years since the "Manifesto" issued by Church President Wilford Woodruff officially ended the practice of polygamy. But in Granite she learned that families deeply involved in the Principle could not quickly change their relationships, and fathers could not be expected to disown their children nor cease to support their wives. A manifesto could not transform a society overnight, particularly when many people disagreed with it. She wisely refrained from comments on the subject and asked no questions about family relationships. The innocent children were as sweet here as anywhere else.

Often on nice days she took her class wandering in the hills. They picked wild flowers, noted unusual rock formations, and enjoyed the beauty of Little Cottonwood Creek, a small but clear, cold stream. The children shared their joys and sorrows with her. All wanted to hold her hand. While eating their noon meal on one of these outings a child asked, "Teacher, are you Mormon?"

"No, I'm not, but remember you love me anyway."

"Yes, oh yes, teacher. We love you."

"Remember that always. I am not a Mormon, but you love me."

She did not try to expand on the idea that they could love someone outside The Church, but sincerely hoped she had taught them an important lesson that they would always remember. Much later she would write of this lesson that love is not restricted "to those of the same cult." She meant it to apply to herself and her children and grandchildren.

Despite her initial despair, in many ways the school year of 1906-07 had proved to be good and valuable. She had made friends in a solidly Mormon community. She had gained experience and become confident in her ability as a teacher. Her religious convictions had remained very important to her despite her inability to attend church services. She realized that she could keep her faith even with limited church association, though she missed it keenly. In her daily Bible readings she often pondered the words of Psalm 137, the lament of the children of Israel who had been carried captive to Babylon: "How shall we sing the Lord's song in a strange land?"

That was a question she would ponder for years to come, one to which she would never find an entirely satisfactory answer.

". . .liberty and the pursuit of happiness."

7 Independence

Liz had sorely missed Marjorie, and the missing was mutual. Letters had not been enough. They decided to find teaching positions near enough to each other so they could live together. Fortune smiled on them. Openings were available in the East Jordan School. They applied and were both immediately hired, thanks to their reputations as unusually good teachers.

They searched for a place to live with easy access to the Salt Lake streetcar and found a pleasant apartment in nearby Murray. It was a small town servicing farmers and a large copper smelter. Liz and Marjorie now looked forward to independence, which they had not experienced in private homes.

That summer and all through the school year the sisters enjoyed a full social life. Liz reveled in being a city girl again, reestablishing her ties with her Salt Lake friends. She and Marjorie took some of their savings to the ladies' apparel store near the Temple and had fun looking at the modern styles—exchanging giggles at some of what they saw, such as bright blue bathing costumes that left the arms naked practically to the shoulder. Attached bloomers hung out in the open for all to see, under a skirt that ended shockingly at knee level.

"Mormons couldn't wear these," Marjorie remarked wryly. "The holy garments would show."

They bought fashionable day dresses, walking suits of sturdy cotton, and afternoon gowns that could be worn to church or musical entertainments. Liz also bought two new hats, one with a modern asymmetrical slant to go with her afternoon frock. She liked the way she looked in the mirror—different from the farm wives in the small towns.

Liz and Marjorie attended plays and concerts, took in lectures at the University of Utah with other teachers, and enjoyed themselves thoroughly. Good looking, vivacious young women, they often received invitations from men. Always they arranged double dates, and neither made any serious attachments. They picnicked in the foothills with groups of people or on double dates. Securely employed for the coming year, Liz relished this free and independent life. But the Symon sisters held to their high standards. Though many young people frolicked at Salt Air, a popular beach resort on the lake, Liz and Marjorie never even considered wearing bathing costumes in public where men and women mingled.

The school term started at the East Jordan School. For Liz the work of the previous year paid off in self-confidence and less preparation. Surrounded by all the innocent, rosy-cheeked faces, she was in her element—and totally dedicated to her career. Her dream had come true: of spending her days in the schoolroom and her evenings with Marjorie laughing over the funny things the children said. In her heart she knew this was her calling.

Neither of them thought about marriage. Marjorie's experience with James was still bitter on her tongue, and what Liz had seen of marriage in Granite held no appeal. The dominance of the husband and the fact that a wife was to be totally devoted to serving him and raising children seemed to reduce the woman to the status of a servant rather than an independent, intelligent person on an equal footing with the man. She read prodigiously and knew that strong-minded women all over America felt as she did. They were working to change the Constitution to give women the right to vote, and this seemed to Liz more than reasonable, it seemed a requirement in any true democracy.

Eager to renew her attachment to her church, Liz begged

Marjorie to go with her. Marjorie finally agreed if the church was Presbyterian, so Liz left her Baptist friends. She and Marjorie attended the church where Liz had first visited on her arrival in Salt Lake, the one that had seemed cold. But Liz was changing, becoming more adapted to American ways. Now that same church didn't seem so unfriendly. This was the First Presbyterian Church on the corner of South Temple and C Street. The pastor was Dr. W.M. Paden, an able preacher and, as Liz discovered when she became better acquainted, a caring and friendly man. Her connection with this church would last for many years, for as long as she lived in Utah, and Dr. Paden would preside over some important transitions in her life.

The sisters found many good friends in the church. It broadened their social life. They also found inspiration in Dr. Paden's sermons. Different from the fervent evangelical preaching of their father, these sermons dealt with themes that challenged people to think. They formed the basis for meaty discussions, which Liz would always find to be one of the most satisfying activities in her life.

Her theology expanded to include a wider range of interest in the social conditions around her. She came to believe that the challenge presented to people of faith was to make the country a more Christian place. This she believed could be accomplished through political action, made possible by a very different form of democracy than the more structured class system in British society. The woman's suffrage movement, the efforts to bring about better working conditions for labor, and the possibility of prohibiting the sale and use of liquor had long been under discussion, but this was the first time Liz saw church people becoming politically active as a way of expressing their faith.

By nature an activist, she embraced these causes. The school years of 1907-08 and 1908-09 would long linger in her memory as highly enjoyable years of her life. She had matured into a truly independent, self confident and strong willed young woman—one to whom others gravitated. She became a leader, known for her fervent beliefs and her clarity of speech, which was often salted with humor. With great rejoicing she and her many friends would see both Women's Suffrage and Prohibition succeed.

During those years she happily watched Salt Lake City become increasingly cosmopolitan. Many non-Mormons were moving there for economic reasons, people of all religious persuasions and many with no church ties. *The Salt Lake Tribune*, which had started in competition with the Mormon owned *Deseret News*, was prospering and offering a forum for those who were disillusioned with the dominance of the L.D.S. Church and its control of the schools and the politics of the region.

In the summer after the first year of teaching at the East Jordan School, Marjorie opened a letter from Alice. She was leaving Scotland to join them! Liz was ecstatic about the coming of Alice, who arrived several weeks later. Alice, who had never sought a career beyond making a home for her siblings, quite naturally fell into the role of keeping house for the two working girls. She made them laugh as she scrubbed the "crud and corruption" from the apartment, flipping her r's with exaggerated determination. She also boiled, washed, starched and ironed their dresses. In this way Alice's presence added another measure of independence to Liz's life.

An interesting after-hours teaching opportunity presented itself. The smelter in Murray and the big Bingham Copper Mine it serviced attracted a great many foreign workers to the Salt Lake area. Many of these were bright men who sought to improve their station in life, men on their way to becoming business leaders. Among them was Constantine Tobias, a Greek known to his friends as Con. He and others organized a night class in Murray to meet twice a week to help ambitious miners and smelter workers improve their English. Their tuition paid a teacher for a few hours each week. The class was located within walking distance of the sisters' apartment. Marjorie promptly applied and was accepted.

She liked the men in the class and the challenge of teaching at the adult level. Nevertheless, toward the end of the school term there were a number of evenings when Marjorie was unable to teach, and she asked Liz to substitute. Liz found that she also enjoyed teaching these well-mannered men who were so eager to learn.

When she had substituted a few evenings, Con began finding reasons to ask for additional assistance, and, when possible, kept her after class to help him with pronunciation, spelling, or sentence structure. Liz didn't mind giving him the extra help. Con was a quick learner who had a good general education and a grasp of several European languages. He was much ahead of most of the men in the class. As she conversed with him Liz took note when he mentioned details of European history, politics and literature. This was no ordinary miner. Darkly handsome and just under six feet tall, he took pride in being a star player on one of the smelter's baseball teams. He was also proud of having worked himself up to foreman. He let Liz know right away that he had no intention of spending much time in "common labor." In this land of promise he would take advantage of every promise America had to offer.

To Liz, Con was a very interesting friend. She liked being with him. To Con, Liz was exactly the woman he needed to share his American dream. She was pretty, had a great sense of humor, was well educated, and approached life with a vitality and enthusiasm that naturally attracted people. Con was in love. This was more than just another good looking girl. Here was a cultured young woman who could help him move into the kind of society he knew he was destined for.

Con was wise enough to know that with a young lady like Liz he must not be too aggressive in his courting. One evening, having kept her for awhile after class, he said, "I would be honored if you would please allow me to walk with you to your home."

Seeing it as a friendly gesture by a gracious young man, she accepted the offer. Never one to be afraid of walking alone at night, she nevertheless found it pleasant to have him escort her. While bidding her good night, he said, "Next Sunday afternoon I would be most pleased if you would accompany me for a ride in my carriage."

Intrigued with the idea of a smelter worker driving a "carriage"— this wasn't the first intimation of class he'd conveyed— she agreed to go with him and see what the day would bring. Many years later she would tell this story to her daughters and granddaughters when they were dating.

On Sunday Con arrived with a nice buggy and a well groomed horse, a rig few smelter workers could afford. On the drive he told her about his home in Greece, the beauty of the sea there, the Aegean Islands and it's importance in the cultural history of the world. His parents owned a large and productive vineyard but as a second son he would not inherit it. Seeing no future in Greece, he had come to America with the blessing and financial help of his father. Some of that help showed in his clothing and his buggy.

In addition to pointing out interesting features about the Salt Lake valley, he conversed easily on many subjects. Unlike most Americans, he was very interested in European politics. He read a Greek newspaper and closely followed developments in Europe. He liked to talk, perhaps, she thought initially, to practice his English.

"For many years good things have been developing in Germany," he told her. "Germans have seemed content to improve themselves at home. They make much of the world's best music. They make big progress in industry and science. They make excellent steel. German products hold the mark, 'made in Germany,' a mark of quality. My watch and my razor announce: made in Germany. American farmers buy seed from Germany, sugar beet seed. German universities are teaching the best in the world. But all is not happy here. The new German king, *der Kaiser*, changes policies now, and not for the good. He is, how do you say, jealous of the colonies of England, France, Holland, Belgium and he is now starting a big program to build a navy. He wants power. I believe Germany will challenge England's navy. They now are building underwater boats, boats that move where you can't see them. Such boats are good for only one use—war! I don't like it and believe me, the other countries in Europe don't like it either. Pay attention, if this continues, there will be a war, a big one."

This sort of talk stimulated Liz's mind and indicated he was a "thinking man," a standard she used all her life. She went riding with him the next Sunday. Again, Con did almost all of the talking. It was good to listen to someone knowledgeable about Europe, but she couldn't escape the feeling that he was very impressed with himself and not very interested in anyone else's ideas. Nevertheless she enjoyed several pleasant Sunday afternoons in his buggy, riding to places of interest in the valley and foothills. They had picnic suppers together, which Con always insisted on supplying. It was springtime. Fruit trees bloomed in pink swaths across the valley, farmers worked in their fields, calves and lambs played on the green pastures. Liz liked traveling through the little towns and countryside with her parasol in the nice buggy beside Con.

She didn't allow herself to consider that she was involved in a romance. Her brother David had never married. Neither had Alice, John or Laurence, and the romances of Nellie and Marjorie were certainly nothing to emulate. Courtship and marriage just wasn't a part of the Symon family experience. But she was enjoying her friendship with Con—though there was something about him that bothered her.

One Sunday evening in early May when the daylight lingered noticeably longer, Liz returned home from a ride, flushed from the bright spring weather. She poured out her happy feelings to Marjorie. "Oh, you should have seen the setting sun paint the tops of the mountains orange and gold. The air is so pure!"

Marjorie brought her up short. "Has he proposed to you yet?"

The bluntness of those words jolted Liz and she couldn't respond.

"You surely know by now that he's not interested in the scenery. He's interested in getting a wife!"

"No, he hasn't proposed. And I don't want him to. I just like going out with him. And in any case, if he is looking for a wife I don't think he would want me."

"Ha! You think not? If you knew anything about men you'd see it in a minute. I see the way he looks at you. You're a good one at fooling yourself. You're exactly what he wants. And the amount of time you're spending with him lets him think you want him too. This isn't Scotland, Liz. It's Utah! You are twenty-two years old, but the fact that this is your fourth year of teaching makes you seem older. Around here you're already considered an old maid. He probably thinks you're afraid no one else will ask you. Wake up, girl! That man is serious about having you for his wife, and from what I heard, he's accustomed to getting what he wants."

The more Liz thought about it the more she realized her sister was right. Many things that Con had said about his plans for the future would be interesting to a woman who wanted to marry him. He was an aggressive, self assured person who liked to be in charge, and it was true that he expected to get what he wanted. She had enjoyed his conversation, his "carriage," and the attention he showered on her, but because she didn't want to think of it in terms of courtship, she had not considered his intentions, or for that matter her own feelings. Was she attracted to him?

She admitted to herself that she was not as attracted to him as the young farm lad on the train four years ago. She hadn't been entirely honest with Con. His self-confidence bordered on arrogance, and he couldn't help but dominate in a way that, she was quite sure, would become more evident if she were a wife instead of a woman being courted. With very mixed feelings she knew she must cool the friendship.

They had not made definite plans for next Sunday; she would make other plans. Thinking this through brought home Marjorie's wisdom. Liz had let things go too far. In simple good manners it would be necessary to let him know in advance. Even the act of telling him was a kind of an admission that an understanding existed between them.

She struggled over the wording of the note, and finally said it as simply as she could: "Dear Con, I will be busy at my church next

Sunday afternoon and so will not be interested in going for a ride. Sincerely, Liz."

As she mailed it she wondered about his reaction. She didn't have long to wonder. Early in the evening of the next day his buggy arrived at the hitching post in front of the apartment. Liz opened the door and met him on the front step.

"What is wrong? What has happened?" he demanded, obviously upset.

Trying to appear unruffled Liz told him, "Nothing happened. I'm quite active in my church. There's a meeting I need to attend. I've been enjoying the rides and neglecting some other things I should be doing. I ought to have mentioned the meeting to you sooner. It just slipped my mind."

A note of anger crept into his voice. "You see those people every Sunday in your Sunday School. Sunday afternoon is my only time with you. Don't do this."

That was a rude order. He should have understood her unspoken intent and gone quietly. Liz felt glad Marjorie and Alice were at home and glad she had not invited Con to come in. "Thanks for stopping by," she said as calmly as she could. "Right now I've got papers to grade and much to do because school ends next week." Each word deepened his color.

She stepped back into the apartment and slowly closed the door. From a window she watched Con return to his buggy. Everything about him conveyed serious anger—the long quick strides, the way he jumped onto the seat, snatched up the reins and grabbed the whip, the way the startled horse broke into a trot. His command had been sharp and threatening. She had not seen this side of him before.

Liz did in fact have many things to do in the few days left before the summer recess. She also needed to make plans for future Sundays. Alice and Marjorie had both heard the exchange through the open door. The three sisters planned several outings. If Con should call when Liz was not at home, Alice and Marjorie were both prepared to explain that she was busy. However, Con made no effort to contact her as spring turned into early summer.

Liz felt restless and troubled—as though she were trapped in the apartment. Surely he would one day confront her again. She wished he could be content just being a friend. She liked Con. She missed him. Or did she miss the rides and the attentions he had lavished on her? But something else troubled her, something about the way her life was going.

She did some serious reflection. She had sought her own enjoyment. She had wanted complete independence without any responsibility for the man's feelings. And Marjorie was right about her age. In Utah most women her age were married or planning to be. Could it be that some devious, buried part of her wanted to get married? She found herself wondering if teachers had to be a citizens to teach school in Wyoming, but chided herself for her foolishness. That young man who had held her hand would be married by now. No doubt he was already a father. She began to think about moving out of Murray where she wouldn't find herself facing Con. Where she wouldn't feel vaguely trapped in the apartment with her sisters.

Alice saw her discontent. "Dear Liz, tell us about it. Maybe we can help."

Liz couldn't put it into words. She prayed for guidance and went for long walks. Lately, in a rather detached sort of way, she had been scanning the employment opportunities listed in the paper. One Sunday after church as she picked up the *Tribune* an item in the classified section seemed to jump out at her:

**Union school is accepting applications for two
teaching positions for the elementary grades.**

For the rest of the day she couldn't get that out of her mind. It seemed providential. A move to Union would be a new start. It would help her deal with her confusion. She had traveled through Union several times—a nice little farm community between Murray and Granite. It had some of the features she had liked about Granite without the isolation. It was near the streetcar line.

That evening as they sat down to a light supper, Liz told her sisters about the notice. "Marj, doesn't that sound like it was meant for us? Two positions in the elementary grades?"

Marjorie looked at her like she was daft in the head. "I like my school. I like this apartment. I thought you did too. It surprises me that you'd want to move to that wee Mormon hamlet. You'd have to board with the locals. Didn't you get your fill of that?"

Alice added, "We couldn't live together."

In silence they ate Alice's crunchy cucumber toast points. Maybe I *am* losing my mind, Liz thought. Was she afraid of Con, running from him? No. That was not it. But she simply couldn't quit thinking of the advantages of moving to Union. All sorts of reasons came pouring into her mind.

The good side of boarding in a private home, as she had learned in Granite, was that it provided more contact with the community. This helped her as a teacher. And there would be a home that would board a teacher in Union—it was the common practice in the rural towns. Con wouldn't feel as free about visiting at the home of a stranger. She wanted a change. Something seemed to be pushing her out of the apartment.

"Maybe I will apply for one of the positions," she told her sisters, who exchanged surprised glances. "Union is only a little way from the streetcar. I could visit you on weekends and holidays. We could continue going places together." Now that Alice was here she wouldn't feel guilty about leaving Marjorie.

After the supper dishes were cleared Liz wrote to the Union address, applying for a position.

A reply soon arrived. They liked her credentials. The salary they offered for a teacher with four years experience was more than what she had been receiving. They asked her to come for an interview.

———

It was a very warm July day. Liz visited the school and liked what she saw. Most of the little town was located about a mile from the streetcar, a pleasant walk if it hadn't been so hot. The principal, who had been involved in selecting her, was friendly, and she felt certain she would like working with him.

By the end of their meeting he assured her that she would find a place to board. She signed a contract made out to "Elizabeth Symon"— since her mother's death there was no reason not to use her actual first name.

"I suggest you go a little ways up the road," the principal said, "and speak to the Smiths, Hyrum and Lucy. My guess is they'd be a good fit for you, being a gentile." In a kind tone he added, "The Smiths don't belong to The Church either."

Liz gave him her most gracious smile. "Thank you, I intend to visit them." Pleased at his kindness despite her being a "gentile," as non-Mormons were called in Utah, she asked, "Is there a church of another denomination in Union?" That would be more than she had hoped.

He shook his head. "Only a little Josephite church. Not active lately." He gave directions to the Smith home, then put out his hand. As they shook, he said, "Miss Symon, I want you to know how greatly pleased I am to have a teacher with your exceptional abilities on my staff."

That pleased her tremendously, and she would never forget the compliment. Later she would learn that this man, an active Mormon, was a personal friend of Bishop Muir of Granite. The bishop had given an excellent account of her work and said he'd hated to lose her.

She arrived at a well built, nicely maintained house of red brick, just where the principal had described it. The big yard was fragrant with clumps of native wild roses in full bloom. Large lilac bushes were past blooming. Several enormous poplar trees shaded the yard. Within the yard grew a small orchard. She saw wee green apples and pears, as well as large purple plums and yellow peaches. The yard was enclosed by a neatly painted fence. A little gate opened off the street to a short flagstone walk, which led to a gracious front porch. The thought of living in this place gave Liz a glow of pleasure.

Anticipating a visit with Lucy Smith and hoping for the offer of something cool to drink, she knocked on the door.

Silence.

She knocked a bit louder. Still no response. Knowing that people in these rural towns seldom locked their doors she tried the door and found it unlocked. Pushing it open a crack she sang out sweetly, "Is anyone at home?"

An irritated male voice grumped, "Yes. But I can't come to the door and you can't come in now!"

That didn't sound a bit friendly. "Did I come at a bad time?"

"Yes!" There was no other sound.

Carefully she closed the door and thought about the situation. She didn't want to return to the apartment without finding a place to live. Then she noticed that the house across the road also matched the principal's description. The two houses were almost identical. Maybe the principal had made a mistake or she had misunderstood his directions. She crossed the road.

A young woman about her age opened the door and gave her a warm welcoming smile.

Liz explained her reason for the visit and described what had happened at the house across the way. The young woman burst out laughing, a delightful good natured laugh that had Liz laughing with her.

"You had the right house all right. My folks' house, Hyrum and Lucy Smith. The voice you heard would be my brother Arthur." She laughed again, then added, "He's really nice. You'd like him. He's going into the city tonight. Likely taking advantage of having the house to himself. Probably in the kitchen sitting in the tub with nothing on and just had no idea what to do!"

Horrors, Liz said to herself, filled with memories of her early training in the segregation of the sexes. Her face heated even more than it had been before.

"My name's Allie Wardle," the amused young woman was saying. "Mom's just up the road visiting my sister Lizzie and the kids. We could walk up there and find her, but I'm sure she'll be home soon. If you're not in a hurry, why don't you just sit a spell? Would you like some lemonade?"

"Too wonderful for me...I do not understand...the way of a man with a maiden."

Proverbs 30:18-19

8 Arthur

The lemonade went down like ambrosia from heaven, and Allie Wardle was a delightful person. Liz took an immediate liking to her. Realizing that this was an opportunity to learn something about a family she might be living with for a year or two, she ventured, "The principal at the school mentioned that your family is not Mormon. Do you mind if I ask what brought your parents to Utah?"

Laughing, Allie said, "It's a long story. But an interesting one if I do say so myself."

"I know very little about Utah," Liz prompted.

"I can hear in the way you talk you're not from these parts."

"Scotland."

"Oh, now isn't that interesting! Over there by England."

Smiling graciously, Liz nodded.

"My grandma's from England. She lives in the little house behind the folks' house. You probably didn't see it. It sort of hides back there. Anyhow you'll want to meet her if you board here. She's a real lady. We call her Grandma Sarah. I guess you might say she's the reason we don't belong to The Church—in a roundabout sort of way. She was one of the first pioneers in this valley, came with the converts in 1851. She married my grandfather, Joe Griffiths, as his second wife. But I think she's always thought the Principle was sinful."

"Well, I should think so!" Liz couldn't help but say. "Why would any self respecting—" She checked herself, remembering that Allie no doubt loved her grandmother.

Allie didn't seem disturbed. "She didn't have much choice. Anyway, Joe Griffiths died. By then Grandma had a little girl, my mother, Lucy Ann. Here's where it gets interesting. Grandma Sarah fell in love with my Grandpa Smith—William P. we call him. William P. had taken ground here in Union in 1852 and built a little adobe house just five years after Brigham Young brought the first settlers in. His wife, my other grandma, was dead by then. 'Course I never met her. He fell in love with Grandma Sarah and they got married. The last of his kids was still living at home, a fourteen-year-boy—that's my dad, Hyrum. At that time Mom was ten. Well, she always did love my dad, right from the start. So later they got married. You follow that?" Allie's narrative dissolved in another cascade of delightful laughter.

Savoring the cool tangy drink, Liz smiled with her and nodded. Mormons certainly had odd marriage patterns, but by now she wasn't surprised. "So your parents grew up together in the same house, because their parents were married to each other?" She tried not to let her distaste show.

"Yup," Allie declared. "Daddy and Mom raised us six kids here: Sarah, William, Lizzie, my brother Hyrum, we call him Hi, me, Mary Alvira—call me Allie—and the kid over there taking a bath, Arthur. He's the baby of the family." She laughed again, a woman who had a real gift for laughter.

"He's just finishing his first year at the University of Utah in Salt Lake," she continued. "Summers he helps Daddy on the farm. My husband Clarence is sort of a partner on the farm with Daddy. Just now the two of them are down in the field puttin' up hay."

"But why did your family leave the Mormon Church?"

"See," Allie said with a mischievous chuckle, "I get off track easy when I'm tellin' that story. Anyhow Grandpa Griffiths was among the first to take up land here along the creek. He had a bunch of kids by his other wife, and when she died Brigham Young thought my Grandma Sarah should take care of those kids and not marry Grandpa Smith. At the time Grandpa was active in the LDS Church, but he was determined to marry Grandma Sarah, so he just ignored Brigham Young and they got married."

"I may have missed something. I still don't understand why they left the Mormon Church."

"Well," Allie said like it was entirely self-evident, "in those days Brigham Young made all the rules. Unless he approved of it you didn't get married. He wouldn't bless the marriage of William P. and Grandma Sarah. So William P. defied him and took Grandma Sarah to Fort Douglas, where the first federal judge in Utah married them. That was 1867. I can always remember that date because it was two years after the Civil War ended." Again Allie let loose with a peal of laughter. "I guess you'd say they were excommunicated." She twisted around on her chair and lifted the corner of the window curtain. "She'd oughta be back any minute now."

"So your parents were not brought up as Mormons?"

"That's right. None of us six was either. I 'spose any of us could have joined The Church later, but we didn't." Draining her glass she poured them both a second full glass of the delicious lemonade, and continued.

"Grandpa Smith took up his land just a few years after Grandpa Griffiths did. And now it's all mixed together, from both sides, this big farm that Daddy owns. All six of us grew up here. Grandpa died about fifteen years ago. Ever since, we all look in on Grandma real often and Arthur helps her a lot, getting in her wood and such. He's real nice about reading to her too. You see, she's lost most of her eyesight. Still sharp as a tack though. She remembers all about when she came from England and the early days in Utah. You'll get to meet her. You'll like her. Like I said, she's a real lady."

Liz found herself anxious to meet the old lady. They had something in common, both having sailed the Atlantic from the British Isles. But old Sarah had spent a lifetime here. It would be interesting to hear what she thought of the Principle. Liz knew that even if she boarded with another family in Union, she would go to that little house and have tea with Allie's grandmother—if she still drank tea. Most Mormons didn't.

"You have a nice home," Liz remarked.

"Thank you. Daddy built it for us. He built all us kids houses when we got married." She smiled. "We all like living together, close to our parents and Grandma. Our own kids are growing up real close too. The only one not living here in Union is my brother Hi. He's in Leamington."

"Do your husband's parents live here too?"

"Yes." She chuckled. "Like I say, we're a real close family." She lifted the curtain again and suddenly got to her feet. "Mom's on her way. Come on. I'll introduce you."

Liz and Allie hurried across the rutted, sun baked road, Allie calling, "Mom, I got someone for you to meet."

Lucy Smith, a pleasantly plump woman of a little more than fifty years, wore the same style of apron over her flowered cotton dress, just like Allie's. The cloth sunbonnet of the American West shaded her face. She had just stepped onto her porch when they caught up.

"Meet Elizabeth Symon," Allie said. "She's going to be one of the new schoolteachers, come fall. She's looking for a place to board."

"Nice to meetcha, Miss Symon. Let's get ourselves inside where it's cool. Lawsey me, it hot out here!" In the shadow of the bonnet, beads of perspiration stood on her forehead. Opening the door she ushered the other two inside a large kitchen, which was indeed much cooler. A puddle of water lay on the floor, but otherwise there was no sign of a man or a washtub.

Allie turned to leave. "I've got to get home and start supper. I told Clarence I'd feed the men when they get in from the field. Mom, you and Daddy come on over too, so you won't need to fix anything. Remember, Arthur's going out. I'll leave you two to talk. I sure did enjoy our visit, Miss Symon."

"Call me Elizabeth." She smiled sweetly.

Before Allie could get to the door a handsome, dark-haired young man appeared. Well dressed and in a hurry he tried to beat Allie to the door.

She stopped him. "Arthur, this is Miss Elizabeth Symon, one of the new school teachers. This here's my brother, Arthur." Allie looked like she might explode with laughter, but held it in check.

Arthur looked shyly at Liz and dropped his gaze, obviously embarrassed. "Pleased to meet you." He hesitated a moment. "You came to the door a while back." It was not a question but a simple statement of an unpleasant truth. "I'm sorry I was so rude. I wasn't expecting company." He hesitated, blushing under his suntanned cheeks, feeling stupid. Of course he wouldn't have expected company while taking a bath. "Sorry to be in such a hurry. If I don't catch the next streetcar I'll be late."

He told his mother, "The math club's having a supper meeting. I'll stay in town tonight. Be home in the morning for work."

Before Liz could think of anything to say he was out the door.

If Arthur had been surprised while in the tub, now it was Liz's turn to be surprised. She had expected to meet a rather spoiled, ill mannered little brother of Allie. Instead he was a remarkably good looking young man who, she was sure, would have had excellent manners had he not felt so embarrassed. In that brief meeting she had seen how well his athletic body filled his clothes, and there was something about the measured way he walked that intrigued her. He was medium height, slim with obviously strong shoulders, possibly from farm work. Later she would learn that he also enjoyed gymnastics at the university. She liked his full head of nearly black, wavy hair. Neatly combed, it was slicked down with water but still held its waves. And his eyes. In the brief instant when he had looked directly at her she saw the fire of intelligence in those warm grey-brown eyes. They spoke of curiosity and a keen interest in the world around him. They were eyes she would like to see again. And she was sure that the square-jawed face that seemed a bit grim would rather entertain a pleasant smile.

Clearly it was an awkward moment for Lucy Smith too, but she took it in stride. "That there's my youngest, Arthur. He's a reg'lar whiz at 'rithmetic. Math I guess they call it." She laughed like her daughter Allie. "That's all a mystery to me. You like math?"

Liz hadn't regained her equilibrium. "It's not my favorite subject. But of course," she added, thinking fast, "I like it." After all she was the new teacher. "But my strength is in writing and literature."

Removing her bonnet, Lucy mopped perspiration from her face. She sat on a kitchen chair and indicated Liz should sit. "Lawsey but it's hot today." She had just walked briskly, as Liz would learn she always did, from the home of daughter Lizzie about a quarter mile down the road. "Sit there now and tell me about yourself. You got a different way of talkin.' Scotch, I'd say."

Liz briefly told about her journey from Scotland and the places where she had taught school.

"Well, we're just plain folks, nothing fancy." Mrs. Smith had Allie's easygoing way of making a stranger feel accepted. Lucy was a short little woman who wore all the challenges of pioneer living on her face, yet anyone could tell she had dealt with them, and she had an optimistic outlook on things to come. She smiled easily, laughed a lot, and could probably be stern when she needed to be. She had borne and raised six children who clearly liked her company, to live so nearby.

"Stick around here awhile and you'll be teachin' my grandkids," she said, laughing. "I've got a big batch of 'em comin' on and a few already past second grade." She flapped a hand toward the doorway through which Arthur had recently emerged. "Room's down yonder."

The older woman rose quickly to her feet and led Liz to a pleasant bedroom with a window looking out on the mountains. It had a nice little desk and a dresser. "We've had teachers here before and they like a desk to work on. You'll eat with Hyrum and me and I'll pack you a lunch. Arthur'll be off to the university again come September, so he'll be no bother. She pointed with her eyes toward what must have been his room. "When school's on, he boards in the city with the

Sears's. Them's Bertha's folks—Bertha's the wife of my son Hi. Arthur'll stay there tonight."

Mrs. Smith gave a reasonable price for room and board, and Liz agreed to the arrangement. She very much liked the room and the easy feel of the place. She thought she'd like this pleasant little no-nonsense woman. And knowing she would meet Arthur again under better circumstances was more than agreeable. She felt quite sure he would be no bother.

—

That evening Liz gave a glowing report to Marjorie and Alice. The school was a fine new brick building, the classrooms large, the Smiths delightful non-Mormons. She would feel much freer living with them than she had with the Mormon bishop. She hadn't met Mr. Smith but from what she'd heard from his daughter, he ran a prosperous farm and Liz felt sure he'd be a gentleman. For some reason she didn't mention Arthur.

A few days later Con stopped by the apartment and invited her to go for a ride. Alice and Marjorie were not present to object, and for reasons Liz didn't understand she now went with him. Con was on his best behavior. It had been a month since their unpleasant meeting. The weather promised a long, warm evening, and she did so enjoy getting out into the countryside.

They made small talk. He had been able to get off work early. She assured him she'd had a pleasant summer. She mentioned her plans for the coming school term, her move to Union, the fact that she would be boarding with a local family.

Con took the news in silence, but by the firming of his lips she knew he didn't like it. "Well, Union isn't so far," he finally said. "Just a few miles. I'll come over and see you often." He cleared his throat rather noisily. "I want to make one thing clear. I don't want you seeing any of those farm boys over there. You understand that?" He was absolutely serious. His tone of voice, the way he implied that he had the right to control her struck like steel on flint.

Sparks flew in her mind. She was angry. The very core of her personality—a fierce independence—had been challenged. In a firm, deliberate tone she said, "What makes you think you can tell me what I can or can't do? You don't own me. I'm not your wife, and you can be sure I never will be. If that's what you've got in mind you can turn this buggy around and take me home. Now!"

He glared at her, his white knuckles clenching the buggy whip. Liz felt fear. Might he lose control and strike her?

"Damn! You're a stupid little fool. With no idea what's good for you!" He swung the horse around and put him into a brisk trot. Staring at the road, he drove in silence. When he stopped at the apartment he made no move to get down.

She opened the buggy gate and quickly stepped down. Not looking back, he drove away. Anger and relief competed within her. She fled through the apartment, glad Marjorie and Alice hadn't returned. Releasing her tension, she flung herself on her bed and had a good cry. It had been stupid to go for another ride with Con. She surely didn't know much about men. Would she ever learn?

By the time Marjorie and Alice came home she had dried her eyes and washed her face. To their inquiry about her day, she simply said, "I went for a short ride with Con. We will not see each other any more."

———

For the move to Union Liz hired an old drayman. He loaded her trunks and other belongings on top of other items destined for Union. A garrulous man with a matched dapple-gray team, he invited her to ride beside him in his wagon, which saved her streetcar fare as well as a mile's walk down Union Avenue. Eager to know more about the Smith family, Liz asked if he knew them.

"Yeah, sure, I know the Smiths, known 'em for years. They're liked in these parts. I heard old William P. and his wife were about run out of town when they first left The Church. But he was a tough old bird and stuck it out. Pretty good doctor too, only one around these parts. Folks needed him. Been dead some years now. His widow's still living. Fine old pioneer lady. And Hyrum and Lucy, the folks you're planning to live with, they're good honest folks. He's a good farmer. Inherited one of the best farms on the creek and turns in a fine harvest. His oldest daughter Sarah married a handyman from Canada, name of Martin Anderson. He's real smart. Ain't nothing he can't fix, but he never holds a job for long. Everyone likes him though, he's a mighty fine singer, a joker too. Not much ambition. If Hyrum hadn't fixed him and Sarah up with a nice house, I doubt he'd have a place for his family to live. Him and Sarah's got a fine little family, smart kids."

"You seem to know them quite well."

The drayman looked pleased. "Yup. Will's the next in the family, after Sarah. I think he does a little farming. Minds his own business and don't talk much. Married a girl name of Lorene. She's a brittle one, does the talkin'. Do business with them, you do business with Lorene. That lady drives a hard bargain—little tough to get acquainted with. Hyrum, Hi they call him, he's the brainy one. Went on to the university. Teaches school south of here, Leamington, I think." He whistled softly in his teeth. "A whale of an athlete, Hi was. Won all the Fourth of July foot races when he was growing up here. He's the only one of the Smith kids to leave Union. Married a Salt Lake girl named Bertha. Never met 'er.

"Allie and Lizzie, now they're real friendly and I know 'em better'n the others. They live right near their folks. It's a tight family. Those two sisters married brothers. Allie and Lizzie married the Wardle boys, Charlie and Clarence. Real nice boys. You'll like 'em. Charlie's a crack carpenter. Built a number of the Union houses. I got to know him haulin' material onto jobs. And that Clarence! A dandy good farmer. He's working with old Hyrum, probably take over the farm some day. Them boys have it figured out. Both got to workin' for old Hyrum and ended up marrying his daughters." He laughed an odd hee, hee,

hee. "Yup, them boys knowed a good thing when they seen it. They all got married just a little while back. Clarence drives a good looking team. I like a man what takes care'a his horses."

He glanced at Liz, perhaps encouraged by her unconcealed interest. "Maybe the girls married the Wardle boys 'cause they ain't in The Church but I'll say this, they're good men. That Wardle family, they used to go to the Josephite Church."

"What kind of church is that?"

"The Reorganized Church it's called. They believe in the prophet Joseph Smith, but got no use for Brigham Young. I think the Smiths are Josephites too. Ain't many Josephites in Utah, not like back east, so I'm told. Most of em split off from The Church before Brigham Young led the emigration out here. I really don't know what all they believe or don't believe."

This somewhat disturbed Liz, to hear that the Smiths believed any of the Mormon tenets, especially the fantastic story of Joseph Smith's visions. She had hoped their beliefs were more like hers. "I think there's another son in the family," she offered innocently.

"Oh, you mean Arthur. He's the only one that ain't married. Went off to the university like his brother Hi. I'd say he's growing into a fine man—smart as all git out and not stuck up one whit. Real good help to his dad. I've hired him a time or two to help me load, or drive. Reliable kid. Good kid. Strong too."

Just what she'd hoped to hear. Clearly this gabby drayman made it his business to know everything about everyone, and he enjoyed having a good listener. Finding out that she was a school teacher, he gave liberally of his opinion about the various teachers at the school, now and in the past. She certainly hadn't expected to get the history of the town and it's people when she hired him to move her belongings.

Well aware that her interest in the Smith family extended beyond ordinary curiosity, Liz looked forward to seeing Arthur again. She didn't have long to wait. The conversation with the drayman had made the time pass quickly, and the wagon was soon in the side yard of the

Smith home.

Allie came running to greet them, and Liz felt as though she were being welcomed home. Arthur stood in the yard, apparently already washed up from the field. He had combed his damp hair but was still wearing a work shirt and bib overalls. Again she saw the strength beneath his shirt. He was talking to an older man, also dressed in work clothes, possibly his father. Liz climbed down as both came forward, Arthur walking in his centered, balanced manner.

The older man extended a large work-hardened hand. "Pleased to meet you, Miss Symon," he said in a friendly but gruff voice. "I'm Hyrum Smith. I think you met Arthur."

Pleasantly and somewhat shyly, Arthur returned her greeting, adding, "I'll carry in your things." He gathered her bags, giving the old drayman a jolly greeting.

———

Soon after moving in, Liz knocked on the door of the little frame house in the back of the larger house and made the acquaintance of Grandma Sarah. The dim light from the small windows softened her deeply wrinkled and pitted face as she walked slowly from her chair to the stove. Quite bent, she was shorter than Liz, who at five feet stood shorter than most women. Years later Liz would write about Sarah:

> Her eyesight was almost gone, so for hours at a time she sat alone with her thoughts. Her granddaughter sometimes dropped in, taking her laundry to be done, or bringing her meals, or helping keep the tiny house in order. She would feel her way to the stove to make herself a cup of tea—so often pouring the water on the floor instead of into the cup. This did not perturb her however, for life had held so many serious problems for her that minor difficulties seemed of little consequence. She had a sweet sympathetic disposition and it was a

joy to visit with her.

As I came to know her better, I volunteered to read a bit to her, and of course it was from the Book of Books. She loved the Bible and was familiar with much of it, explaining to me that she had learned to read by reading the Bible in the Wesleyan Methodist Sunday School in Lincolnshire, England.

From the beginning Liz and the housebound old woman felt a bond, both having crossed the high seas and the prairies and mountains to Utah. However Liz could not imagine why this woman had consented to live in the barbarous condition of polygamy. But she wasn't yet comfortable asking the sweet old lady such a question. Over the next year she would piece together Sarah's story.

Mother Lucy, the old woman's daughter, was then at the peak of her matriarchal powers. Bright and observant, she spoke in a manner unaltered by education and learned in the limited atmosphere of this isolated Mormon community. Her speech bristled with regional colloquialisms that Liz found fascinating. Equally interesting to the Smith family was Liz's perfect English colored by a light Scottish lilt.

Most of Lucy and Hyrum's ever increasing band of grandchildren lived within walking distance. Liz observed that they all adored their grandmother. She also noticed, during their shared meals, that Hyrum found it hard to express his feelings, but cared deeply for and respected Lucy. A frugal, hard working farmer, he often sought Lucy's opinions on matters of farm business. Obviously life was good for this large three-generation family.

A week remained before the fall term would start and Arthur would move back to the city for his second year at the university. Sharing meals, he overcame his shyness and Liz found him an excellent conversationalist. They talked about community affairs, politics, his studies at the university and his grandmother. Liz hesitated to mention religion to Arthur, but noticed that no one in the family went to church on Sunday. However, they all seemed to respect Liz for her daily Bible readings with old Grandma Sarah.

Arthur had a fine singing voice—pure and on the tenor side. Sometimes in the evening he played his mandolin, which he did very well, and sang American folks songs, many from out of the days of slavery and the traditions of the South. Liz loved to hear him sing *Old Black Joe,* which was new to her. She sang him some of her favorite Scottish songs. He quickly picked out the chords on his mandolin and accompanied her, apparently never tiring of hearing her sing the songs of the Highlands. It thrilled her to make music with him.

One evening Arthur told her about William P. Smith, the grandfather who had defied Brigham Young to marry Grandma Sarah. "Like Grandma, he was converted to Mormonism by missionaries in England. He and his family settled in Nauvoo, Illinois, at the time Joseph Smith was at the peak of his power. Grandpa knew Joseph and named my father Hyrum for Joseph's brother. Grandpa was quite a leader in The Church, but when the Mormons left Nauvoo, in 1847, to come to Utah, Grandpa was detained for five years because Brigham Young put him in charge of running a ferry boat across the Missouri River near Council Bluffs, Iowa. William had a large family by then, but never practiced polygamy. My father was one of his two youngest sons. Grandpa finished his trip west to Utah in 1852. One story says my father was born while they were crossing the plains in a covered wagon, but most likely he was born in Council Bluffs just before they started the last leg of their journey.

"I was four years old when Grandpa died, but I remember him. That was in 1893. He was housebound several months before he died, in bed most of the time. His mind was good; he'd been active all his life and was very tired of being shut in. He wanted me to come every day and sing for him, and he told me interesting stories of his early life. I always liked being with him. He'd ask me to sing some of his favorite songs over and over. It helped him pass the time." He smiled his somewhat shy smile. "Grandma always had cookies and milk for me."

Picturing the earnest little boy standing by his grandfather's bed singing in the clear sweet tones of childhood brought tears to Liz's eyes. And there was something almost as touching about the young man he had grown to be. It seemed to Liz that some of the charm of the little boy remained in him.

She had never been in such an informal relationship with a young man, and found herself irresistibly drawn to him, though she was more than two years older. She was a mature woman well along in her teaching career. She tried to tell herself that her feelings for him were nothing more than a sister would feel for a younger brother.

After his school term began she saw him only on weekends, and many weeks he did not come home. She found herself looking forward to his coming and chided herself for feeling disappointed when he failed to come. When he was there he was talkative and eager to share his college experiences. Liz found herself telling him many of her personal memories of growing up in the manse. She told him about her schooling in England and Scotland, and her experiences with the first and second graders in the Union school.

He was a good listener regardless of the subject. He always made an effort to understand what lay behind the words. It also pleased her to discover that he was an avid reader, loved poetry, and could recite many passages from such works as *The Lady of the Lake* and *Elegy Written in a Country Churchyard*. She felt herself bonding with him and he with her in their love of poetry. As part of their schooling on opposite sides of the Atlantic, each had committed a great many poems to memory. One would start reciting a poem and the other would join in. It was a wonderful experience having Arthur for a close friend without any implication that they were courting.

He came home for several days at Christmas time. The intense pleasure she felt when he gave her a small Christmas gift surprised her. One evening during the holidays a number of young people organized a hay ride on a big sled. It felt quite natural for Arthur and Liz to join the party. In Mormon towns even very young people paired into couples. Liz found herself next to Arthur sharing the same hot brick placed in the hay to keep their feet warm. Everyone sang Christmas hymns. Harmonizing with him—his tenor, her soprano—sitting close beside him on the crowded hayrack, she felt a pleasure she had never experienced while riding beside Con in his buggy.

That night as they walked home in the crisp cold air with a canopy of stars twinkling overhead he took her hand in his. A pleasant shock ran through her. After he said good night and went to his room, she lay awake in her bed reliving the evening. It was then that she finally admitted to herself that what she felt for him was something intense, quite different than any affection she'd had for her brother Laurence, quite different than she had ever felt for anyone before.

When Arthur moved back to the city at the start of the new term he found more reasons to come home on weekends. They began taking long walks in the evening and, when alone, always found it natural to walk hand in hand. Every time, Liz felt the spark. In the willows by the creek he took her in his arms and kissed her gently. Almost trembling, he said, "I love you, Libby"— the affectionate name her father had called her mother.

"I love you too, Art." With all her heart she knew it was true.

Spring was in the air. They felt a restlessness living in the same house, wanting more of each other, yet, when the parents were present, having to act as though nothing had changed in their relationship. But the change was very evident to the perceptive Mrs. Smith, who had seen the courting of her five older children. Her attitude toward Liz chilled. Mother Smith was not willing to see her youngest, not yet twenty, seduced by an older women, one she saw as the aggressor. She resented Liz coming into the house as a school teacher and apparently taking advantage of her inexperienced son.

Tensions grew for Liz, both the uncomfortable change in Mother Smith, whose friendship she had come to treasure, and living in the same house with Arthur without being able to openly acknowledge her feelings. She found temporary relief in the little house behind the main house, having tea with old Grandma Sarah. This she often did after school. They talked of things distant, such as the terribly crowded conditions under decks on the creaking old sailing ship in which Sarah had crossed the Atlantic nearly sixty years earlier.

One late afternoon in early May, Liz was washing their cups at the sideboard—the old lady sitting in her chair with her thoughts—when Liz suddenly knew she must write Sarah's remarkable story. By now she had heard most of it and it seemed historic to her, important. She knew it should be committed to paper so that future generations would understand this woman's experience with polygamy. If Liz didn't write it, who would? Then if she left Union and never saw Arthur again, a heartbreaking thought, she would first give him the written story.

Old Sarah's scratchy voice startled her. "You're fond of Art, 'ent you, dearie?"

Stunned, for they had never discussed her feelings for him, Liz assumed Lucy had told her mother. The idea embarrassed and hurt her. Lucy might have complained that she, Liz, had been too forward. Yet she couldn't deny her feelings. "Yes, I am fond of him."

"'E's a bright one, Art is. Pullin' himself up like 'is brother Hyrum. I'm very fond of Art too. 'E thinks about others, not just 'imself. You'd be good for 'im, dearie. A fine talking wife like you could give 'im a little nudge, if you know what I mean. Lucy and Hyrum, they think farmin's good enough for 'im. But 'e should try for better. Dear Libby, ye could search the whole world over and never find a more thoughtful 'usband. Nor one so talented."

Liz was glad that Grandma, as she now called her, couldn't see her blush. Grandma had called her Libby, as Arthur did. Clearly he and old Sarah had talked about her. But what prompted the old lady to advise her to marry him? Arthur hadn't broached the subject. Far from it. Yet despite her embarrassment Liz felt comfort in Grandma's attitude. Here was another of the Smith family, besides Allie, who seemed to feel that she and Arthur had a right to care about each other.

The following week she spent the late afternoon with Allie, who long ago had recognized the obvious. Allie came right out and said it. "You and Arthur are made for each other. It's wonderful that circumstances brought you together. I'm really hopin' to have you for a sister-in-law. You're a wonderful person. I've never met anyone quite like you before."

Liz blinked back tears and, in wordless thanks, put her hand over Allie's.

Allie continued, "Clarence and I have talked about this. We know it's hard for you to live in the same house with Arthur and Mom. It's probably not a good thing. I know Mom pretty good. She's just doesn't want another woman taking her little boy, the last of her family. She won't admit that Arthur's crazy about you. And you're different from the local girls. You'd never be happy as the wife of a farmer. That's one of the things Arthur loves about you, your interest in so many things. He really doesn't want to be a farmer either, even though he's good help to Daddy. But farmin' is all Mom knows. She still can't understand why Hi had to go off and teach math. Can you understand how Mom sees things?"

"Well, maybe." But she didn't like it.

"See, my situation's different. I'm happy as a clam right here on the farm, right next door to the folks. Dad and Clarence farm together. Dad's still the boss but he trusts Clarence with a lot of decisions. Clarence is part of the family. But Mom knows it's different with you. You're educated. You appeal to a lot in Arthur that Mom can't understand. She's seen him changing since he went off to college. She can't understand why anyone would want to leave the farm and read poetry written by a bunch of snooty Englishmen." Allie laughed her wonderful laugh. "That's the way she sees it. But I can sure understand Arthur, and I'm pleased as punch you two found each other."

"But what am I to do? I can't go on living this way. I have to teach school. And Arthur has to get his degree. That's two and a half years away! He isn't ready to take on the responsibility of a wife and I won't push him into it. I don't think anybody should be talking about marriage." Nonetheless, she often allowed herself to imagine it.

"Well, for now, do what you have to. Sign your contract to teach another year and board somewhere else. If you'd be comfortable with us, Clarence and I'd be happy to have you here. Mom might make a fuss and get after me about it, but she'll get over it. I love her." Allie gave Liz a wise smile. "Like I said, I know her pretty good. We've had our little quarrels but always got over 'em. She's faced a lot in life that didn't work out the way she wanted. She can be sorta gruff, but underneath she's a kind person. But if Arthur marries you, she'll do anything in the world for you. You'd be family. And she loves him dearly. For her, family comes first."

Allie's candor and understanding of her mother impressed Liz. She knew she would always cherish her friendship with Allie. "I'm very fond of your mother," Liz said. "I guess that's why it bothers me so to have her acting like she does. But I'll keep your kind offer in mind."

Despite Allie's friendship, Liz felt relieved when the school term ended and she moved back with Marjorie and Alice for the summer. Arthur was home for the summer, working on the farm, but from time to time arranged to make the short trip to Murray to see her, including the evening of July 1, when he turned twenty-one. He obviously enjoyed meeting Marjorie and Alice. Liz was delighted to see how easily he visited with them.

As the summer progressed, she considered her situation in a more detached atmosphere than in the Smith home. She prayed about it and discussed it with Marjorie, who encouraged her to stay in Union.

Marjorie had a very romantic side. A teaching career was not all she wanted from life. "If you love Arthur as much as you say you do," she told Liz, "and he has all the qualities you claim he has, don't give him up. Don't jump into marriage too soon, but go back to Union, continue to teach while he goes to school, and let your love for each other grow."

Alice wasn't so sure. "You mustn't sacrifice your career. I don't want you to become a Utah wife tied down with too many children and a man telling you what to do."

But Arthur was a gentle sort, Liz explained.

"But marriage might change him."

"No, I really don't believe that would happen with Art. His father respects his mother. I saw that every day I was there. When a child grows up seeing that, it makes a lasting impression."

Still there was much to ponder. She didn't want to give up teaching, but felt very glad Marjorie didn't disapprove of her being in love. Marjorie usually gave her good guidance. Alice's concern was understandable, but a bigger worry was whether she could teach if she were married. She had heard that there was often a rule against it. And if she couldn't teach, Arthur would feel obliged to quit school and work. She would be responsible for damaging his future. But he had never even mentioned marriage. Why think about such things? Anyway, she had always been able to work things out and felt sure this would be no exception.

She made her decision. Overshadowing all her thinking was the fact that never in her life had anything made her as happy as Art holding her in his arms.

—

The school term of 1910-11 began, Liz boarding with Allie and Clarence. She saw little of Mrs. Smith. They greeted each other when they met and visited no more than necessary. But Allie continued to assure her. "I can tell Dad likes you, sort of admires you. He doesn't say much because he doesn't want to rile Mom. They both know you're a fine person. Don't you worry about it. Everything will turn out fine."

But something else that Liz didn't want to acknowledge finally became all too evident. The desire that she and Arthur felt for each other was far more than intellectual, something much different than a beautiful friendship. It was a part of being human, a force as old as creation. It could not be satisfied by holding hands and having pleasant discussions on long walks. As the autumn leaves turned gold and Indian summer colored the Wasatch Front, as she sat up at night making her lesson plans and saw Clarence and Allie seek an early bedtime, she knew it was a desire not to be denied.

Then in mid September Grandma Sarah fell ill. Lucy and her daughters took turns trying to get her to take a little broth. They kept the fire burning in her house to keep her old body warm, but the fever did not abate and her lungs rattled as she breathed. Sarah rapidly slipped away.

Arthur returned for the funeral, which was held in the little Josephite Church in Union, reopened for the occasion. He sat with his brother and sisters while Liz sat in the back. She rose to view old Sarah Pidd Griffiths Smith one last time—so frail in her bones, a grand old lady who had endured so much. Silently Liz promised, "I will write your story."

As the large family and all their friends assembled in the cemetery—a new one with only a few graves, later to be called "Cottonwood"—Liz had a chance to exchange some quiet words with Arthur. "Why isn't she being buried beside William P.?"

He looked down, sorrow smoldering in his gray-brown eyes. "I'm not sure exactly, but I don't think she wanted to be buried beside his other wives. They're in the old pioneer cemetery with him."

Liz felt the shock register on her face. "Other wives? I thought she was his one and only."

Arthur quickly disabused her of what she was thinking. "My grandfather's first wife died. He divorced the second one but they had been sealed, and she insisted on being buried beside him. I guess they were both sealed to him. I don't know, maybe Grandma thought somebody would think they were plural wives if they were all buried side by side."

"Sealed? You mean those other two are sealed to him in heaven?"

Liz had heard of this Mormon practice, which she thought was ridiculous. Now it appeared that Josephites believed it too, and maybe Art did.

"Yes, sealed in heaven." Because the graveside service was starting, he leaned over and whispered, "That was before Grandpa left The Church. Let's talk later."

After the service the crowd gathered in Lucy and Hyrum's house. Liz found more time to be alone with Arthur. They went behind Grandma Sarah's old house, a late September wind heralding the coming winter. Checking to be sure they were unobserved, he pulled her to him. She loved the feel of him in her arms and knew she always would. "Lib," he said, "I just learned this morning that Grandma willed me her land. Along the creek. You remember we walked there?"

"Yes, of course. That abandoned mud cottage. What did you call that building material?"

"Adobe."

"Yes, adobe. I often pictured your grandmother living there with William P. and your mother and father when they were children." For some reason she no longer thought it was immoral that those two children who had no blood relationship had fallen in love and later married. "You said William P. selected the best land in Union when the first pioneers were settling."

"That's right. Just before his death Grandpa deeded five of those acres to Grandma, the best acreage on the entire place, and gave the rest of the land to my father. But that little five acres is very fertile from centuries of the creek flooding. It's still the best homesite in Union. Dad and Clarence have been farming it and giving Grandma some of the proceeds for her upkeep. I can hardly believe it's mine now. It came as a complete surprise. I'm afraid my brothers and sisters might be disappointed."

"Will your father give you the proceeds from that land?"

"I guess so. Of course he and Clarence should get the lion's share for doing the work."

"Of course. I'm glad for you, Art. I know your grandmother loved you very much. She told me that. I think you were her favorite."

"Well I loved her too, and she was fond of you, Lib, very fond. That means a lot to me."

—

Libby never remembered a formal proposal. It was simply something that both of them recognized as the proper next step. They decided the ideal time would be Christmas Eve. In addition to peace and goodwill, romance was in the air. Even Alice, who at age thirty-five had resigned herself to the single life, had found love.

"Let me not to the marriage ot true minds admit impediments."
William Shakespeare, Sonnet 16

9   Marriage

With Liz and Marjorie away at school so much of the time, Alice had found herself unhappily alone at the midday meal. At no other time of the day was she more aware of the fact that she was alone in life. Often she took the late morning street car into Salt Lake to do her shopping and stopped at a pleasant coffee house for her cup of tea and a "wee bite" to eat. She enjoyed the sociable atmosphere there and made the acquaintance of a few of the "regulars."

John McQueen, the dapper little Scottish proprietor, noticed her. When his cafe was uncrowded he often served her himself, delighted by her Scottish accent. Soon he was making excuses to sit awhile at her table. This was not unusual behavior; he was a friendly man who made a point of knowing his patrons on a first name basis.

It delighted him more to learn that she had grown up in Perth and had lived in Dumbarton, his home town. "My mother was Free Church Presbyterian, and your father, Reverend John Symon, was a fine preacher, well known. My mother told us about him."

Alice was ecstatic to hear that her father was known these many miles away.

The more John learned about Alice the more time he spent at her table, enough so that his hired help began to speculate. For Alice, being with John was almost like a visit home. She dropped by the coffee shop more frequently, making an effort to go at times when she knew John wouldn't be busy. Neither had much social life, and their friendship filled a hunger that each had denied. John wanted her to know more about him and she was eager to listen. These two quiet, dignified people were reaching out to each other.

Realizing how close Alice was to church life, he explained his own lack of involvement. Years later Liz would put some of this on paper.

"My father was never much interested in the church," John said, "and I just never seemed to have time for it. Father died when I was quite young. I got too busy working to help support the family. Then I started a little business of my own and found myself working long days, seven days a week. My brother Sam joined me. We had a cafe, and as you know, people like to eat on Sunday as well as any other day. I did most of the cooking. Mother always wanted us to go to church—took us when we were lads. But when we started working, we just thought we were too busy. Mother didn't nag us about it.

"Sam and I always wanted to go to America. We worked doubly hard and saved our money. Ten years ago we came to Salt Lake and started this shop. America's been good to us."

Shyly, she asked, "Did Sam ever marry?"

"Neither of us has ever married."

Blushing, Alice told him of her sisters being busy school teachers and how she had come to keep house for them. "Our Mother died when Liz, the youngest, was only eleven. I've always felt a responsibility to be a mother to her." John caught the wistful note as she added, "But she's doing fine now by herself. I guess I need her more than she needs me."

He understood loneliness. "My sister lived with Mother and made a home for her, then Sis married and moved to a home of her own. Mother was lonely. Sam and I talked her into coming over here to live with us. We have separate apartments, so she lives with one of us awhile, then the other. I know she'd be proud to meet the daughter of John Symon."

John arranged for his mother to have lunch with Alice, and the two took an immediate liking to each other. Alice and Annie McQueen began shopping and attending church together—Annie having transferred her membership from the Dumbarton Free Church to the First Presbyterian soon after arriving in Salt Lake City. Marjorie,

Liz and John occasionally attended with them. Liz and Marjorie liked John McQueen, a proper sort of fellow, not only well mannered but prosperous.

After church one Sunday, Alice admitted to Liz and Marjorie that John had proposed marriage.

Said Marjorie, always quick and free with her opinion, "Don't think about it too long. John's a fine man. If he's thinking about marriage, don't give him time to start thinking about someone else."

Liz told Alice how happy she was that Alice would have John's good company and would be well cared for.

On a sunny day in early October, Alice and John went quietly to the Justice of the Peace—John being uncomfortable asking a minister to conduct the service when he was not a church member. Afterwards Sam hosted the wedding reception at the cafe, in the dining room reserved for special occasions.

Liz and Art attended the reception. It felt natural that when they revealed their intention to marry on Christmas Eve, John and Alice offered to host the ceremony in their apartment. "And since Alice has been like a mother to Liz," John added, "I suggest that she and I play the part of mother and father of the bride. Your guests will be my guests. They'll eat with us afterwards."

"That would be wonderful," Liz agreed. "Don't you think so, Art? We could ask Dr. Paden to officiate."

Art smiled his agreement, very much preferring an intimate celebration to a large church wedding.

———

Doing his own planning for the wedding, Art made a decision that marked the new direction of his life. He would sell his horse. He needed money for a wedding ring, a new suit, and a night in a hotel in the city. As a student able to work only at odd jobs, he used what little money he made for his books and streetcar fare, and at this time of year there was no income from his five acres. But he didn't want to get married without a little money in his pocket.

Besides his land, which he wouldn't even think of selling, his only asset was a fine saddle horse, one that also worked well with a buggy. He was very fond of this horse, which he had raised and trained. The gelding had provided him with transportation and a great deal of independence while he was growing up. Art was an avid fisherman and "Joshua" had taken him to many choice fishing streams in the hills. He had transported Art on pleasant camping trips with high school friends, traveling in the hills and forests that he loved. But since Art started college Joshua had been little used. He wasn't really needed any more. Art didn't even own a buggy. While courting, he and Libby had done all their traveling by foot or street car, she being a cultured city girl.

Art had never mentioned his horse to Libby. She was hardly aware of him. He knew she probably wouldn't understand a person's fondness for an animal. As a girl she had briefly had a cat but had no other experience with animals, and she seemed to feel something of a dislike for them. She associated "filthy beasts" with the uneducated working class who used them to make a living. Although he had worked with farm animals all his life, he would never discuss them with her.

Knowing a man who admired his horse and would pay a good price for him, Art sold Joshua. Now he had the money he needed and a little bit more. But as he watched the new owner mount and ride away, a sadness and sense of heavy loss surged through him. He felt suddenly aware of the complete break with his past, much of which he had truly enjoyed.

Could he ever really fit into the kind of life that his Libby would expect? There was no question about his eagerness to marry her. He adored this remarkably gifted, intelligent, attractive woman who was not only willing to marry him but seemed as eager as he was. She had dropped into his life like a shining gift from heaven, and he knew he was the luckiest man in Utah. But might this be the fairy tale of the princess and the swineherd? Could he possibly live up to her expectations and keep her love in the years to come? He felt quite certain that for all her love, she would never be able to turn him into a prince. But he could do his best to make something of himself that she could be proud of. He could get his degree and teach advanced math. They were from two different worlds, but surely love would build any necessary bridges to bring their worlds together.

———

On Christmas Eve, 1910, Art and Libby exchanged their vows in a small but deeply intimate ceremony in the McQueen's apartment. Dr. William Paden of the First Presbyterian Church conducted the service. Marjorie was the maid of honor. A good friend of Marjorie's, George Irvine, acted as best man and the two of them signed the marriage license as witnesses. Afterwards two of John's best waitresses brought in a very fine wedding supper.

The wedding belonged to Libby. It was gracious. It was proper. She could see that Art was as deeply moved by the meaning of the vows as she was.

He thought the ceremony was just right, though the absence of anyone from his family or any of his friends from Union troubled him some. For the rest of his life he kept that to himself. He and Libby had planned the wedding without consulting his parents. They had known the McQueen apartment was too small to host the Smith clan, and Art had mentioned the date to his parents knowing they would realize that they had been excluded from the planning. He never mentioned his reasons to his children, perhaps not even to Libby. But some explanation can be surmised from the nature of the situation and the people.

He loved Libby more than anything or anyone on earth, and wanted to protect her from unpleasant feelings at her wedding. Always one to avoid confrontation, he too looked forward to an atmosphere of happiness and love at his wedding and felt a strong desire to avoid any coldness. Being legally of age, he did not require parental

Elizabeth Dewar Symon and Arthur Thomas Smith
December 24, 1910

consent, and having wanted Libby for so long and suffered the disapproval of his mother toward her, getting married apart from his family felt like a declaration of independence as a man. It was part of his break from the past. Asking a relative or neighbor to stand up as his best man might have been seen as rubbing his parents' noses in it, so he let Libby pick the best man. He made the excuse that Christmas Eve was the best time for the wedding and the Smith custom of observing Christmas Eve in Union precluded them from attending anyway. He told Libby, who later told her children, that in Utah at that time weddings were not typically social events. But when all was said and done, getting married was the main thing. The details didn't seem to matter much.

When Art informed Lucy of the time and place of the wedding, Mother Smith's comment had been brief:

"There's no reason we should have a part in it. We'll have Christmas Eve here with the grandkids. We think you're making a mistake to get married when you can't support a wife." Always one to deal with the practical aspects of life, she added, "You'll need a place to live. Grandma's house is empty. Take good care of it and you can live there till you decide what you're goin' to do about makin' a living."

This brief conversation, hurtful though it felt, eased Arthur's mind. His mother never minced words, but he believed she would adjust. They had not disowned him, and the offer of the house solved an immediate problem that had worried him. The old adobe, the only house he owned, was too broken, dirty and drafty to be considered a home for a wife like Libby. His father had built Grandma the newer cottage when her eyesight began to fail, closer to her children and grandchildren. So the house that Art and Libby would live in belonged to his father, and Art felt grateful that his parents were willing to provide a home for him and his bride for a while—he hoped until he finished his education.

The newlyweds moved into Grandma Sarah's house on Christmas day. That night as they retired, a "fearful din commenced just outside the window." Terrified, Libby peered out to see a large group of people, including some of her pupils, yelling and banging pots and pans together. Most wore big smiles. "It's a chivaree," Art informed her, "an old American custom. Sometimes they break in and kidnap the bride or groom."

To Libby's relief they refrained from that. Forty years later as she told her granddaughter about the loud and lengthy chivaree, she could hardly contain her laughter.

Being completely together at last brought a blissful new dimension to their lives. The sense of having their union blessed by the gentle old lady before she died added a quietude about living in her house. They shared some laughter and tears as Libby, who had never in her life done much housekeeping, attacked the new adventure. Being the last child at home, Arthur had often helped his mother and knew how to cook a little. He had helped Grandma Sarah a great deal in the past few years, and, under her direction, prepared meals. Libby's comment on cooking:

> To me it's like a foreign language. I'll study it
> and do my best. I did learn to speak some French
> but was never very fluent in it.

At the end of the holidays Art returned to the university, commuting daily on the street car. He enjoyed walking briskly the mile from his stop. Libby was back in her classroom, happily rehearsing the first graders in the fact that she was now to be called Mrs. Smith, not Miss Symon.

The second day after school started, the principal asked her to stop by his office. She had always liked him; he ran a good school and treated her well. Still, she worried about whether this district had a rule against married teachers, and, if so, whether an exception would be made for her. The children had progressed well and the parents had praised her work, so she had reason to hope for an exception.

"Congratulations," the principal said without a smile. "The Smiths are a fine family. Arthur is a bright young man. I taught him in the eighth grade, always liked him. I'm sure he'll go far." He cleared his throat. "I guess you know we will not be renewing your contract come spring."

That struck like ice water. She forced herself to listen as he continued, "The district has a strict policy against hiring married women. A married woman should not take a job away from a man who needs to support himself and his family. I'm sure you'll understand."

Libby did not understand at all. The policy seemed completely unfair. The job should go to the teacher who could best inspire the children to learn, and she knew people said she was one of the best teachers the school had ever had. Besides, she desperately needed to support her husband. She felt angry and hurt, but held her tongue as the principal continued:

"I'm supposed to let you go as soon as possible, but I can't find a qualified teacher to take your place in the middle of the year. I'm going to let you finish the term, so I'll have the summer to look for your replacement. You've done good work. I'm going to miss you next year. I thought you should be aware of our policy as soon as possible so you could make other plans."

The interview was over. There was simply nothing more to say, nothing to discuss. She excused herself and began the short walk home with the cold wind knifing through her coat. She felt physically ill facing the reality that her teaching career was coming to an end—the work she truly loved, the activity that had given meaning to her life. In a few months she would see the last of her schoolchildren, their little faces glowing with the joy of understanding. Yet she knew that she would not exchange being with Art to have her career back. Some part of her had been trying to adjust to this possibility, but now that it was real, it felt as though, deep inside, a vital part of her were dying.

In a detached sort of way she went about fixing supper. Art would come home soon, generally on the five o'clock streetcar. She had a cold roast she could warm up. Potatoes to peel and boil. She had been learning to make biscuits on the wood stove. The last attempt had failed utterly, but she would try again.

The biscuits turned out better. She was tasting one when Art opened the door, threw down his coat, cap and books, and exuberantly embraced her. She held him close and began to sob, something she had assured herself she would not do.

"Libby! You're crying! What on earth is wrong?"

She struggled to get control of herself. "It's hard to explain. I don't know why I'm crying about it. Put out the plates and we'll talk while we eat."

He set the table while she washed and dried her face. The food was good and he was hungry. "Tasty biscuits," he said, "You're getting to be a fine cook."

She was glad he liked the biscuits, yet the compliment didn't make her feel any better. She knew that with a little practice she could learn to be an acceptable cook. But few people could take a classroom of raw kids and make them want to read the way she could.

She told Art what had happened. "I suppose I should have expected it. But I hoped they would make an exception for me. He stated it so bluntly!" Forcing back the tears, she tried to explain how much she enjoyed teaching and why it was so important to her. "And we need the money! You'll be a wonderful teacher, I know, but the level you will teach requires your degree—that's two and a half years away. And anyway, there's no good reason we both can't be teachers!"

Art couldn't think of anything constructive to say. He tried to comfort her, hoping not to say the wrong things. He realized he hadn't understood the intensity of her desire for a career, her need for an identity of her own. He knew she was strong willed and very able to make decisions. These were qualities that had attracted him to her. He hadn't thought much about how this side of her nature might be in conflict with being a contented wife and happy homemaker. All the women he had known seemed very comfortable making pleasant homes and caring for their children. He felt confused and puzzled.

"We're together," he said. "We'll work things out. There are likely other school districts that aren't as narrow minded as this one."

Little more was said about the subject, but her extreme reaction to the rule against married teachers continued to bother Art. He wondered if she had second thoughts about their marriage. He would be glad when he had his degree and a good teaching position, though he felt none of her passion for teaching. He thought of it as just a job where he could use his math and make a living—a lot easier than farming. If accounting paid as well, he knew he could do that too. He liked working with figures.

The coming of spring, 1911, brought happiness nonetheless. Libby poured herself into her teaching. Art crowded in all the extra jobs he could find and saved his money. He appreciated his parents for letting them live in Grandma Sarah's house, and felt pleased about the strong friendship between his Libby and his favorite sister, Allie.

The relationship between Libby and Mother Smith warmed a little too. Lucy was not one to stay angry, and Libby was doing her best to be friendly. Then summer arrived.

To gain credits and hasten his graduation, Arthur signed up for summer school. Libby was determined to enjoy the summer months without brooding over the fact that no job waited for her in the fall. She attended a few classes at the university, riding the street car with Art. Unlike most of the women in Union, she didn't plant a garden, but on nice days worked some with Allie in her garden and shared the produce. Allie was a good teacher for Libby. Together they canned vegetables and fruit. Libby was pleased to see the Ball jars lining up on her pantry shelves. Allie constantly asked to help Libby in the kitchen as a quiet way of giving her cooking lessons. The two couples shared many pleasant suppers together, sometimes inviting other members of the Smith clan to join them. Art and Libby were often invited to have meals in the homes of his other siblings.

Libby also made friends with Art's other sisters—Lizzie and her Charley, and Sarah and Martin. She developed an especially strong affection for Sarah's boys, Floyd and Ervin. They were only ten and eight years younger than their Uncle Arthur, whom they idolized. Little Lucy, Sarah's daughter, was a beautiful and bright child who eagerly looked forward to starting school. Libby couldn't help but love her. She also found Sarah's husband Martin to be delightful company. Having come from Canada, his parents had given him some British ways of saying things. His vast sense of humor always lifted her spirits.

It was Martin who read a Canadian newspaper and made her aware of the tensions building between Germany and the British, which Con had predicted. "If something doesn't change pretty soon," Martin declared, "I'm afraid there'll be a terrible war over there, pitting Germany against England and France. That will drag in Canada and affect my brothers. I don't like it."

Libby knew that a war involving the British would also draw in her beloved brother Laurence. Single and living in Canada, he would be among the first to be recruited. Marjorie also worried about the situation in Europe. Quite alone again after the marriages of Alice and Libby, she was talking about returning to England to become a nurse so she could help her country in the event of war. She was still a citizen of Scotland, a very loyal one. Her life and Libby's were taking very different directions. Marriage had made Libby a citizen of the United States, and she was beginning to feel that this was her country.

Libby spent a lot of time alone. Art was at school for long hours and the in-laws busied themselves with children and farming. The memories in the house around her brought alive her promise to write Grandma Sarah's story. Now that she had the spare time, she sat at the table and began to make notes, deciding to tell it as though Grandma were in the room dictating her story all in one piece. Libby realized that her wording would reflect more education, but that couldn't be helped. Recalling the little things Sarah had emphasized, Libby wrote them down as they came back to her, knowing she could later cut them apart and rearrange them in chronological order.

Six or seven decades later she would edit those notes and complete the following chronicle of Grandma's coming to America and her early experience with marriage:

> After we closed the Bible one evening I said, "Tell me about yourself," and bit by bit she told me of her life. As she talked she presented quite a picture—practically sightless eyes, shabby clothing, a kerchief on her head, and a way of holding her hands together with the first fingers touching. Her accent was so completely English, with the "h" put on or dropped on certain words, as was the way with her section of the country.
>
> 'My dear, it's a long and sometimes painful story. I was born [March 4, 1825] in Lincolnshire, England. Lincoln was a busy town. There were many towns in that shire and many cotton mills, where most of the people found employment. Father and Mother had three children: William, myself and Elizabeth, who was seven years my junior. Poverty was our lot. Perhaps because everyone around us was very poor, we did not feel poverty our condition so much, for we demanded little and entertained no hope of ever becoming wealthy. All our friends were much as we were, only many worse, because many men spent their small earnings in the grogshop. We were fortunate that our father, who made such a small pittance in the mill, brought his earnings home to Mother.
>
> 'Mother was an excellent seamstress and sometimes helped eke out the family income by sewing for the neighbors. At an early age she taught me to sew and

make over clothes, often given us by charities. Everything of course then we sewed by hand. There were many very wealthy British who gave money and clothing to help the needy, and although we often envied them, yet we appreciated the things given the poor through "the church." When William was about 13 or 14 he also had a job in the mill, and soon I, too, joined him.

'In the very early morning the cobblestone pavement resounded with the clatter, clatter of clogged feet as hundreds of workers reported for their jobs. Tea and bread, or tea and porridge had been our breakfast—and we carried a meager lunch. Somehow we accepted our poor fare, for we knew no other life.

'By birth we were members of the Church of England, but we seldom attended services. My chief pleasure was the Wesleyan Methodist Sunday service and the reading class. They taught us to read so we could read the Bible and I'm so thankful for that. They also gave me this Bible that I've kept all my life. Reading has helped me through some lonely times.

'Time passed and Lizzie, as our little sister was called, joined us working at the cotton mill. Every penny she made eased our situation a little.

'Then tragedy struck. A fearful sickness—the dreaded smallpox struck England. There was no amelioration for the disease and hundreds succumbed to the scourge. Mother and Lizzie escaped its ravages, but Father, William and I became ill. I have little recollection of those days. Everything seemed far away and dark. When I finally became conscious I learned that Father was gone, and a look at William's face struck horror to my heart. Yes, mine was the same.

'I do remember the unbearable itching. Mother would dip a feather in kerosene and we would apply this to our tortured faces and bodies. When first I saw my face in the mirror I moaned in unbelief.

'Sheer necessity gave us no time to bemoan our fate. Somehow we had to live. We had to face the world. I suppose it was poor consolation to know that thousands more scarred faces came out of that epidemic.

'A few months later William drifted away from home, and in those days it was difficult to hear from other countries. However, we later learned he had gone to America.

'Lizzie, Mother and I tried to keep going, but it was increasingly difficult, for Mother was frail from the long siege of illness and Father's death, so when an offer of marriage came, she accepted. For her, we were glad, but as it often happens, having a stepfather around was very different. By this time Lizzie was 19 and I, 26. Often on Sunday evenings Lizzie and I would walk, perhaps out a way from town two or three miles where the hawthorn in its beauty scented the evening air, or perhaps just down to the town square where we would mingle with the throngs of others like ourselves looking for some sort of diversion.

'Maybe a political orator, maybe a Punch and Judy show—maybe a religious meeting. On this particular night, noticing a little crowd, we joined it, thinking it was a revival meeting. Yes indeed it was a religious group, but somehow the leaders looked a lot different from those to whom we were accustomed. Who were they? Their accents, too, were unfamiliar. This difference appealed to our sense of adventure. There was a drunken man in the crowd who kept interrupting. During a pause in the meeting we heard him say, "What about polly-gammy?"

"'Oh she's all right,'" replied the speaker, "but to us that conveyed no meaning. After the meeting we waited around awhile, and one of the speakers spoke to us. What a thrill that someone should notice us! Lizzie was rather personable, and unscarred, and made friends more readily than I.

'After that first meeting we made it a point to attend whenever these men were to speak. After one of the meetings, they invited us to come to hear more at the house of Sister Hilton. What a thrill!!! New friends! There we learned they were Latter Day Saints. *Saints?* We didn't know people were called saints in this world. Well, we were told, Paul wrote "to the Saints' at Corinth, Rome and other places. We are the saints of today—so Latter Day Saints. Some people call us Mormons on account of our main historical publication, the Book of Mormon." We found close friends among these folks who came to listen to the elders. All of us were hard working poor folks feeling elated that God should so favor us.

'Then we heard of Zion, in far off Utah, where God's saints were gathering together, having been persecuted and driven out of Nauvoo. They were building God's Empire in the West—God's country—for God's chosen people. There, in an atmosphere of love and understanding we could serve the Lord. All were brothers and sisters in the Gospel. All were equal. All were loved.

'We listened spellbound! Oh, the utter joy after our poor restricted lives of poverty. Our love for this new group grew by leaps and bounds, and, Oh, could we ever attain? To think we should be called of God! Could we ever gather to Zion? Finally we began to harbor the idea of going. It would cost us 20 pounds apiece. So we began saving every penny. Our stepfather thought perhaps it would be a good idea and offered us a bit of financial aid—one of the elders said he had a good friend who could loan a few pounds. So several months passed, and then came the day we had been working for—we could actually go to Zion! Mother seemed heartbroken. "How can I let my girls go," she sobbed. But feeling that perhaps life in the American West offered a better living, she tried to make us feel all was well.

'Our stepfather said, I remember, "Well Lass, who knows, they may find rich husbands there. I've heard tell there's often gold found way out there." [Ed. note: The California gold rush started three years earlier.]

'Then came the parting. We tried to tell ourselves Mother would be consoled by having perhaps a little more with which to do, and a husband unworried by two grim stepdaughters. The morning we left for Liverpool Mother kissed us good-bye. She did not accompany us to the Liverpool docks, partly because money was scarce and maybe partly because actually seeing us sail into the West might be harder for us all.

'Transatlantic crossing was in a process of change at that time. Some sailing vessels were being converted into steamships. Many of the older vessels were still sailing vessels, and a few were a combination of both. Whatever ours was, under decks, I knew nothing about, except for the towering sail spars, but I realized later that had she been a rowboat open to the whims of the Atlantic, our fears and terrors could not have been greater. We had paid 20 pounds, yes, but of course that was to cover expenses to Utah, food etc. Twenty pounds was a veritable gold mine to us. We tried not to worry, and now we were meeting our new friends in the Faith: Swedish, German, Danish folks, mostly young women under thirty. I wondered at the predominance of women — well maybe women accepted the teaching of the Bible more readily than men. Even in the Wesleyan Methodist, I recalled, there were often more women than men. In later years I rethought these things often.

'We were given some instructions: the Saints would congregate together often, sing and pray, thus we would get to know members of the Household of Faith. At last the vessel was loosed from her moorings and slipped out toward sea. Then tears came as I saw the distance widen between old England and the boat, the distance growing greater between myself and all I had loved in the past. I went to my cot in the crowded steerage and sobbed bitterly. Would I ever see Mother again? At last sleep took over and when I awakened it was early morning.

'Lizzie's feelings were less intense, perhaps she had a greater sense of adventure, or perhaps already some fellow travelers had caught her interest. Many passengers showed little grief. Perhaps some had a greater faith than I, and also life had been extremely hard and exacting; perhaps now they felt better things lay in the future.

'The first part of the trip was fairly smooth and uneventful. Often the group of Saints would sing together and found an interest, too, in learning songs of our new Faith. As we sang "Beautiful Zion, built above, Beautiful City that I love," a feeling of kinship settled on us. Another hymn we came to know was, "Oh, my Father, Thou that dwellest on the High and Heavenly place, When shall I regain my presence or again behold thy face?" As we sang, "In the Heavens are parents single—No, the thot makes Reason stare. Truth is Reason, Faith Eternal tells me I've a mother there"— "Oh, Mother," I thought, "Won't I meet you before we reach Heaven?" How completely I was misunderstanding! Mother referred to here was not my mother—it was the Mother God, later I learned. Adam was the God of this world, and the only God with whom we have to deal.

'I really knew almost nothing of the Mormon theology, nor did my companions, but this at the moment didn't seem to matter. We were traveling to God's country where a warmth and recognition in kinship in the church were awaiting us. So we in our hearts thanked God for permitting us to be part of this added enlightenment that would forever guide us through life's perplexing pilgrimage. Some of the elders returning home spoke to us of the oneness we would find in Zion.

'They had filled missions in various countries, as this New Gospel was now reaching out—these converts aboard had been taught the Gospel, or part of it, by these young men, and the converts had implicit faith and love for them. Many of these people had loyally shared their bare existence with these preachers, and made life more comfortable for them while they preached. My sister Elizabeth seemed to be enjoying the trip more than I, but she, being younger, often sought my advice. She had a greater capacity for making friends than I, being spared the facial disfigurement of smallpox. I began to notice that she had become quite a friend of a young man aboard. He was an easygoing friendly fellow, smiling and affable, clever with his hands, could bandage a cut or dress a wound. He read many books, medical books seemed to attract him and before long he earned the name of Doc. Because of poverty in England he had seriously contemplated making medicine his career. In later life I learned he did accomplish this goal.

'About fourteen days out sailing conditions changed. A terrific storm ensued, and now indeed our Faith was tested. The velocity of the wind increased, and our none-too-substantial craft began to be tossed hither and yon upon the crest, down in the trough. A terrifying two-week ordeal ensued. All except the crew and a few of the strongest men were ordered below decks. Nerve wracking days and nights followed—women screaming, children wailing and moaning, men and crew swearing.

'The religious on board prayed loud and agonizingly. Overhead one heard the continual command, "All together boys," as the men sought to bale water from the upper decks and compartments that were being inundated or seeking to salvage necessary equipment in danger of being washed overboard. Often we heard, "Oh God, save my babies!" The continual damp, the cold, the bad air with so many sick, and the poor food took its toll, and several times we saw little bodies being committed to the sea. A mother also, because of a premature birth—both of her infants. Sorrow often bonds friends together and in this case, this was certainly true.

'During these experiences Elizabeth and Frank grew to care deeply for each other. Often he had asked her to help him care for some of the very sick passengers. Finally, the storm lost its savagery and gradually abated.

'In about eight weeks from the time we left Liverpool our badly battered vessel limped into the harbor of New Orleans. Then we realized even more fully what our vessel had been through—The cries of dismay and wonder as we reached the docks! "A miracle," some said. "How ever did she make it?" Her battered hulk, her ripped sails and broken spars—surely a miracle. Our spirits rose as we went ashore. "Oh!! Is this Zion?" "No, indeed," we were told, and as we viewed this town around the docks, we too felt that this could hardly be the dwelling place of the Saints. No, our journey was only really starting.

'Our group stayed together and found temporary lodgings. We had a brief period to bathe, wash and sort again our pitiful supply of clothing.

'In a couple of days we boarded another vessel for the ride up the Mississippi—a smoother and more comfortable trip. Soon we were in Council Bluffs, Iowa. Surely now, this is our destination, but no, we are still far from Zion. But now something different. Here are the wagons that are to take us to God's country and our long cherished hope. But to those of us who had come from Europe and had been long used to railroad travel this did seem a bit strange. How crowded England, Germany had been! This was different. But then God's ways are not always our ways, and also it seemed like an exhilarating experience—riding in wagons.

'To Lizzie it seemed wonderful, for by now she had lost her heart to the young English lad and to her, life presented no difficulties. She was happy and life seemed rosy to her. She was unafraid. Love seemed to ease out from her mind all fear of the future. Her optimism was good for me too—she cheerfully talked of the lovely friendships we would always have in Zion. I, too, would meet a good man, she said, to share with me in life's joys and sorrows. So Westward Ho, the Wagons!

'Would we encounter Indians? Would we have enough to eat? Oh yes, there will be enough, we were told, "and later good buffalo meat." Feeling secure with passage paid, we faced West on our long trek toward the City of the Saints. I saw some doubt and fear in the faces of some of the older people—although there were not many in our company over forty years of age, a few intrepid souls who had not wanted separation from their families.

'Elizabeth's friend had really intended to leave the group in New Orleans, but she in her love and enthusiasm had helped bring the Truth to him, and having no very definite plans he decided to go on to Zion. Perhaps for him this would indeed be a new life— a sweet wife, friends, land of his own. The daily journey for weeks was peaceful. The roads not too difficult, fair food. The evening stopover, the circled wagons, the rest after a tiresome day, the hymns of faith, sometimes dancing, and, oh, the exhilaration of pure clean air!

'How well we slept! We were all good friends now in our company, and kindliness seemed to prevail. Customs of our various countries did not make barriers between us, for we were all tied in a common bond of Faith, faring forth to do God's will. But as we journeyed further westward dangers began to be encountered. Soon now we must ford the Platte River, where even at the best chosen places the waters were turbulent and menacing.

'None of the women could swim, and few of our men, for we were all mostly from inland towns and swimming in these days was not considered a pastime, certainly not one in which women ever indulged. Now this river test! The drovers yelled at the horses urging them on. Most made it across. Some women, terrified, refused to stay in the wagons. They saw wagons tip into the water, some splinter, horses in panic. Men in the group tried to find the shallow place, and attempted to carry some of the screaming women over. Horrified, we saw one man stumble and fall, and the woman he was aiding went down quickly. Before others could help she was swept downstream—beyond our help.

'When we gathered on the other side of the river to assess the damage, we mourned over Kate. She was a gentle soul who often tried to help others, urging us to be patent and trust the Lord. Now this incident over, we must go on—distance had to be covered—so we had no time for remorse. Next morning a band of frightened, subdued people continued quietly on their way.

'By now we were in Indian country. Each night as we circled our wagons I and several of the young girls huddled together, for earlier in the day we had seen Indians on the surrounding hills, stringing along in the direction we were going. But we were confident that our watchmen were on the job while we tried to sleep. One night terror seized us, for one of us saw a dark hand feeling around under the tent flaps of the wagon. Evidently her scream frightened him, for he ran—probably a lone Indian scouting for the rest.

'How weary we were at night, for often to lighten the load, the able bodied walked ahead of the wagons for many a mile on the trail, leaving the wagons for the older people, the sick and the children. How fortunate we were to have escaped cholera, then sweeping through some settlements. We heard a report from some eastbound wagons that it had taken a heavy toll in some camps. One day we spied what seemed to be stacks of wood. Some group ahead must have done this—strange to take the time for this. When we came close to the stack, imagine our horror to find that these white logs were white bodies—scalped victims of a recent Indian raid. No wonder sleep was almost impossible that night. No wonder the howling of the coyotes sent shivers of terror through us. But there was only one path for us: Forward, no matter what our fears.

'That evening we gathered together to sing, trying to buoy up our spirits and the courage of others. Under the stars we sang:

> Come, come ye Saints, no toil nor labor fear
> But with joy wend your way
> Tho hard to you this journey may appear
> Strength will be as your day.
> Gird up your loins, fresh courage take
> Your God will never you forsake.

Somewhat comforted, we slept fitfully and with the optimism of Youth and Faith we trudged forward next morning.

'At last we were in Eastern Wyoming. Supplies were running low. After breakfast we were rationed two slices of bread for the rest of the day. At noon sometimes Lizzie would say, "I'm so hungry I'll eat both slices." "No, no," I would say, "don't do that. You'll need the slice at night." Along the way we would look out for wild berries or edible plants. One day I took a little dish and wandered off a distance, and to my joy I found some wild strawberries. Suddenly as I picked, I heard a rustling in the bushes. I literally froze in my tracks. I was paralyzed. Was it an Indian? No, a huge animal stood near me and I guess all that saved me was that I was rooted to the spot staring at it, unable to move a muscle. We stared at each other—finally it turned and lumbered off. When it was on its way, I soon was running back to the camp. Never again did I go foraging for food. Later I learned it was a cougar or mountain lion. My experience dampened the desire of others, and the wagon master advised us against leaving camp.

'About a week later further troubles arose. A friendly woman in the company became ill. She rode in the wagon. Various "sisters" ministered to her and the elders prayed, but still she showed no improvement. Perhaps the terrible tensions accentuated her illness—for she knew there was no real medical help available and then only the barest supply of what then were drugs. Her husband stayed by her side continuously and the other wagons cared for their three little children. At last the jolting and rough roads became unbearable for her. Her husband pled for stops and at times we came to a halt so that she might rest a bit. Her condition grew very critical. The train stopped longer. When after a two-day stop her death seemed imminent, the wagon master said, "John, we will leave the wagon now and later you can catch up. Supplies and water are running low." Some of the "brothers" went a distance ahead, dug a grave and hauled rocks for cover. So we left him sad and alone on the vast plains, while we rolled on. We were all thunderstruck when John caught up so very soon. But no one questioned the terrified man. On, on to Zion and Hope.

'Finally the great day came when we gazed down

Emigration Canyon to the Valley of the Great Salt Lake. The very place Brigham Young had stopped and declared, "This is the place!" There, wending its way was a river named Jordan by Saints who had arrived before us. So this was Realization!

'As we rolled down the trail into this valley we wondered. Here scattered around were a few adobe houses, a couple of small stores and stables. Rain had fallen the previous night and I heard one Saint whisper to his wife, "They said this was a land flowing with milk and honey. Looks more like mud—a land of damned mud." But we realized he was weary and impatient, for truly time and effort made the desert blossom like a rose.

'So this was our destination. The culminating months and years of hope—the time we had longed and prayed for. Well, time would tell. We had a new sadness now, knowing that we fellow travelers would soon have to separate. Surely we would often meet—church meetings. Oh, this now would be Fulfillment. Together we could learn God's way and live in love and harmony with our brethren. We unloaded in "The Square." Later this would become Temple Square.

'In a sense, now we women were on the Auction Block. Many people had gathered there, meeting relatives, some looking for women to help their wives. Frank, Elizabeth's friend, soon got a job to help in a store and smithy, and was on his way with his new boss. Elizabeth was hired to help in a home. Perhaps because I was older (27) and disfigured by smallpox I was slow in "being chosen." Finally a man came along and asked me what I could do. I assured him I was a good seamstress and could work in a home. Soon then, I was jogging west with him in his wagon. Six miles from town was his destination.

'Arriving at his little adobe shack I met a gaunt look-ing woman with five small children around her. I was amazed that she showed no enthusiasm for me—I would help her and ease things for her. Her extreme coldness was hard to bear, while there I sewed, patched, cleaned, did all I could, the only remuneration some food and a place to sleep.

'Then, very soon another family took me over and the same cool treatment resulted. I was received almost bitterly. Again a few weeks later I was shunted off, this time to an adobe with a man, woman and seven chil-dren. That night I wept bitterly. What was wrong? I was doing my best. Wasn't this Zion for which we had prayed and longed? At this third home the woman was less hostile, and when one day she found me in tears, she said, not unkindly: "What ails you? What all are you crying for?"

'When I told her of the coldness I found so hard to bear she said, "What? You mean you ain't wanting to marry and be his second wife?"

'I recoiled. "What are you saying, Mary. What do you mean? Are you mad?"

'She continued, "You don't know he brought you here, to marry ye?"

'I quickly disabused her. "Why, your husband has you. Do you think I want another woman's man?" Oh, God, I moaned, how could I be a wife to a man already married? I thought of the English law where a woman could separate, but divorce was practically unknown.

'After this encounter Mary treated me more kindly and in a sense a friendship grew between us, although we had little time to exchange ideas or talk. How I

longed to see Lizzie! To tell her my troubles and find
out how things were going with her! She was miles away.
I knew, too, she had a friend in Frank.

'Clouds of dissention soon gathered again. Joe
Griffiths himself broached the subject of marriage to
me. In a storm of tears I repeated to him what I had
told Mary—and temporarily he dropped the subject.
A few days later Joe mentioned he was going to make a
trip across the valley near where my sister lived. My
heart jumped. Perhaps to help win me he offered to
take me along to see her. Oh, how grateful I was! I could
see her and talk with her. Quickly I changed my dress
and smoothed my hair, and we were on our way.

'At last we arrived at the little store where Frank
had been working and eagerly I asked for him. The
storekeeper eyed me quizzically, "Why, Frank ain't been
here for a week. Ain't you heard that him and that English girl got hitched and left in the night?"

'"Gone, gone you say? What do you mean?"'

'"Well, one night after work he claimed he had to
deliver some goods. That's the last I ever seen or heard
of him. Maybe just as well, too. He ain't a good Saint,
nor she neither."'

'I rode back with Joe, stunned and speechless—even
tears refused to come. I felt completely sure something
or someone had frightened him to make him risk traveling alone with Lizzie in that hostile country. When I
got back to the adobe shack I went to my sleeping place
and threw myself down to think, but I have little recollection of the ensuing hours. I felt completely alone.

'I remember Mary trying to be kind to me. One
day soon after Mary came to me. "Sarah," she said,
"Joe is bound and determined to take another

woman. You and me get along. Won't you have him?"

'My will power was broken. Hope was gone. I cared not, now, what happened. I seemed completely up against a stone wall, so I simply told her, "If you want me to marry him, I will." So we were married for Time and Eternity in the Old Endowment House in Salt Lake City. Mary dutifully placed my hand in the hand of Joe, as was required by the ceremony.

'Life continued. But I had a sense of guilt and restlessness. One day as we talked a bit, Mary said to me, "Sarah, ain't I glad that it isn't with us like it is between some women."

'"What do you mean?" I asked.

'"Well, now, look at Katie and Maggie and Annie. What a ruckus goes on there. He likes Annie the best. Of course she's the youngest and best looking. He brings her little things from the store, and it sure do make the other two mad. Yes, Hell's sure a poppin' when they find out he's bought something just for her. Then there's Gretchen and Nellie, William's two. I heard tell he bought Nellie a big gunny sack of apples. Gretchen got so mad she went into Nellie's end of the house—she's got so many young 'uns they gave her that side—Well, she went in there and throwed the applies around. They throwed 'em back and forth till they ruined most of the apples. William got a fearful smack in the eye too, and the swearin' sure was bad. But Sarah, ain't it good we get along so well?"

'One day I asked Mary why the men wanted more than one wife, especially when they were all so very poor and couldn't get ahead. Is it just their lustful natures?

'"Well," Mary said, "I think with some it is, and an

excuse to change around among women, but I've heard tell by the elders that the reason is that the greater number of offspring born, the greater will be our exaltation in Heaven. This is why they call it a Divine Principle."

"'How do you mean Divine?'"

"'Well, the Lord has created millions of spirits. These here spirits need bodies. Every spirit must have a body, else they cannot go on to a higher glory. So the Lord gives special blessings to those who help give the spirits bodies. That's why men want more than one woman, to help the Lord out. Men want glory, you see."

"'Mary, do you really believe that?'"

"'Well, yes and no, but maybe believing this makes life easier here."

"'Well, I could never believe that, nor understand what you are saying."

"'Sarah, don't you see that if the women do believe these things—and millions of spirits are needing bodies before they can progress eternally—then maybe it is our duty to let our husbands have many children. A one-wife man is thought of as a slacker. Children are accounted for as payment toward the Salvation of their parents. We will have our husbands in Heaven. That is, if we are sealed to each other in the Temple."

"'What about people with no children, or men and women who never marry?'"

'Mary thought a while. "I believe they are to minister to the rest of us. I think the Bible speaks of ministering angels. But also, Sarah, women who are married can be sealed for Eternity to men who want them. I don't know, though, whether they can bear children in Heaven."

'How sad and utterly bewildered I felt, but Mary

was kind and the months passed drably and uneventfully. No word came to me from England, and now that Lizzie was gone—later I learned they had made it to the Missouri—and I had become the second wife to Joe, I just lived one day at a time, mostly with my own thoughts.

'After I had been married a year, our first baby, a little girl was born, a daughter we named Lucy. A year later another baby came, but he soon left us. He was a frail child. Lucy was a comfort to me. She was mine. Something of my own. Mary, in her own way, was kind. But her tasks were many, taking care of her seven children. We helped each other. We felt the children were all brothers and sisters, and tried to show no preferences. How bleak the days and months were! And I found myself longing deeply for home—Mother, and crowded conditions, hard and poverty-stricken as they had been.

'But somehow through it all, I kept telling myself that the God whom I had come to know in England still cared for me even out here in the far off desert country. How I did appreciate being able to read. Some of the women could not, but I owed this ability to the little Wesleyan Chapel, and I so treasured the Bible given me. Had I sinned? Daily I prayed to be forgiven, and to find some way out of this perplexity.

'Later another baby boy came to us. We called him Georgie. Perhaps I was overly anxious about him, because the other boy had died, but Georgie was healthy and happy and easy to care for.

'Joe felt the burden of such a large group to support. He didn't complain, because he was proud to be now the father of nine children. But when a brother in the Faith offered him a job ten miles away, he readily responded—a job on the road gang trying to make roads a bit easier to travel.

'Mary and I tended the little patch of land, taking care of potatoes, vegetables and milking the cow. Also we had a few eggs. At times, cured pork and dried venison. One day after Joe had been gone about three weeks, a horseman rode in very fast and excitedly. "Sorry Ma'am, to tell you Joe's been took awful sick. The men are following behind bringing him home in the wagon."

'"Oh, what's the trouble?"

'"Well, we were afeared it might be cholera, but we don't know yet."

'We hurriedly prepared for his arrival and soon had him in his own bed. Of course there were no doctors available in those days, so we ministered to him as best we could, but not for long. What his illness was we never knew, but perhaps violent food poisoning. We were glad, at least, we had been spared cholera, which had been prevalent some time before among the immigrants. Two days later we laid him beside his little boy "up the creek," and again Mary and I faced the future together.

'I was confused, so often I went by myself and prayed for a solution to this predicament of marriage. No, I felt sure this was not an answer. I felt God didn't work this way.

'Mary's grief was much keener than mine, for he had been her husband—and even if he had married me, her earlier memories remained.

'I had a kind of liking and respect for him. He tried to be fair and was not unkind. Now we were hardly able to go on. Joe's work was gone. Others, very poor themselves, helped us when they could. I began to go out again sewing for neighbors. Lucy, now six, stayed with Mary and usually Georgie stayed and played too. Sometimes he begged me to take him with me, and at times I did, for he seemed to be little trouble and was quiet and contented.

'One morning I took him to the home of Sister T, and I settled down to sew. Suddenly a scream and a splash. My baby had fallen into a tub full of boiling soap! Sister T. had pushed the hot soap behind a curtain to cool and hide it from view, but Georgie had stumbled into it. No help. No hope. Nothing as an alleviation of pain. Soon unconsciousness. He too sleeps "up the creek" beside his father and brother. But life still had to be lived.'

In the grip of this horrible memory, Sarah had been unable to continue her story. Libby remembered that tears had glistened in the furrows of her eighty-five-year-old face, and that they always reappeared any time Sarah mentioned little Georgie's death. This was, Libby realized, the end of the story of Sarah's first marriage. Afterwards came her marriage to William P. Smith in defiance of Brigham Young. They had nearly been forced out of town. She had given birth to twins by him, one who died within a few days and a girl, Sarah, who lived for seven years before she died of a disease, possibly encephalitis—yet another devastating tragedy. But William P. and Sarah had endured and become respected pioneers in Union. He knew how to set bones, pull teeth, and care for people with various kinds of illness. He had been friends with the Indians, and his family had stayed safely on his land while Indians attacked other settlers and everyone else fled inside the protective walls of Fort Union.

Putting down the pencil, Libby realized that the writing had stirred her own emotions—she had put herself in the place of that gentle, hopeful woman who had been so cruelly misled. Marjorie had also been enthralled by Mormon missionaries, but Libby and Marjorie had a profession that gave them independence. Libby picked up her pencil and added to her notes as though Sarah were still speaking:

> My dear, things were very different when I came. I
> had no money and no way to leave. In many ways I was
> a captive. I had to do the best I could in the situation I
> was in. As you grow older you may find times when you
> have to do the best you can do, not just what you would
> like to do.

Libby stacked the papers on the shelf and went to bed. Art was waiting. She hoped Sarah had found half as much happiness with William P. That bright little lady had been entitled to some happiness. She had dealt bravely with a reality not of her choosing. She had lived an honorable life under the circumstances. She had raised a fine daughter and kept her faith in God. Surely she had heard the blessed words spoken to one who had worked hard and made the most of her talents: *Well done, thou good and faithful servant. Enter into the joy of thy Lord.*

There was more to ponder here. Sarah's story made Libby reassess some of her own idealistic, perhaps rigid, standards. She could no longer think of the wives of polygamous husbands as immoral. And she saw the rule that prevented her from teaching in a somewhat different light. Just as Grandma, seeking a fuller and better life, had long ago set a new course that determined her future actions, Libby, in her marriage to Art, had set a course for her life from which there was no turning back. She would find it necessary to be less judgemental in the way she related to good people who simply looked at life from a different set of standards. She was part of Utah now. She could no longer make decisions based solely on what seemed right to her, but would face circumstances that determined what she must do. She felt she could surmount the challenges and, like Sarah, make something good come out of whatever tasks God assigned her.

After all, she had Art. Their love would get them through whatever the future held. She felt sure of that.

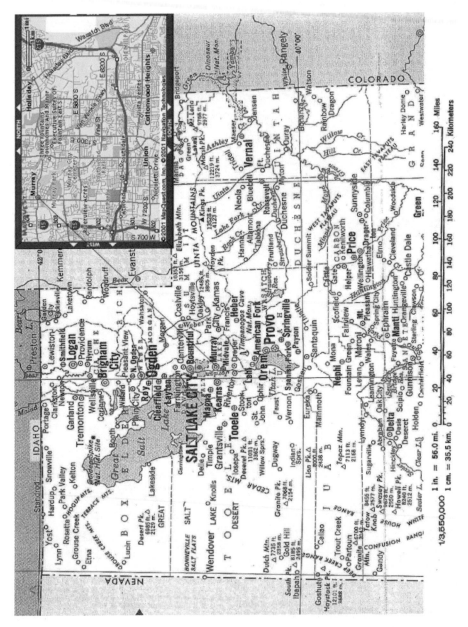

Base map from These United States, published by Reader's Digest Association, Inc., 1968. Insert from MapQuest.com Inc, 2001, showing modern Union between Murray and Midvale, just west of Cottonwood Heights.

". . .a book of verse—and thou beside me singing in the wilderness."

The Rubiayat of Omar Khayam, rendered into English verse by Edward Fitzgerald

10   Yost

In November of 1911, Libby became certain that she was pregnant. This was not entirely unexpected, but not planned. In his third year of studies at the university, Art insisted that now, with the responsibility of a wife and child, he could no longer continue as a student. He must get a job to support his family. Libby wept to think of him giving up his schooling when he was doing so well, but understood that it had to be done. Hyrum and Lucy had been generous, but a child changed things. Libby and Art discussed their options. She wanted him to find a job in education. If she could not be a teacher, she felt that he should be one.

Without further education he couldn't teach math at the level he wanted, but he could be an elementary teacher and keep studying in summer school and taking correspondence courses to obtain his degree. Meanwhile he could easily pass the examination required for an elementary certificate. This he did. He also began looking for a position to open in midyear.

Soon it was evident that nothing was available. Midyear openings around Salt Lake were quickly filled by experienced teachers with letters of recommendation. Finally, when they were about to despair, they found a notice in the newspaper. A community called Yost, Utah, was seeking a teacher for the upper grades in their two-room school. The salary was acceptable. A furnished teacherage was provided. Why the vacancy had occurred at midyear was not mentioned.

Though he had lived in Utah all his life, Art had never heard of Yost. None of his family had either. They found a map of the state and finally located Yost to the west, on the Utah-Idaho border and only twenty-five miles from Nevada. The map indicated no other towns anywhere near it. The nearest rail stop was Kelton, about forty miles south and east. From its location it appeared that Yost would be a small supply center for a vast ranching area of forest and grasslands.

Art corresponded with the school board and learned that they were pleased to have an application from a married man who would bring his wife. In answer to the question of transportation from Salt Lake City, the school board suggested the train to Kelton, then "other transportation" to Yost. If there was no one to meet them at the train with a buggy or wagon, they could ride in a freight wagon that brought supplies to town. It ran at least once a week. If the Smiths accepted the position they would be advised of the day the freight wagon would run. There would be no charge. The driver was always pleased to have company.

Art, who had been raised a country boy and had always enjoyed the out-of-doors, was intrigued with the prospect and accepted the job. For Libby, Yost was not so inviting. She liked living near a street-car or a train. The year in Granite, when she'd had no easy access to the city, had been a trying time. Furthermore, transportation by freight wagon sounded a bit too much like Grandma Sarah's experiences, but she kept her doubts and fears to herself. A teaching job was necessary, and the job in Yost seemed the only chance to get one. She was comforted by Art's confidence that they could manage just fine.

The trip to Yost was a venture into the unknown—a little like the day she left Scotland. They took the train to Brigham City, then switched to the westbound train. Before long they were gazing from the train window at the vast blue lake. For a long time the water stretched farther than they could see. Then they sped into a desolate and frosty landscape, supporting nothing but an alkaline scrub. For hours not a creek nor sign of human habitation interrupted the monotonous vista. Stopping the conductor as he made his way up the car, Libby asked about Kelton, where they planned to spend the night. The conductor sat across from them and gladly shared his considerable knowledge.

For twenty years prior to the building of the transcontinental railroad, Kelton had been a service stop for wagon freight and miners trekking west to the California Gold Rush. When the railroad was finished in 1869, Kelton became an important railhead for the westward freight, as well as for wagon freight and stagescoaches northward to the Boise area. With the discovery of gold in 1862, the Boise Basin mines opened and Idaho City was suddenly one of the biggest cities in the West. Additionally, farming and ranching were expanding in the Boise Valley. Supplying this booming area, Kelton Road became one of the busiest freight routes of the West. Kelton, the transportation hub, was itself a boom town.

Things changed with the 1884 completion of a railroad across southern Idaho. The great old Kelton Road was largely abandoned, as were many Kelton businesses. The town shrank into a sleepy existence, though remnants of the earlier activity were still in evidence.

Art and Libby spent the night in one such remnant—a once-fancy hotel now in need of paint. They arrived just before dark on a very short winter day. The hotel proprietor introduced them to Fred, the operator of the freight wagon who was waiting for them in the lobby. He would drive them to Yost.

In his rough western manner, Fred, a hugely bearded man in a red-plaid flannel shirt and leather suspenders, packed most of their luggage on his wagon, then asked them to "get some grub" with him. In the hotel dining room, a room like Libby had never seen before, Fred sat across from them. He explained that his custom was to load his wagon for Yost, then, after a night in the hotel, get an early start. Libby tried to look squarely at Fred as he spoke, not behind him where a large gilt-framed painting of a reclining nude gazed across the room without a trace of modesty. The painting hung above a sideboard that had a brass rail across the bottom, as though it once had been the bar of a saloon. Thick golden ropes held back the purple draperies on the tall windows, though dust dulled both the gold and the purple. The linen napkins had been washed and ironed too many times, and were now quite frayed.

As the good roast beef and potato dinner was served, Fred told a story about a cowhand named Wildcat, whom he had known in his youth. Wildcat became jealous of his horse on account of its metal shoes, while he, Wildcat, wore out his boots very fast on the rocky, sagebrushy land. It seemed he was always riding a long way to town to buy expensive new boots. So he went to a blacksmith and had a pair of soles made of solid iron, curving up around his feet, with nail holes around the edges. He took these "soles" to the shoemaker, who attached leather boot tops by means of thongs though the nail holes. Concluded Fred, "Ol' Wildcat clomped around in them metal boots for many a year, and was mighty proud of 'em too." Fred chuckled as he methodically wiped his plate with a slab of bread.

Libby couldn't imagine a man being jealous of his horse. She found every aspect of the story disturbing and unsettling, but smiled politely.

Laughing, Art clearly enjoyed Fred, who was stuffing his mouth with the soaked bread. "I had some colorful relatives myself, "Art said. Libby made a mental note to ask him about those relatives.

The freighter talked with enthusiasm about the country around Kelton and its people. The people were so different from her experience that it seemed she had entered a mystical realm. He told about prospectors, one driven crazy by the isolation, another married to an Indian whom he left in Kelton while he headed for the "gold fields of Alaska."

Tired, and knowing they would leave at first light, Art and Libby rose to go to their room.

"Come morning," said Fred, "we leave at dawn. Put on everything warm you've got. Wagon's open to the weather, you know. It's been good weather up to now, for December, dropping to only eight or ten degrees above zero at night, some above freezing on these sunny days, but it could turn cold." He squinted at them as though to emphasize the point. "Sometimes a wind comes up and it gits downright miserable. We'll have to hope no blizzard comes through here. I'll have the hotel cook heat some bricks for your feet."

The Old Kelton Road was as good as could be expected of a rutted dirt road, frozen where it would have been muddy. The trip would long be remembered, the story retold many times. A breeze came sharply through the sunshine, and it became difficult to keep warm sitting on the wagon seat. Art and Libby warmed up by walking behind the wagon, but only briefly. They couldn't match the walking pace of Fred's spirited team. When they got back in the wagon, Fred brought out some old buffalo robes for them to wrap up in. "Some folks don't realize how cold it is ridin' in an open wagon. I never travel without my buffalo robes. Ain't nothin' like it to keep a body warm."

Libby had heard of such robes but had never dreamed she would ever be wrapped in one. Soon, however, she understood why the Indians and pioneers had valued them.

Around noon Fred stopped the team at a spot where a cold fire indicated other travelers had camped. Needing a rest stop, Libby had, for more than a half hour, become increasingly uncomfortable but couldn't imagine how to mention it. She was relieved to see that they had stopped quite near some thick brush. Tracks in the snow indicated that other travelers had availed themselves of the privacy of the brush. She realized that for all his coarseness and rough speech, Fred was a thoughtful man. Nevertheless, this would be the first time she had bared herself in the open air like a primitive person.

When Fred and Art returned from another clump of brush, Fred said, "We'll have a bite to eat now and stretch our legs. Mary and Joseph need some grain."

"Mary and Joseph?" Libby repeated, immediately linking that with the fact that it was late December and she was with child. "Aren't those names a wee bit unusual for horses?"

"I reckon they might be, but they fit. They're fine horses. I bought 'em from a Catholic fellow who said he got 'em at Christmas, and those were the names that first come to him. Them Catholics put a lot of store by Mary and Joseph. I've never had cause to change their names. They sure do pull together like a good couple should."

He began rummaging in the wagon for his sack of oats and the nose bags for the horses. When they were munching their grain, Fred and Art went out to "rustle some firewood."

Libby looked at the desolate scenery. The sagebrush and scrub grass gave the appearance of nappy upholstery on the rolling hills, and beyond the hills snow blanketed a range of distant peaks. No sign of human habitation could be seen in any direction. Silently she said a prayer that they would be delivered safely from this journey through the wilderness and she would give birth with the assistance of a doctor and nurse.

Fred built a campfire, brought out a blackened coffee pot, and soon had coffee boiling. "This'll help warm you up," he said handing them steaming tin cups. The noon meal had been packed by the hotel cook, a courtesy the hotel offered to teamsters who spent the night with them. Libby felt better after eating a hearty sandwich—the sliced roast beef no doubt from last night's supper.

After lunch they stood warming themselves while Fred waited for the bricks to reheat in the fire. "Don't mean to be snoopy, he said to Art, "but I noticed a little rifle case in your baggage. You do some shooting?"

"Some. Targets and small game. That's a little 22. It's big enough for anything I do."

Throughout the journey they had seen jack rabbits leaping in the sagebrush, and now a large one stopped about fifty yards from the wagon and was sitting there watching them. Fred walked slowly to the wagon and produced a rifle from beneath the seat. "See that big 'ol Jack sittin' there. He's just waitin' for us to go so he can see if the horses spilled any grain. The jacks're hungry this time ayear and travelers drop a little grain where the horses feed." He handed the rifle to Art. "See what you can do with 'im."

Art heard just a bit of a good natured challenge in Fred's tone. He took the rifle, felt it's weight, balanced it in his hands. "Mighty fine little gun." It was a 250-3000, named for its 25-calibre, very high speed and generally very accurate bullet. He released the safety, aimed carefully and squeezed the trigger.

The rabbit jumped straight in the air and fell to the ground. Fred looked surprised. "By God, that was some head shot at that distance! Not many men could do that. Man, you'll do!"

Art realized he had passed a test—shooting ability was highly valued in this area. He was pleased with himself. Shooting was something he excelled in. He was glad to be with someone who appreciated good shooting. With his characteristic shy smile he handed the gun back to Fred. "I always like a head shot. That way they don't suffer."

Libby, who had been alarmed when Fred produced the gun, was pleased because Art was pleased, but she was as surprised as Fred. She knew Art had a gun, but he had never talked about it and she had never seen him shoot. She had always associated guns with ignorant, uncivilized people. Sensing this, Art had refrained from speaking about it. Libby would soon learn that no one traveled these roads without a gun. There were coyotes, a few wolves and an occasional cougar— none of which were friends of the ranchers. Here, guns were simply a part of everyday life.

As they continued their trip toward Yost, Libby noticed a new warmth between Fred and Art. Fred began speaking on a more personal level. "I guess you know why there was a teaching job open this time of year?"

"No, I really don't," Art said. "They didn't mention that."

"Well, the teacher just quit. Folk's said the kids ran 'im off." That sent a shiver through Libby.

"Do you know what happened?" Art asked.

Fred hunched over the reins, squinting past Mary and Joseph as they stepped smartly along the road. "Well there's some big boys in that school. The law around here says a kid has to go to school till he finishes eighth grade or turns eighteen. A lot of 'em live on the ranches, real scattered out. Them big fellas go to school when there's no work to do. A number of those boys, why they're grown men afore they finish the eighth grade. Puttin' up hay and doin other fall work in September, October. When bad weather commences, they show up at school. Well, some of 'em ride horseback a long way." He squinted over at Art. "One big fella rides about ten miles. Naturally they bring their guns and don't want to leave 'em in the barn with their horse. Cloak room neither."

"Well, the way I heard it," Fred continued, looking back at the road, "this teacher was pretty much a city dude. The guns scared the sh—scared him to death and he told the boys to leave 'em in the barn." He looked over at Art, "He downright ordered one boy to leave his gun in the barn or leave it to home."

"'The hell I will!' that boy told 'im, just like 'at. "'Just try and make me! I'm not leaving it in the cloakroom neither.' He parked his rifle by his desk." Fred chuckled. "That dude teacher was so scared he up and left town."

"How long ago was that?" Art asked.

"Oh, a couple months I'd venture. The lady that teaches the lower grades did the best she could to keep things going till Christmas. She's a dandy good teacher. Older lady. Married to a rancher that lives not far from town. Raised a few kids herself."

Noticing that in Yost a married woman was eligible to teach, Libby was nevertheless struck with horror to hear about big gun-toting young men defying a teacher. What was Art up against? Would his classroom turn into an armed showdown? Terrible scenes raced through her mind.

Recalling the innocence of the school children in the rural towns of Scotland, Libby snuggled against Art, who sat quietly on the buckboard obviously giving the story some thought himself. She feared for her gentle husband in the wilds of America. It was getting colder, the bricks having lost their heat. The very short winter day would soon end. She wondered how this Yost segment of her life's journey would end.

Darkness settled over the wagon, but Mary and Joseph seemed to know the way, and soon Fred pulled up before a cluster of buildings. "This used to be a stagestop," Fred said, jumping off the buckboard. "Hard Up, they call it. You bunk over there." He gestured toward the largest building with light showing through the windows and a door just opening. He set down the luggage, Art helping Libby down. The dark silhouette of a man approached from the lighted building. Fred introduced Art and Libby to the proprietor, a broad shadow, then led Mary and Joseph to a nearby stable. *At least there is a room at the inn,* Libby thought to herself.

The man made no move to shake hands, but silently led them into the building. Somewhat alarmed at his unfriendliness, Libby followed, then stopped in her tracks inside a large room. Two gas lanterns suspended from the ceiling illuminated the man's bloody hands and bloodstained apron. He picked up a huge butcher knife in one hand and a meat saw in the other. About to run for her life, Libby realized he was approaching one of two large tables upon which lay the halves of two hogs. He returned to his muscular work of butchering them. Bad as that looked—she'd never seen the bloody mess of a "beast" being butchered—she now felt very grateful that the man had made no attempt to shake hands.

The proprietor looked up. With a nod of his head he drawled, "You'll find your bed over yonder. Gotta finish with this so the missus can fix your supper." At the back of the room, on a sagging wire stretched across it, hung a curtain that Libby had at first mistaken for the wall.

Art picked up their luggage and carried it behind the curtain. Libby followed. The narrow space contained a bed, two chairs and a dresser with a mirror. Art stepped to a back door and opened it. A path led to an outhouse. He closed the door and sat on the bed, putting an arm around her. Knowing that anything they said could be heard by the man, they said nothing. It didn't matter. Art didn't know what to say and Libby was speechless, but running through her mind was the constant thought: *We're a long way from Perth, or even Salt Lake. I wonder what Mother would say if she could see me now?*

Exhausted from the day's ride she pulled off her shoes and stretched out on the bed. Art drew a blanket over her. The gas lanterns delivered a little light through the space between the top of the heavy curtain and the ceiling. Art rummaged around in the semidarkness, found a kerosene lamp on the dresser and lit it. About two hours later, around seven o'clock, they were called to supper. One of the butcher tables had been moved to the side of the room and was now heaped with the bloody hog parts. The other was cleared off and covered with a cloth. A pleasant woman laid a good supper upon it and sat down to eat with them.

The two dollars they paid at supper included the "room," the supper, and breakfast the next day. Art and Libby were both hungry. Fred came from his "room" in the stable and joined them. All very tired, they ate in silence and retired immediately. Libby and Art were grateful for each other, for the warm bed, and a good sleep.

The next day was a repeat of the day before. They no longer followed the Kelton Road, but a road in fair condition that branched off to the west. Fred continued his visiting and his stories, and by the time they reached Yost they felt they knew everything about the town and most of its people.

They had a chance to look around as they entered the town, for it wasn't quite dark. The schoolhouse was the most prominent building. Two saddled horses and a team stood at the hitching rail of a general store. Light glowed in the windows illuminating several people within.

The scattered houses reminded her of Granite. Most homes had a small barn. In the corrals she saw horses and cows eating their evening hay. One look at the tiny town verified what Fred had said, that most of the children would come from neighboring ranches.

Libby told Fred she was anxious to see the teacherage and Fred obligingly drove them directly to it. He unloaded their baggage before returning to the store to unload his freight. She looked inside the little log house and felt relieved to find it quite well cared for. After the past two days nothing would have surprised her, and she realized she'd been apprehensive about her new home.

The logs were well chinked, the house soundly built. It had a kitchen-living room combination with a sideboard and sink. Obviously water would have to be brought in from the pump outside the door. There was one small bedroom and a combination storage closet and pantry with shelves. The kitchen range would provide heating and cooking. Art's one comment: "I don't think it will be hard to heat."

To Libby it seemed that during this last two days they had somehow traveled back in time, like the famous Alice in Wonderland. Here was a world that she had read about in novels but never expected to move into. It seemed disconnected from the way things really were in the world. She wouldn't have been surprised if the Mad Hatter had walked in and offered her half a cup of tea or a fairy godmother had appeared to straighten things. All she knew was if any rabbit appeared it would likely be gray and very long-eared.

As she watched Art kindle a fire in the stove, go out to the pump with the bucket, prime the pump and fill the bucket, she suddenly realized that he was making himself quite at home. Indeed he *was* quite at home in this place where she felt herself a stranger. His relaxed movements were reassuring, but could she ever feel at home this far from civilization? She had no choice.

She loved her husband and had chosen to share her life with him. He was the father of the child she carried. If he could live and work here, she could make it her world and keep her doubts and fears to herself. The furnishings were spare but adequate. With a fire started in the stove, the room soon became quite comfortable. She had much to do to get settled. It felt good to be off the jolting wagon and it was time to start supper, but they had no food.

They went to the store for food and supplies. The friendly store-keeper seemed delighted to meet them, as were the customers in the store. Obviously these people had been eagerly waiting to make the acquaintance of the new teacher. Art felt proud watching Libby greet them as though she had just stepped out of Buckingham Palace—grasping their hands with her head cocked in genuine interest as she looked into their eyes and gave them a little smile. He sensed that the people they met were well pleased.

The next day was Saturday. School would start on Monday. When Art visited the schoolhouse and met a few more people around town, it became evident that the wagoner had lost no time in spreading the word that the Smiths were friendly, interesting people and that Art Smith "sure knew how to handle a rifle." Everywhere he went people kept assuring him that "Yost is a very friendly town—you'll really like it here." Assuming he encountered no trouble in school, he was in total agreement with them.

———

"Oh Art," Libby moaned as he left for school early Monday morning, "be careful. Don't risk your life. We can always go back to Union. You could find some other kind of work."

He hugged her reassuringly and smiled. "I'll be all right. I've given some thought to this."

He had a plan. He started the fire in the big heating stove and wound the clock on the wall. This he would do each day. By previous arrangement, Mrs. Johnson, the teacher of the lower grades, also came early and helped with his questions about the curricula for the various grades, roll books and procedures. He had already spent the previous day going over what the former teacher had left and found things pretty well in order. He felt confident as far as the school work was concerned, however he wasn't sure about a number of things. He realized that much would depend on his own common sense and instinctive reactions in dealing with people.

As the students began arriving he found them polite but reserved. They left their coats, overshoes and lunches in the cloakroom—he heard the sounds of rifles being put down— and gathered around the stove to warm themselves. There was an informality much like one would expect entering the home of a good neighbor for a social visit. For some time the boys and girls had been out in the cold winter morning; their ears and faces were red. The warmest place in the big room was near the stove, and it was not yet time for school to start, so Art saw no reason for them to sit on cold benches at cold desks.

In days to come when it was extremely cold and a wind was blowing, he would allow them to remain around the stove after nine o'clock, when school was supposed to start. But now, eager to keep order, he realized that no rule said he had to wait until nine to call the roll. He picked up his roll book as each student arrived, introduced himself, asked his or her name, checked it off on the attendance chart and asked them to tell him a little about themselves. He was gratified to have all twenty-four marked present a few minutes before it was time to ring the bell, which he did mainly to notify the town that all was well. He noted with interest that no student wanted to miss meeting the new teacher.

The room had warmed nicely and everyone seemed in a pretty good mood. No rifles had been brought into the classroom. He also noticed that several boys stood larger than his own compact five feet and six inches.

He did not say, "Take your seats." Without thinking about it he said what came completely natural for him. "Do you think it is warm enough now for you to go to your seats?"

A big, apparently good natured boy answered, "Yes sir, I reckon so." They all promptly went to their desks, and Art realized the boy had the characteristics of a leader. A sudden warm feeling came over him that he understood these kids and was going to like them. They had been brought up very much like he had. They were country kids.

"Now that we're all here," he began. "I want to make a few suggestions on how we'll start our days. If it's too cold to be outside till the bell rings, come in and get warmed up like you did today. You might like to go to your desk and check on your homework or go to the reading corner and read. We don't want to make a custom of a lot of visiting in the classroom. Of course, as long as class hasn't started there's no harm in a little visiting if we keep it down so we won't disturb someone who might like to study.

"We'll begin our day by pledging allegiance to the flag. Each day I'll ask a different student to lead in the pledge. Then I will call the roll by grades, starting with the fifth, and review the subject that each grade will be working on so you can study for that day's discussion or test. That way you will all have something to do while other grades are reciting."

"Now, one other thing. I want to make a suggestion about your guns." He had their undivided attention.

"One of the most cherished possessions a man or boy can have is a good rifle. We wouldn't want someone to slip into the barn and steal one of them. I'm going to suggest that first thing when you get here, those who bring guns to school come and stack them against the wall right here behind my desk. And I'm sure you will all agree it will be best not to have them out in the cloakroom where one might get into the hands of a younger child who doesn't know how to properly treat a rifle. I know those of you who have guns have been taught proper respect for them. I'm sure you've all been taught to unload them before entering a building. If the guns are here in the front of the room, we can all keep an eye on them. Does anyone have a problem with that?"

There was no response and Art felt that the boys all were comfortable with that plan. He didn't mention the feeling of security it gave him to have the guns near his desk where he would be the first to reach one in the event of serious trouble, which he really did not expect.

"If there's no objection, I'll excuse the boys who have guns to take a few minutes to check to make sure none of them have cartridges chambered up, and bring them in."

Several of the larger boys left their seats and in an orderly fashion retrieved their guns from the cloak room and stacked them against the wall behind Art's desk. The large boy who seemed to be a leader paused to say, "Thank you sir. I think this is a good idea."

Art smiled. "Maybe some time you can show me some good places around here to go hunting."

"I'd be proud to do that, sir."

This story of Art's first day teaching would be told and retold many times in years to come.

—

Libby worried all day about Art. She finished her settling-in chores, finally mastering the art of keeping a good fire in a wood-burning stove, then decided to take a brisk walk in the bright winter sunshine. Passing another log house, she was hailed. A woman stood in the doorway, waving her to come in. Libby thought a visit with a neighbor might take her mind off Art. Over a cup of chickory tea, she and Doris talked, Doris obviously eager to learn what she could about the new teacher's wife.

From Doris, Libby learned that though there were no churches in Yost, a group of Mormons met for worship in one of the homes. Some of the families around town were gentiles. The nearest town was Almo, about twenty miles north, in Idaho. "You know," Doris laughed, "Yost and Almo just might be the most isolated towns in these here entire United States!"

Silently Libby marveled to find herself in such a place. She reminded herself: *God's ways are not always our ways.*

Doris said the nearest doctor was in Oakley, Idaho, a Mormon settlement about forty miles north. It was a bit larger than Yost. A number of polygamous families had moved there about 1880, when polygamists were being hunted down and sometimes jailed. They felt safer outside of Utah.

Libby didn't like the sound of it, and learned enough from Doris to know that Brigham City was the nearest town where she might feel comfortable giving birth. Surprised how much she enjoyed her visit with this neighborly woman, Libby looked forward to meeting others in the town.

Walking back to her own little home, she prayed that all was well in the schoolhouse. The absence of a church meant that, at least for the present, her faith must be an individual effort kept alive by regular Bible reading and personal prayers. This she promised God she would do. By now she knew that Art had almost no experience with religion, either as practiced in church or family worship. However it seemed to her he had a private religion of his own, and whatever his faith, he didn't share it easily with another. He had disliked too much of what he'd observed in organized religion. She was right in thinking he would never be one to lead his family in daily Bible readings and prayers.

On the walk home from school on that first day of teaching, Art had to restrain himself to keep from breaking into a run. He had good news to share with Libby. The sunset fired the few puffy clouds with a rosy brilliance, imbuing the little village with soft light that seemed to blanket it with contentment and hope. His foreboding was gone. The worry had lifted from his shoulders. Life was wonderful. He now knew he would be a good teacher. He looked forward to getting to know his students better—country kids he liked and understood. And something about the landscape exhilarated him.

Libby threw open the door before he got to it. Seeing the concern on her face, he swept her up in his arms and, before she could ask, poured out his enthusiastic account of his day. The students were well behaved. He had solved the problem of the guns. Everyone was pleased with the way he handled it. He assured her he would get along well with the big boys. He knew they carried their guns on long rides to school to be prepared in case they could take a deer for the family table, or harvest a valuable coyote or bobcat fur. "Yost is going to be a fine place to live," he promised.

Despite the friendly neighbor, Libby lacked his enthusiasm. In fact, his being so pleased caused her a twinge of concern. Did it mean she would be stuck here forever? Would he forget about finishing his college work, forget about a better job in the city? Again she was aware of the differences between them. She and Art cherished memories of totally different cultures and ways of living. He did not miss the church or the amenities of city life, and she would find no joy in the opportunity to hunt and fish. But she wisely kept this to herself. His happiness made her happy, and her day had been good. She liked being mistress of her own home. She told him about Doris.

His happy mood made for a pleasant evening. After their supper, he spent an hour planning his work for the next day, and before bedtime they popped corn while he described to her some of his more interesting students. But what most pleased her was his mention that the lack of other distractions here in Yost would give him plenty of time to work on correspondence courses and progress toward his degree.

The days passed quickly for Art. On Saturdays he took his rifle and spent a few hours hunting. The jack rabbits were so abundant and caused so much damage to the crops in the summer and haystacks in winter, that the state of Utah tried to control them by paying a bounty—five cents per rabbit. The hunter took the ears as evidence of his kill and collected his bounty. In Yost the general store was authorized to collect the ears and pay the bounty. Art was such an outstanding shot that he was able to increase his spending money from a sport that was recreation to him.

The storekeeper was soon boasting to his other patrons that the new teacher was the handiest man with a rifle that he had ever met. Bullets for the 22-caliber came in three sizes: shorts, longs, and long-rifle. Shorts, the least expensive, had the shortest range, but were adequate if one could get a shot at close range. A box of shorts, with fifty to a box, sold for fifty cents, a bit cheaper in a carton of ten boxes. Generally a hunter walking along would flush a rabbit at very close range but had to wait until it ran a good distance and stopped before he could hit it. Art could shoot the rabbit running at full speed, at close range. The storekeeper proudly informed all who came into his store: "Can you believe it? That Art Smith is getting up to thirty-five rabbits with one box of 22-shorts."

Most men didn't believe it. Though they were all skilled with a rifle, they were pleased if they hit one out of three running shots. Generally they didn't even try, preferring to wait till the rabbit stopped running, which meant using longer range, higher priced ammunition. Art's shooting was the talk of the town. The men and older boys wanted to see it for themselves. So they planned a community hunting day for a Saturday in February and invited Art to join them, which he gladly did, not realizing it had anything to do with him.

The event was well organized and much enjoyed, and years later Art's children would greatly enjoy the story. For safety the men walked across the fields in a fairly straight line, walked at the same pace, keeping all shots out in front. This same arrangement was sometimes used for a rabbit drive, when a whole community would turn out, no guns allowed, and drive rabbits into a catch pen.

It turned out to be a bright sunny day. The number of ears taken would score the total success, but they also kept count of the number of shots fired to collect the ears. A lot of good natured banter followed missed shots, and Art found this a perfect opportunity to make the acquaintance of new friends.

And what a day it was! He had never lived where shooting ability was held in such high esteem. Men in these parts were judged by it. He had always taken his marksmanship for granted as something that came naturally to him, and he never talked about it. He had simply been blessed with remarkable coordination. He could juggle five apples, do all sorts of balancing acts and all his life had entertained at family picnics. He never suspected that on this rabbit hunt he was putting on a special performance. But he enjoyed a challenge and did some of his finest shooting, counting the number of his shots. He didn't realize that the man nearest him in the line had been given the responsibility of keeping track of his shots so that there would be no chance of his mis-reporting them.

The man doing the counting heard two shots so close together they almost sounded like one. Sure Art had missed a shot and followed up with a second, he was wondering whether to report both shots. Then to his surprise he saw Art take the ears from two rabbits. Two rabbits had jumped up at the same time and Art, with his little slide-action repeating rifle, had taken them both with split second timing.

At the end of the day when the hunters gathered to report scores and enjoy a friendly campfire, Art reported thirty-eight rabbits and forty-five shots fired. In his good natured way he admitted: "I missed a few. Tried some running shots that were just too far."

Trying not to be obvious, several of the men glanced at their appointed scorekeeper. Enthusiastically he obliged them. "I never seen anything like it. He took two rabbits runnin' with two shots so close together it sounded like one." Looking at Art: "Why ain't you travelin' with a circus or something? You're just as good as Annie Oakley!"

In his quiet way Art said, "I'd rather be teaching school in Yost." Cheers and hand clapping responded. Obviously these men wanted their children to be taught by a man who could handle a rifle.

He would never fully understand the extent of the respect he gained that day. For the rest of his time in Yost, men would go out of their way to speak to him. He was the first to be invited to any shooting contest, a popular form of recreation, and he was never bested. Men also looked to Art for advice on estimating the number of tons in a hay stack or grain in a load, measuring the flow of water in an irrigation ditch, or figuring the number of acres in a field. In those matters too, he had exceptional ability. All his life he would enjoy helping farmers with math problems.

Libby always felt uncomfortable seeing her husband with a gun. But she rejoiced in his popularity and the satisfaction it brought him. It also opened doors for her. Art liked the men of the community, and he liked what she saw as "primitive" in Yost. He felt much more at home here than in the city. But she managed. She had time to write letters to her sisters and Laurence in Canada, and visit the neighbors. She sorely missed her church, but here, where there was no church, she felt no guilt about her inability to interest Art in it and therefore could relax about it.

They enjoyed Sundays together. As springtime brought warmer weather they took long walks and shared good conversation. A new dimension had come into their lives. She told him how disappointed she had felt in Scotland to be the only one in her family without a little brother or sister. She told him of her intense feelings for the babies brought for baptism, and now she was to have one of her own to love, cherish and nurture. It pleased him to hear her talk like this.

A few things bothered her but she tried not to complain. The first time Art brought in a cottontail rabbit with the intention of having it for supper, she felt repulsed. "We're going to eat that filthy beast?" she exclaimed.

Seeing the startled look on his face she smothered her inclination to say more. She recalled that she had eaten rabbit in Scotland, but always it had come from the market, dressed and ready to cook. She hadn't been the one to cook it either. She had simply never stopped to think about the fact that someone had killed it, skinned it and cleaned it. She realized that her reaction was irrational. Nevertheless, after that Art always gave her rabbits that were skinned, well cleaned and soaking in a pan of cold saltwater. She soon found that cottontail rabbit was one of her favorite foods, and it had the advantage of costing nothing. The time would come, when her firstborn was learning to talk, that the child would call them dogs because of their fur, and Libby could have a hearty laugh when little Grace asked for "more dog" at the dinner table. This became one of many Smith classic stories.

Libby's sense of humor was such that, though conditions disturbed her greatly, she could report them later in a way that made people laugh until their sides ached. Subtly and interestingly, these vignettes poked fun at herself for her upper class manner and expectations— the effect enhanced by her delivery in proper English with pulled back chin.

The spring countryside seemed to make Art all the happier in his work. Libby found time to read the theological and literary books she'd brought with her. She also did a lot of walking and thinking about the coming of her baby. The increasing awareness of the child helped her lose the anger and frustration she had felt about the termination of her teaching career. She knew she would greatly love the child, and was beginning to believe that God's purpose for her was teaching and guiding her own children.

However, she would not give birth in Yost. Several good women assured her they would help when her time came. They assured her that a number of dependable women in the area presided over Yost births. It hadn't helped when one of them remarked: "I seen a lotta lambs into this world, and it really ain't all that different."

Libby and Art discussed the matter. He completely agreed with her wish to have her baby where there were doctors and trained nurses—civilization in a word. The baby was not due until late May or early June, so they planned to leave as soon as school was out and spend the summer on the "outside."

———

Art signed his contract for a second year in Yost, and in mid May they made the trip "out." Parley and Wilma Johnson drove them to

Kelton in their light spring-wagon, the springs making it much more comfortable than Fred's freight wagon. Even with the awkwardness of her advanced pregnancy, Libby found the trip "out" much more pleasant than the trip "in." The May weather was ideal, she knew the road, and had none of the apprehensions she had harbored on the first trip to Yost. She and Art enjoyed Parley's company, Wilma's too. The wagon was fitted with a canvas to shade them from the direct rays of the sun or from rain. Such "white-tops" carried light freight and passengers, and were much in use by families who could not afford a buggy or carriage for riding exclusively.

After a night at the Kelton Hotel they boarded the morning train to Brigham City, about 150 miles from Yost. It was the nearest town of any size. They would spend the summer there, and with the good train connection, Alice would join them to help Libby. By correspondence Art had arranged for a furnished two-bedroom apartment and a summer job at the general store.

Before noon the train stopped at the busy station in the middle of town. The station master let them use a luggage cart to take their bags to their apartment, which was only three blocks away. Blooming roses surrounded the building and they were delighted with the airy rooms. "Oh to be in England, now that April's here," Libby quoted playfully. But, with a glance at Art, she revised Robert Browning, "No. I want only to be in Brigham City with you, now that spring is here."

In the privacy of their new room Art kissed her, helped put their things in the closet, then left to make the acquaintance of his new employer. Libby sat down at the table and dashed off a note to Alice, telling of their arrival and new address. She returned to the station to post the letter and make sure it would be on the afternoon train to Salt Lake. The postman told her where to find the offices of the two doctors in town.

The doctor Libby called on gave her a great sense of confidence, and she liked him as a person. He seemed pleased to have a new patient, assuring her, after an examination, that she was in good health and carrying a baby with a good strong heartbeat. "When you need me," he said as they parted, "I will be here. And if for any reason I might be out of town at that time, Dr. Jones will be here to take over. He is also very competent and experienced. We work together."

Deeply contented now that she was safely back in "civilization," Libby walked the long way back to the apartment so she could see for herself the small frame Presbyterian church the doctor had told her about. It had a simple cross on the peak of the roof. Tears blurred her vision as she gazed at this evidence of Christian fellowship. She had convinced herself that she had adjusted to the isolation of Yost, but now as she quietly thanked God for bringing her safely to this place before giving birth, she realized that just a year or two earlier, looking for civilization, she would not have seen it in Brigham City. It even struck her as funny. Now in her mind she was comparing this little town with Perth.

This thriving little city served a fairly large surrounding area. She saw stores where everything she needed could be bought. Her outlook on life, her standard of judging a town had changed. Instead of being concerned about what the town didn't have, she was rejoicing in what it did have—not the least of which were two doctors, two trains daily from Salt Lake City, and a dentist whom she needed to visit about a toothache.

Loud goose-honks drew her attention to the street. Two newfangled horseless vehicles—shining black with gold trim—were passing each other. Their jaunty owners waved at each other like delighted little boys. She laughed with them. The world truly was good and her baby would soon be in her arms.

The next morning while Art was shaving for his first day of work, a boy came to the door and handed her a telegram from Alice. Art came out and they read it together: BE THERE TOMORROW STOP MORNING TRAIN STOP

Inhaling the heavy purfume of the roses, Libby thanked the boy and watched him trot back toward the station. She took Art's elbow and quoted Robert Browning, "The year's at the spring, and day's at the morn."

Understanding her playful invitation, he carried the poem forward: "Morning's at seven; the hillside's dew-pearled;

"The lark's on the wing;" she added.

He smiled. "The snail's on the thorn."

Joyfully they proclaimed in unison, "God's in his Heaven, and all's right with the world!"

"Oh, I can hardly wait to see Alice!" Libby exclaimed.

The apartment was convenient to Art's work. His job included clerking in the busy mercantile and feed store, which stocked a wide range of general merchandise and all sorts of feed. In the mid afternoons he delivered orders to nearby farms and ranches. He enjoyed both parts of his work—the numbers, which seemed more like a game to him, and seeing the countryside and visiting with the farmers. He also enjoyed lifting the feed bags. At the university he had won a lifting competition for his weight class, and it felt good to use his muscles again. He handled the well-trained team with pleasure. He had a way with animals, bonding with them quickly. Life for him was as good as it had ever been. His beloved Libby was content with the arrangements. She seemed completely free of the worry that had been apparent the last few weeks in Yost, when she feared the baby might come early, or worse yet, on the trip "out." But now her spirits were high.

With Alice caring for Libby, Art could enjoy his job and devote more of his evenings to summer school correspondence courses. Driving the country roads with the obedient team gave him time to reflect on the fact that he had a wife who depended upon him and he was about to be a father. His lack of interest in religion troubled her. He knew how important her faith was to her, and he respected her for it. The fact that they avoided the subject of religion in their conversations bothered him. It wasn't right.

In his analytical way of looking at things, he realized that she might very well interpret his dislike for her church in Salt Lake as an indication that he had no faith at all. That he didn't miss having a church in Yost would have reinforced that belief. Actually he had a very meaningful faith but had never been exposed to any form of organized religion in which he could express it. He did not believe Joseph Smith was a prophet of God, and certainly not Brigham Young. Faith in Joseph Smith was a stumbling block for him in both Mormonism and its reorganized form, to which his parents and many of his relatives subscribed. As he reflected about this he realized his hours spent reading the Bible to Grandma Sarah as her eyesight failed had shaped his faith. The two of them had enjoyed many long conversations. She had confessed to him that she had never believed in Joseph or Brigham or the Book of Mormon. She told him of the joy she had known in her Sunday School classes with the Wesleyan Methodists in Lincolnshire, and of the awe she'd had for some of the great traditions of the Church of England. He knew that his own rather strict moral code must be based on those religious beliefs. With his habit of committing to memory many passages of literature he had also memorized the Ten Commandments, large portions of Psalms, and could remember many of the parables of Jesus, having read them over many times for Grandma. If he had a religion, he presumed it was what his wise old grandmother, whom he loved and respected, had grown up with in England.

Then he recalled the few services he had attended with Libby at the Salt Lake First Presbyterian Church. Actually he had often appreciated much that was said in the sermon. He also liked and respected Dr. Paden, who had provided a moving wedding ceremony. What bothered him was the formality of the church services, the upper class atmosphere. It made him feel out of place, like he'd sometimes felt when he investigated the clubs and sports teams at the university. He had no desire to be a part of it. He just didn't fit in. And now, driving the team, he laughed aloud to recall what had really stopped him. It was the ushers behaving with all the formality of high-toned butlers in some high society home, wearing their formal afternoon dress of striped trousers, bow ties, swallow tailed coats with a flower in the lapel. They reminded him of penguins in the Salt Lake zoo. He recalled thinking that if one of them smiled his face might crack. Unfortunately, instead of discussing the sermon or commenting on the fine music, he had told Libby how funny they looked to him. He realized now that he had given her a false impression of his actual beliefs. He decided he didn't want her bearing a child thinking it had a heathen father. He must do something about this.

The next Sunday, when Libby and Alice were hurrying to get ready for church, Art announced that he would go with them. The pleasure that radiated from Libby was his reward. He thought that if she had been a puppy, she would be vigorously wagging her tail.

"Oh Arthur"—she seldom called him Arthur—"I'm so glad!" With a happy giggle she added, "I really didn't want to show up at church in this condition without a husband."

That bit of humor would long live in the family.

Alice's reaction was skeptical. Art realized he had, in her eyes, already marked himself as an unbeliever, though she had never put her thoughts into words in his presence. She had a sadness of her own with regard to men and churches. Her husband, John McQueen, would not attend church. His attitude had been greatly influenced by a recent and unfortunate experience. From the time John and Alice had started seeing each other, Libby had taken a keen interest in John's religious life. He had attended the church with her and Alice on several occasions, and had seemed to enjoy it. Libby talked with him at length, and he finally agreed to join the Salt Lake church. Libby personally proposed his name to the Session. In the custom of the Presbyterian Church, the elders who comprised the Session voted on the qualifications of those proposed for membership. They voted not to accept John. No reason for the rejection was given, and John never again attended church. A proud man, he never discussed the rejection. Feeling crushed, Alice withdrew her own membership.

The decision of the Session had amazed Art, and though he didn't discuss it with Libby he knew his own pride would never let him submit his name for membership for fear of the same rejection. In his own private thoughts he wondered just why those people thought they were so righteous. What gave them the right to judge the faith and feelings of someone else?

That Sunday Art truly enjoyed the service in the Brigham City church, and he knew he would continue attending throughout the summer. Since they would be returning to Yost when school started, the question of membership was never considered. This was the only non-Mormon church in the town, and people attended whose background was other than Presbyterian—Methodist, Baptist, Congregational and others. The friendly pastor had grown up on a farm. Art appreciated his plain speech and farm metaphors. He and Libby found that the sermon provided themes for interesting discussions. It added a wonderful new dimension to their lives. She felt a special thrill when they stood up to sing the hymns, his tenor and her soprano making beautiful harmony. People welcomed them, and a couple their age invited the three of them to Sunday dinner. In a short time they made many friends in that church.

On the walk home that first Sunday Art commented, "I wouldn't mind belonging to a church like that."

Libby stopped in her tracks, understanding the significance. "Oh Art," she said taking his elbow. "It makes me so happy to hear that!" She would cherish that remark for years to come and pray that they might some day live in a place with a church like this one.

If the baby was a boy, he would be named Arthur, with the middle name Laurence for Libby's brother. If a girl she would be Grace, for Libby's favorite aunt—her mother's sister who lived in Perth and sang off key in church, much to the delight of the Symon children. On June 8th, 1912, Grace Elizabeth made her appearance. To Art's relief the delivery was not unusually difficult and they had a healthy baby. He thought that maybe Libby's sense of security of late had eased the birth—a doctor she liked, Alice's loving care, and Art's presence.

When the squirming, eager child was placed in Libby's arms, she experienced a great surge of joy, a feeling of fulfillment that exceeded anything she had felt before. In Yost she had struggled with uncertainty concerning her purpose in life. She knew she was born to be a teacher, but had spent her days at home doing what any servant girl could have done. But now, as she held her own child to her breast, she knew that God had given her a calling, a responsibility to be the mother of wonderful children—children who would do great things in the world. She would nurture and guide them with the special teaching skills with which God had blessed her.

Art agreed with Libby to have Grace baptized by Dr. Paden. A month after Grace's birth Libby felt quite able to travel. They took a Saturday train to Salt Lake and spent the night with Alice and John. On Sunday, July 8, Grace Elizabeth was presented for baptism at the Presbyterian Church. As Dr. Paden dipped his hand in the font, Libby suddenly felt herself transported back to old Free St. Paul's in Perth. It seemed to her that the Reverend John Symon took the child in his arms and blessed her, and that this beautiful daughter of Libby's was her father's child too. And wonder of wonders, she and Art were the parents! She would always cherish that moment and sometimes relate it to people with whom she felt very close. She pondered it in her heart, even as Mary in the sacred story of long ago had pondered the wonder of the birth of her first born. On this special day, the church that had once seemed cold and overly formal seemed very warm— almot an inviting home to her.

John McQueen did not attend but was delighted with the baby. He liked the idea of being Uncle John and determined that he would be a good uncle, something of a godfather, even if no one ever called him that.

Following the baptism and a festive dinner supplied by John, Art and Libby took the streetcar to Union and introduced little Grace to her Grandma and Grandpa Smith. All the other relatives hurried over, and it was a joyful homecoming for Art. His nieces and nephews crowded around and everyone was talking at once. Mother Lucy took baby Grace in her arms and hugged her to her breast, closing her eyes. Hyrum looked on with a smile that transformed his careworn face. "Well," said Lucy with tears in her eyes as she glanced at her husband, "one more Smith baby to love."

Libby realized that the baby bonded Art and his mother ever more tightly together. Libby felt accepted more than she ever had before, now that she was the mother of a Smith baby. However she realized that the difference between Union and Perth was vast, and the first eighteen years of her life had so powerfully shaped her values and her ways of thinking and expressing herself that she would never really feel in her heart that this Utah family was hers. Hyrum and Lucy had been fair and helpful in many ways. They were honest, hard-working people. But their formative years had been spent under the domination of the Mormon Church, because it dominated the entire community. They had been shaped by it since birth. And though they now were no longer active in the Reorganized Church, they sometimes attended services in the next town and still considered Joseph Smith the Prophet of God. That would always seem a heresy to Libby. Two years after being excommunicated from the Mormon Church, Art's grandfather William P. Smith had been baptized in that "Josephite" church—not much different from the un-reorganized, Libby thought—and was elected an elder. Art's family had no real knowledge of any other church. Furthermore, Mormons encouraged dancing, even among children, right in the church building. The Smith clan saw nothing wrong with that. Libby knew she could love and respect the Smiths, but could never get over or around the great invisible wall of culture and religion that separated her from them. She did not want to live in Union and have Grace or any future children raised in Union. Yet, never having known for herself the joy of grandparents, she felt a sense of guilt in her desire to deny her children the influence of these warm and loving grandparents. This was a burden she would bear, a matter about which she would often pray in years to come.

—

The visit to Union was brief. On Monday they took the train back to Brigham City, then packed and left for Yost. School would start after Labor Day—an interesting American holiday set aside about fifteen years earlier for workers in the railroads and factories to discuss their working conditions. Libby had learned that one of their leaders, Eugene Debbs, had been jailed. A tremendous hew and cry had arisen across the country. Congress finally recognized the needs of labor by establishing the holiday. She doubted whether the common people of Britain could ever influence the government in that way. How miserable the wages and long working hours had been for Sarah Pidd in Lincolnshire! And the working poor in Perth and Glasgow! The mining and smelter workers were now agitating in Utah, as well they should, she thought.

Now she found herself looking forward to getting settled again in her little log house. She proudly showed her baby to Doris, Wilma and other friends. They helped her when she had questions about caring for a baby. Alice had greatly helped but now a new era had dawned. Libby was on her own.

Though it wasn't her choice of places to live, she took some pride in how well she had been accepted in Yost and how well she had adapted to it. Soon after their arrival, however, an incident occurred that shook her confidence. This story she would tell many times in years to come.

The autumn days were pleasant. Along the creek the wild plums had ripened. The locals called them pottawatomie plums. On a sunny Sunday afternoon, she and Art took baby Grace on an outing, finding and picking a quantity of plums which she later used to make pies. Having many more plums than she could use in pies she canned a few, and then decided to make a very large batch of plum jam. When she finished boiling down the jam in her dishpan, she realized she would need to get more small jars to put it in, and that meant waiting until tomorrow. Needing the dishpan for its usual purpose she poured the jam into a three and a half gallon crock and placed it at floor level under the sink where it could keep for a day or two.

That night Libby, Art and baby were invited to supper in a house some distance away. As they walked home after a pleasant evening, an almost-full harvest moon was rising. Grace slept in Art's arms. They had been discussing the good points of the hosts, but as they approached their house, sounds from within startled them. There was a loud crashing and banging that sounded as though men were fighting and breaking up the furniture. The house was totally dark. Handing the baby to Libby and instructing her to remain a safe distance away, Art gingerly stepped to the door shouting, "Whoever you are stop what you're doing." At the same time he struck a match, opened the door, and stepped inside to light the lamp. Fearing the worst, Libby backed behind a tree and began to pray for the safety of her little family.

There was an immediate increase in the crashing sounds. The lamplight flooded the room just in time, she later learned, for Art to sidestep what appeared to be a living battering ram charging toward him. It smashed into the wall. Finally figuring out what was happening, he stepped quickly outside again to avoid the terrified animal. He left the door wide open hoping it might remove itself from the house, but to no avail. The crashing and banging continued unabated.

Trembling, Libby called to him. He came to her and described the situation. As was their custom, they had closed their door when they left, but had not locked it. It was a door that opened easily. A large feral pig had wandered by, smelled good things in the house and nudged the door open. It had followed its nose to the sink, found the crock of jam, and shoved its head into the crock. Unfortunately, when the sow tried to remove her head by backing away, she discovered that the crock was a perfect fit and came right along. With her head in the crock up past her eyes, she dashed blindly around the room breaking chairs. Every time she hit a wall the crock drove farther onto her head, up past her ears, making a very snug fit. When she bumped the door, which opened to the inside, she closed it, leaving herself shut securely inside. Unable to see and finding it difficult to breathe with her snout in the jam, the panicked animal simply rushed madly around.

Art assured Libby there was really nothing to fear. As they talked, the commotion in the house seemed to be subsiding. Once again going to the door, Art noticed that the pig was very nearly exhausted, perhaps dying from suffocation. Taking a short piece of rope, he quickly tied her hind legs together and dragged her outside. The pig gave up the struggle and was barely breathing. There was no way to remove the crock—one of Libby's cherished possessions—so Art broke it with a rock.

The "beast," as Libby would call it later—using the same distasteful inflection she had heard as a child when that word signified the Devil—lay on its side, so still that Libby thought it was dead. Its nose was completely plugged with her delicious jam.

"There's a little breath coming through the mouth," Art announced.

Frightened as she had been, Libby found herself strangely touched by the way Art squatted and patiently cleaned out the pig's nostrils with a small stick. He showed no anger, only concern for the well being of the unfortunate pig. After a few minutes the animal inhaled a deep breath, let it out with a long sigh, slowly staggered to her feet, and wobbled off into the night.

For a long time Art held Libby and the baby in his arms. Then they surveyed the destruction. Nothing was left undamaged in the main room. The table was upset, dishes and chairs broken. Fortunately the pig had not found the door to the bedroom; the bed was undisturbed. Libby put the baby down and lay beside her, giving way to great uncontrolled sobbing. Could she go on living in a place where wild beasts roamed at will and were free to enter her house? Could she bear to raise Grace in a place where she might be attacked if she played in the yard?

By the time she gained control of herself Art had the worst of the mess cleaned up. She pitched in and helped finish the job. Her only comment: "So much for pottawatomie jam." Wisely she stifled her urge to fully express her views on rural living.

Autumn turned to winter. Baby Grace was growing rapidly, and Art was happy. Libby made the most of Yost and found many things to enjoy—among them the low cost of living. She was fond of fish, and Art so enjoyed fishing that he kept them well supplied with trout—always cleaned before he brought them into the house. Neighbors supplied them with all sorts of produce from their gardens. Ranchers brought prime cuts of beef and lamb. She marveled at the generosity of these country people, who found a joy in sharing and often used the delivery of food as an excuse to visit. They clearly enjoyed her tales of Scottish history and her fine sense of humor—the story of the beastie in her house having been added to the repertoire. And though she didn't dance—the main entertainment in town—she liked the community events, such as pie suppers and school programs.

Libby was asked to help with the school Christmas program. Happily she plunged into organizing a pageant. She instructed the children in the singing of the selected hymns as they rehearsed daily after school. Glad to find herself in charge again and at the piano, Libby nodded out the rhythm with her head as she sang with the little ones. On the evening of the performance her efforts were rewarded by many people who commented that it was one of the best programs ever seen in Yost.

At the end of the school term the teacher of the lower grades announced her desire to retire. Libby felt elated when the school board president asked her if she would be willing to teach again. A lady in the community who was a good mother assured Libby that taking care of one more child during the day would be no problem. Libby was thrilled, knowing the woman would provide good care for little

Grace.

Art was just as enthusiastic. The idea of teaching together as a team appealed to both of them, and Libby once again realized how much it meant to her to be a teacher.

They spent a pleasant summer back in Union living in Grandma Sarah's small house, Art advancing his course work and tending the sugar beets on his own land. When they returned to Yost, Libby felt elated to walk into a classroom again and see the eager young faces. Each morning she led the children in a cheerful song: *Good morning Merry Sunshine, How did you wake so soon?* But a dark cloud began to shadow her teaching.

Within a few weeks of the start of school she knew she was pregnant again, this time suffering rather severe bouts of morning sickness. The school board assured her that if she could manage, they would be more than pleased to have her continue teaching, and they would give her some time off when the baby came. Her teaching style had impressed them, as well as the way the children loved her and responded to her. This deeply gratified her.

But by mid November she knew she couldn't handle the job. She kept a bucket in the cloakroom, and from time to time had to excuse herself to go vomit. She became just too miserable. Two other factors added to her resolve to resign. The stress of forcing herself to keep going when she longed to lie down increased the severity of her attacks. And "a few days off when the baby came" would mean giving birth in Yost. She was determined that no child of hers would be born in a place without a doctor.

Once again her dream of a teaching career was shattered. She had to face the fact that her feeling after Grace's birth was the right sign. God had called her to be a mother, not a teacher. She vowed to fulfill that calling, to rear her children to be the finest and best.

*From the famine of her isolation, like the family of Jacob, she "came
into the land of Goshen."*
Genesis 46:28

11   Goshen

Art and Libby discussed their situation at length. Art didn't see how
he could go "out" with Libby in March for the birth of the baby. For
Libby, with Grace not yet two years old, a trip by herself to Kelton
and another day on the train to Salt Lake seemed daunting. But for
Art to accompany her would require a four day trip to Kelton and
back to Yost, just to get her to the train—two days off from his teaching. He didn't feel comfortable taking the time off. They hoped they
could find another solution.

They did. Parley and Wilma Johnson offered to drive them to
Kelton again. Grandma Sarah's house was still available in Union.
Libby and Grace could move in there, and ever-faithful Alice would
come and care for them.

In a spell of good weather in early March—three weeks before the
baby was due—Libby looked deeply into Art's eyes and told him good-
bye. This was difficult for both of them, never having been apart since
their wedding. Sensing the mood of the departure, Grace clung to her
daddy, then cried loudly when Libby pried them apart. Libby handed
her up, screaming, to Wilma, then climbed up to the buckboard herself. Art waved. Libby waved, and tearful Grace, somewhat comforted
on her mother's lap, moved her little hand up and down. As the white-
top made the turn in the road that shut off their view Art still stood in
the road waving.

Libby later said she experienced a strong premonition that she was
seeing Yost for the last time. If it were true, she would miss a few
friends and Art would miss the open country and the friendly rural

way of living, but she was leaving without regret. She had survived, she had managed to make a good impression on the community, but it was not her kind of place.

She and Art had discussed the possibility of his getting a better paying job now that he had teaching experience. They had come to no definite conclusion and he had made no applications. She worried that he was reluctant to leave Yost. She could only hope that while she was gone he would write letters of inquiry and find a teaching position with access to the city.

Good traveling companions, Parley and Wilma Johnson had both grown up in Yost, the children of ranching families. Now they owned their own ranch. A strong, considerate man, Parley was an excellent hand with horses and drove a fine team, according to Art. Libby didn't make it her business to know the difference. Wilma had been "out" only a few times in her lifetime, never farther than Brigham City. She admired Libby and envied her fine education and experiences in far away places. Her many questions kept the conversation lively. Her help with baby Grace eased much of the concern that Libby had felt in anticipating the long wagon ride. After a night with "the butcher," Parley pushed his team along at a fast pace that made it possible to catch the evening train, so there was no need for Libby to spend a night in Kelton.

Libby knew the train would put Grace to sleep, and she could get some rest too. She would be in Salt Lake around midnight. As Wilma and Parley helped her get settled in her seat, Wilma's eyes filled with tears. She did not speak what she must have felt, that this would be the last time she would see Libby. She simply gave her a hug, looked at her a moment and said. "Take good care of yourself and the baby that's acomin'. You've made me laugh more than I ever laughed with anyone before, and I'll never forget you." Then she was gone. Libby would never forget those words, or her puzzlement about Wilma.

The train sped into the dusk and as she ate the supper Wilma had packed for her, Libby thought about Wilma's kindness. Before she dropped off for a much needed nap, she pondered the question: how could a place like Yost produce such a beautiful spirit? How could this uneducated woman who managed a busy ranch family, who involved herself with cattle and sheep, rode and roped with the cowboys, and helped with the birthing of beasts be such a fine and sensitive individual? And as such, wasn't she wasting her life? Lines from Thomas Gray's *Elegy Written In A Country Churchyard* ran through her mind, favorite lines that she would quote to her children and grandchildren when she advised them to develop their talents in a place where they could be appreciated:

> Full many a flower is born to blush unseen,
> And waste its sweetness on the desert air.

Surely anyone as kind, thoughtful and intelligent as Wilma Johnson was wasting her life in such an isolated place. Just why that meant wasting a life, Libby never really thought about. She just knew that it did.

The train stopped in Salt Lake just before midnight. Faithful John and Alice were there ready to take care of her and Grace, and take them to Union the next day. What a comfort they were! John could have shown no more affection for little Grace if she had been his own child. Once again in the role of mother, and now as grandmother, Alice stayed in Union to be Libby's housekeeper and nurse until after the baby was born.

Again Arthur Laurence failed to appear. On March 26, 1914, Constance Alice was born, a beautiful baby with an excellent voice with which to announced her displeasures. The birth was no more unusual than Grace's, but Libby developed a fever and remained very ill for several weeks. Additionally, her milk didn't seem to agree with the baby. The doctor was never sure what was causing the illness in either mother or baby, and could do nothing to help. The situation became critical.

Knowing that childbed fever was the great killer of young women, Libby prayed for God to restore her strength and allow her to live to care for her little daughters. She believed she had much to offer as a mother, and she couldn't bear to think of leaving Arthur. Mother Lucy Smith stayed with her, piling on blankets to keep her warm, wiping her face with cool cloths, and bringing cleansing washes. She brewed special teas, one to encourage the milk. For the same purpose she made plenty of fresh oatmeal with raisins and cream, frequently coaxing Libby to eat a spoonful or two during the day and night. Additionally she made regular meals of healthy soups and custards that Libby could tolerate. But despite these measures, Connie, as Libby called her, turned her little face away from the breast and cried like her heart was breaking. She cried almost constantly when awake. Sometimes Libby simply cried with her. Alice or Lucy, whoever wasn't watching Grace, would take the baby away and try to get her to suck a little whey or oatmeal water from the tip of a soft rag. In these matters Mother Smith proved to be an invaluable source of wisdom. Libby deeply appreciated her unpretentious administration of procedures gained from her vast experience.

At last Libby recovered. Connie became more contented, nursed better, and began to gain some weight. Alice, who had never been fond of Art's mother, had developed a new appreciation of this rough talking, down to earth country grandmother who had spent her life with babies and difficult circumstances. She had cared for Libby like a true and loving mother. Alice would never feel close to this "uncouth" farm woman who had made Liz so miserable before her wedding, yet she felt very grateful to her.

When things were going better and Alice felt rested, she tried to thank Lucy and tell her she couldn't have done it by herself.

"Oh pshaw!" Lucy said with a dismissive wave. "We just done what we had to and pulled 'em through." She grinned in her satisfied, closed-mouthed way. What for Alice had been a terrible crisis seemed to have been all in a day's work for Lucy.

It was late May and two-month old Connie was about to meet her daddy for the first time. They dressed her in a long white dress given to her by one of her aunts. Art had written Libby many times. He knew she didn't like living in Yost. The day she left he had begun writing letters of inquiry to various school boards. In his most recent letter to Libby he explained that he would be delayed for a few days after the end of the school term, getting their household goods and other belongings packed and shipped via Fred the freighter. He would store them in Union for the summer and save making another trip to Yost. He had located a good position in Goshen, a farming community about seventy-five miles south of Salt Lake, a place he remembered well from a visit after his high school graduation.

He wrote, "It's on the railroad to Salt Lake. The town has only about six-hundred people, but it's a service center for a much more populated area than Yost. It has a four-room school. I'll teach 7th and 8th grades and serve as the principal. I guess the school board liked my recommendation from Yost. They were willing to hire me without a personal interview. I thought you'd like the town, so I accepted the position, but I haven't signed a contract yet. I said we'd go down there together and meet them and look around first, in early June. Dear Lib, I hope you'll be happy with this news."

Libby was pleased, and anxious to tell him so. Though she would have preferred Salt Lake, she hadn't wanted to return to Yost. She also didn't want to live in Union in close proximity to all the in-laws. She thought Goshen would be a satisfactory compromise. It wouldn't be difficult to get into the city to see Alice and John, and Alice could easily come and visit her and the children.

Art opened the door of the house, eager to see his new daughter. Grace ran to him and embraced his leg. Smiling, Libby held the baby out for him to take. He reached out to take her, but was met with a piercing scream. The screaming continued with such force that Libby could not even speak to him until she had walked with Connie, quieted her and placed her in the crib. Meanwhile Art picked up Grace and gave her a hug, but the reaction of the baby was one of pure panic and fear. The experience unsettled Art for a time. It was hardly the homecoming he had anticipated. It took him several days to gain Connie's confidence, which was just fine with two-year-old Grace. She had been feeling neglected since the birth of little sister and was happy to reclaim her Daddy.

They had a busy summer. After a day trip to Goshen with the children, the signing of the contract, and a look at the teacherage, Art immediately began commuting daily by streetcar to attend summer school classes at the university. Alice had left Union by now and Libby was caring for the two small children. Two of Art's older nieces, Sarah's daughter Ruby Anderson and Lizzie's daughter Hazel Wardle, dropped in often to help with the baby and were such good help that Libby found herself occasionally wondering why she was so reluctant to live around Art's family. She still couldn't put it into words. It was an instinctive feeling deep inside. Was she really uppity and snobbish as she was sure her in-laws considered her? Did she think she was better than they were? She didn't think so and would have denied it if someone accused her of it, yet despite the kindness shown her, she did not want her children to grow up as typical Union people. It was something about Mormonism, which she felt very intensely, something more diffuse and cultural than pure theology, something at odds with who she was. She wanted her children to love their Smith relatives but not be "of" them.

With the good train connection, the move to Goshen was easy. By the first of September, 1914, they were settled in the teacherage—modern compared with the log house in Yost. This would be the first house Grace would remember. There were two bedrooms and an indoor pipe feeding into a tank attached to the kitchen range, for hot water. The range burned coal, providing much more steady heat than wood. Libby was pleased with the house. Her only regret—a quiet, deep regret that she decided not to talk about—was the absence of any Protestant church in town. A large, very active Mormon church stood at the center of all community social activity.

A small weekly newspaper printed in Goshen provided local news, and the two daily newspapers came on the train from Salt Lake: *The Deseret News,* the official paper of the Mormon Church, and *The Salt Lake Tribune,* which had always been such a satisfaction to her.

The *Tribune* brought troubling news of war in Europe, and Libby followed the events closely. On June 28, 1914, an assassination in Bosnia triggered a series of events that brought one nation after another into armed conflict. On August 4, Great Britain declared war on Germany and the terrible "Great War" exploded into the headlines. A year earlier, fearing this, Marjorie had returned to England to enter nurses' training in a large hospital in Manchester, where she would serve her country.

A letter from Laurence gave Libby a strange and gloomy premonition about him, which she would relate the rest of her life. Still single, he had enlisted in the newly organized Royal Canadian Regiment. For most Americans the war was someone else's business or it was seen as a potential for a great economic boom that would create huge markets for goods to supply the Allied Forces. But with the companion of her childhood training for combat and Marjorie training to be a war nurse in England, the war became a personal reality for Libby—much more than economics or politics.

The work at the school went well for Art. He enjoyed being principal. The people of Goshen were basically country people, the kind he understood. Discipline problems were occasionally referred to him, but most problems were handled by the teachers in their own classrooms. He encouraged them to do so with the assurance that he would support their actions. The few cases that required the involvement of parents he found he could handle very well, meeting with the parents at the school or at their home. The school board consisted of a businessman from town and two farmers, all with children in school. They concerned themselves with the quality of the education and were easy to work with. When repairs or improvements were needed these men would assess the problem and arrange a work party to fix it.

Though Art and Libby were seen as a bit strange for not being involved in the many activities of The Church, otherwise they were well accepted in the community. Once again Art was being called upon by farmers for help with estimating tons of hay in haystacks, figuring the number of bushels in a bin of wheat, and giving advice on the growing of sugar beets, a subject he had studied and practiced. Libby was soon helping with school programs.

The school year of 1914-15 was hectic for Art. Besides his teaching and administrative duties, he worked on his correspondence courses. He signed a contract for the following year, and the family stayed in Goshen during the summer of 1915, Art making good use of the train connections. In order to complete some concentrated summer courses, he spent eight weeks on campus in Salt Lake, staying the nights in Union and commuting to Goshen on weekends. He was an excellent student, and with more correspondence courses in the fall of 1915 and the spring of 1916, arrangements were made to permit him to graduate with the class of 1916, his diploma to be signed after one more summer session on campus.

It was a proud day when Arthur Thomas Smith walked across the stage to accept his "sheepskin" from the University of Utah. He also received a citation for outstanding work in the field of mathematics. Attending the graduation were his older brother Hyrum, the other college graduate in the family, Allie and Clarence, and Alice. Sister Lizzie contributed by tending Grace and Connie in Union. Libby and Alice sat with Hyrum. Meanwhile John McQueen prepared a celebration feast at his restaurant.

This was one of the happiest days Libby had known since her marriage. Her pride in her husband, the respect she had for his determination and persistence in pursuing his education, knew no bounds. She could not have described exactly the cause of her unparalleled joy, but somehow it involved the fact that his degree was tangible proof that he had risen in status. He was now a college graduate in a society where a high school diploma was a notable achievement. Besides that, he would qualify for a teaching position in a high school in the city, a big step up from where he had been, socially and financially.

Art, however, enjoyed teaching in Goshen and signed a contract for the school year of 1916-17. He looked forward to being a father and husband without the pressure of correspondence work and the urgent need to finish his degree. After only a week of vacation, he started his last intensive summer school course on campus, again spending the nights in Union.

Libby was pregnant again. In the early months she suffered some from her morning sickness, not too severe, and with Art at the university, ever-faithful Alice moved in to help her with the housework and the care of her girls until Art could return in August. Grace would always remember this as a wonderful summer in which Alice spoiled the girls as only a loving aunt with no children of her own could do. In good weather Alice would spend hours walking them around the little town and amusing them in a park near the schoolhouse, where there were swings and a slide. Now four years old, Grace took pride in her ability to push two-year-old Connie on the swing. Alice was a constant source of stories, some of which she told from memory and many she read from children's books. She helped Grace in her eagerness to learn to read. Alice also insisted on doing most of the cooking, giving Libby plenty of time to rest and catch up on her reading.

John McQueen and his brother Sam worked out an arrangement at the restaurant so both would have a day off each week. John visited Goshen on his free day. He took a morning train, spent a full day in Goshen, and caught a night train to Salt lake. A loving uncle, he always arrived with a gift for each girl and a supply of candy treats in his pocket. All their lives Grace and Connie would fondly remember the quaint little Scotsman, always impeccably dressed in a suit and black derby hat. He would walk around the town with Alice and the girls, seeming to enjoy the outings as much as they did.

The United States did indeed experience the predicted economic boom as the allied countries went to war. Art's contract for the next year included a salary increase. With easy rail access, Libby no longer felt isolated. The Goshen general store carried most of the family's daily needs, but she also made shopping trips to the city, where it seemed anything on earth could be found. On those days, Alice stayed with the girls and spoiled them even more. Libby noticed increasing numbers of "motor cars" on the city streets. They frightened the horses and caused dangerous upsets, but many people believed that motor cars would, ultimately, be a great boon to cities, reducing the pollution of manure. In this, Libby agreed, and not just because of the smell. Cars would end the "fearful" air pollution caused by dried, pulverized manure blowing in the wind. All her life Libby took pride in being a "modern woman" who approved of "progress."

She felt a deep sense of fulfillment in her rapidly growing and very bright little girls. They gave her much to write about in her regular correspondence with her brother David in Scotland, sister Marjorie in England, and brother Laurence on the front lines in France.

In August Art returned from the university and Alice said good-bye. Late the following day, August 15, they received a telegram from Clarence: FATHER SMITH VERY ILL STOP COME IMMEDIATELY STOP

After a restless night, Art and Libby and the girls caught the early train. In Union the gathered Smith clan was somber. The doctor gave no encouragement. Family members took turns joining Mother Lucy at Hyrum's bedside. Once when he regained consciousness, he told Lucy, "Something broke inside of me. I can feel it draining out."

Libby and the girls spent the night across the road with Clarence and Allie. Art and his sister Lizzie were sitting with their mother at four-thirty in the morning of the 17th when Hyrum breathed his last. Lucy, who handled almost any crisis with stoic courage, cried inconsolably. Hyrum's death had been too sudden and unexpected. He had died of a perferated ulcer.

At sixty-three, Hyrum had been a powerful and seemingly healthy man. He had hardly slackened the pace of his hard daily work. From time to time he had complained of pain in his stomach, some indigestion, but nothing interfered with his work. On the morning of his final attack he had eaten his breakfast and gone out to work as usual. In warm harvest weather he was putting in long hours on his grain binder, a fine new horse-drawn McCormick reaper, the machine that in his own lifetime had replaced the scythe and the sickle. It also tied the cut grain in neat bundles.

He had come in for the noon meal, eaten and discussed with Lucy his pleasure in the harvest, his eagerness to get it all in while the weather was good. He had rested briefly, then returned to the field with only a brief comment about his "old stomach acting up again." Soon after that, when Clarence was working in a nearby field, he noticed Hyrum's horses standing quietly, not moving briskly as they should have been. Thinking Hyrum might be having trouble with the binder and could use some help, he went to investigate and found his father-in-law lying on the ground. He had apparently stopped his team, struggled off or fallen off the seat of the binder, and was in such pain and shock that he could not stand.

Clarence took him to the house, sent for the doctor and returned to the field to take care of the horses. By the time the doctor arrived, Hyrum was running a high fever and slipping in and out of consciousness. He was unable to speak.

Lucy could hardly remember life without Hyrum. She wasn't yet ten when Hyrum's father had started courting Lucy's mother. Hyrum had been a husky thirteen-year-old. She idolized him from the beginning. Some time after their parents got married, Hyrum went to Wyoming to work on a ranch for his relatives. Lucy dreamed of him and wrote him letters, and she looked forward with eagerness to his occasional visits home. When he was twenty-three and she was nineteen he courted her briefly and asked her to marry him. Her dream had came true. She cared for him and bore his children.

He had been a loving husband. Determined to prevent her from suffering and dying like his mother had after a life of constant childbearing, he had made a solem promise that after the birth of Arthur, her sixth child, they would have no more children. Now she felt that she had died with him. She sat beside his bed for a long time holding his large calloused hand. She would not have moved except that her children finally insisted on helping her up and walking her to bed. They assured her they would "take care of things." It was several weeks after the funeral before her devoted children and grandchildren made her wake up to the fact that she was still very much alive with a great deal to live for.

Libby's little family stayed in Union until after the funeral. During those days of mourning Libby, who had appreciated much about Mother Smith, felt a sympathy for her very near to love. The day after Hyrum's death, when she put her arms around Lucy to comfort her, there was a warmth in the embrace that brought them closer than they had ever been before. Art loved his father very dearly, and in his profound and silent grieving Libby gained a further appreciation for this rough cut little pioneer woman who had given so much to make her Arthur the fine man that he was.

Art, Libby and the girls returned to Goshen. Summer slid into autumn and the start of Art's school. Libby's pregnancy slowed her down and she was grateful for Grace's help in amusing Connie. Precocious herself, Grace was already trying to teach her little sister to read. Libby often took one girl beneath each of her arms and read to them or told them stories.

The Goshen doctor was friendly and seemed competent. His presence comforted Libby as her pregnancy progressed. She knew he would be available for the delivery in late November or early December. After a rather short time in Salt Lake, Alice returned to Goshen to help when the baby came and stay until she was no longer needed.

During the wee hours of the morning on the 5th of December, 1916, Libby gently grasped Art's shoulder to wake him. "The baby's coming," she said. "Maybe Arthur Laurence." He hurriedly pulled on his clothes, tiptoed into the other bedroom where Alice slept with the girls, whispered to Alice what was happening, and trotted through the cold dark town to rouse the doctor.

Back at the house he put kindling on the coals still glowing in the stove and blew the fire back to life. Then he shoveled in a little more coal. When he had the stove going, he filled the water tank, then started boiling water for oatmeal. The sounds had awakened the girls. They stood behind him on the cold floor shivering in their night-gowns. "There's a man in your room with Mama and Aunt Alice," Grace informed him.

"He's the doctor. He's come to help your little brother or sister come into the world."

"If he's a boy will he be wearing overalls?" Grace asked.

Art smiled. "No. He won't be wearing a thing. Now Grace, you and Connie go put on your warmest stockings and leggings and boots. Can you help Connie do that?"

"Yes Daddy."

While they were gone he peeked in the bedroom and told Libby. "I'm staying home today." This was Wednesday, a school day, but he was needed here. At eight-thirty when the teachers would be starting the fires in the school stoves, he would go over and ask the teacher of the 5th and 6th grades to assign his class the special work he had prepared and send the class home early. Libby had been ill after Connie's birth. Today he would be with her to help in any way he could.

Art dished out the hot oatmeal and poured the half-frozen milk on it—cold from the windowsill where they stored it. Once again he felt grateful to the farmers who kept them supplied. Through the bed-room door he heard Libby moan. The girls looked worried. Telling Alice what he was doing, he bundled the girls for a long walk. By the last of the early morning moonlight they slowly walked around town, their boots squeaking in a scatter of frozen snow. "Your mother is fine," he explained to them. This is how it always is when babies are born." Each time they circled near the house, he listened.

Daylight finally broke and by then he thought it was all right to take the girls back in the house. The baby was crying and he was as anxious as Grace and Connie. "Wait here," he told them. "I'll see if it's all right for you to go in."

Arthur Laurence had indeed made his appearance, obviously a strong healthy baby with a good set of lungs. Alice was wiping him down with a cloth. The doctor had more to do with Libby, who smiled at him, so Art returned to the kitchen and told the girls they must wait a little longer. "You have a baby brother," he said, so proud that his voice cracked. "His name is Arthur."

"But Daddy, your name is Arthur," Grace informed him.

"Yes," he is named for me. And his middle name is Laurence, for your mother's brother who is far away in France fighting a war."

"I don't know him," Grace said.

"He played with your mother when they were children. She thinks about him a lot now."

Alice stayed in Goshen until Libby was well enough to take full charge of her household with the two little girls and a tiny baby. Fortunately she remained healthy and her milk agreed with the baby. Now Libby realized as never before that God had truly called her to a full time job of motherhood. Christmas, however, presented an unanticipated challenge.

Four-and-a-half-year-old Grace, who later wrote this story, had impressed upon two-and-a-half-year-old Connie the wonder of Christmas and the magic of Santa Claus. Both girls were intent on making the first Christmas for baby brother Arty, who was three weeks old, a great occasion. They had his little sock ready to hang on the mantle next to theirs when the great night arrived. But a problem developed. Before Christmas, Daddy had kissed them good-bye and taken the train to the City. He would be gone three days attending a teachers institute, but had assured them he would be home on Christmas Eve in time for Santa's arrival.

He and Libby had seen this trip to the city as an opportunity for him do all the Christmas shopping for the children. The city offered a much better selection of gifts. A dozen times Grace had asked him, "You will be back in time to see what Santa brings us?" A dozen times he had assured her that he would. But soon one of Libby's favorite lines from Robert Burns began running through her mind:

> The best-laid schemes o' mice an' men
>
> Gang aft agley. . .

The winter of 1916-17 was turning out to be very severe. There was snow on the ground when Art left. The next day heavy snow began to fall and didn't stop until it piled up a little past the window sills. A kind neighbor, knowing that Art was away, came and cleared the front door and removed the snow from the roof, since there were some roofs in town that had collapsed from the weight of it. Two days before Christmas Eve word came that no trains were running. The snow was simply beyond the capacity of the snow plows.

Libby had never felt so alone in her life. The day of Christmas Eve arrived and the little girls were singing: "Daddy will come today and Santa tonight, Daddy will come today and Santa tonight." Libby felt desperate. Not only was Art delayed but there were no gifts to put in the stockings.

The children ate their morning oatmeal. For three days the snow had been so deep there had been no chance for the girls to get outside to play and they were feeling the tension of being housebound. At breakfast Grace, who was pestering her mother for assurance that all was well, could tell that Mamma was troubled and all was not well. Libby did her best to explain. "The snow is so deep the train can't run. Men are working hard to clear the tracks and maybe they will get it done before tonight." But she did not feel a bit confident.

Grace wanted more assurance. "But what if they don't get the tracks cleared? Daddy will miss out on Santa and the stockings in the morning, and all because of an old teacher's institute!"

This posed another serious problem. The girls expected Santa whether Daddy was here or not, but without the gifts that Art would bring there would be no Santa. The reputation of Santa was at stake. Libby felt helpless. When the children hung up their stockings, including the little one for Arty, and she tucked them into bed, she knew she had to say something but what she said puzzled Grace more than it helped her. "This is such a terrible storm, it could be that Santa might have some trouble, too. If he hasn't been here when you get up in the morning, don't feel too bad. He *will* come just as soon as he can."

Grace laughed a bit to herself. *It is terrible to think that Daddy might miss Santa but poor Mamma. She is very wise in most things but I know some things that Mamma doesn't seem to understand. Santa is magic, and besides, he has a sleigh and can come even if a train can't get through the snow.* With this confidence about Santa, but fear that Daddy might miss Christmas, she finally drifted off to sleep.

The weather had turned very cold and it was hard keeping the house warm. Libby slept little, having to feed the baby, add coal to the stove several times in the night and check on the children to be sure they were adequately covered. At five in the morning Art had not come. Added to her concern for the children was a growing fear that Art might be stranded somewhere in a rail car with its heating system shut down.

She was building up the fire in the kitchen range and beginning to prepare the oatmeal for breakfast when she heard the patter of little bare feet on the ice cold floor. The girls had heard her working in the kitchen, popped out of bed and came running to inspect the stockings that hung as empty as they had been the night before. Grace stared in stunned disbelief. Connie let out a wail that pierced Libby's heart. Gathering the girls in her arms Libby spoke very softly. "Now listen to me. Santa will come. I promise you he will come. We must wait a little longer."

Finally Connie sat down at the table and slowly ate her cereal. She was hungry and she had not suffered the shattering of her faith as

Grace had. Grace tried a spoonful but could not swallow it, something she had never experienced before. She naturally had a vigorous appetite. Seeking some shred of hope she went to the window to look out but it was still quite dark and the snow was piled so high she could see nothing at all. Libby fed Arty, gave him his bath, then sat by the stove to cut out paper dolls for the girls. It was Christmas day. Santa had not come. The day passed slowly. The weather grew even colder. Two teary eyed girls climbed into bed. Libby piled extra blankets on them and took Arty into her bed to be sure he would be warm enough. It was a house of mourning.

Some time past midnight Grace was awakened by a noise and a light in the house. Mamma was laughing. And just as Grace was pulling Connie out of bed their door burst open and there were Mamma and Daddy and Mamma saying, "Get up quick. Santa Claus has come!"

For Grace there was no more cold, no sadness any more. Stockings were stuffed. There were doll buggies, a toy kitchen set with little pots and pans and skillets, all filled with candy. And Grace would always know that Santa was not only magic, but very kind and had waited until Daddy could be there.

—

The winter was long and cold but it finally passed. Except for Hyrum's death, the year had been a good one. Libby, the girls, and the baby were all thriving. Art had his degree and had saved a little money. He had also inherited land from his father to add to the land from Grandma Sarah. He now felt like a substantial family man, but was beginning to feel the pull of his land upon him.

On April 6, the United States declared war on Germany, thus entering the "Great War." Art's nephews, Floyd and Ervin—about ten years younger than Art and presently attending the University of Utah—were eligible for the draft. For Libby, with Marjorie working as a war nurse in England and Laurence on the front lines, the participation of the United States brought a certain sense of relief. Much as she abhorred war, it seemed a sign of hope that Britain might be saved from defeat and the war's end hastened.

During the Easter recess, to Libby's great joy, Art secured a position to teach math in a Salt Lake City high school, starting in September. His salary would be increased again. With the contract in his pocket he stopped to look at the new motor cars in the Ford dealership. A shipment of Model T Touring Cars had just been delivered. A sign taped to the window advertised the cost as $360. The salesman showed him how to work the crank, then they both got in and the salesman showed him the various levers and the steering wheel that controlled the car. Art wanted the flexibility of such transportation, and knew that improvements had been made since the first motor cars had been sold. But he was a methodical and conservative man. A more important financial matter had to be dealt with first. He thanked the salesman and took the streetcar to Union to see his brother-in-law Charley, the Union homebuilder.

Art had a vision. It had developed slowly in his mind over the past several months. In this vision his family lived on the property Grandma Sarah had bequeathed him—the best homesite in Union—surrounded by the additional property his father had recently left him. The land from their new house would slope down to the very same trout stream where he had learned to fish. Little Arty would run happily with his sisters. The children would pick fruit from his trees and play with their cousins who lived a short walk away. Libby would be freed to a great extent, not needing to take the children to parks and push them on swings. Instead they would watch the animals and the raising of crops. Everything of interest to children was right there in Union, including their loving Grandma Smith.

Libby wanted to live in Salt Lake while Clarence sharecropped the land, but Art felt sure that she would like what he had in mind. And he wasn't one to dream uselessly. This he could afford. This was the right thing to do. Not taking advantage of that building site and not farming the land his father had given him would be like the Biblical parable of the man who buried his talents.

A few days later when he came home from the Goshen school, Libby handed him the mail: a more finalized version of the contract he and Charley had rough-drafted. Now it was filled in with the actual costs of materials. He turned the pages, smiling. "We'll have a house built to our specifications," he told Libby. "Your specifications, my dear Lib. The living room will be as big as you want, big enough for meetings, a piano, singing, entertaining."

Libby couldn't remember seeing him this happy. His enthusiasm for building a house on the Union property showed in everything he said and did. He walked with more spring in his step, laughed more readily, and could hardly wait to start the spring planting. "I'll have an orchard and garden well up by the time school's out," he declared. "I'll get the sugar beets started too. It'd sure be too bad to let a whole growing season go to waste just because school didn't let out in time for planting."

"I won't see much of you," she said.

"For a couple of months, but then we'll have the summer, and Union isn't far from Salt Lake. We'll see more of each other than ever. Think how the girls will love watching their own house being built!"

Not having the heart to dampen his joy, she watched him sign the final papers.

Art immediately embarked upon an ambitious program of planting and building in Union. At the same time he finished his end-of-term work in Goshen—preparing the students and teachers for tests and grading, and organizing the eighth grade graduation ceremony. Libby was busy with her children. All she could do was watch while her life took a dramatic turn to where she hadn't wanted it to go.

On a Sunday evening in May, Libby heard three loud goose-honks. Grace and Connie looked up from their paper dolls, then scrambled to peer out the door with Libby. There, parked in front of the house, was Art in a shiny new 1917 Model T Ford Touring Car. He climbed out, shut the door, and stood smiling at the three of them, resting his elbow on the side of the car, which was open to the air. The two little girls ran to greet him. They hit him running, and he threw back his head laughing. To Libby he looked like the handsome man in the advertisement for just such "family touring cars."

It was then that she began to think it might be all right, after all, to move to Union.

"They shall sit every man under his vine and under his fig tree."
Micah 4:4 KJV

12   Union

Art's father had drawn a will dividing his landholdings among his children. Possibly to keep his youngest son in Union, the land he left Arthur fit nicely with the homesite Sarah had left him—several acres of good hay land just across the creek from the higher ground that they spoke of as "the hill." He also left Art several acres of well irrigated land very near his and Lucy's house, just across the road from the land he willed to Allie and Clarence.

Art had no intention of becoming a farmer; he didn't have enough land to make a living as a farmer. But he loved the land that his pioneer grandparents had settled, and he would have time in the summers and on weekends to be a "gentleman farmer." He saw it as recreation—his favorite kind. His new home would be located very near the historic old adobe house where his parents had fallen in love. When school started in September he would commute to Salt Lake in his Touring Car, which he had learned to drive by studying the instructions in the booklet—later joking with Libby and the children how fortunate it was that so few cars and horses had been on the road that day. He looked forward very much to touring with the family. The car was big enough for all the family with room to spare for bedrolls and picnic baskets.

Libby tried to look on the bright side. Living in Grandma Sarah's small house while the new house was under construction, she remembered how dear old Grandma had lived with courage through hard circumstances. In comparison Libby was richly blessed. She told herself it was simply not her lot in life to live in a city. Instead, her children would live the healthy life she had lived as a young child near

Crathie Parish. But she would be vigilant about teaching them her Christian beliefs and ethics, and she would make certain that they spoke proper English despite the crude English that was spoken all around them. Then they would have the best of both worlds.

She had helped Art draw up the detailed plans for the house, and now, after all the weekends he had spent with Charley and the Danish cabinet maker, the house was almost finished. A fashionable yellow brick, it had three bedrooms—one large room for Art and Libby in the back of the downstairs and two smaller upstairs bedrooms for the children. It had a big living room with a dining area on one side. Taking advantage of the power from the dam in Cottonwood Canyon, the house was wired for electricity. Indoor plumbing delivered heated water through the tank on the stove to the kitchen and bathroom, which had a white porcelain sink and tub. No longer would the family bathe in a washtub in the kitchen. Art was proud of his system for running water to a high tank to provide the pressure and downward force for an indoor flush toilet. Later he would explain the workings of the septic pool and leach lines to his sons. The house stood on a lot that sloped down to cold, clear Little Cottonwood Creek, a year-round stream with a forest of willows and cottonwoods along its banks. Art happily commented: "This is where my children will learn to be fishermen, right here in their own back yard."

Before school was out Art had carefully marked out places for an extensive garden, an orchard, a small barn, and pens and houses for a few hogs. Now the orchard and garden were doing well and the corn and sugar beets were crisp and green. He housed a flock of chickens in the old adobe house. Libby had never before seen how much he loved working with the land and making things grow. In the next few years she would see him grow one of the finest gardens in Union—his fine white cauliflower being particularly admired. He would also raise and butcher hogs, keep a milk cow and a team of horses. To give their new home something of the graciousness of the manse, Art planted a large lawn with a stand of lilac bushes, and he made beds for roses and flowers, all of which he tended with the caring of Old Duff. She discovered that his joy and energy in being a homeowner and a "gentleman farmer" brought them close together, almost like newlyweds.

During July and August Art worked from sunup to sundown with brother-in-law Charley, racing to finish the house by the time his school started. His two varieties of apples, twelve peach trees, plums and pears thrived. His crops were prospering in the rich soil. He would succeed in getting a full growing season his very first year.

By Labor Day the beautiful new house was finished. All the relatives gathered for a housewarming picnic. Libby participated wholeheartedly in the festivities. She even raced with the children, hiking up her skirt and letting her long, curly light-brown hair steam out behind her, a sight Grace and Connie would remember all their lives. Art entertained the crowd by walking on his hands, doing running handflips, and backflips, and by balancing things on his nose—sticks, a chair, and a broomstraw standing on end. He told the fascinated children that he would pay any of them a dollar if they could balance a broomstraw on their finger. They all tried very hard—Libby fearing they would tear off all the straws from her broom. His own children would continue trying for many years, including those not yet born, but none of them would ever be able to perform that difficult trick.

The men and older boys began to throw horseshoes, a game Art excelled at. The rest of the cousins played "Run Sheepy Run." Mother Lucy sat in the shade of the new house rocking Arty while Libby visited with Allie, Lorene, Lizzie and Sarah—all cutting lemons and squeezing them into a crock for lemonade. A block of ice had been brought from the underground icehouse near Lucy's house.

Sarah, Art's oldest sister, said, "It's such fun to see Art with his children. Why, I had no idea he'd be so good with kids!"

"He's got 'em helpin' in the garden," Lizzie quipped, stirring sugar into the lemonade.

"He can't wait to teach Arty to catch trout," Libby said, adding, "Art has trained me to favor trout."

Lucy smiled wisely from the rocking chair.

"Well, we're pleased as punch that you and Art are living here," Allie said, breaking ice with the pick.

"I couldn't be happier," Libby told them. Silently she had grieved over the lack of a church in the community and prayed for guidance about it. Now, watching a dozen children streak across the yard in laughing pursuit of the one who was hiding, an inspiration came to her.

"I'd like to start a Sunday School," she announced.

"What do you mean?" Allie asked. "In what church?"

"First I'll have to go to Salt Lake and see about it, but I think we could have a wonderful little school here right here in my house on Sunday mornings. The children could sing and learn Bible verses. I think they'd enjoy it."

"Well, if you're teaching, they will," Sarah agreed.

———

On Tuesday morning Libby left her children with Allie and went to Salt Lake to discuss her idea with Dr. Paden at First Presbyterian. Grace and Connie loved spending time with Allie, whose daughters Donna and Sarah were almost exactly their ages. The two pairs of girls would be favorite playmates for years to come. Libby's visit to Dr. Paden turned out to be a most enjoyable experience. She told him of her idea, and he assured her that his church would supply any study materials or song books that would be needed. In effect she would be forming an extension of his church, but, knowing her, he had no misgivings. In fact he was delighted with her idea of a Sunday School in Union.

Dr. Paden was always happy to visit with a person with such a grasp of church history and policy and such sincere interest in religion in general. He was fascinated to hear of her experience with the Mormon community and the story of her husband's Josephite background. For Libby, visiting with this well educated, devout man who accepted her as an intellectual equal was more than a satisfying experience. She realized she had been starved for such companionship. He invited her to lunch, prepared and served by his wife. The planning of the Sunday School extended their friendship and formed the basis of a deeper and more enduring relationship, though opportunities for visiting would of necessity be limited.

Before leaving the city, Libby went to a music store and signed the papers for a big upright piano. The proprietor of the store said it would be crated and shipped to her in two days. Art's higher salary and the money from the excellent crops they would soon harvest made them comfortable buying a few needed items.

The next Sunday morning Libby was ready for her first Sunday School class. As arranged, Allie came to serve as the teaching assistant, and would continued to do so for the next six years. All the sisters-in-law came with their children. Grandma Lucy marched through the door, scooped Arty off the floor, and announced, "I'll mind the babies." She took Arty and Allie's youngest into the back bedroom to give Libby and Allie the freedom to teach unhampered.

Libby couldn't have been more surprised or grateful to Lucy, who would continue to care for the babies every Sunday that the school was in session.

The Sunday School turned out to be a source of pleasure and learning for all the cousins. Unrelated children began coming, not wanting to feel left out. Either their parents didn't know where their kids were or did not object. Everyone knew to be in place promptly at nine-thirty for Libby's opening prayer. She was as faithful and devoted as any minister. The Sunday School was a vital and important part of Libby's life. For Grace, Connie, Arty and later-to-be-born Donald, their first experience with organized religion was in their own living room.

True to its promise, the Presbyterian Church in Salt Lake kept her supplied with age-level study material and story papers for the children who were starting to read. She put an emphasis on memorizing

Lucy Griffiths Smith (center) with 26 grandchildren, about 1922. Standing in back are Floyd and Ervin Anderson, the eldest. The four children sitting in center front are (l-r) Connie, Donald, Arthur, and Grace.

favorite scripture passages in an atmosphere of friendly competition. She taught a new lesson each week, covering all the beliefs of Christianity, and that "Love is not restricted to those of a particular belief." Almost all the Smith children had excellent singing voices. To the accompaniment of Libby's piano playing they sang hymns. Very often Libby organized little programs of recitations and songs for their parents, thereby, in a sense, bringing a semblance of church to the parents too. For many years to come that bright spot in the week would be remembered as "Aunt Elizabeth's Sunday School."

Art recognized it as Libby's compromise in living in a small town surrounded by Mormons. It was also her way of answering Grace's questions, prompted by her Mormon classmates who said things like, "You will not go to heaven and your grandpa never went to heaven because your family doesn't belong to The Church." The Sunday School helped ease Libby's fear that her children and their cousins would become Mormons. Despite the Sunday school, however, in later years several of the cousins did join The Church by marriage.

By 1924, with so many babies being born in the Smith clan, Lucy's grandchildren formed the large and faithful core of the Sunday School. Once a year Libby put on a special presentation, attended by Dr. Paden and a few members of the church in Salt Lake. All of the proud parents looked on: Martin and Sarah, Will and Lorene, Lizzie and Charley, Clarence and Allie, and, of course, Art. The only ones missing were Hyrum and Bertha, who lived in Leamington, a Utah town quite far to the south. Grandma Lucy beamed with pride and happiness as she gazed upon the performances of her brood gathered together. And indeed, they were an impressive and talented group.

The special programs were presented on a summer day, and always finished with a picnic. Libby would wear a bemused smile as she watched the dignified and proper Reverend William Paden complementing Grandma Lucy, who had never been in a Protestant church in her life, on her grandchildren's remarkable knowledge of the Bible. Seventy years later, at a reunion of Art and Libby's descendants, Grace and Connie entwined their two clear soprano voices in moving harmony as they sang *I saw my Savior*. They had learned it in their mother's Sunday School.

The summer of 1917 had been busy and pleasant for Libby. Besides settling into her new home and watching her children enjoy the farm, her mind was filled with ideas for the Sunday School. To increase her enjoyment, in August she received a letter from Marjorie that surprised and pleased her very much. Marjorie had found love. She had married a Scotsman named Ernest Hill. It had been a quiet little wedding in the chapel of the hospital in Manchester, England, where Marjorie worked as a nurse. The news came to Libby as a surprise because Marjorie had never mentioned any courtship.

Ernest was a soldier who had been serving with the Royal Canadian Regiment on the front lines in France. He had never met Laurence Symon, who was also serving there with the Regiment, but it was that commonality that started Marjorie and Ernest visiting. Marjorie said he described life on the front lines in France as "indescribably horrible." He had dived into a trench just in time to protect his body from the full force of a grenade. It destroyed one leg below the knee. After the amputation in a field hospital he'd been shipped to Manchester for recovery and rehabilitation. He went through a period of depression in which he had wished the grenade had killed him instead of making him "completely useless and no longer a man."

Marjorie, his nurse, tried hard to convince him that he still had much to live for. Having spent some time in Perth before moving to Canada, he had much to talk about with Marjorie. Their friendship helped him regain an interest in living. When his leg was healed sufficiently to be fitted with an "artificial lower limb," a term Ernest despised, Marjorie helped him learn to use it. She then proved to him that he had much to live for by agreeing to marry him.

Libby was just savoring the happy news of Marjorie's wedding when shattering news came in September. A telegram from brother David in Scotland transmitted the message from the British Army

that Lance Corporal Laurence Symon had been killed in action somewhere in France.

It was small consolation that he was being awarded the British
War Medal. While training in England, before being sent to France,
he had met and married a gracious young woman and had written
Libby sharing with her his joy. In her silent and personal prayers,
Libby had prayed daily for his safety. The news of his death devastated
her. For the children's sake she felt she must not show her emotions.
To the best of her ability she kept her weeping private. Art tried to
comfort her, for which she was grateful, but for a long time she
struggled with the loss of this brother, even though she had not seen
him for many years.

Sensitive to her moods, five year old Grace asked, "Mama why are
you so sad?"

She finally realized that she would have to share the facts with the
children. She explained as best she could that their Uncle Laurence,
the brother who had played with her when she was a little girl, the one
whose name Arty bore, had been shot and killed in the war. The girls
knew more than she realized about the war, having listened to many
adult conversations. When they tried, in their sincere and childish
way to comfort her, she did finally weep in their presence. They seemed
to understand death more than she thought they did. Grace said, "He's
gone away to heaven just like Grandpa Smith."

Libby desperately needed someone to talk to who could relate to
her sorrow. She found a source of comfort where she had not expected
it. Almost directly across the road from her new home lived the Jensens,
an older Danish couple. Karl Jensen was the skilled cabinetmaker who
had built her new cupboards. Knowing they were Mormons she had
not expected that they would be a source of close friendship. But one
morning Gudrun came over to see the new house and her husband's
handiwork. Libby was drinking a cup of tea. By reflex, before she
remembered that Mormons didn't drink tea, she offered Gudrun a
cup. Gudrun gladly accepted. As they visited an immediate bond of

friendship developed between Libby and the woman old enough to be her mother.

Gudrun had known grief and sorrow. Two of her three children had died, one of whooping cough and one of typhoid. The third, their first born, had grown up and left The Church; he had left Utah. He was a businessman in California with a wife and young family. Like Libby, Gudrun hoped and prayed, and felt quite confident that family men would be the very last to be called into war service.

Gudrun was a Mormon, but something about her quiet faith and her ability to accept life's disappointments reminded Libby of Grandma Sarah. Her friendship was most helpful to Libby as she struggled with the death of her brother. It would be a bright spot in her life in Union for years to come.

The friendship grew over many shared cups of tea, sometimes in Libby's house, sometimes in Gudrun's. They were both lonely for someone who shared memories of an "old country." Gudrun rarely attended church. When she and her husband were newly married in Denmark, they had been converted by missionaries who gave glowing accounts of life in Utah, but mentioned little about Mormon theology or the Divine Principle. A thoughtful man and good husband, Karl was now an indifferent Mormon, not a religious man by temperament, but went along with The Church for the sake of his business.

Gudrun had grown up in an active Lutheran family and had been confirmed in the Lutheran Church. Remembering her devout parents and her Lutheran Bible, which she still read in Danish, she couldn't accept the idea that all the other churches were apostate, or "false." She couldn't believe that Joseph Smith was a prophet of God who had found and restored to earth the one and only true Church of Jesus Christ. She had come to realize that there was much about The Church that she "just couldn't and didn't believe." Libby saw that she was a kind and gentle person who disliked upsetting people. "I go along with things," Gudrun said. "I never argue about religion with my friends. That is best for Karl and his work." But privately Gudrun found a great deal of pleasure in visiting with deeply religious Libby.

The year 1917 had brought many changes—moving to Union, the Sunday School, the marriage of Marjorie, the death of Laurence, and Libby's increasing political action. Throughout the year she did everything she could to support the Temperance Movement, writing letters to newspapers and political representatives, giving talks at meetings in Salt Lake, and encouraging people in Union to be more active. For the past several years Libby hadn't had an opportunity to be involved in causes with other church members, and this activity satisfied her need to work for a better world.

On December 18, 1917, to Libby's great joy, both houses of Congress approved the 18th Amendment to the Constitution with the required majority, and it was transmitted to the states for their ratification. Libby knew the pertinent language by heart.

> **Sec. 1. After one year from the ratification of this article the manufacture, sale or transportation of intoxicating liquors within, the importation thereof into, or the exportation thereof from the United States and all territory subject to the jurisdiction thereof for beverage purposes is hereby prohibited.**

Her father had preached against the liquor business, and she had seen the destructive effects of drinking, particularly among the poor. She believed with a passion that liquor should be outlawed. Now, even though women had not won the right to vote and many thought the women's vote was essential to the success of Prohibition, she saw that her dream was likely to become reality after all. One after another, the states were ratifying the amendment. It gave Libby a strong sense of fulfillment.

Her family was rapidly changing. Early in 1918 she found she was pregnant again. When school started the following September, Grace, who had already learned to read, went off proudly to the first grade. A precocious child curious about everything, Grace had been constantly demanding Libby's attention, and she was surprised to find how much the absence of one child opened her day. Connie amused Arty, who wasn't yet two, and Libby had more quiet time to write her letters and read. She closely followed the activities of the Suffragists, people agitating for a constitutional amendment to give women the right to vote. She knew that under different circumstances she would be marching beside them.

On October 16th, 1918, with Alice in attendance once again, Libby's fourth child and second son was born. A much more sophisticated Grace didn't ask whether he arrived wearing overalls. Libby, who always felt a need to put a light touch on serious matters, would later tell her friends: "On Monday the old sow had ten pigs. On Tuesday the other sow had eleven pigs, and on Wednesday I had Donald."

They named him Donald Ian, a good solid Scottish name—Ian being the Gaelic form of John, for Libby's father. It was a normal birth and a healthy child. Libby quickly regained her strength, and Alice left after only two weeks.

On a Monday morning in November, less than a month after the birth, Libby was singing to Arty and Connie, who were in the kitchen with her while the baby slept. She was also starting to fix a big noon meal for Art and his nephews. Floyd and Ervin Anderson had been putting in long days harvesting sugar beets with Art. They had just finished their military training in Fort Douglas and in a few days would be "shipped out" to action in France. This had been the subject of many grave conversations within the Smith clan. Libby and Art were particularly fond of Floyd and Ervin, who were bright, ambitious young men. Having lost Laurence in France, Libby had developed a deep and abiding horror of war, and she worried terribly about these nephews—Sarah and Martin's boys.

At eleven o'clock she was startled by the sound of horns honking, sirens screaming, and the school bell ringing. Connie cried, "Mama, what's happening!" Libby's first thought was concern for Grace at school. Something terrible must be happening, maybe a fire, the school house burning. In the next room the baby started to cry.

Snatching up Donald, Libby ran outside, Connie and Arty with her. She was amazed to see, in the nearby sugar beet field, Art, Floyd and Ervin throwing their hats in the air, hugging each other, and dancing about like madmen. Seeing her, they ran to the house. They grabbed Libby and the children, picked them up, and did more dancing—all the time shouting. "The war is over, the war is over!"

It was a moment of great joy, long to be remembered, long to be talked about— a moment they would relive for many years on November 11. Armistice Day would become one of the greatest national holidays. The war to make the world safe for democracy, "the war to end all war," had been fought and won.

Floyd and Ervin were free to follow their dreams of completing higher degrees. They would finish at the University of Utah, then Yale Law School, ultimately becoming prominent attorneys in Ohio. They would return to Union only for occasional visits. One of their favorite relatives was their "Aunt Elizabeth." They kept in touch with Art and Libby through all the coming years.

On Christmas, 1918, peace actually did prevail on earth. One month later, January 29, 1919, another great social goal of Libby's came to pass. The necessary thirty-sixth state ratified the 18th Amendment. Only one year in the future it would be illegal to manufacture or sell liquor. She had dreamed of this and worked very hard for it. Now, brimming with hope and joy, she expressed her strong feelings on paper. In poetic prose, almost in ecstasy, she rejoiced in the knowledge that her children would grow up in a society without the demeaning influence of liquor and her sons would never face the danger of serving their county on the battlefield. They could peacefully contribute to the welfare of the country. The "poem" as Donald thought of it when he saw it among her papers decades later, made a strong impression on him. Unfortunately it subsequently disappeared.

Libby's was the typical idealism of the times. The scourge of war had ended, people were prospering, rapid improvements were being made in medical research, education and living conditions. Electricity had spread to most cities and work-saving appliances made life ever easier. The theory of evolution was being applied to society, a concept of "social evolution." A popular phrase used for practice in typing classes expressed it well: "Every day in every way we're getting better and better."

The emphasis in Christian churches continued to shift away from changing individual lives by conversion to Christianity. The new emphasis was on changing society by political means, on the assumption that a good society would make good people. The Gospel was becoming the "Social Gospel." A high quality religious magazine was born with the promising name, *The Christian Century*. Many devout Christians were caught up in this wave of idealism which would make political activity a primary expression of missionary action. Libby, whose very nature called for action, and who under different circumstances could have devoted her life to being a "missionary to the heathen," was caught up in this new kind of religious thinking.

A 19th Amendment to give women the right to vote appeared to be making gains, though acrimonious debate continued around the country. Women everywhere were becoming more active. Frequently Libby read accounts of legislators changing their votes after their mothers begged them to, one from her deathbed. Libby worked hard, writing letters and speaking. In Utah, this struggle was far more difficult than the fight for the 18th Amendment had been. The Mormon Church opposed the use of liquor, whereas it encouraged the submissiveness of wives to their husbands. In Utah most people seemed to believe that a man's vote represented his wife's preferences too, as though she had no mind of her own. With newspaper reports of each victory, Libby felt her voice joining those of thousands of women cheering in kitchens across the country. And she knew she was more fortunate than many. Art also supported women's suffrage.

Then early in February, 1919, she experienced one of the most stressful times of her life. It was a month that stretched the limits of her physical strength, her emotional endurance and her faith. Her beloved Art contracted a severe case of "Spanish influenza," a strain that was killing hundreds of thousands of people around the country. It may well have been her faith and her habit of personal prayer that brought her through it. She discovered the practice of "prayer on the run," when there was no other time for it. Art's fever raged and he could hardly breathe. The doctor looked in on him briefly, wrote some prescriptions and gave her directions on caring for him, but the care was up to Libby. She knew that doctors and nurses everywhere were overworked. The only nursing help had to come from family members.

Grandma Lucy was some help, but her time was divided between several of her children and grandchildren who had fallen ill. All the in-laws who would have helped gladly were struggling with illness in their own homes. Besides trying to get fluid into Art and keep his fever down, Libby was caring for a tiny baby and three young children. Part of the stress came from keeping the children from getting close to Art. Doctors were quoted in the newspaper saying that the influenza was easily contracted; they advised people not to travel lest they spread the disease. Alice could not come to help. Libby sat up in a chair with Art several nights, afraid if she let herself sleep she would lose him.

Just when she felt she had surpassed the limit of her endurance, Donald whimpered and turned hot to the touch. Only three months old, he rapidly became so congested that as he violently choked and coughed, he turned blue. She had to hold him upside down and strike him on the back to dislodge the mucus. Even then his breath came weak and ragged. Grace was in school, so Libby sent Connie for the doctor. The doctor briefly examined the baby and said it was a severe case of whooping cough. Libby felt her legs go weak. This killer disease targeted children, particularly the very young. Gudrun's child had died of it. The doctor left some medicine and promised to check again in two days.

Now Libby had to keep Arty, Grace, and Connie away from Donald. She set up a cot near the kitchen stove where she lay with him. No longer could she ask the girls to help with things that exposed them to him. She spent a night in constant crisis, fearing every few minutes that he was dying. For his fever she gave him small amounts of dissolved aspirin in an eyedropper with warm water. Art coughed in the bedroom but she didn't dare leave the baby. Before school the next morning she sent Grace for the doctor again.

The doctor looked at Donald and sadly told Libby that there was nothing more he could do. A naturally kind man, he was very weary. He hadn't meant to sound harsh when he added, "I have to give what time and energy I have to patients that I hope to save."

Those words fell like a blow from a fist. Her reaction was similar to that of her own mother years ago when the specialists recommended amputating Libby's lower leg. Clutching Donald to her breast she told the doctor, "My baby will not die!"

Exhausted as she was, she set herself to the day and night task of keeping the kettle pouring out warm vapor, clearing out the tiny congested throat, and helping her little one breathe during his fierce coughing and choking spells. He couldn't nurse. Reluctantly relying upon four-year-old Connie to amuse rambunctious two-year-old Arty while Grace was in school, she dropped warm water into Donald's mouth. She lost track of time. When she felt at the end of her strength she asked God to help her, and kept on going. Finally she saw that her baby was breathing easier and beginning to nurse a little. Her milk responded. He began to recover. She knew it was unlikely that he could have recovered with any less care. Her prayers and total dedication had saved him.

When Art was awake and Arty was napping, Libby could begin to leave Donald under the watchful care of serious, dependable six-year-old Grace and steal short periods of sleep. It was evident that Art, too, was gaining strength. Her care and his exceptional physical condition and naturally strong constitution had pulled him through an ordeal that had brought death to so many strong young men and women. A prolonged nightmare had passed.

—

Libby resumed her Sunday School, and Art went back to teaching math, planting crops, and caring for his animals. There was much to be thankful for. The children were all healthy and growing fast. On June 4, 1919, Congress adopted the 19th Amendment to the Constitution. Libby and Art rejoiced as each state ratified the amendment. Then on August 24, 1920, Tennessee became the needed thirty-sixth state to ratify Women's Suffrage. In November, with great pride, joy, and diligent preparation, Libby savored the moment when she walked into the precinct voting booth for the first time. Until her death she would never miss an election.

A year passed quickly as she cared for her children—telling them stories, teaching them songs, bandaging and bathing them. She cooked regular meals, tried to keep some order in the house, washed clothing in her new tub on legs with an automatic agitator and a switch that made the wringer rollers turn, and she hung out endless loads of wash on the clothesline. A concern about Donald began to niggle her mind. He had cut his teeth and learned to walk but never tried to speak. The other three children had spoken their first words at around a year. With two doting sisters Donald got what he wanted by pointing or received more serious attention by crying. His second birthday passed and he still had not tried to speak a single word. At his age the other three children had developed impressive vocabularies. Libby began to fear that such a serious case of whooping cough might have damaged some area of his brain. She researched and found a specialist who might be able to diagnose the trouble. She composed a letter to Angelo Patri, a doctor who had a column on child rearing in *The Salt Lake*

Tribune. They said she should wait, that many children do not speak until they are well over two years of age.

But Donald's third birthday arrived in mid October and still he had not spoken a word. Now almost sure that he was mentally impaired, she suffered in pained silence. Then on a cold Saturday in November, Art, with the help of some neighbors, began the fall hog butchering. He was an expert in making hams and bacon and did his own butchering, something Libby never imagined he would do back when, years ago, they met "the butcher" on the way to Yost.

She didn't like her children to witness the process, but Donald escaped her notice and was outside giving it his careful attention. A hog's throat was cut, producing copious amounts of blood. The hog was scalded in an enormous tub of boiling water, scraped clean of hair and hoisted, strung up by the hind feet and left hanging on a pole between two trees. Fascinated, worried for the pig, and very excited, Donald came running into the kitchen shouting, "Mama, Mama, piggy hangy!"

Libby was ecstatic. She picked him up and hugged him. Not only had he spoken a word, he had put together a whole sentence. She would have preferred a less earthy subject to inspire him, but her son could speak! He was not mentally impaired. If her prayers were answered by a naked hog hanging in a tree, so be it. She would later tell the story many times, adding that once he started talking he never stopped. He had accumulated a vocabulary, but with all the talk that went on between his parents and three talkative siblings, there simply had been no reason to get involved. This became one of Libby's classic stories, told in her inimitable way.

The school district insisted that Arty had to be six by the 15th of September to be enrolled in the first grade, even though he could read. Libby pointed out that he would be six in less than three months, but learned that there were no exceptions to this Utah practice. The previous summer, when he was five, she had reluctantly cut off the blond ringlets that had made him look so angelic, and now he looked terribly grown up in his knickers as he joined his sisters walking toward the Union School for the first time.

Connie trotted back and told Libby in a confidential tone, "Don't worry, Mama, I'll watch him on the playground." She too was a beautiful child with serious blue eyes—a daughter who would always be close to Libby. Connie returned to the others, and Libby stood on the doorstep watching her precious band of three walking up the road, sober little Donald standing at her knee.

With three children in school and only one to care for at home, Libby became more and more involved in the affairs of the school. Education was a top priority in her life, and the quality of the education her children received was very much her business. She was pleased that Arty's teacher advanced him to the second grade soon after his admission, but all was not well at the school.

Grace came home in tears, telling about a "missionary class" and how she had been teased and shunned by her classmates for not attending it. Righteous indignation took hold of Libby. It was not in her nature to quietly accept what she felt was wrong. Her dear, precocious Grace was feeling like an outcast, a terrible experience for an eleven year old girl. Being well ahead of her class in all her subjects, she had been moved up a year, skipping the fifth grade. She already felt somewhat different from her peers because of being younger, and she longed to be accepted as an equal among the sixth grade girls. She poured out her troubles to her mother. Each week the class was taught in the school—instruction in the tenets of Mormonism. Grace was excused during that period because she was not Mormon. It was the last period of the day, and she was told she could go home or go to the library to read and study. But increasingly she felt herself the object of scorn on the playground. She didn't want to be different.

Something had to be done. Libby believed that the use of the public schools for religious education was not legal in the United States. It had been done by the Established Church of England and Scotland, but this was America where there was to be no established church.

Leaving Donald in Allie's care, she went to Salt Lake to visit with Dr. Paden and exchange a pile of Sunday School materials. She told him about the trouble in the school. He said he thought the Utah Constitution prohibited such a practice. She went to the city library and read the first ten amendments of the U.S. Constitution. The one about religion wasn't very specific, protecting the right *to* worship, but the Utah Constitution contained a specific protection *from* established religion. But what could one mother do?

She discussed the matter with Art. Never one who liked to make trouble, he nevertheless agreed that the Union school was likely doing something illegal. As far as he knew, it was not being done in the Salt Lake City schools.

What could anyone do? As the year progressed and Grace continued to feel extremely unhappy over the "missionary" class, Libby decided she could do something. She had a voice and she could write. She would launch her campaign with a letter to the editor of the *Salt Lake Tribune*, which continued to provide news and opinions separate from the church-controlled *Deseret News*.

On Thursday, April 5, 1923, Art came home from teaching and picked up the *Tribune* on the front doorstep. As usual he sat down to read it, but then got up, joined Libby in the kitchen, and silently showed her the article. They stood reading it together, though the children were clamoring for their supper.

CHARGE OF CHURCH CLASSES IN SCHOOLS WILL BE PROBED Jordan Officials and State Superintendent promise Investigation of Alleged Unlawful Practice

———

A charge that religion is being taught in the schools of the Jordan District is made by Mrs. E. S. Smith of Union in a correspondence sent to the Tribune. She alleges that in many of the schools in our district religion classes are held weekly, immediately following regular class work, the pupils remaining in their respective rooms and the grade teachers conducting the classes. These classes are designated as Junior Missionary Classes.

. . .The president of the Jordan School board admitted that he had heard reports of such classes but he had no personal knowledge that such reports were true. He also stated that the board had received a request to hold such classes and the matter had been referred to the board's attorney. The attorney stated that in his opinion such classes would be illegal and the board had never given its permission. If such classes were being held it was without the approval of the School Board. . . Persons familiar with the situation hold the opinion that the question of whether religion can be taught in the schools will be settled finally by rulings of the courts.

Libby's accusation stimulated a great deal of discussion in Union and in all of Utah, for similar "seminary" classes were held all over the state. The papers carried denials about the interpretation of the law and arguments about legal technicalities. One Jordan board member said that if there was no objection from the community, the practice should be continued. Upset parents from solidly Mormon schools appreciated the religious classes. They said they were the taxpayers, and if that's what they wanted it should it be legal. People in Union groused about the unfairness of one person trying to control everyone else. The effect of this was that it pointed a finger at Libby as an undesirable troublemaker. No one in the community stood up to agree with her. Only Art, in his quiet way, was on her side.

Libby had touched a very sensitive issue. A few days later a larger headline declared:

RELIGION CLASS WORK STOPPED
Jordan District President Orders
Discontinuance Until Board Meeting

"Religion classes, which have been held in many of the schools of the Jordan district, will be discontinued until the board of education can meet and act on a permanent abolishment," W.W. Wilson, President of the board said last night.

"On account of the agitation which has been caused over the question, I tried to call a special meeting of the board today," he said. "However I learned that one member was away and I think that all should be present."

The absent member had made public statements in defense of the religion classes and implied that the board president agreed with him. However, Mr. Wilson now denied any such agreement.

On the following Thursday the board convened. Keenly aware of the hostility on many faces, Art and Libby entered the assembly room and sat in the back. People whispered and turned around to look at them. Many were from other towns. Art hated being the object of controversy. Some of these people were friends and neighbors. Their parents had been friends and neighbors of his parents and grandparents. President Wilson banged his gavel and called Libby to speak.

She walked forward with a straight back and great determination. Quoting the relevant sections of the Utah constitution, which prohibited the use of school property for religious purposes, she added that the state legislature had adopted special laws to assure that the public schools would "be open to all children of the state and be free from sectarian control." The author of the *Tribune* article had researched that and Libby thought it should be mentioned to those who read only the *Deseret News*. She also quoted the *Tribune* that the State Superintendent of Public Instruction had stood squarely behind the ruling of A.C. Nelson, State Superintendent of Public Instruction twenty years ago. "In ought-four," she pointed out, "he was constantly in receipt of letters from around the state protesting the use of public school buildings for religious purposes. Often, contrary to the law, religious classes were taught immediately following regular school classes. He therefore sent a letter to all schools in the state summarizing the various prohibitions and ordering the classes cancelled. That ruling still stands. The law still stands. As a mother of three children in this district, I protest such use of the public school and call upon you to abolish it. Thank you, gentlemen, for the opportunity to provide my testimony."

In turn, others went forward, all insisting that the religion classes furthered the morals of the students and did no harm, since gentile children were not required to attend. Person after person from solidly Mormon communities said that Mrs. Smith ought not to have the power to stop religion classes where everyone else wanted them or had no objection to them.

Libby realized that she had opened a hornets' nest. She glanced at Art, a peaceful man gazing at his trouser knees, and felt an urge to put an arm around him. She looked at the speaker and winced at the anger in his words. A premonition came to her that things would not easily settle down, and though she might eventually bring back the smiles to the faces of her Mormon acquaintances in Union, other confrontations would arise sooner or later as her children progressed through the schools. Perhaps the only way to save Art from this embarrassment and assure that her children would be spared estrangement from their classmates was for the family to move—either to Salt

Lake City or another state where Mormons did not predominate. Her preference would be Salt Lake City, where Art could visit his relatives and they could rent their land but still have some oversight of it.

The hornets did not settle down. Later the courts would rule that conducting religion classes on public school premises violated the law and the state constitution. Libby would win her fight, but the Arthur Smith family had become very unpopular.

It became increasingly uncomfortable for Libby and the children to live in Union. The children were being teased by other children who repeated things they heard their parents saying at home. To a greater extent Grace, Connie and Arty were excluded as gentiles. In normal times they had been left out of the many parties and taffy pulls held in the Mormon Church building. Libby knew that it was normal for children to feel closer to friends who attended both church and school together, and that this explained why her children were not selected first on playground teams. But now that the Smiths were seen as disruptive spoilers, the sense of exclusion grew worse. Grace and Connie complained that classmates stuck out their tongues at them. It became harder for Libby to believe herself when she told them, "Just ignore that. Everything will be all right." When shopping at the general store, she too encountered coolness from people whom she had formerly considered to be friends. She too felt excluded.

When she had a few minutes to herself, she took Donald and visited Gudrun. Over tea, Libby poured out her sorrows and mentioned that maybe the family should leave Union, though that would hurt Art. She told Gudrun how hard it was to broach the subject with him.

Gudrun was a sensitive woman. She understood the dilemma. Sadly she advised Libby that in her opinion it was not possible to escape from all the Mormon ways of thinking and living without moving away. She and Karl had chosen the path of silence in order to keep his business and their home in Union. But she knew Libby well. She knew the situation would only create more problems in years to come.

The reaction of the community hurt Art deeply. He knew Libby felt that she had done the right thing. He admitted to himself that she had, in fact, done the right thing. He gladly told her that some of his friends—non-Mormon teachers in Salt Lake—had congratulated him on the courage of his wife for being willing to stand up for what was right. "Tell her for me," one man said, "that what she did was important and well overdue. My kids were unhappy when all their friends went to Mormon classes in the sixth grade. I made sure my voice was heard when 'Seminary' was proposed in the high school."

Libby appreciated knowing that there were many people who agreed with her, though she wished they weren't so far away. She appreciated Art's repeating to her what his friends had said. But that didn't erase the shadows from his face. Her poor Art was suffering. When she forced herself to talk to him, he agreed in principle that the family should move. He never argued about that. But Union was his home, the place where he had grown up and had so many friends. This was where he wanted to live. The family legacy of land had been bequeathed to him and he wanted to pass it down to his children.

Before the 1923 school term ended Libby went to the city to return materials to Dr. Paden and pick up new materials for the summer. He praised her for writing to the *Tribune* and seeking support among her many allies in the city. He told her that non-Mormon pastors and leaders all over the city had spoken publicly of her courage under the circumsttances.

Riding back to Union in the streetcar, Libby felt better. A few hours later Art drove up to the house, and she told him what Dr. Paden had said. He was glad for her but continued to find it hard to discuss the subject—a rare and painful gap in their otherwise talkative relationship. She tried to tell him that she understood what it was like to leave family and old friends, and that she too would be leaving friends in Union. But nothing seemed to salve the hurt that Art felt.

He was torn between loyalty to his wife and the attitude of the townspeople, between loyalty to her and what he felt inside. She wanted to move to Salt Lake. But he loved the home he had worked so hard to build. He loved his land, the farm, his mother and all his extended kin, and he didn't want to live in the city. He had never felt comfortable there, but couldn't explain it to himself, much less Libby.

On one of the last days in April, Arty's teacher told him to stay after school. The other children looked at him like he must have done something wrong. When they were all gone, he sat in his chair, alone in the classroom with his teacher. Several other teachers came in and looked him over from different angles, talking among themselves—some who had taught the now-suspended religion classes. Terrified, Arty didn't understand what was being said, except that he was a gentile. He knew that meant he was different. He thought they were looking at him to see if something were physically wrong with him. He was six years old, isolated in a room with powerful people and sensing that they didn't like him. They released him after a few minutes but to him it seemed like hours. He ran home and told Libby.

She listened to Arty's story and hugged him. To her he was a perfect child. "What exactly did they say to you?"

Obviously very upset, he looked up at her with eyes as blue as the clear sky, but couldn't remember anything in particular. She felt anger building inside her. Here was an intelligent little boy who deserved to go to school feeling normal and included. No teacher worth her salt would treat him that way. She felt herself losing control, wanting to march down to the school and tell them what poor examples of teachers they were, but she didn't trust herself not to make matters worse for everyone.

That evening she and Art talked, keeping their voices quiet, but Arty knew they were talking about what had happened to him. Decades later he would tell his own children that he thought the teachers had looked him over to see if he had horns—something ignorant people in other parts of the country believed Mormons had. As an adult he never forgot the sense of being isolated in a room with suspicious adults and "examined," nor the sense of unfair discrimination.

For Libby, this incident drove home what she had known all along—that she did not want her children brought up in Union. The Mormon church building was used for dances that children as young as Grace attended. Libby knew that Grace would soon be asking to go to the dances along with Mormon children and would be very unhappy when Libby forbade it. Some of Grace's classmates were already dating. Early marriages were common and looked on with approval.

"Imagine," Libby told Art one evening, "what will happen when Grace and Connie want to date and the only non-Mormon boys in the entire town are their cousins!"

"We will move, Lib." But he hadn't looked for a house in Salt Lake. He was busy winding down his classes for the school term and planting crops.

In early May school let out for the summer and the tensions in town settled down a bit. Libby felt relieved not to have to get the children dressed for school every day. The weather was ideal, everything lush and green. Art's little trees had grown bigger and were setting good fruit. More than a dozen Smith cousins roamed barefoot around the big family farms like a happy band of vagabonds. Now five years old, Donald ran with the gang. They waded in the creek and played "castle" in the large wooden piano crate behind the house. Sometimes they ate lunch at Libby's, sometimes at Sarah's, sometimes at Lizzie's, and sometimes at Allie's. Libby had time to read her books and theological journals. At the end of the day the children came home filled with stories about things they had found and seen, such as new kittens or extra large pollywogs. Connie and her favorite cousin Sarah examined the loft of the old adobe chicken house and found an ancient spinning dobbin under the dust—old Great-grandma Sarah's. They helped their father weed the straight rows in the garden. They watched him brush his work horses, soap the harnesses and hang them neatly in the barn. They brought in the rhubarb that he cut for pies—

Art's favorite. They helped him carry bags of plums to the upstairs bedroom and spread them on the floor where the sun poured in so strongly, to make prunes. On Sundays they sang lustily in their mother's Sunday School.

A family outing that summer would be long remembered. Libby and Art packed food and bedrolls in the car, which was now dubbed "Old Flivver." With Grace, Connie, Arty and Don aboard, they drove up the dirt road into the mountains—the upper reaches of Little Cottonwood Creek. Every now and then the car's engine would stall. Libby and one of the older children would immediately grab a brick, two of which were always in the car for this purpose, leap out on opposite sides of the car, and put the bricks behind the back tires to keep the car from rolling downhill while Art cranked the engine back to life. When he returned to the driver's seat and applied the brake, they hurriedly retrieved the bricks and scrambled into the car. The excited children held on tightly, half expecting the car to careen backwards down the steep mountain.

The mountain meadow beside the creek was green and inviting. The children fished with their father in what he called "the best little trout stream in the country." Soon they had a mess of trout. Libby unpacked the food while Art helped the children clean the trout. Then he fried the fish in his homegrown bacon. All savored the taste of fresh fish and bacon. Then they spread out their bedrolls. Art and Libby told stories as the family lay beneath the bright stars, Donald between his parents. The children would never forget falling asleep beside the bubbling stream. In the night Donald awoke wondering where he was. Afraid, he reached over and felt his father's arm, and knew everything was all right. Many years later he would fashion a sermon around that theme.

At daybreak Art and the boys were back at the stream catching more trout.

In September Art began his series of harvests—corn, potatoes and sugar beets. He had not searched for a house in Salt Lake, and Libby didn't press it. By then she knew she was pregnant again.

With the start of school, another problem developed for Grace. She was in the seventh grade, having turned eleven in June. Each week seventh and eighth grade students boarded the school buses to go to Salt Lake City for "temple work." Sometimes they were excused from school to be transported on these busses to be baptized for the dead—baptized in lieu of deceased people who had never joined The Church and were thus barred from heaven. Naturally Grace was never asked to go. But seeing her classmates leave on those exciting buses, she felt left out. After the trips her classmates talked about the fun they'd had. They looked forward to it all week. She felt like an outcast. On these days she would burst into the house crying and demanding of Libby, "Why can't I go to Temple with my friends? It just isn't fair! I have as much right to go as they do!"

This was not easy to explain to a girl who was at an age when being accepted by her peers meant everything. As Art and Libby discussed the situation they both understood that there was no satisfactory solution as long as they lived in Union.

Libby knew that using public school buses for religious purposes was no different than using school rooms. That summer she had followed a case aired in the *Tribune* in which a high school in the Fillmore district was accused of allowing a Mormon "seminary" on the public school grounds. Students were excused from their regular schoolwork to attend religious classes. The faculties and monies were commingled—the main issue. The school board had been directed to move the religious classes off campus and make sure the monies were separated.

Now Libby got involved in the school bus issue, but not as visibly as before. She wrote letters to her friends in the city. Several non-Mormon religious leaders took up the matter of school busses being used for Temple work. Another round of *Tribune* articles appeared. It was reported that the busing practice was widespread. Again the issue attracted attention, but this time Libby kept abreast of it without seeing her name in print.

Many responsible Mormon leaders felt that the publicity was harmful to The Church. Private transportation was substituted for school busses. But having to give up the busses increased the community's resentment toward Libby for having started the trouble in the first place.

"Art, I don't know how we can stay here any longer," she said one evening. "I'm sure we could find a good place to live in Salt Lake." Both girls had come home from school in tears, and Arty had grown oddly quiet about school. Now, with the children in bed, she and Art had been reading in the living room.

Folding the paper, he let out a long breath and said, "I guess I have to say this the best way I can."

Filling with trepidation, she waited.

"I don't really like teaching in the city. I had another discipline problem today. I guess I don't understand those city kids. They're different from farm kids. So many of them don't respect adults and don't care about math. I can't seem to make them interested in it. They aren't there to learn; they're there because their parents want them to be. I doubt if their parents have any more control over them than I do. They don't support me when I tell them about the problems their boys cause. The boy today was insolent. Like he was daring me to strike him." He looked at the dark window. "I guess I liked teaching in the rural schools, but not in the city. Not the big kids."

Libby's mind raced through the possibilities of where this was leading. She knew that by nature he was a quiet, patient person who disliked any kind of confrontation. He would go to great lengths to avoid it. She was the disciplinarian in the house. He never liked to tell anyone else what to do or what not to do, and she could well understand that just one student who enjoyed disrupting his classes could ruin his day. She also understood that too many ruined days could make anyone want to quit.

"You could be an accountant," she suggested. "There are many big companies in Salt Lake that could hire you."

"I've thought of that, but I know I couldn't stand working in the city and living there too. I need to work the land. It clears my mind. A little like prayer is for you. The farmwork helps me face the city again. I don't know what I'd do without my land, or—" his voice became almost too quiet to hear—"some other farm.

"You're not saying, are you, that you want to be a full time farmer?"

"I think I do, Lib," he said quietly, "but I know that's not what you want for me."

She swallowed the lump in her throat and with great determination held back the tears pushing to break free. "You should be teaching at the university level."

"Yes I'd like that. But I'm not eligible. I'd have to do some higher university studies, and we've already been through that. It's just too hard. I'd never see the children, and with the baby coming in March, I just don't see how I could. I wouldn't have time to work the land. And when I got through with my university work, if I ever did, I'd probably have to teach somewhere else anyway, away from my land." For a moment she thought he might weep. But he did not. Art was an orderly man with a great deal of self control.

It always came back to the land. She knew he meant it when he said he couldn't work in the city and live there too. He didn't see how he could give up his land and go on teaching, and he couldn't study and support the family at the same time. So what were they to do?

"Lib, he said, "We've got to be practical. We'll leave Union, and when we do that, the best chance I have of making a living, the way I guess I need to live, is in farming."

She took a breath. "Where?"

He pushed to his feet. "We'll have to ponder that. For now, I'm tuckered."

"But Art, we wouldn't have a regular monthly check, and with five children to feed—" She stopped, hearing the whine developing in her voice.

"Farmers grow all their own food," he reminded her. "And you know how to put up vegetables and fruit."

That was true. "Art, you go on to bed. I'll be there in a few minutes." She saw by his expression that he knew where she was going.

Closing the back door she shivered as she stepped into the moonless October night and went to her private place behind the barn. Nothing could be seen but the glittering fishnet of stars spread across the blackness above. The heavens seemed cold, yet shone as constantly here as in Scotland. She felt herself surrender her smallness before the Lord who piloted the ship of the universe, felt again the invisible bond of faith that sometimes seemed too fragile or too mysterious to depend upon, that sometimes she, with her verbal facility and force of personality, pushed away as though she could find her own way through the treacherous shoals of this life. But she was not alone. He was always waiting for her to knock on His door. She bowed her head in humility and spoke softly, praying for the wisdom and humor to face the risk of selling everything and taking five children into a new life where the family might be beggered by insect plagues or bad harvests. But the good side was that they could find a place where Mormonism was not dominant. She could actively participate in church life again. If the only way to leave Utah was to become a farmer's wife, she would do that. She had to smile at little at herself. In many ways she was already a farmer's wife. There was nothing that could be done about this but hand over her troubles to the Pilot at the helm of her ship. She settled into the peace of her faith, knowing that she would be the best mother and teacher she could be—a farmer's wife with an educated twist.

—

They agreed not to move before the baby was born. However they must move in time to plant crops and get a harvest their first year. And so it was decided. Art would finish out the school year. They would save money, look for a farm the next summer and work out the details of buying it. They would move the following spring, as soon as possible after the baby arrived.

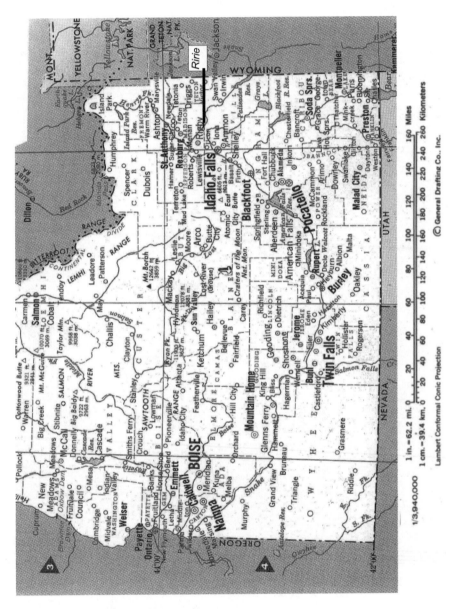

Map of southern Idaho from These United States,
published by The Reader's Digest Association, Inc., 1968

"We will go with our young and our old; we will go with our sons and daughters and with our flocks and herds..."

Exodus 10:4

13   The Exodus

Salt Lake City newspapers often carried stories about the developing farming communities in southern Idaho. It seemed to Art and Libby an ideal area to search for a farm. The first stage of the Minidoka Dam Project had been completed in 1907, making irrigation possible on thousands of acres of otherwise arid land. Now, after the sagebrush was removed, the high desert was blooming. Large numbers of farm couples from Kansas, Nebraska, and Missouri had seen the advertisements and settled in the Project area. They wanted the dependability of irrigation instead of rain. They also wanted electricity, which was not yet available in the Midwest. Some of these new settlers were homesteading farms, others buying farms that had been put into production, then sold. These people brought their churches and culture with them, and the majority were not Mormon.

Art and Libby learned more from *The Minidoka County News*, to which Art subscribed. He studied the real estate ads and notices encouraging families to buy electrical appliances and install electric lights to ensure the continuing prosperity of the Minidoka Dam power company. At last he began to feel a spark of interest in moving. They had saved enough money for a down payment, and he and Libby agreed that they must sell the Union property for working capital.

A logical thinker, Art fully understood the risk of selling his assets and investing everything in a venture that depended almost entirely upon his own physical strength. But he was quietly overcoming his worry about whether he had the endurance to farm full-time. Seeing the unremitting hard work of his father, he had planned early in life to follow his brother Hi into mathematics, and not be a farmer. So this took courage. But he had his Libby, and he trusted her instincts about the children's needs.

On March 14, six days before Libby's birthday, David Symon made his appearance—a strong and healthy baby boy with Libby's fair complexion. They named him for her beloved older brother. Fortunately Libby recovered quickly, and by the middle of June felt ready to travel. They left the girls with their Grandma Smith and the boys with Aunt Allie. Clarence drove Art, Libby and baby David to the train in Salt Lake. Faster and much more reliable than out-of-date Old Flivver, the train put them in Pocatello by evening. In the morning they boarded a connection to Shoshone, then Rupert. The real estate agent had suggested they stay at the Caledonian Hotel. That seemed a good omen—there was a street by that name near the manse in Perth. Surely, Libby thought, the owner had been a Scotsman.

In a holiday mood she walked with Art from the Rupert station to the hotel, the baby in her arms. The early afternoon air felt pleasantly warm, a few fleecy white clouds stretching across the blue sky. The little town looked new and clean. Checking into the Caledonian, they got directions to the real estate office. Libby changed into her new day-dress with the hemline partway up her calf. Like most women nowadays, she liked the freedom from long skirts.

To their pleasant surprise they discovered that instead of the usual main street, Rupert's town center was a park. One block square, it had a well kept lawn and many shade trees. Wide streets bordered the park, and stores and offices faced the "Square" from four directions, all located on the far side of the streets. Libby and Art strolled the sidewalk around this park, Art carrying the sleeping baby. Walkways angled to the center of the Square, meeting at a picturesque white bandstand.

"This speaks well for the people of the town," Libby said with a nod to the bandstand. She sensed that Art, free from his teaching duties, felt as liberated and happy as she did—a young couple on an outing with only one baby who slept most of the time. She smiled at Art and took his arm. "It looks quite civilized here."

She read the signs on the stores—grocery, hardware, clothing, sundries, candy and ice cream, a restaurant, a doctor's office, and many more. On a diagonal across from one of the park corners the marquee of the Wilson Theater displayed the title *The Lost World.* She saw a dentist's office she no longer needed, all her teeth being false now. As they crossed the street to the real estate office, they glimpsed another street radiating out from the park where new buildings were being built, but most of the business core of the town faced the park and would continue to do so for many decades to come.

They planned to spend several busy days "farm shopping." The realtor drove them around the "Project" area in his new model T Ford, one that had an electric starter and required no cranking. Unlike Old Flivver, this was not open to the air. It gave Libby the privacy she needed to nurse the baby while the man showed Art the fields. Afterward they looked at the houses. Between farms, the realtor extolled Rupert as an area with a great future and a wonderful place to raise a family.

Some of the farms had nice houses but were beyond their means. Art had impressed upon Libby the credo of the farmer—that it would be the land that paid for itself, not the house. Some farms required more down payment than they felt they could afford and still have enough money to survive the first growing season. Some were farther from town than Libby wanted to live. Art asked questions about yield, markets, water availability and cost. She asked questions about schools and churches.

June was the perfect time to shop for a farm. The crops were flourishing and irrigation water flowed in the ditches. On the second morning the realtor met them in the lobby of the Caledonian and drove them to a farm barely three miles from town. The land was bordered by a line of fine Carolina poplar trees—tall trees now intensely green, planted close together for a windbreak. An excellent stand of second cutting alfalfa was growing. The selling farmer assured Art that a third cutting before winter would bring the total alfalfa yield to over four tons per acre. That was exceptional. Art knew enough about sugar beets to see for himself that the crop in the field would likely make more than an impressive twenty-five tons per acre. In addition, a potato field thrived, and the barley was already starting to turn the golden color of ripeness. The farmer said his last year's barley crop had yielded a hundred bushels per acre. "A few acres of that will fatten a lot of hogs," he added in the flat tones of the Midwest.

They looked at the elementary school—Hopewell School, an easy walk from the farm. That was appealing, but Libby didn't like the house. She didn't see how anyone could squeeze five children and two adults into that one-bedroom place. Knowing Art could see that for himself, she kept quiet and felt a twinge of alarm at his obvious pleasure in the quality of the soil. She knew how determined he was to make a farm pay for itself.

The next day the realtor met them at the hotel again and drove them to two more farms. They took their time getting information and looking at everything, but on the way back to the hotel Art wanted to stop and see again the farm with the poplar trees. The price seemed right—$7,000 for sixty acres. They wouldn't be investing much in the house.

That evening, eating meatloaf in the restaurant across from the Square, Art explained why he wanted that farm. It boiled down to the numbers working out best.

"The house is inadequate," she said quietly, not wanting to break the spell of these happy days together.

"We'll add rooms and indoor plumbing when we see our way clear."

Despite her worry about caring for the family prior to a remodel, she had to trust his knowledge of the numbers. She reflected that it was she who had been eager to leave Utah. It was she who had gone public with her criticism of The Church and made it almost mandatory that they leave. Art had stood beside her, though it meant forfeiting much that he cherished. Now she must do her best to stand by him. With serious misgivings about what lay ahead, Libby agreed to the purchase.

She went to the restroom to nurse David while Art read the evening paper and drank another glass of lemonade. Afterwards, they stepped out into the warm evening air and heard the band playing. It was Saturday night and many families had come to picnic on the lawn of the park. The street lights around the perimeter had been turned on, though the summer twilight would linger for another hour. Adding to the festive atmosphere, the stores were all brightly lit, the doors wide open. Young women with shopping bags were going in and out of the shops. Groups of them laughed and chatted on the sidewalk. On the grass of the Square men sat holding their knees in conversational groups or lay propping their heads on their elbows, while all around them happy children jumped to the music or darted around the park. Captivated by the music and the neighborly atmosphere, Libby and Art went to a candy store and ordered ice cream cones.

Libby smiled at Art while the man scooped. "Remember, your mother wouldn't eat an ice cream cone when they first were sold?"

He chuckled. "She called it eating the ice cream and the dish too."

Strolling across the grass toward the bandstand, the baby in Art's arm, they licked their ice cream. "Remember Mom the first time we took her for a ride in the car?" Art asked, "Holding onto her hat for dear life?"

Libby laughed at the memory of Mother Smith's wide-eyed expression of terror, flattening the hat on her head as they drove down State Street at the great speed of thirty-five miles per hour.

They found places to sit in wooden folding chairs set in rows before the bandstand. The band was just beginning a spritely waltz that would have made the dourest old maid tap her toes. Libby saw Art's excitement about the farm. He sat straight in his chair, every part of him approving of the band. Some couples were dancing on the grass.

"We could dance a little," Art ventured with speculative brows raised. "Hold the baby between us?"

"You know I don't dance," she said good-naturedly. It continued to feel sinful to think of holding a man that way in public, even a husband. Understanding her meaning, Art would never ask again.

The older couple sitting next to Libby acted friendly. Libby introduced herself and learned that they were staying with their daughter's family on a nearby farm. They said the band played every Saturday night in the summer, and the stores stayed open till ten o'clock. Women did all their weekly shopping simply by walking the four blocks around the Square.

For many years to come Libby and Art and their children would look forward to summer Saturday nights in Rupert. Dad, weary from a long day in the fields, would visit with the other tired farmers who were resting in groups on the cool grass. While the women shopped, the men discussed the weather, irrigation methods, livestock, politics and all their farming concerns. Libby liked shopping in the cool of the evening, and in this way she made many friends outside her usual circles. Sometimes these sidewalk visits were quite deep and meaningful, a very satisfying experience for her. Meanwhile the children played on the grass with their friends. Sometimes by prearrangement the Smith family would join other families with their picnic baskets and share a meal topped off with a freezer of delicious homemade ice cream. The older children took turns with the cranking. The volunteer band, which often included members of the high school band, played some tunes better than others, but what they lacked in technique they made up in enthusiasm. High school kids gathered to talk and flirt and compare notes about whatever "picture show" was playing at the ever-popular Wilson theater. Saturday night would become a highlight of the week for the Smith family, and this concentration of farm families on the Square made for friendship and good neighbors, enhancing the cohesive nature of the Project community.

"Art," Libby said as they walked toward the hotel that first night, the music fading behind them, "Providence must have brought us here on a Saturday night. I'm so glad we had a chance to see this. I can't help but have doubts about the house, but now I believe this is the right place for the children. I will make do with the house." Wryly she added, "Until we can add some rooms."

He smiled down at her with his sparkling brown eyes, David asleep in his arms.

The next day they put down earnest money on a purchase contract. They made arrangements to complete the transaction and take possession early the following spring.

Back in Union there was much to do. They needed to sell their house with the proviso that they could continue living in it until March of 1925. Most of their property sold quite readily, the house and ten acres of irrigated land for $3,000. However, no one was interested in the land on the hill, which had only a high water irrigation right and would produce only one hay crop per year. Art agreed to let Clarence take it on a crop-sharing arrangement with the hope of selling it later. A few years later Clarence finally found a buyer, and Art sold it for $22.50 per acre.

To keep an income for as long as possible, Art asked his school superintendent if he could teach until mid year. The district authorities liked his work and hated to lose him. Graciously they agreed to his request to teach only half the school year. His contract terminated December 31, 1924.

One by one, the Smith clan tried to persuade Art and Libby not to go. Lucy grieved to see her Arthur planning to leave the family and the old homestead. Allie, Libby's best friend in Utah, shed tears. At a get-together to wish them farewell, the long sad lines in Clarence's face wordlessly conveyed his feelings. Only Will's wife Lorene took a different tack. She had been a good neighbor, but she and Libby were very different and had never been close. A good-hearted woman, she nonetheless had a naturally caustic tongue. She said something that Libby would long remember and remark upon in years to come.

Libby had cheerfully commented, "When we prosper on our farm and get a new car, we'll come back and see you all."

Lorene snapped, "You'll never have a two-bit car."

Libby hoped that was not prophetic. She thought it was just Lorene's awkward way of advising her not to move to Idaho. But the way the comment continued to replay in her mind, hinting of doubts about Art's farming ability and the lack of means to remodel the house, made her realize that once again she was moving into an unknown world. It frightened her more than she wanted to admit. Her up-bringing dictated that she show a happy face to the world and do her weeping alone in the night while others slept. Her intuition told her that many such nights were waiting for her in that tiny little farm-house in Rupert.

⸻

In March the weather in southern Idaho can be nasty—a cold wind hurling dust and fine sand from the newly plowed fields. Or it can be soft and gentle—shirt sleeve weather so pleasant a newcomer might think she had arrived in Paradise. The latter face of springtime greeted Libby and four of her children. Grace had stayed in Union to finish the eighth grade; she would join them in June. Art, or "Dad" as Libby and the children called him, had arrived at the farm a few days ahead of them, to get the place ready.

Libby sighed with relief as she herded the three excited children off the train at the Minidoka transfer station and carried fussy year-old David into the waiting room. A big baby, he had spent the entire trip trying to wiggle off her lap and crawl under the seats on the train. He was also teething and drooling. Meanwhile, the three other chil-dren had explored everything on the train and transfer stations. She'd hardly had time to think of what lay ahead. Connie had just turned eleven and was a big help keeping track of eight-year-old Arthur and six-year-old Donald, but sometimes couldn't control their exuberance.

While Libby sat on the oak bench humming and bouncing David on her knees, waiting for the spur line train to Rupert, the boys investigated how far the fountain in the waiting room would squirt when partially closed with a finger. She gave them a stern look and they slipped outside to explore the tracks and the switching mechanism for diverting cars off on a siding or a train off the mainline onto the spur line. Connie ran out to find them.

Libby was beginning to feel a strange mixture of exultation and apprehension. Much relieved to be leaving Utah, in later years she would refer to this day as "The Exodus." But like those involved in the original exodus she was leaving what she knew and entering a wilderness. Like them she would need to trust God and move forward by faith. If she'd had only herself to think about, she could have faced it with the same confidence and courage that had carried her through other trying experiences. But with her brood of children so young, so dependent, so trusting, the uncertainty of the days ahead filled her with anxiety. However, for their sake she hid her emotions.

She had trusted Dad's judgement about the fertility of the land and the desirable water rights. Spoiled by the nice house in Union, she nevertheless had lived in farming country long enough to know that it was up to the wife to make a home out of whatever house came with the package. Many nights since the decision to buy the farm she had lain awake rehearsing how she would fit her family into the cramped spaces.

She knew that a farm was a good place for children to live and grow, learn responsibility, and have plenty of room to play. Rupert had other advantages. Mormons did not predominate. The school was nearby. The Square would have everything she needed to buy, and Grace would attend Rupert High, by all accounts a very good school. But it was the daily caring for the family that continued to bother her—pumping water by hand, washing diapers and clothes every day, heating the wash water, bathing the children, and expecting them to sleep in the living room and kitchen. And once again, with her Victorian sensibilities, she would be using a primitive outhouse. Located rather far from the house, this one would present a difficult challenge for little children, particularly in winter.

Here in Rupert there would be no helpful Grandma, no friendly sister-in-laws down the street who were willing to watch the children and help in many ways, no host of cousins for the children to play with, no Alice to come in case of emergency. Alice, who had advised them not to move away from "civilization," couldn't be expected to leave John and join them in a dwelling that could hardly house its principal occupants. Dad would be busy tending the crops so they could make the mortgage payment in the fall. He couldn't be expected to drop everything and help with things that other farm women did by themselves. What would she do if one of her children became gravely ill? Or if Art seriously injured himself?

Perhaps it was fortunate that she had so little time to brood over it. She told herself she would simply handle situations and solve problems as they presented themselves.

The little "town" of Minidoka was nothing more than a service point where a branch line left the main line of the Union Pacific Railroad to serve the rich farmlands along the Snake River—the so-called Magic Valley. With a whistle and a lot of clanging, an odd little engine-car combination—more trolly than train—hissed to a stop. Libby carried David to the track, where the boys were jumping up and down, Connie making corralling motions with her arms to keep them from scrambling on the train before they were told to do so. The engineer signaled Libby, and in a frenzy of movement everyone was in the car, the boys exploring this latest conveyance. The little engine car would carry them the twelve miles to their destination at Rupert, after which it continued on a branch line that ran quite near the farm. For years to come it would be a familiar sight as it passed the farm each day, whistling and chugging. For some strange reason that was never explained, it earned the name of Ping Pong.

Libby watched the passing farms, relieved that David seemed to be falling asleep. She wondered how Dad had fared on his trip to Rupert. His telegram had informed her that he had arrived several days earlier, but had he encountered any trouble? With all their worldly goods he had made the trip inside an "emigrant car." Many such cars were in use at that time—a boxcar leased by the railroad to a family moving all its livestock and furnishings. The car was switched off on a siding where the traveler could have a few days to make modifications inside, such as temporary stalls for the livestock. Dad had built the pens and stalls for his horses, cows, chickens and pigs. He loaded his big farm wagon, his tack, implements and tools, the piano, the household furniture and the many boxes of linens, books and clothing. He also made up a bed to sleep in. Thousands of families who settled the West after the building of railroads had traveled in this pattern—women and children following behind a husband and father who had traveled with the goods and animals.

Later Libby and the children would hear fascinating stories about Dad's trip. It had been a trying experience shut in the dark box car. The two nights were cold. He could have ridden in the caboose, but few men did because, like him, they didn't want to leave their animals unattended. Boxcars on freight trains were not treated as gently as passenger cars. As freightcars were coupled to a train or put off on a siding, and as the train stopped or started, there was a great deal of jolting and bumping. Animals in such strange surroundings sometimes panicked. Dad had not expected it to be quite as bad. He described for the children the way his team, faithful Bess and Doll, had trembled in their stalls as they anticipated the shock of cars being coupled and uncoupled. Heavy furniture and farm machinery could shift in dangerous ways. It was like living through a continuous earthquake—mild most of the time and then a period of violent shaking.

Fortunately, Dad, being a careful, methodical man, had loaded the car with great care, tying down the piano and other heavy items. The load traveled well. The chickens continued to lay eggs and Old Mustard continued to give milk, which Dad had given to hobos who were always present on freight trains. During long periods when his car had been parked on a siding he had enjoyed good visits with the hobos, who were grateful for the eggs and milk. Young Arthur listened spellbound to these stories of life on a freight train.

Now the yellow passenger depot next to the larger freight depot became visible out the window. Dad stood beside the track, smiling and waving. Shouts of joy went up from the children, who had been watching. The moment the door opened Connie, Arty, and Donald jumped off the engine-car and rushed to greet their father. With the exuberance of the children, Libby could barely speak to Art.

One more link remained to complete the journey to the farm. For the children it was just one more exciting adventure, but it caused Libby to silently pray that this was not a preview of her new circumstances. The team and wagon would be the family's only transportation for the next two months because Dad had left Old Flivver in Union. When Grace finished school at the end of May, he would return by train and drive her to Rupert in the car.

Dad had parked his farm wagon near the freight depot with Bess and Doll, his span of horses, tied at the hitching rail. The wagon was equipped with a unique box called a "beet dump." Raised above the wagonbed, it was a high platform designed to haul a load of sugar beets from the field to the railroad. Its sides could contain a load of beets, then be let down on either side to allow a hoisting device to dump the beets onto the conveyer belt and drop them into a waiting rail car. The children were familiar with the wagon and delighted at the prospect of riding in it. Dad had securely tied a kitchen chair for Libby in the center of the beet dump. Newly purchased sacks of seed wheat made comfortable seats for the children. A number of Rupert citizens watched curiously, some from nice motor cars, as Libby climbed awkwardly into the wagon and sat on her chair in the beet dump. Perhaps the lines of Robert Burns occurred to her, lines she often quoted:

> O wad some Power the giftie gie us
> To see oursels as ithers see us!

As Dad set the horses into motion, she felt deeply humiliated but refused to allow it to show. Much to the delight of the children, Dad stopped at the railroad livestock yard where he had arranged temporary care for the cows that had made the trip from Utah. He tied the two gentle cows to the back of the wagon where they would follow along to their new home, dropping occasional cow pies. One of the cows was presently milking and would provide the family with milk. Her odd yellow color had inspired the name Old Mustard, after an ox in a story the children had been reading about the Old Oregon Trail. The ox, the hero of the story, alerted the pioneers to a surprise Indian attack before the attackers closed in on the wagons, thus saving the lives of all the party. The other cow, a younger animal, had not yet calved. Dad simply referred to her as "the heifer."

As the wagon creaked slowly up the road, Libby's straight-backed chair affixed squarely in the middle of the raised platform suddenly gave her an idea. Sitting proudly as though on a throne, head held high, she announced to the children, "I am Queen Victoria. This is my royal coach drawn by six white horses. You are the princes and princess, and we are driving through the streets of London being admired by all my loyal subjects." The children were delighted.

As they drove out of town a number of cows in a roadside pasture came running, as cows often do, to check out the strange cows behind the wagon. The curious cows crowded against the fence, mooing, pushing and shoving each other. With a sweep of her hand, Libby said, "See, the roadway is lined with our loyal subjects, cheering their beloved Queen. Your father, on that fine elevated seat, is my faithful coachman. See how well he handles the prancing steeds." Gesturing proudly toward Old Mustard and the heifer, she said, "Here is my royal guard, mounted on their chargers."

The children cheered as the farm wagon creaked up the dirt road, followed by what Libby normally called "the faithful beasts." Never in her life had she felt less like a queen, but the children never suspected. For many decades they would tell the story of their ride with Queen Victoria.

As the wagon neared the farm, young Arthur jumped up with delight, pointing and crying out, "There's a bunny rabbit!" Everything seemed wonderful to him in this enchanted new place.

Dad called over his shoulder, "You'll be seeing plenty of those. Rabbits are a nuisance here. They eat the crops. The young cottontails are good and tender, but the jackrabbits aren't nearly as tasty. But I don't think we'll be eating rabbits. We'll have plenty of good pork and beef and chicken." He didn't know that his sons would later participate in jackrabbit drives, and Donald would raise rabbits for food.

Driving into the yard, Dad stopped the team near the back of the house. As the excited children jumped down, he helped Libby and the baby from the wagon. Quickly setting the baggage down, he drove the short distance to the barn and stopped to put up his horses and introduce the cows to their new home. By then Arthur and Donald had tried out the long-handled pump on a cement slab near the back door. They then ran inside the house to explore with Connie.

Dad had placed all the furniture that would fit in the little house. What didn't fit he stored in a small shed behind the house—soon to be called the "annex." The annex had been built over a root cellar, which, like a Midwestern tornado shelter, was entered by a very heavy door that sloped upward from ground level. When that door was lifted, a person could go down the concrete steps to the dirt cellar. The first owner, who had developed the homestead only a few years before, had probably distrusted the reports that there were no tornadoes in Idaho. The annex itself was entered by a conventional door, with three steps up from the ground.

Much heavier than needed, the door to the cellar would be lifted very often, since many food items were stored in the cellar. It was a struggle for the children to lift that door, which soon came to be known—and would henceforth always be called—Portcullis. Libby named it for the heavy gates of wood and iron with sharp teeth on the bottom that were lowered with chains and used to bar the entrances to Scottish and English castles. The cellar, cool in summer and frost-free in winter, stored fruit, vegetables, canned goods, milk and butter at a time when there was no refrigeration. It was constantly in use, and "raising Portcullis" would contribute to the building of muscled young bodies. Connie and Arthur were proud of being able to lift it; Donald would need help for the first year but saw it as a challenge.

Dad had worked long hours getting the place ready for the family, repairing fences to contain the cows and pigs, and starting the spring farm work. He knew it was imperative to make a good harvest so he could meet the mortgage payment—due annually in October. He had no financial reserves. One summer without a good crop would mean losing the farm, a threat that would hang over them for years like the sword that hung over the head of Damocles as he sat at and tried to enjoy the King's banquet. That great sword was supported only by a hair. As they tended their crops in the summer the Payment would never be far from their thoughts.

Now Dad brought in a bucket of milk from Old Mustard and built up the fire in the coal-burning range. Since it was only mid-afternoon, he went to the field to get more plowing done. Many of the neighbors had already planted their sugar beets. With a price guaranteed by the sugar company, for many years beets would prove to be their most dependable cash crop.

Libby and the children turned to the task of putting the house in order. The davenport in the living room would serve as a couch in the daytime and unfold into a double bed where the boys would sleep at night. The baby's crib stood in the small bedroom beside the double bed where Dad and Libby would sleep. A simple curtain served as their bedroom door. Libby and Dad would need to walk through the living room to get to the kitchen. The house had only those three rooms.

Since arriving at the farm, Dad had been sleeping on a metal cot placed in the kitchen. Now Connie would sleep there. In addition to that bed, the crowded kitchen contained a sideboard and cupboard, boxes of pots and pans, the kitchen range that Dad had brought from Union with the coal bucket beside it, and a table with six chairs. In the daytime the cot would serve as additional seating and a place for Dad to rest when he came in tired from the field. Connie, having reached the age where she felt modest in front of the boys, realized she would have no privacy. She was accustomed to sharing a private room with Grace. But now she would sleep where the family meals were eaten and the stove drew everyone to the kitchen to get warm in the mornings and evenings. In addition, much of the family living and visiting was done in the kitchen. Being a good-natured child, Connie made the most of it, keeping her clothes in boxes under the cot.

Libby prepared supper from the supplies Dad had laid in: eggs, milk, sugar, potatoes, and hamburger just purchased from the Rupert butcher. Fortunately familiar with the stove, she knew how to get the best performance from the dampers and drafts, and knew how to get the oven heated evenly. Whipping several eggs in her pottery bowl, she added sugar and cream, then put the custard into the oven—a favorite treat for the children. Cooking would not be a problem, but keeping the family properly dressed would be. There was only one small closet in the house and little space for dressers with drawers. Clothes would have to be kept in boxes. Libby would learn that the continuing organization of personal items for all the children was virtually impossible.

The electric washing machine had come with Art from Utah, but all water had to be pumped and carried inside to be heated on the range in a boiler—an oval ten-gallon vessel with a handle on either end so it could be carried by two people. To keep faces and hands washed, Libby tried to keep water heating on the range at all times, so the family could dip out hot water as needed. In winter, when it was brutally cold on the screened back porch, they would push the washer into the kitchen and squeeze it between everything else.

Once again, bathing would be primitive—in a large round wash-tub in the kitchen, close to the stove in cold weather. As in Union, baths were taken on Saturday night. In the summer the family would bathe before going to the Square. Libby would bathe first, then join the rest of the family in the living room while Dad bathed. Grace, when she joined them, came next, then Connie and so forth. To reduce the amount of water to be pumped and carried, two or more children bathed in the same water, adding a little more hot water between baths. If the tub became too full, the excess was dipped out with a bucket. After the last person finished, the water was dipped out until the tub was light enough to carry. The climate was dry, the soil porous, so waste water was simply thrown onto the dirt of the back yard, or, in summer, on the flower bed that Dad tended near the house, where it was difficult to run irrigation water.

Libby couldn't help but recall the hot water piped from the tank behind the kitchen range in Union, indeed the Perth manse a quarter of a century ago. Her parents had been very proud of that modern convenience, but Libby had taken it for granted. Just as she had taken for granted the indoor flush toilet. Now, as though to ridicule her 1918 surge of ecstasy over world progress, an outhouse stood in the orchard.

"At least it will be fragrant in apple blossom time," she quipped. Retold over the years, this comment would bring many smiles, but no one smiled when the wind blew and temperatures dropped below freezing. She had returned to a situation as primitive as Yost, but though some things appeared to be stalled in their march toward "getting better and better," she firmly guided her children toward the highest educational and moral standards.

On Sunday morning she sat at the piano and led the family in their favorite hymns. Art was resting for a time before going out to plow.

"I thought we would go to church on Sunday," Connie said. "I want to meet some new friends. Why don't we go?"

Art and Libby exchanged a glance, then Libby said firmly, "We will not go to church in a farmwagon."

"But you can be Queen Victoria," Donald offered, trying to be helpful.

She gave him a look that ended the discussion. Much as she yearned to find a church home and worship with like-minded people, Libby would wait until June, when Art brought the car from Utah.

On the farm, many situations that meant a great deal of very hard work for Libby were viewed by the children as new adventures—though the novelty of working the pump soon wore off, especially on wash days. Arty was big and strong for his age and proved a great help with the pumping and carrying of water. Very soon he also relieved Dad of the chore of milking the cow. In turn, Arty taught Donald to milk and pressed him into being an assistant milker. Very wisely, Libby never learned to milk a cow. Remembering the Scottish jokes about milkmaids, she drew the line at turning herself into one. Connie was excellent help with household chores, Donald eager to help wherever his six year old muscles could handle a job. Soon the family settled into something of a routine.

Overwhelmed with plowing and planting, Dad had to leave almost everything else to Libby. Much of the heavy farm work required a three-horse hitch, so he bought an additional work horse named Dick, and soon after that another horse named Bally. He used the three-horse hitch for plowing, and with four horses, each one got a regular day off. This helped them stay in good condition. Physically Dad's work was much more demanding than schoolteaching and farming on the side. He worked as long as daylight allowed, and, for the first time in his life, had no father, brothers and brothers-in-law working nearby to assist when harnesses snarled or horses balked. Single-fur-row plowing was grindingly slow, hard work. On some spring days a bitterly cold wind blew. Riding the plow hour after hour in his schoolteacher's coat left him chilled to the bone. But with so much to be done to get the crops planted, he hated to take time off to go to the house and warm himself. He had not yet invested in a fleece lined work coat worn by most farmers. Often he came in at night too tired to be sociable and too weary to listen to the children as they clamored to tell him of their day's experiences. Libby, too, was working harder than she had ever done before. By the time the last child was asleep she and Dad could hardly speak to each other.

On the first Monday after their arrival in Rupert, Libby walked with the children to Hopewell School, pushing David in the baby carriage. She enjoyed the half-mile walk down the tree-lined dirt lane—a pleasant break from her work—and reflected on the orderliness of the layout of the farms and schools. The Project area had been surveyed and laid out in mile sections with eight farms in each section so that each school served thirty-two farms. The schools stood at the junctions where the four sections met, so no child had to walk more than two miles. The Smith farm was the third farm from the school, the house on the side of the farm nearest the school. Without hurrying, Connie and Arty had about a fifteen minute walk.

The school had two rooms, with thirty children in the lower four grades and twenty-six in the upper four. The teachers seemed to be bright women. After enrolling Connie and Arty, Libby headed back toward the farm with Donald—David enjoying the bumpy ride in his carriage. With a twinge of envy she had seen that both teachers wore wedding rings. They didn't spend their days keeping a toddler away from the stove or stopping him from eating everything he found on the floor, while at the same time trying to cook and wash diapers and work clothes. Much as she loved her husband and children, she found herself wishing for a servant girl to do the work at home while she taught in the school—work that she loved.

Donald was troubled about a different matter. The busy school had looked interesting. "Why can't I go to school with Connie and Arty?" he asked.

Libby patiently explained. "In Utah you had to be six years old by the 15th of September to start school. You were still five."

This was a totally unsatisfactory answer for the practical-minded Donald, who had turned six in October. "But I am six years old now. And this is a different school. It isn't fair that Connie and Arty can go and I can't. It just isn't fair!"

All Libby's explaining failed to persuade him. At home he missed the older children terribly, and now his mother had so much work caring for a baby who had reached what Libby called the "suicide age," that she hardly had any time to visit with him. Donald spent a few days exploring the farm from one end to the other.

Feeling very lonely and left out of the family's activities, he decided to take the matter into his own hands. "I'm going to the school so I can walk home with Connie and Arty," he announced to Libby.

She saw no harm in it. She had worried about him wandering around the farm by himself, possibly getting in the way of Dad's farming operations. She was too busy to notice that he was leaving a little earlier each day. He would arrive before school was out and sit forlornly on the front step. One day he got there before the last recess.

The teacher noticed. "Aren't you one of the Smith children?"

"Yes."

"How old are you?"

"Six."

"Why are you wasting your time out here on the steps? Why aren't you in school?"

"They won't let me in."

"That's ridiculous! You come on in here and we'll talk about it."

By the time the recess was over, Donald was enrolled in the first grade and introduced to the class as a new student. Mrs. Snyder, an excellent teacher and herself an understanding mother, called on the Smiths that very evening and the whole matter was properly resolved.

Donald had learned his letters at home from his older siblings, was reading a little, and spoke without the "aints" and "I seen yous" that rural elementary teachers spent so much time trying to eradicate. She thought he would fit right into her class. That was the end of March.

Libby felt pleased and relieved to have him safely off to school each morning with the older children.

By mid May when school was dismissed for the summer, Donald was promoted to the second grade and was in love with Mrs. Snyder as only a first grader can love a teacher. He would always remember her as one of the best teachers he was privileged to know in the entire nineteen years of his academic life.

Art and Libby were both well pleased with Hopewell School—a bright spot in their arduous new life. The teachers and the community support for the school were excellent. The school served as a center for community life. The local Grange, which they soon joined, met in a large upstairs room above the classrooms. While many Mormons lived in Minidoka County and had a church in Rupert, they did not join the Grange and were far from a majority in the community. Never feeling like outsiders, the children became very involved in school activities.

By moving to Idaho, Art and Libby had achieved their primary goal: a better school environment for their children. The parents were paying the price in much harder work and much less financial security, but soon they would discover a more pleasant and satisfying social life for themselves as well.

Grace, however, would take a different view.

Pharaoh's dream interpreted by Joseph: "The fat cows are the good abundant years that will soon be eaten up by the starving cows, the lean and hungry years."

Genesis 41:26-32

14 Rupert

In late May, 1925, Grace graduated from the eighth grade and was recognized for having achieved the best academic record in the class. Knowing he couldn't let her be the only graduate without a parent at the ceremony, Dad made a special effort to attend. He planned the trip so that he would be away from the farm the least time possible and be back for the critical first cutting of alfalfa. He arrived in time for the evening graduation ceremony. The next day he left with Grace. Fortunately Old Flivver didn't break down. Dad didn't regret the little time spent with his Utah family. Until he felt more secure in his new venture, he didn't like responding to their questions.

On the long drive home there was plenty of time to visit with Grace. He had been so busy the past year that he had not had time to pay much attention to what was happening in Union. Hearing her tell about the wonderful time she'd had doing things with her girl cousins, he realized that this was no longer his little girl. Though she was only twelve years old, she would enter Rupert High School in the fall, and she talked and thought like an independent young lady. She made it plain that she didn't look forward to living on the farm.

"It's unfair that I have to leave all my cousins, and Grandma," she grumbled.

Dad tried to describe their new life in positive terms, but he sensed a new hostility in his eldest daughter. He told her she would not need to sleep in the kitchen as Connie was doing. He described the annex and explained that it was being cleaned up and made into sleeping quarters. "Of course, with no way of heating it, when the weather turns cold you and Connie will have to spend most of your waking time in the house."

"You mean I will have to sleep in a room with Connie! At Grandma's place I had my own room."

"Yes you and Connie will share a room like you did in Union, and we expect that you will help with some of the chores, like running the cream separator and feeding the pigs. We all need to help on the farm."

"I might run the cream separator but I sure don't plan to feed pigs or milk any dirty old cows."

Dad felt a growing irritation bordering on anger, but he was not one to show anger. He was a peace maker, one who wondered whether his deep and abiding avoidance of confrontation would plague his role as a father as it had marred his high school teaching career. He had been able to quit teaching, but he couldn't quit being a father. Grace would turn thirteen in a a little over a week. Would he fail as a father of young teenagers? And how would Libby, who had excelled as a teacher of first and second graders, cope with Grace now?

"You won't have to milk cows," he told her. "The boys do that. But we all have to work hard together, to pay for the farm."

Grace did have a great respect for Dad. She was not about to talk back to him, but wanted to say, "It sure wasn't my idea to buy that dumb old farm. We were all getting along just fine in Union." They rode in silence for a time until Dad, wanting to continue the visit on a happier note, returned to the subject of Grandma.

Grace brightened and began telling of all the nice things Grandma had done for her and the good times she'd had, especially with cousin Donna, Allie's oldest daughter, and Amy and Alice, daughters of Aunt Lizzie. She didn't mention that they had introduced her to the fine dances that were a regular part of Mormon family entertainment. These were good clean dances sponsored by The Church and attended by entire families. Grandma Smith had seen no harm in them nor had Allie and Lizzie. Grace didn't think Dad would disapprove—she'd heard stories of his attending such dances when he was young—but she was certain her mother would.

Correctly sensing the start of a stormy chapter in his life, Dad felt apprehensive as he approached the farm. He loved his children and wanted them to love him and respect his decisions. Did their growing up mean that would end?

After the long separation Libby and the four children warmly welcomed Grace. Grace pitched in and helped Connie move her things into the annex, but Connie confided to Libby that something had changed. Grace didn't act like Connie was her good buddy any more, but just a little sister. Libby loved Grace passionately and was extremely proud of her academic ability, her fine soprano voice, and her progress on the piano, but she too felt a difference in their relationship. She realized it might have been developing the previous year when Libby had been so involved with her differences with The Church, the new baby, and the problems of moving to Idaho that she had failed to notice. But now as Grace looked around her new home with obvious displeasure, complaining about the loss of her cousin chums, the change in their relationship was painfully noticeable. Libby sensed in her daughter a restrained hostility, a coolness, and an unwillingness to share her thoughts. Libby found she couldn't talk to her without making it worse, and it deeply troubled her.

When she got a rare moment to talk to Dad, he simply said, "I know. I felt it on the trip home. I don't know what we can do about it."

Grace did try, reluctantly, to fit into the family schedule. She learned to operate the cream separator that stood on the back porch beside the washing machine. It took a lot of vigorous turning of the handle at a certain speed, but she was strong and could handle it. It also required a good deal of careful washing of all the separate parts. She did that without complaint, often keeping her mind off the work by singing. She carried the skim milk out to the pigs as instructed but showed no interest in them, unlike Connie and the boys who had named all the adult pigs and enjoyed watching the baby pigs at play. Dad gave each of the older children a pig of their own to care for and to sell for personal spending money. As instructed, Grace fed her pig each day, but for some reason it died. The other children, in telling of the incident, said that she had gone on feeding her pig. Only on the third day did she notice that the food was heaping in the trough and her pig was lying in the far corner of its pen, four feet in the air.

She claimed it wasn't that bad, really. "Why should I have to look at a dumb pig every time I feed it? I have better things to think about than a dirty old pig that dies for no good reason."

She did do her share of the household chores and helped some with the garden, but always in a detached manner.

In mid summer a family crisis developed when a cow bloated; it was in danger of dying. The children watched Dad run for the bicarbonate of soda to mix in a bucket—a well established remedy. To give the cow a liberal amount of the solution, he needed a long necked bottle that he could force into the side of the cow's mouth. The only one was in the cellar.

Excited and in a hurry, he said, "Grace, go get that bottle." It came out in a tone of voice that sounded like an order.

She ran to raise Portcullis. Unfortunately, at that time of year about a foot of cold irrigation water stood in the cellar. Grace had to pull off her shoes and socks, and wade in on a packed earthen floor that was now slick and slimy. She got the bottle, but with the possibility of "creepy crawly" things in the cellar, she found it a horrifying experience. The more she thought about it the more she felt she had been insulted and abused. It was an errand that Connie or Arthur might have done without a second thought, but somehow it fed her feeling of having been victimized by the move to the farm. It insulted her sense of being a lady. In later disputes she began referring to it as an example of her dislike for the farm. Dad never said anything in response, but thought, "How I wish I had sent one of the other kids!"

Another problem developed. Emmer Bowman, the next farmer up the road from the Smiths, had a fine barn with a large hayloft. In the spring and most of the summer the hayloft was empty. Emmer loved music and dancing. He played the piano by ear, mostly simple cords, and had a number of relatives in the area who played various instruments. They formed a little band that sometimes played for dances, so it was natural for Emmer to hold dances in his own hayloft. In May, June and July his band played every Saturday night, and many people attended these dances. The large door in the end of Emmer's loft, nearest to the Smith farm, was open for ventilation. So were the windows of the Smith house. Thus on many nights the toe-tapping music sounded almost as clearly in the Smith home as in the barn, and it continued long after the Smiths returned from the Square.

There were rumors about drinking, though Mrs. Bowman would never have condoned it. The rumors were never proved, but the Bowmans probably would have found it impossible to keep some men from slipping into the darkness of a stall in the barn, below the loft, and passing a flask.

One Saturday as they were planning to go to the Square, Grace said, "Mom, I'm going to the Bowman's dance tonight instead."

"Certainly not!" Libby said in a horrified tone that she later wished she had moderated. With her upbringing, such forms of entertainment could not be tolerated.

Grace retorted, "Grandma let me go to the dances with Donna, Alice and Amy. That didn't hurt me one bit and I don't see any reason I can't go to our neighbor's dance!"

Libby spent some time in a shocked silence, sorry she had allowed Grace to stay in Union. Then her anger flared. She leveled her gaze at her daughter and spoke in a firm, deliberate voice not unlike one her own mother would have used. "You will not go to any dance as long as you live in this house."

Grace envisioned what seemed a lifetime of unjust imprisonment. But she was a fighter and her face showed it. "Why not?"

In her agitated state Libby couldn't begin to explain something that ran so deep and defined her very identity. What came out sounded insubstantial even to her, colored by anger. "It's for your own good. How could I hold my head up in church if people saw my thirteen-year-old daughter at a dance?"

"What do I care if you can't hold your head up! That's stupid."

"You're not going to that dance and that's final!"

The only good thing about this exchange was that it happened when none of the other children was present. Knowing she had precluded reasoned discussion, Libby went out behind the haystack, where she wept and prayed for guidance. *I just can't understand that child. How does one raise children in this country?* It seemed to her that Grace lacked the respect and restraint that Libby had shown her parents. She had expected to receive that respect from her daughter, particularly when the restrictions her children lived with were far less than what she and her siblings had experienced. Where had she gone wrong? What could she do to restore the respect and love Grace had shown her only a short time ago? She would try, but the rift never completely healed. Well into her eighties Grace would recall what her mother said about holding her head up in church and feel again the sense of being wronged. The restrained hostility continued in the house, and Libby's inability to cut through it pushed her away from this daughter in whom she took so much pride and loved so very much.

Years later, Connie would fare better. Also a pretty, vivacious girl, Connie was popular in her school activities. In high school she became president of the Girls Home Economics Club and was therefore responsible for planning a school dance with the boy who was president of the Boy's Agricultural Club. Together they worked out the details of decorations and refreshments. When Connie explained this, Libby responded in the kind and reasonable tone that she had been rehearsing in her mind for just such an occasion. "I'm sorry, but it won't be possible for you to attend."

Connie, who was over two years older than Grace had been during their first clash over dancing, spoke in a rational and adult way, which was characteristic of her. "Mom, it would be very irresponsible of me not to be there. I must see that everything goes well and the chaperones are all present. I can't let my club down. This is my job. People are depending on me. I know you want me to behave in a responsible manner."

The conversation continued and Libby finally relented, allowing Connie to go to the dance. However she couldn't help but add, "But it breaks my heart." It also broke her heart that Grace had distanced herself from the family. Libby doubted whether she could bear to lose Connie in that way.

After that, Connie went to many dances, and so did all the boys in their turn. Though she continued to disapprove, Libby gradually came to understand that dances were an important part of American social life and that prohibiting her children from attending was probably an unnecessary hardship on them. Grace had been the intrepid pioneer.

—

Until Dad brought the car from Union, Libby had stayed at home. She hadn't even gone with the family to the Square on Saturday nights for much needed shopping trips. But the summer of 1925 brought a new life that made her believe the move to Idaho had been very good, indeed, for the family.

On the first Sunday after Grace and the car arrived, Libby dressed the children in their Sunday best to go to church. There was no Presbyterian Church in Rupert, so they visited the Rupert Methodist Church, not far from the Square. By now Libby knew this was a very active church, well attended and very friendly. They arrived before nine o'clock and learned that there were Sunday School classes for men and women and all ages of children. Art went to the men's class, the children to all the appropriate rooms, David to the nursery, and Libby to the women's class.

"How did you like it," Libby asked Dad when the family reunited at the entrance to the sanctuary.

"I enjoyed it," he said, smiling at her.

This pleased her as much as his comment long ago in Brigham City. She had been praying for a friendly church where he would feel at home. The children too were in good spirits, and she and Dad led them down the aisle to a pew about a third of the way from the front. The choir was robust and skilled, and the pastor delivered an interesting sermon.

On the way home Dad spoke well of the sermon and the friendly church atmosphere. Delighted, Libby asked for details about the men's class. In an animated way Dad told how he had found himself one of the major participants in a discussion about the Scopes trial, a major news item that summer. The men discussed whether public school teachers should be allowed to teach the theory of evolution. Art had a good knowledge of the Bible, gained from reading to his Grandmother, a good education, and a logical mind that respected scientific inquiry. He also had a quiet, personal respect for the wonders and workings of the natural world. The men in the class had obviously appreciated hearing why he thought the evolution of so many life forms was all the more wonderful for unfolding over a long time, and why he felt it was important to share Darwin's thinking with children in school. Some may have disagreed with him, but he had their respect. It was a new experience for him to be sharing such ideas with a group of men. He truly enjoyed it.

Libby felt the women's class had been a bit mundane, but she knew she could overcome that by attending regularly. Even Grace, who had been less than enthusiastic about going to church, mentioned meeting some girls she liked. Arthur, Donald and Connie also liked their classes and looked forward to going next Sunday. They had sung some of the songs that Libby had taught them at her Sunday

School in Union.

Hearing all the good comments, Libby silently said a prayer of thanks. If she had found a church home for her family, the move from Utah would have been well worth all the pain and struggle it had cost. And it wasn't lost on her that the Methodists had taught old Grandma Sarah to read the Bible. Maybe events were somehow coming full circle.

Most of the members of the Rupert Methodist Church were farmers, but a number of them were business people. The Sunday School superintendent owned a company that operated the grain elevator and was the major grain buyer for the farmers in the Project. Two doctors, a father and son, were active members, and the husband and wife who owned the Caledonian Hotel. They had been in the men's and women's classes that first Sunday morning. These rather well-to-do hotel owners would become friends of the Smiths.

After that, the Saturday night baths were more on schedule. And Libby saw to it that the Sunday morning preparation for church was done promptly and that everyone looked presentable. Tardiness was not tolerated. Having had her hair "bobbed" to the nape of her neck in the fashion of the Twenties, she spent less time on her own appearance. She felt freer and cooler, and never allowed it to grow out again, although the sight of those long tresses on the floor with the last remnants of her golden brown hair gave her a pang of sorrow. Now, with the exception of a streak on top, she was snow white—prematurely white like some of her forbearers.

The family never missed a Sunday in church. The pastor made an evening visit at the farm. Knowing the Smiths, he brought his wife and three children. One was a girl who would be starting high school in the fall, as would Grace. Libby was glad to see that the two girls enjoyed each other's company. All the children had a good time, and with their parents having a fine visit, were allowed to play outdoors until it was dark on a very long summer evening. When it was time to go, the preacher's kids didn't want to leave.

"I wish we could live on a farm," said a child about Connie's age. "Me too," the others added.

Later, Libby asked Grace, "Did you hear them say that?"

Her comment: "That was stupid."

On the next visit the pastor discussed church membership. He stated that since the family had all been baptized he could simply receive them all into the church as a family. Without hesitation, Dad replied. "I'm sure we will all be proud to be members of your church." Libby was elated.

The pastor said he would write Dr. Paden at the First Presbyterian Church of Salt Lake for a letter of transfer for Libby. When Dad mentioned that he was not a member there, the pastor said: "We'll just receive you on profession of faith. Dad never bothered to mention that, as a child, he had been baptized in the Reorganized Church of Jesus Christ of Latter Day Saints. Years later Donald, as he was being ordained as a Methodist minister, reflected on the interesting fact that he had become a church member without ever having professed a belief in anything except the wisdom of his parents.

Becoming members of the Methodist Church opened channels of social life that the family had never enjoyed before. Church families made a practice of entertaining one another in their homes for a home-cooked supper and an evening together. Children would play outside in summer and enjoy indoor board games in winter. The adults discussed religion, politics, economic concerns and farming—Libby happily leading the conversation on religion and politics. She and Art both relished these visits and realized how starved they had been for adult friendship and conversation.

The active boys gave Libby some concern. On one occasion they were walking barefoot along some narrow branches of a tree, pretending to be circus performers on tight ropes, when Arty slipped and landed on the rusty tines of a rake in the grass below. When he lifted his foot the rake came with it. Donald shimmied down the tree to look. One tine had passed all the way through the foot and stuck out the top, another passed through the fleshy side of the foot. Like the Spartans of old, whom Arty very much admired, he clenched his teeth but made no sound. Donald stood on the rake handle and pulled his brother's foot free. This time the boys decided that medical attention might be called for. Relieved that no more serious injury had occurred, Libby soaked Arty's foot in a pan of hot water with Epsom salts. The foot healed without incident. Hot salty water was her effective remedy for all puncture wounds and infections on the limbs. Aspirin for headaches and fevers, Noxema for itches and rashes, and a dark elixir called Syrup of Figs for constipation completed her medicine chest.

Grace began to make friends. Her preference was for girls who lived in town, but she found one or two among the farm girls who shared her dream of moving to a city. They talked about the entertainments they would attend and how they would dance the Charleston all night—a passion of "the roaring Twenties."

Grace became an eager participant in the church's youth group. Here she could mingle with older, "more sophisticated" girls and boys. Her intelligence and verbal facility belied her actual age. She would never be reconciled with living on the farm, but Libby rejoiced in seeing how these outside contacts helped diffuse Grace's resentment about being forced to leave Union.

There were no school busses at that time. Grade school children walked to their schools. Older students either walked to the high school—two blocks from the Square—or managed as best they could. Many were driving trucks and cars by the time they entered high school; farm boys drove from the time they could see over the steering wheel. Driver's licenses were not required. Parents judged their child's ability and trustworthiness. Most kids arranged car pools, usually with boys driving, but Art and Libby didn't feel that they knew any of the neighbors well enough to make such an arrangement for Grace.

To Grace's joy, Libby arranged for her to board in town with Mrs. Gooch, a woman whose own children were grown. Grace was active in the church youth group and often stayed in town after the morning church service on Sunday so she could be a part the evening activities. Then she would remain in town for school Monday morning. From her point of view, the longer she was away from the farm, the better. Dad would pick her up on Friday, sometimes late in the evening when she had a Friday evening school activity, and often the family saw her only on Saturday. Libby worried about Grace being so young and so much on her own, though Mrs. Gooch was a good housemother. But this worry was offset by the easing of tensions in the house and the fact that Grace had found friends who were active in the church. Grace's being in town made it possible for her to practice with other young people who sang duets or trios in church on Sunday, which always gave Libby a surge of pleasure and pride.

But she also grieved. Grace was rapidly cutting her ties with the family. And in her grieving, Libby had to admit to herself that she would not have freely chosen to live on the farm either. In Grace she saw something of her earlier self, transformed by youthfulness and a certain American brashness. God certainly did move in mysterious ways to teach his lessons.

—

The Grange was another bright spot in the social life of Libby and Art. The National Grange had been organized in 1867 and originally named the Patrons of Husbandry. It was something of a fraternal organization to bring farmers together to exert political and economic pressure to improve the lot of farmers in their relationship with railroads and industrial monopolies. It also formed cooperative enterprises, such as farm machinery co-ops and credit unions. It grew rapidly. By 1925, some of the other activities had ceased being so important and the Grange's primary value was the improvement of rural life in general. In the 1930s it defined itself as follows:

**The Grange is a great farm fraternity: build-
ing character; developing leadership; encour-**

aging education; promoting community betterment; instilling high ideals; teaching through work and play the value of cooperation and service in the attainment of happiness.

The goals of the Grange strongly appealed to the idealism of both Art and Libby. They joined the Hopewell Grange and in the next few years would become active at the county and state level. They were pleased to note that the master of the State Grange was a Methodist preacher serving a rural church.

The Hopewell Grange met in a large hall built over the classrooms of Hopewell School, conveniently near the farm. The regular monthly meeting was conducted much like a lodge meeting, but it was always followed by an enjoyable program and a pleasant social hour. The farmers were always hungry to visit neighbors. Libby, with her piano playing and song leading ability, enjoyed organizing programs and soon was elected "lecturer," an officer whose duty was to do those very things.

She and Art entertained by singing duets such as the humorous Scottish songs they knew, often in Scottish dialect—*Soldier, Soldier Won't Ye Marry Me* was a favorite. Their contributions were enjoyed and appreciated. The Grange greatly expanded their circle of friends. Neighbor Emmer Bowman was also a "Granger," and, with his musical relatives, enjoyed entertaining during the social hour. This meant that he and the Smiths were often involved in the same program. He had a rough, good-natured sense of humor and enjoyed poking fun at "the school teachers who thought they knew how to farm."

Libby returned jab for jab, and in a grudging sort of way they became friends, though she never forgave his very expressive, almost lyrical gift for swearing. When working in his fields, he sometimes lost his temper over an obstinate piece of farm equipment or troublesome horse. He had a powerful voice. On a calm summer day his bursts of profanity could be heard anywhere on the Smith farm. Libby resented these outbursts, especially when her children were working in the fields. But she realized that they were growing older and she was changing, becoming more tolerant and less protective. In the interest of friendship, she never mentioned his swearing to Emmer. Just a few years earlier she would not have been so constrained. He never swore in public, at least not in the presence of women. She shared with him an exuberant sense of humor, and these two totally different people often found themselves being the life of the party at a Grange oyster supper or picnic.

One bit of his humor she never enjoyed, however. It was almost a religion with him to be very early in the fields in the summertime. He managed two farms, and in driving between them passed in front of the Smith house. Sometimes he would be driving by in his wagon before there was evidence of activity on the part of the Smiths. At such times he would stop and call out in a loud voice: "You can't farm alying in yore beds."

With the windows open, every syllable could be heard, even his soft laughter and the clip-clop of the hooves as he continued up the road. He obviously thought of the Smiths as people who could take a joke. Perhaps, Libby thought, his heckling stemmed from the fact that he really liked them and secretly admired their broader knowledge of the world.

Increasingly, the Project area experienced a problem of disease in the wheat, commonly called smut. It reduced the yield and greatly reduced the value of the harvested grain. The foul black fungus that grew on the heads flew up, becoming a dark dust cloud when thrashed. Dad, who had taken courses in agriculture in Utah and was always on the cutting edge of new developments in farming, was first in the community to treat his seed wheat by dipping it in a solution that contained copper sulfate, commonly called blue vitriol. This effectively controlled the disease, which was carried by spores on the seed wheat. Emmer chided him at planting time on his "school teacher newfangled ideas."

At threshing time Art had beautiful clean wheat. But on Emmer's farm a dark, ominous cloud followed the thrashing machine all day, making it appear from a distance like the whole operation was going up in smoke. That was a bitter day for Emmer, and Art and Libby were careful to never mention it to him.

The next planting season Emmer remarked casually, "Reckon I'll dip my seed."

Art, though never an enthusiastic farmer, was a careful, scientific one, something Libby admired. Each year the sugar company offered a prize for the best essay on growing larger yields of sugar beets. Each year Art submitted an essay and won the prize—two hundred pounds of sugar. This was a great boon to the family, which was always short of cash. Candy-making became a hobby in the Smith home. It also made for good parties. Libby and Dad encouraged the Methodist youth group to meet at their home. They enjoyed the "taffy pulls" as much as the young people did, and there was never a concern over the cost of the main ingredient, sugar.

Grace became interested in candy making and excelled in making divinity. Another favorite candy was panacha. At the nearby sugar factory, a certain amount of sugar was unavoidably burned into something resembling the clinkers from a smelter furnace. The factory workers had to clean it out. They gave it away to farmers who would bother to pick it up. The flavor was not damaged and many children sucked it for candy. In candy making it could be substituted for brown sugar, the main ingredient in panacha.

Even the boys learned how to make fudge and peanut brittle. All that needed to be purchased were flavoring, coloring, peanuts and the cocoa for the fudge. Cream, butter, egg whites and milk came from the farm.

Hosting get-togethers for the church youth group and seeing her children having fun with their friends proved to be a great source of pleasure to Libby. On many summer evenings the spacious front lawn was the scene of twenty or more young people vigorously playing outdoor games—Kick the Can, Run My Sheepy Run, Steal the Bacon, and plain old Hide and Seek. Happy laughter prevailed for hours and hours, starting before the sun sank behind the Carolina poplars. Often these evenings closed with a marshmallow roast, and the ever-popular singing around the campfire as darkness fell and boys and girls could sit close together and hold hands. Grace was not interested in this type of social life, which was too closely associated with the farm, but during her high school years Connie relished it, made many friends and, after finishing high school and college and after teaching school a number of years, would marry a man who had participated in those events.

The years of 1925 through 1929 brought extremely hard work for the family. Crop yields and reasonable prices made it possible to make the Payment. But there was very little money left for the necessities of life and none at all for any recreational spending. With no money for hired help, Dad and Libby kept the family cared for with limited resources and were both tired much of the time. But the nature of farm life created a great deal of family time. The children worked in the fields with Dad in the summer, and worked with Libby in the great amount of work that it took to keep the family going. After her freshman year, Grace lived at home too, with a ride to and from school arranged by neighbors who had a high school student who could drive.

With their interest in academic and cultural subjects, Dad and Libby, in the daily rounds of their work were constantly honing their children's minds. They did it without thinking. This was a family in constant conversation. If the girls were helping can fruit or prepare vegetables, Libby would likely be telling them fascinating stories of Scottish or English kings and queens, castles and battles, or explaining the meanings behind the common nursery rhymes. All the while, without knowing it, they were being schooled in "the King's English." If she recited *Little Jack Horner* to David, she might explain to the older children that when Jack stuck his thumb in his Christmas pie and "pulled out a plum," it was originally meant as commentary on a corrupt government granting benefits to favored people—thence the term "political plum."

In the field hitching a three-horse team, Dad might well be explaining to the boys the mathematics involved in designing a triple tree, as contrasted to the usual double tree, with a system of levers that would require each horse to pull exactly one third of the load. Or he might be explaining the surveying and engineering involved in designing a system of ditches, dikes and furrows that made it possible to spread the irrigation water evenly over all sixty acres of the farm, even though it was not perfectly level. Or he might be discussing the remarkable way that tadpoles trapped in a ditch when the water was turned off turned more quickly into frogs who could live on dry land.

At butchering time, he might be explaining the principle of the block and tackle with which he could hang up a hog that weighed much more than he did. Or he would carefully explain the chemical process by which the salt and "curing compound" turned raw pork into choice ham or bacon. All the while the children were receiving practice in the use of perfect English.

Then there was the family practice of memorizing poetry and reciting it at every opportunity. While the farm work was being done, lines from Longfellow's *Evangeline* led naturally to additional commentary on the brutality of the British as they removed French families from Canada.

Libby encouraged the reciting of poetry, singing of songs, and telling of stories as the children spent hours on monotonous farm work such as hoeing sugar beets or beans, or cutting seed potatoes into the small chunks or "sets." The children already knew that potatoes were not grown from seeds but from a buried potato, and that no one would waste a whole potato to grow a new plant, a potato having a number of "eyes" any of which could put out a sprout. They knew that an average potato could be cut into six or eight pieces, and each set would start a new plant.

Each spring as Dad ran the potato planter, the children had the task of keeping him supplied with potato sets. He devised a unique system to make the work go rapidly. On each side of a table he affixed a knife with the blade sticking up, sharp edge toward the center of the table. He would dump a sack of potatoes in the middle of the table. Each child reached out for a potato, took it in both hands and pulled it toward himself or herself, across the knife, first cutting it lengthwise, then repeating the process and cutting it crosswise, once or twice, or even three times, according to the size of the potato. The sets were then dropped into a sack attached to the table just behind the knife and between the child's legs. With practice, a child could cut sets very rapidly, but it was also possible, if one became too concerned with speed, to slice the skin off the side of a thumb.

While working at this table the children enjoyed breaking the monotony by seeing who could best recall the lines of a long poem, or by singing a song with a chorus, each child taking a turn making up a new verse. Libby encouraged and applauded such efforts. A song might go something like this:

> Poor old Robinson Crusoe,
> He sure was a fool to do so,
> He climbed up a tree to look out at the sea,
> Poor old Robinson Crusoe.

Each child added a new third line with another foolish activity for the lonely man.

Another favorite way to break the monotony was to tell a story. One person would make up an opening paragraph, then each would add as much to the story as his creative powers could produce. Often he or she would add a new setting or character. Some of these stories became quite interesting, went on for hours, and sometimes were enthusiastically picked up the next day. It was not unusual to add a known character like a school teacher or neighbor, keeping that person's behavior in character. While washing clothes and putting them through the wringer on the back porch Libby overheard these stories, glad to hear her children's fine use of language. They were not only developing their imaginations, they were honing a sense of comedy—making the others laugh was prized—and learning the complexities of good tragedy.

For the rest of their lives the Smith family would contemplate the way in which the tragedy about to befall the country affected their family.

It was the dark night of the soul.

15   The Lean Years

The 1920s and 30s were troubling times for a deeply devout, intelligent and thoughtful woman like Libby. Following the Great War, the traditional religious certitude and unquestioned moral values with which she had grown up were being openly questioned, even scorned. Books, news media and moving pictures featured a blatant materialism and passion for "worldly" pleasure—a little less felt in rural areas than in the cities, but nonetheless pervasive in American culture. The quest for personal gratification and the pursuit of wealth seemed to be replacing concerns about good character, personal virtue, and strong families.

Perhaps it was during this time that Libby developed more of an antipathy toward the "filthy rich." It came to some extent from the Bible: the teachings of Jesus, the purity of those who give up worldly goods for a spiritual life, and the notion that it is easier for a camel to get through the eye of a needle than for a rich man to get into heaven. But it also had something to do with the British sense of "noblesse oblige," the obligation of the upper classes, who were ideally circumspect and private about their wealth, to help the less fortunate. Few of those who were helping the less fortunate made the social pages during the 1920s. Instead, the papers featured people ostentatiously displaying wealth and immorality, and Libby judged them unworthy of any respect.

Great and confusing changes were rocking American society. Newspapers and newsreels brought constant reminders of the flouting of Prohibition, the proliferation of "road houses," gangsters, the uninhibited behavior of many of the "newly rich"—who, to Libby's dismay, were widely viewed as trend setters. Serious scholars and writers questioned the motives of the political leaders who had made the decisions during the war, thereby tearing away some of the national pride people had felt in their country. The belief that "we are getting better and better" now seemed naive. Popular literature examined the apparent breakdown of morality and lack of a sense of purpose in life. In their excellent work: *The Growth of the American Republic,* Morison and Commager discuss the period between the wars:

> **Meantime, inspired by Sigmund Freud of Vienna…the revolt against Puritanism and rationalism flared all along the literary front. . . The most significant and most widely read writers of this generation were those who confessed that theirs was a 'lost generation'…The writers of the lost generation…had passed beyond rebellion into acquiescence, and beyond that to a kind of nihilism.**
>
> **The most gifted writer of his generation was F. Scott Fitzgerald, who became the chronicler of the peculiar disillusionment that afflicted the very rich, idle or otherwise, in the postwar years that he taught us to call the Jazz age. *This side of Paradise,* published in 1920, became a kind of Baedeker [guide book] of the new cynicism. . . In Fitzgerald's books the beautiful are always damned, the young men always sad, the night is tender but mornings bring disillusionment.**

Disillusionment reached even into organized religion. Libby would never lose her passionate faith in a personal God or her strong belief in the importance of prayer, but biblical scholars whom she respected were writing on subjects that made her realize that she could no longer simply turn to unquestioned scripture for guidance for herself and her family. A prolific reader of literature as well as scholarly material, Libby recognized that she had no sure formula to lead her family past those powerful outside forces. She would always love the Bible, but recognized that her children were heavily exposed to a society that questioned all authority, and she could not use biblical precepts in bringing them up the same way her parents had done with her.

One day while tidying up in Grace's room, she noticed a book that Grace had been reading. Seeing the title, *The Flapper Wife,* she leafed though it and tears came to her eyes. What could she do? She didn't want to further strain her relationship with Grace, who continued to feel that the family had betrayed her by moving to the Rupert farm. Quietly she returned the book where she found it. *How does a mother rear children in such a world? With God's help I will just have to try to be a good example, and beyond that I will simply love them and accept them and not drive them away from me by trying too hard to make them conform to my standards.*

Arty also began to show signs of impatience and distance. Handsome, strong and curly haired, he cut an impressive figure for his age. At the top of his class in his schoolwork despite having skipped two grades, he was two years younger than many of his classmates and, though Libby knew that he often felt small compared with his classmates, he clearly didn't want that known within the family. He insisted on being called "Arthur." She noticed that he sometimes bullied Donald. The fact that they still slept together on the davenport didn't help. Young Arthur occasionally drove the team for the harvester and planter, and mowed the alfalfa. But though he helped increasingly with the heavy farm work, at thirteen and fourteen he began to run with a crowd in high school that Libby didn't like, boys who were fifteen and sixteen years old, not church boys.

The crystal radio set was an exciting invention. Young Arthur

learned enough about it to make a set of his own. It received a little
scratchy music from time to time and seemed a magical thing to the
children, but the younger boys knew better than to touch it. Down
the road the opposite direction from the Bowmans, the Goff family
bought a store radio in the late 1920s. Their son was older, but graciously invited the Smith children to come from time to time and
listen to the radio with him. Seventy-five years later Donald could
still sing some of the jingles:

> With Blue-Green gas,
> Not a car on the highway you can't pass,
> Unless he's using Blue-Green too.

In the election of 1928, Libby and Art did what they could to
combat the assault on morals by working for Herbert Hoover, who
supported Prohibition. Al Smith, the Democrat, advocated repeal of
the 18th Amendment. That marked him as a "Wet," a supporter of
the liquor industry. Libby worked hard for the Women's Christian
Temperance Union (W.C.T.U) and voted against Al Smith, as did a
great many church people.

Her growing family desperately needed more space. In the summer of 1929, Dad found an old two-room house that had been vacant
for years and cost only a hundred dollars. It measured fourteen by
twenty-four feet. He moved it with blocks and tackles, the farm wagon,
and the help of friends. One room was placed against the window of
the living room. Dad made that window into a door. The other room,
the one young Arthur and Donald would share, jutted out from the
house as a separate wing. There was no provision for heating in these
two new bedrooms. When the door to the living room was left open,
some heat circulated into nearest one, but virtually none reached the
room surrounded on three sides by cold air. After years of enduring
freezing winters in the annex, Grace and Connie slept in the room
nearest the rest of the house. Both rooms were brutally cold in winter,

but the family had heavy quilts and all were accustomed to the cold. Often a dusting of snow blew in under the door in the boys room and remained on the floor all day. David continued to sleep in the parents' room.

Grace had finished high school in May of 1929 a month before her seventeenth birthday. Home for the summer, she then went to the College of Idaho in Caldwell two hundred miles away. After that, the room was Connie's, except when Grace came home for holidays and for one more summer.

The older boys slept on old army cots on opposite sides of their room, and had their own door for when they needed to go to the apple orchard. This was a vast improvement over the cramped conditions they had known, and for the first time the family had a living room with no one sleeping in it. Libby felt much freer about inviting people to visit—an activity that she regarded as essential to civilized life.

The last year of good farm income was 1929. The October 29 stock market crash had no immediate effect on the family, nor any of the neighbors. Few of them paid attention to the stock market or had any understanding of it. As usual, in mid October Dad had sold his potatoes right out of the field, the choice Number Ones going for $4 per hundred pounds. At a Grange meeting he visited with Emmer Bowman, who had some exceptionally fine potatoes and a spud cellar. "I'm putting my spuds in storage again," Emmer said. "Holding out for $4.25 per hundred pounds." That had worked for him in the past, and Dad wished that he too had a spud cellar so he could outwait the annual October glut. He harvested his sugar beets, hauled them to the plant, and received his full contract price.

The full force of the crash became evident in early 1930, when the *Minidoka County News* began to report farm foreclosures and bank failures. It was hard for farmers to realize just what was happening. But the buyers of farm produce had grown cautious, not doing much buying. By mid November the market for potatoes had plummeted.

Emmer couldn't get anyone to make an offer, and by Christmas there was no market at all. In the spring of 1930, potatoes were rotting in the cellars. Emmer and other farmers loaded the foul smelling gunny sacks into trucks and dumped their contents into the Snake River. Having managed well in his farming business, Emmer had paid for his farm and was therefore able to keep it, but the financial and emotional shock devastated him. At Grange meetings his usual cheerful attitude and sense of humor were noticeably absent.

Dad approached the spring work with none of his usual optimism. The hard work seemed much harder when there was no real reason to do it. All the farmers felt the despair. Not the slightest rumor of an economic turnaround was heard. Dad couldn't get a contract for his next crop of sugar beets, but he had to plant and hope things would change before fall. The memory of farmers dumping potatoes in the river stayed with him. Would all his crops rot in the field? The cold spring wind, which had always been a hardship for him as he did his spring plowing and planting, seemed much colder, the grit in his eyes more painful. He tired more easily.

When school started that year, Arthur, who was twelve years old and a freshman in high school, regularly drove the team after school. In the mornings he and Donald milked six cows. The milk and cream check, which in the past had proved to be a good source of supplemental income, continued to come on a regular basis, but in a greatly reduced amount. Fortunately, the family belonged to a cooperative creamery that provided butter and cheese to members. An order could be left for those items when the can was set out for the milk truck, and the items would be delivered the next day.

Libby read the increasingly sad news of city workers who were unemployed and the terrible news about long lines of hungry people waiting for a bowl of soup. She thanked God every day for the blessing of farm life. Her family had an abundance of good food, and with a ten cent block of ice and the sugar from Dad's essays, they could make top quality homemade ice cream. As the summer progressed, hungry men began to appear at the back door asking for a meal in exchange for work. They were good men, family men who had taken to the road to search for employment. Libby fed them, glad she could do this, and sent them on their way, often with a bag of potatoes, some apples, or a cabbage. She tried to visit with them, but they were defeated men with little to say. Their lives were shattered, the pain so deep that they couldn't bear to talk about it. They simply ate, expressed their thanks, and walked on.

She was living her own quiet despair. By summer it was clear that the Payment could not be made in October. Where would they go when they were evicted? The possibility of returning to Utah and begging help from relatives seemed a pill too bitter to swallow. Art wouldn't talk about it. Lorene's words came back to Libby: *You'll never have a two bit car.*

With almost no cash income from the farm, Libby struggled to clothe her children for school that fall. She patched and sewed and tried to put on a cheerful face to help them cope with their austere life. David was six years old and starting school. She couldn't buy him new shoes and had to let him wear a pair of old tattered shoes that Donald had long since outgrown but were too large for David. She couldn't buy Grace and Connie new dresses. It seemed to them that all the other girls in college and high school wore better clothes. Libby had a treadle sewing machine that her in-laws had taught her to use. On that machine she made serviceable cotton dresses, but not with the skill or style that many mothers had. Every morning when she opened her eyes she wondered how she could possibly find the strength to keep going. But hers was not a job she could resign. Meanwhile the frequent contact with the men at the back door, especially family men who had been evicted from their farms with nothing but a few personal belongings, kept her constantly aware of the impending fall of the sword of Damocles.

Perhaps Dad felt it even more keenly. These were by far the darkest and most difficult days of his life. Deeply discouraged, he sank into depression. He made an effort to put water in the irrigation ditches and bring in a harvest, but without hope. He was going through one of the worst experiences a proud man can face—the inability to support the family he loves and the prospect of losing the farm into which he had put all his money, every ounce of his energy, and every moment of his planning for the past seven years. He was losing his family heritage all over again because the Utah property had paid for the Rupert farm. Soon he would have nothing. The newspaper carried stories about men in this situation who ended their pain with suicide.

Even when he read of the plight of millions of hungry people, he couldn't rejoice in the fact that his family had food to eat because that too would soon end. He had led his family on a collision course with disaster. His dear Libby had trusted his decision to farm full time. But even in the beginning he had seen through her cheeriness to an underlying fear that they would be forever poor, living a life she was not meant to live, a life she had not imagined any child of hers would live. Now, her brave demeanor in the face of utter ruin intensified his judgement that he was a failure as a husband and father. No matter how hard he worked, he could not provide for his family. All spring and summer his hayfever and asthma had been particularly bad. Though he'd had allergies all his life, in earlier years he'd been able to keep himself going by looking forward to harvest time. Now, hardly able to breathe, he sank into a kind of darkness, losing interest in life itself. There were days when he could not get off the sofa.

This was a lonely time for Libby. Art's depression made her feel all the more desperate. Her efforts to cheer him with humorous asides failed, as did her attempts to convince him "Don't worry, Art, we will endure." There was nothing she could do for him. She was at the end of her rope, but the demands of motherhood kept her hanging on. She had meals and lunches to prepare, clothes to wash and mend, children to cheer up so they wouldn't feel the hopelessness.

As always, she hid her fears from the children by making light of bad situations. If there was a mouse in the bread drawer, she referred to it in mockingly respectful tones as *"Monsieur la rat,"* though her skin crawled at the thought of a furry beastie in the house. She composed amusing little rhymes to help the children get through the necessary chores, and one that stoked their courage when they walked to school past the fence of a vicious looking bull who sometimes feinted a charge at them. Seeing their bravery, little David among them, as they chanted her rhyme and marched away together brought tears to her eyes.

> Marching off to the Hopewell School,
> Marching down past Kennedy's bull,
> This is the way we keep the rule,
> Marching off to the Hopewell School.

Hope well, indeed, she thought. Perhaps it would have surprised her to know that over seventy years later they would remember that rhyme.

She had a place between the barn and the haystack, sheltered from the wind, where she went to pray and weep, but only for short periods. There was always a child needing her or pressing work to be done. Every night she fell exhausted into bed and when morning came, got up and repeated the day before.

Then she received what seemed the knockout blow. It was something she thought would never happen again. At forty-three years of age she learned that she was pregnant with her sixth child. She knew her strength would be sapped. They would surely be evicted from the house. Would she give birth in Old Flivver? With its eisenglass and canvas long since broken and tattered, it provided no shelter from the snow or sun. And how would they buy gasoline to get from place to place to beg for jobs? Or would Mother Smith take them in again?

Not long ago she had thought that being a farmer's wife was beneath her, but now she prayed to remain just that—a farmer's wife. She had learned a painful lesson in humility. She wanted Dad to trust again that the crops would sell for a living wage. But when she told him she was pregnant, he became even more despondent. She mentioned going back to Utah. He only stared dully across the room. This sent her outside for another round of weeping and prayer.

Seeing their father's strange behavior and their mother's hidden desperation, the older children took turns getting up in the morning to start the fire, relieving Libby of that task. She appreciated that they were trying to lighten her burden, but that was not the same as having a willing and cheerful helpmate, a person with whom she could share her feelings.

For the second time in her married life Libby was unable to keep hiding her tears from her children. At odd moments, especially when she looked at Dad on the sofa, those streams of salty water betrayed her. Ashamed though she was, it brought an unexpected source of comfort and hope. Connie, Arty and Donald came to her aid in a remarkable way. They assured her that they would take over most of the washing, cooking, cleaning, and, when the new baby came, caring for the baby. David joined in. "I will bring in the eggs every morning."

Libby found even more hope in the extent to which the children carried out their promises. The older children continued to take turns getting up in the morning to start the fire. At sixteen, Connie was a competent cook, and now she greatly increased her efforts to keep meals on the table. She was dependable and willing to sublimate her personal interests to the challenge of survival facing the family. Mature for her age, she also provided companionship for Libby. In addition to their outdoor work, the boys made sure there was always an adequate supply of water pumped and ready for use. Six-year-old David brought in the eggs and handed up the clothespins when Libby hung out the wash. This willingness of her children to be of help in every way they could gave Libby the feeling that together they just might make it through whatever would happen. Later in life, looking back on "that dark night of the soul" Libby knew that it was her children, her faith in God, and her powerful sense of humor that sustained her.

The baby crib had long since been given away, and Libby was deeply touched when eleven-year-old Donald, who had been raising rabbits for the family table, said he would remodel a rabbit hutch to make a bed for the new baby. He said he could make a bed like the manger baby Jesus slept in. It was crude, but when the time came it was put into use. Many years later, when that child was running for U.S. Senator from Idaho, Donald assured him he would never be allowed to forget that he had started his life in a rabbit hutch.

In October, 1930, the due date for the mortgage payment arrived. The grain had sold for twenty cents a bushel—hardly worth selling. Meat producers knew there was no point in feeding it to hogs that were selling for two cents a pound. Dad had harvested the sugar beets though they were never contracted. In the spring the sugar company did its best to pay a fraction of the amount of previous years. Most of the work had indeed been futile. Even the essay contest was cancelled, there being no point in teaching farmers how to increase sugar beet production.

Putting on his hat, Dad drove to town to sign the foreclosure notice. To his surprise, the former owner of the farm met him there to "talk things over." An interesting situation had developed, something that was happening in quite a few similar cases. For a time the former owner had looked forward with anticipation to repossessing the farm, then making money on a resale. But he learned that no one was interested in buying a farm at any price. He didn't want to farm it, and he knew that if he turned the Smiths out, the farm would grow weeds and fall into disrepair. To keep the value of the farm for a time when the economy recovered, it was necessary to have it cared for by a good farmer. Dad was a good farmer. They made a deal. Dad would stay on the farm and make a little money on crops as best he could, pay a little of the interest on the mortgage if he could, and together they would wait and see what the future would bring.

He returned home with some of the burden lifted. Libby and the children would have a roof over their heads and a place to grow their food. They would not become beggars, at least not immediately. Nevertheless, Dad did not snap out of his depression. The newspaper headlined dire predictions about the country's economic future. There were rumors of civil war. A Progressive Movement grew strong in farming communities like Rupert. Like blue collar workers, many farmers looked to socialism or even communism to restore the food distribution system. Lacking markets, Dad felt little incentive for doing the wintertime work of mending harnesses, repairing tools, and repairing fences and outbuildings. He didn't enjoy the work any more, like he had when he'd been a gentleman farmer in Union. He couldn't keep feeding all his hogs, and butchered more of them, bartering the pork and bacon to people in town in exchange for services.

The hard times didn't stop the decline in morals. On the contrary, it seemed that reports of horrible crimes increased. Bonnie and Clyde careened around the countryside and many people apparently cheered them on. Hollywood churned out film after film depicting grotesque killings, often associated with the illegal liquor business, which was thriving. How could a mother compete with so much immorality, trashy moving pictures and books?

But in the darkest days of winter a new source of cheer arrived. A new pastor was appointed to the Rupert Methodist Church. Libby invited Reverend Phillips and his family for supper and a visit. An Englishman with a rollicking sense of humor, he had not been in America for long and had not bothered to become a citizen. Libby enjoyed his very Cockney style of speaking.

During the church service, he read Matthew 11:15—"E oo as hears to ear, let im ear." Young Arthur and Donald both giggled. Libby shot them a stern look, but at home when the children gleefully repeated that line, she knew they saw the twinkle in her eye. "Phillips," as Libby referred to the minister, was neither a great preacher nor a theologian—the kind of "thinking man" Libby enjoyed sparring with—

but being British, he had something in common with her. She became very fond of him. He liked the Smith family, and over the next years the two families spent many pleasant evenings together. He had an infectious sense of humor. Almost every week he had a new joke about the extreme thriftiness —stinginess—of the Scotch. He brought out Libby's sense of humor as she engaged him, giving as good has she got. Years afterward, speaking of him, she said: "He taught me how to laugh again."

During those long winter nights the family sat together reading aloud from library books. Soon after the move to Rupert Libby had started this practice, and she felt very pleased that it had become a favorite family activity. Aloud, Libby would read a few pages from a book, Dad, if he felt like joining them, would read a few pages, Grace, when she was home from college, and all the other children would follow, regardless of their reading level. In this way the children learned about the world outside their home and gained an appreciation for literature. All of them made an effort to bring the stories to life by putting emotion into their reading. In this way they read many different kinds of books over the years. Donald was particularly riveted by one suspenseful novel in which an Indian spy was caught between camps and punished by having his tongue cut out.

They also played *Authors*, a card game in which the object was to be the first to assemble four books written by the same author. In this way they learned about Sir Walter Scott, Mark Twain, and many others. Often they later read aloud from the books they first encountered in the card game. Once in a while Dad would bring out his mandolin and accompany himself in a song. He also had an old violin, a "fiddle" that he could play a little. Or the family would play caroms, having brought the carom board from Utah. It was a big, square wooden board with netted side pockets in the four corners—a game resembling pool in which flat wooden "caroms" were flicked in turn by the player's index finger, using the thumb to generate force. On the reverse side was a big checker board.

During the worst years of the Great Depression common people in all walks of life rose to the challenge, doing what they had to do to hold their communities together. Doctors and nurses worked for subsistence pay to serve their friends and neighbors. They accepted small amounts for service when it was available. Farmers paid for services in produce, which the townspeople appreciated. Grace was able to continue in college because of the devotion and sacrifice of professors who stayed on their jobs even when they were not paid. There were no other jobs available, and dedicated teachers felt they would rather teach than sit idle at home.

The College of Idaho functioned somewhat like a large, poor but loyal family, each member pitching in to help the group survive. Good students had work scholarships, performing almost all of the non-teaching work needed to keep a college open. In that way Grace was able to attend for two years and earn a teaching certificate in 1932. At nineteen, she became entirely independent as a teacher in a rural school in a ranching community two-hundred miles from Rupert.

—

On May 26, 1931, baby Robert was born, named for the Scottish hero "Robert the Bruce" with the middle name of Lindsay—the maiden name of Libby's Grandmother Symon. As promised, the children continued to help, Connie changing diapers in addition to doing her many other chores. She made extra porridge, which Libby forced herself to eat to keep her precious milk flowing—something Mother Lucy Smith had taught her. For the first time in her childbearing years, the quantity of her milk was a problem. Connie continued to cook for the family and, when Libby was too tired, bathed the baby in the evening. Arthur, Donald and little David continued bringing in water, eggs, produce, fish, and skinned eviscerated rabbits. That year Dad's hay fever was very bad again, and Arthur and Donald helped with the difficult farm work. In the fall Dad butchered a hog, a few of which he continued to raise and use like money.

By that time Herbert Hoover was in the second half of his term. The Great Depression was in full swing, and people blamed him and other Republicans for the economic disaster. Politics took a sharp turn to the left as the collapse of banks and businesses overshadowed all other matters. Though they had once supported Hoover, Dad and Libby now turned against him along with millions of other people. The unsightly collection of makeshift shelters that appeared in every city and town in the country—patched together by hungry, discouraged people—were called "Hoovervilles." In the West, jackrabbits earned the name "Hoover Hogs," pork being inaccessible to most people. In that spirit the Smiths referred to their shabby extra bedrooms as "the Hoover Addition." Libby was nonetheless grateful they had bought it when they did, for they could not have afforded it later.

As the depression wore on, little Bobby toddled, then ran around the farm. David and Donald walked to Hopewell School, and Connie and Arthur found rides to Rupert High School. The family stayed together and survived, though Dad remained listless about his work. He decided that farming was not for him, and with Libby's encouragement began to talk about other ways to make a living.

They were able to buy enough gasoline at fourteen cents a gallon to get to church on Sunday—if Old Flivver would start on the winter mornings, Dad cranking so hard he would perspire profusely in the bitter cold before he could coax the motor to turn on its own. In summer the car took them to the Square on Saturday nights. There, Dad listened to other farmers sharing their fears and discussing their difficulties. At church, he became the regular teacher for the men's Bible class. This took his mind off farming for a while and helped him regain a little self respect. The fellowship of the church helped many farmers keep their emotional equilibrium during the long financial depression. The friendship of the English pastor with his everlasting good humor also continued to provide a beacon of light for Libby.

But it was the election of 1932 that turned Libby's world around— not because Franklin D. Roosevelt promised new ideas to get the economy back on its feet, but because Dad would run for office on the same winning ticket. Poverty being so widespread and painful, the liquor issue took a back seat in the national campaign. Libby and Art supported Roosevelt, a "Wet," whose promises were seen by some astute political leaders as a big step toward socialism—feared in the United States since the Russian Revolution thirteen years earlier. But people were so hungry and desperate that they were ready to embrace anything that promised hope.

The Smith family had become well known and respected. They held leadership positions in the church, the schools, and the Grange. All who knew Libby loved and greatly admired her. Dad was respected for his clear thinking, good education, and quiet friendliness. The County Assessor, a Republican who had held the office for several terms, was not very efficient and took his reelection for granted. Dad's friends began suggesting that he would sure make a fine assessor. By now he had helped many farmers in the Project solve math problems. Dad was not a politician, not one to push himself forward, but those friendly suggestions got him thinking that this elected job might be the career change he'd been looking for. He knew he could handle the job. In fact, he knew he could handle all of it very well. Though not a "public man," he related well to people on a one to one basis.

His interest in running thrilled Libby. She recognized that this could be the beginning of a better life. With her enthusiastic support he registered as a Democrat and filed for the job. The campaign that summer and fall was a family affair. Libby managed the politics, Dad's speaking schedule, and the printed matter. Dad simply was himself, the quiet but extremely well qualified candidate. Connie, who had just finished high school, Arthur ready to start his senior year, and Donald in his freshman year, all eagerly knocked on doors or stood on street corners handing out piles of "Smith for Assessor" cards. They campaigned informally on Saturday nights at the Square. It was great fun and they enjoyed sharing their experiences over meals. Dad's opponent in the Democratic primary was not well known. In the November general election Dad would likely have won by a comfortable margin regardless of the Roosevelt landslide, but with it he garnered an overwhelming victory. Most people in the county, indeed the United States, simply voted a straight Democratic ticket.

Dad became the Minidoka County Assessor elect and a Democrat for life. The backing of so many voters did wonders for his self esteem. He began studying the records of the previous assessor. Consistent with his approach to life, he would not just be the County Assessor, but in his own quiet way would be the best assessor in the state. This determination to be the best at whatever he did was a characteristic that, by example, he passed on to all his children.

On January 1, 1933, he began his new job at the then magnificent salary of $125 per month. The Great Depression had only just begun, but this salary brought a bright new sunrise for the Smith family. Recognizing his regular income, the newly organized Federal Land Bank refinanced the debt on the farm with a lower annual payment, a longer payment schedule, and a lower interest rate. Now the fear of losing the farm evaporated. Fields that would grow row crops Dad rented to other farmers. Young Arthur and Donald would manage the hay, cows, and hogs. Arthur would graduate from high school that spring and leave home after the summer, but Donald, with the help of a neighbor at haying time, would continue as a share cropper, raising cows and hogs until his graduation from high school in 1936.

Dad's attention now shifted, to a great extent, to his new job. He enthusiastically performed the work. At age forty-three he had fallen into a career for which he was perfectly suited, one that also gave him a measure of local stature. Everyone liked him, and he was reelected every two years for the next sixteen years, until he accepted a better job with the State Tax Commission.

Farm commodities remained low, but Dad's landlord share from the sugar beets, potatoes and beans paid the lowered annual mortgage, all without hard work or any further cost. Additionally, the farm continued to furnish the family with meat, milk, and produce from the garden and orchard. It also furnished jobs and a little cash income for Arthur and Donald. With their share of the milk and cream checks they could buy their own clothing, put gas in the family car, and have more spending money than many other high school students.

Immediately after Dad took office in January, the family moved into a rented house in town. This would be their temporary home while the farm house was being remodeled. Libby and Dad were entering a very different phase of their lives.

"She opens her hand to the poor, and reaches out her hands to the needy."

Proverbs 31:20

16 Missionary In Her Own Town

For the first time since her teaching days, Libby felt in control of her destiny. The family was far from wealthy but she felt comfortable and secure. She walked easily to most of the places she wanted to go in Rupert and was able to buy some things the family had desperately needed. She even bought a radio. Now they could hear President Roosevelt's "fireside chats" as well as the daily news and musical programs. She found it wonderful to sleep at night without worrying about what the next day would bring.

Dad bought a 1929 Model A Ford, a virtually new car with all the updated features. He didn't need it for work—the county supplied him with a Model A Coupe to visit farms and other properties—and he usually walked to his office in downtown Rupert. Working nine to five, he generally took his lunch to the office and returned home at a regular hour for supper. He had the freedom to put in extra hours when he needed them or leave early to spend time with his family. Sometimes he left early and went fishing in the Snake River or read— an activity he enjoyed all his life.

Arthur, a senior in high school, continued to be very precocious both physically and academically. He was a linebacker on the varsity football team, which held practices after school. He also attended school dances, took a leadership role in the church youth group, and played a part in the school play. Living in town made these activities convenient for him. Donald, small for his age, did not participate in high school athletics. Feeling some sibling rivalry, he wasn't interested in getting involved in any school or church activity where he felt socially in the shadow of this very popular older brother. He liked the farm and the animals, and was proud to be entrusted with the family car. Taking over the regular farm chores, he commuted the three miles twice daily to milk the cows, feed the hogs and see that all was well. His interests kept him working in close contact with "Mom." Libby affectionately called him "Hank, the hired man."

Living in a house with a flush toilet and hot and cold running water, Libby now had some personal time. She utilized it fully, walking to weekday meetings in the church and community. David, a quiet, thoughtful nine-year-old, was doing well in the Rupert elementary school, and often she could take little Bobby to meetings or find a dependable baby sitter a few doors away.

Dad continued to be active in the church. Delighted about that, Libby took a more active role in church work herself, not only teaching Sunday School but serving as a delegate to the annual conference of the Methodist Church—the Idaho Conference, which included Southern Idaho and Eastern Oregon. Elected by the members of the Rupert Church, she felt honored and took her responsibilities very seriously. Delegates, who included ministers and lay people, participated in week-long meetings to help set church policy. She had always wanted to serve in such a position, and this activity became a vital part of her life. Libby was an admired member of the "Conference," advocating that the church support social and economic programs to better the world. For the rest of her life, even when she was no longer a delegate, she would read the Conference reports. She and Art would enjoy many lively discussions generated by them.

But for Libby, a Christian life meant getting beyond intellectual issues and church politics. It meant devoting herself to the less fortunate. She gave much of her time to visiting with the housebound and lonely members of the church. She befriended and counseled unwed, pregnant girls of any faith. Sometimes she arranged places for them to live until their babies were born and could be adopted. She also gave direct assistance to people who were suffering hardship as a result of the continuing Depression.

Trying to relocate, one such family found themselves in Rupert with hungry children, a broken down old car, no money and no place to live. Libby undertook solving the problem. A German bachelor who lived near the farm had a chicken house but was no longer raising chickens. Libby persuaded him to let the destitute family use it. With very limited resources she organized a work party to clean and disinfect it, and make it weather tight. An old stove was moved in, and though it wasn't much as a home, the rehabilitated chicken house provided shelter for the grateful family, who lived there for some time. The father worked on nearby farms, earning food for his family. Libby visited this family often, and her friendship was a comfort to them. When one of the children became ill she persuaded a doctor to make a call.

The illness was serious. The doctor left medicines, and Libby helped the distraught mother care for the child. The little girl had been undernourished for a long time and lacked the strength to overcome the illness. Libby was there with the mother when the child died. The parents, complete strangers in the community, were at a loss concerning what to do next. Though the farmer would have allowed it, the grieving mother and father could not emotionally bring themselves to bury the child on a private farm in an unfamiliar area, which had been the frontier custom. They had no church connections and no caring pastor to comfort them.

Libby simply took over. She made arrangements to have the child buried in a section of the county cemetery where people without funds were buried. She found volunteers to dig the grave. The parents said they did not feel free to ask a minister, none of whom they knew, to conduct a burial service, and would be much obliged if Libby would do it. Glad to do it, she delivered a sincerely felt graveside service. Several neighbors who had become friends of the destitute family later told Libby that her service was one of the most meaningful they had ever heard. She was deeply touched by that, however it came as no surprise to her children, who knew her way with words and her desire to do missionary work.

Several years later, when David was old enough to drive, he would become her chauffeur, sometimes driving Libby to the cheaply built apartments on the other side of the tracks. There he read books or did his homework while she visited the poor and distraught. On their drives together they shared a closeness, often discussing the circumstances of the poor of the community and the reasons for the continued economic depression. They also discussed pacifism, her belief that war was an unchristian behavior unlikely to solve the problems it was meant to solve and very likely to create worse problems in its wake. In this belief she was not alone. Partly as a reaction to the disillusionment after WWI, the Peace Movement had grown strong and politically powerful in the 1920s and 1930s. Libby made sure it remained on the agenda of Methodist conferences.

For enjoyment, she wrote articles for the *Minidoka County News* and would continue to write them for many years. For a time she wrote a weekly social affairs column. This kept her in close touch with people of all religious persuasions and political interests. Meanwhile she continued reading the theological journals to which she subscribed as well as theological and philosophical books.

Despite her broadening social contacts and her satisfaction with her intellectual and church life, Libby continued to feel troubled by a growing distance between her and young Arthur, and the continuing distance between her and Grace. Arthur often came in late at night. Her sources in town mentioned a group of senior boys who were doing some drinking. It hurt her profoundly to suspect that her son was one of them, but she could not maneuver him into telling her what he did at night any more than she could get him to share his thoughts and plans. She wondered: *"Why is it that my two brightest children are the ones I understand the least? Why are Grace and Arthur determined to move away from my influence and out of my reach, when so many other people hope to elicit my advice and counsel?"* It seemed to her that loving them had not been enough, yet she didn't know what more she could have done.

Grace had become a respected young school teacher in a small cattle town. She knew that Libby viewed dancing, and certainly drinking, as sinful, but Grace believed dancing was no more sinful than sharing a meal. She loved to dance and was an excellent dancer. Dancing was a popular form of social activity. Often there would be some drinking, but if people behaved themselves it was tolerated and overlooked. Now Grace, unknown to Libby, was in love with Stanley Jenkins, a man six years her senior whom she had met at a dance.

In one of her rare letters Grace pleased Libby by mentioning that she was teaching a Sunday School class in the community church. But she included little more information about her life. Grace never felt free to share with her family the details of her personal life. She didn't mention her romance with the handsome, good-natured young rancher. In 1934 she would marry Stanley Jenkins in a private ceremony, and it would be many months after the marriage before Dad and Libby would find out about it. Knowing she would lose her job, Grace also kept her marriage a secret from the school authorities. Neither Libby nor anyone else in the family ever knew for sure exactly where she lived, but she probably took lodging in Grand View, the little town where she taught school. This was near the Jenkins ranch.

Meanwhile Donald was enjoying his classes in high school and his job with the livestock. Connie faithfully wrote letters, came home during vacations, and in 1933 was progressing at the College of Idaho toward her teaching certificate.

In 1933 A letter arrived from sister Alice in Utah with the startling news that David lay very ill in Scotland. Alice wrote that she was on her way to Dumbarton to care for him. "I owe it to the family to care for our dear brother, and I don't plan to return to Utah." Puzzled, Libby read on. "John and I are parting ways."

Grieved to hear of David's illness, Libby wrote him a letter to thank him for all he had done for her during her youth. She told him she was praying for his health. Regarding Alice leaving John McQueen, she didn't know what to say, and wrote only that she was sorry to hear of it.

———

As soon as the remodeling was finished on the house, the family moved back to the farm. In no way was the house luxurious, but it was quite adequate. They now had two good sized, well made bedrooms downstairs, a full attic, hot and cold running water, and a flush toilet.

A stairway led to the attic, which was roomy enough for two bedrooms if they ever decided to finish them, which they did not. This attic of bare studs and uncovered rafters provided a great deal of needed storage space. Donald chose to put his bed up there, and had his own private sleeping quarters for the first time in his life. One day while preparing clothes for the wash, Mom found, in one of his pockets, a very melancholy poem about his lonely nights in the attic. She wept. Later she gently questioned him about it, but he assured her that he liked his attic. He was, at times, simply a melancholy person. He also assured her that he loved his mother, enjoyed his home, and appreciated all that she and Dad did for him.

In 1933 Arthur finished high school and Connie finished her first year of college. They both lived and worked at home that summer, and in the fall Arthur entered the College of Idaho. To save on living costs, Arthur and Connie shared a small converted garage in Caldwell. They had always been close friends and enjoyed each other's company. Both had rather exceptional singing voices, and they enjoyed singing the duets of the popular film stars Nelson Eddie and Jeanette McDonald.

Arthur was sixteen and would not turn seventeen until December. Although he was well prepared academically and impressed people as being exceptionally mature for his age, Libby and Dad were both concerned. Would a sixteen-year-old have the judgement and experience needed to do well in college?

They soon had evidence that their fears were well grounded. Arthur turned out for football, a sport that he had managed well in Rupert High School. But college competition was different. Across the line of scrimmage he faced older boys and grown men, all of them more experienced, many of them bigger and stronger. He was not accustomed to being dominated on the field or anywhere else. The coach didn't allow him to play as much as he wanted. In practice he received an injury to his knee that caused him a great deal of pain. Misguided pride kept him from reporting it and admitting he was hurt. Not receiving the treatment he needed, he suffered while he continued to practice. The injury was slowly becoming more bearable, but the hurt to his pride lingered. He realized that he needed more size and experience to be a college football star. The season ended with the traditional Thanksgiving game. Since he would not be playing, he made a quick decision to skip the game and go home for the two-day holiday.

Connie worked on campus and was unable to go home. Arthur had no money for a train ticket, but, having studied the ways of some daring hobos, he made a very foolish and dangerous decision. As the fast passenger train left the station, he jumped on the engine to "ride the blinds." He thought if others had done it, he could too. It meant clinging to a narrow space on the side of the engine shielded from the engineer's view. This was a very fast train with only one brief stop before it reached the junction town of Minidoka, a high speed run of two hundred miles.

Donald was at home alone when the telephone rang five short rings—the Smith signal on the sixteen-family party line. Dad was at work, having driven his county car, and Libby had gone somewhere with a neighbor. Donald picked up the tubular earpiece on the wall phone and spoke into the jutting mouthpiece.

It was Arthur, barely able to speak. "I'm in Minidoka, at the train depot. Can you come and get me?"

Donald left at once in the family car to drive the fourteen miles to Minidoka. Though it was nearly noon, the temperature on that late November day was just above freezing. Frost lingered in the shadows of the trees and buildings. He found Arthur in a state of near shock, sitting on a bench beside the depot. Why he was not inside trying to get warm, Donald never figured out; Arthur didn't answer him. Perhaps hypothermia had advanced far enough to cloud his thoughts. Perhaps, having been involved in an illegal act, he was avoiding the risk of being questioned.

On the way home Arthur sat in silence. In the house he began to shiver. Donald sat him in a chair, wrapped him in a wool blanket, and fixed him a mug of warm milk. In about an hour he began to get control of his shaking. He had dressed warmly but admitted he had underestimated how cold it would be on the outside of a steel engine traveling at seventy miles an hour. He admitted that he could not remember much about arriving at Minidoka or making the phone call. He mentioned that there had been a time when he seriously wondered if he could hang on any longer.

"But I guess I did so it turned out all right. It won't be necessary to go into detail telling the folks about it."

From long experience Donald knew that this was not a suggestion, but an order.

When the folks arrived home, Arthur was quite himself again and simply said, "I decided to come home for Thanksgiving and rode the blinds of the Portland Rose. Guys do it all the time."

He spent much of the holiday sleeping. At Thanksgiving dinner he had very little to say about his experiences at college. He said he was doing fine in his classes and liked his professors, but Libby noticed that he seemed quite discouraged. He assured the family that Connie was doing well.

After the holiday, at Libby's insistence, Dad bought Arthur a bus ticket back to Caldwell. Connie had not worried about him, rightly guessing that he had gone home for Thanksgiving. She assumed he had hitchhiked or arranged a ride with friends.

He returned to his usual routine. When school was dismissed for the Christmas holidays, jobs were hard to come by and he made no effort to find one, nor did he go to Rupert. Connie's work continued through the holidays. Each day when she returned to their room, she would find him reading a little or doing nothing at all. He seemed depressed, moody, and not interested in visiting or doing anything. She began to worry. The last night of the Christmas break he sat up very late, making no effort to prepare for school the following day.

"Arthur, classes start in the morning. You've got to get some rest," Connie told him.

"I've decided to quit school. There's no future in it. There are no jobs out there anyway. I'm going to ride the rails and learn about life that way. I'll see America. A lot of fine men do that. At least they're learning something about the real world. There's a freight train going through about midnight. You don't need to say anything to the folks. I'll write when I can."

"You can't just leave! You've got to stop in Rupert and tell the folks what you're doing."

"I don't know what I'm doing. And I won't know till I do it. There's nothing to tell them."

Strongly disagreeing, she finally said, "You'll need some identification."

"I don't want any. Guys will know who and what I am when they meet me. That's all that counts. Where I come from and who my parents are won't mean a thing to anyone."

When Connie left in the morning, Arthur was still sleeping. He had prepared a "hobo bundle," and his coat lay beside it. Quietly she slipped an identification card in an unused inside pocket of his coat and went off to her classes, later her work. When she returned in the evening Arthur was gone. Sorrow and loneliness washed over her. During the first weeks of school, the two of them had enjoyed some good times together and shared many long discussions about school and life. Now she wondered if she'd ever see him again. Being close to her parents, she understood how great a blow this would be to them.

It was night and she knew her parents had gone to bed. Hoping Arthur might take her advice and stop to say good-bye to the folks, Connie waited until the next day to go out and find a phone to call Rupert.

Mainline freight trains didn't stop in Rupert. Having had more hours to think it over, Arthur knew it wasn't right to leave without telling his parents, particularly when they assumed he was in school. But he didn't want them to question him. When the train stopped in Minidoka to switch off some cars and pick up more from the branch line, he took the risk of being seen, jumped off and phoned them. By now it was in the wee hours of the morning. Libby finally answered.

"Mom, I'm leaving school," he said. "I'm just wasting my time there. I'm riding the rails and will be gone a long time. I've only got a minute before the train leaves."

Stunned and half asleep, Libby asked, "Where are you?"

"It doesn't matter. I'll drop you a card in a few days. I'll be OK." The line went dead.

Early the next morning, the five short rings sounded again. Libby went swiftly to phone. It was Connie, relieved to learn that Arthur had called but angry that he hadn't stopped to see them. Over the phone, Libby and Connie shared a good cry. Dad stood in the room, his dark face showing a mixture of grief and anger.

Libby was beside herself for fear of what might happen to her son. She had read stories about killings on the rails and accidents—men run over, their legs cut off. Yet many young people viewed that illegal means of travel as exciting. Thousands of poor men and young people were riding the freight cars, risking beatings by the "bulls" and injuries getting on and off of moving trains for what one radio commentator called "the romance of the rails." There was absolutely nothing that Libby, Art, Donald, Connie or David could do but share their fear and despair.

True to his word, about every two weeks Arthur wrote home, a short message on a post card. He also wrote from time to time to Connie. Libby always rejoiced to learn that he was alive, but felt very frustrated to be unable to write to him. He said that he was never in any place long enough to receive a letter. She laid out a map of the United States on the kitchen table and over the next months charted his progress with straight pins—down through Utah, where a January cold snap must have nearly frozen him to death. Years later his children would hear how he stayed alive by running in circles all night. The train took him south through New Mexico, east to Texas and across that vast state. For a time he worked as a longshoreman on the Gulf Coast, then caught a freight across the deep South and finally to Florida. He wrote that he liked the weather in the South and that hundreds of men were spending the cold months there.

In early April, 1934, he was again riding freight cars, moving up the east coast. The Depression continued to foster crime and stir up the unemployed population. Men were killed for their shoes or coats— Arthur had a good coat and a pair of new leather shoes paid for by his farm income. Libby lived in a constant state of fear. In addition to vicious railroad authorities, "bulls," there were reports of brutal behavior among the hobos themselves. In some places in the South, hobos were arrested and put into chain gangs without a trial. What would be the fate of a handsome, inexperienced boy? A boy riding for days in box cars with unsavory characters and sleeping in "hobo jungles?"

Dad tried to comfort Libby by mentioning that Arthur was an excellent athlete, weighed nearly 170 pounds and was stronger than most men his size. But she was not consoled. Her beautiful and talented boy seemed determined to get himself killed.

They all looked forward to his next postcard, but none came for another six weeks, during which time Libby was frantic with fear. What had happened to him? Who could she write who could try to find him? Then a card from Florida simply stated that he would go west. "All is well, don't worry about me." How typical of Arthur, she thought. In grave danger and telling them not to worry! Much later he would tell his children about a narrow escape during a knife fight when a hobo enclave erupted in a race riot. Libby did what she could: prayed for her wandering son.

Dad continued to say things like, "He's a tough kid. He's taken care of himself so far. He'll be all right." But Libby could tell that in his heart Dad was hurt and grieving. This was his fine, bright first born son. How could this be happening? How could he do such a thing to his parents who loved him? Why would he want to be a hobo? Why would he deliberately associate with "low" and criminal elements?

A month later another card came from a small town on the Mississippi. "I'm living with a family on a houseboat on the river. I've been sick but they are taking care of me and I'm feeling better." There was no return address. Then, after more weeks of worry and wondering, a card came from a small town in Missouri, and ten days later, in early July, a phone call from Minidoka. "Will someone come and pick me up?"

Libby and Dad welcomed him home like the Prodigal Son. With tears of joy she embraced him. In a very uncharacteristic action, Dad also embraced him. Arthur's hair had been cut in the past month, not professionally, but it was neat. "Somebody washed and mended your clothes," Libby observed, "And who cut your hair?"

"There was a girl on the houseboat. I guess she did a pretty good job. She cuts the hair of everyone in her family. She seemed to like me." Libby silently thanked God that he'd had the sense to leave. Later his children would hear a sketchy story about a "pretty quadroon" who lived on a houseboat with her family. A wandering artist came by and painted her—a painting Arthur thought worthy of the best museum. It was hanging in the living room of the houseboat when he left.

Libby could tell he was glad to be home, but he treated his absence as nothing exceptional. Parrying most questions, he had very little to say about his adventures. He treated the whole thing as if he'd been visiting friends for a few days. Libby soon realized it was pointless to ask questions.

Connie, having finished two years of college, was attending summer school at the teachers college at Albion, not far from Rupert. She came home every weekend and looked forward to starting a teaching job in the fall in a rural school not far from Rupert. Much as she loved her brother, she was indignant and gave him a heartfelt scolding. "Why did you just walk off and leave? You didn't even talk to your professors, people who could have helped you understand what was going on inside that head of yours. What a horrible way to treat your parents! And me! Why didn't you talk about your trouble in school, or whatever it was, at least say something?"

"I just wanted to leave." That was the end of the discussion. Over the next few years bits and pieces of his strange experience would come out. He had traveled over 36,000 miles. He believed he had learned a lot more about people, himself, the world, and life in general than he would have learned in school. He told of a few bad experiences, such as coming into a hobo jungle where a group of men had just killed a particularly mean "bull" and nailed him to a tree. He told of trying to sleep in swamps where all night he heard the roaring of alligators. He told a little of how he ended up in the riverboat. He had seen some men unloading grain, carrying heavy sacks up a steep ramp from a boat to the top of a levee. The men were not very strong and were having a hard time. When he stopped to help, they were amazed at how easily he could shoulder a hundred pound sack and walk briskly up the ramp, not having to rest after each trip. When the job was finished he was invited to supper on one of the boats. They were friendly and hoped he would stay, marry the eldest daughter, and become part of the family. He said she was nice but that kind of life didn't appeal to him. Then his sick spell, during which she took care of him, caused him to stay longer than he had planned. He headed west as soon as he felt well enough. All of it disturbed Libby.

Over fifty years later, Arthur told his daughter that he had gone first to the Gulf Coast of Texas to work as a stevedore at the docks and save money to sail to South America, Brazil in particular. He hoped to acquire land and make his fortune as a pioneering farmer, much as his great-grandfather William P. Smith had done in Utah. But news of a revolution in Brazil arrived on one of the ships, and he changed his mind.

He seemed content to simply slip back into his former life. Libby knew she would never understand this son whom she loved so dearly, this son who seemed to be driven by alien forces. He had a passion for knowledge and was constantly checking books out of the library. He read philosophers she had never heard of, seemingly searching for something. To her sorrow, she noticed he was also reading books that questioned the basic tenets of Christianity. She remembered how, when she was his age, she had yearned for something more in life, a sense of assurance, and found it in her father's faith. Would he find assurance? She knew she couldn't help him, so she kept her thoughts to herself.

In September, 1933, Arthur, now three months shy of his eighteenth birthday, resumed college but at the Southern Branch of the University of Idaho located in Pocatello. He teamed up with a brilliant pre-law student and they set a remarkable record as a debate team. Both were persuasive speakers, each having almost total recall to speak without notes. They defeated many of the major colleges and universities on the west coast. Libby revelled in collecting newspaper clippings about their successes. Often they argued current political issues, taking one position then arguing the reverse. *At last*, she thought, *he has found himself and will have a distinguished career in politics or law.* But that was not to happen soon. Money was scarce and the family could give him little help. But he was eager to be independent and planned to teach school for a while to support himself. Later it would be revealed that he was doing a good deal of drinking, a habit that would hurt him in years to come and nearly break Libby's heart.

In September, 1934, Connie began her teaching career in a rural school not far from Rupert. She boarded with a farm family who also had a daughter teaching in the school, all active members of the Methodist Church. Often Connie returned home to attend church with her parents on Sunday, much to the delight of Dad and Libby.

David helped around the place, mowed the lawn and helped build Donald's rabbit hutches. Dad commented about David's remarkable patience. In the evenings he would sit motionless in the kitchen for an hour with his beebee gun waiting for a mouse to make an appearance. Other farm families had indoor cats for that purpose, but Libby couldn't abide animals in the house. The report of the gun would nearly bring her off her chair in momentary fright, until she remembered David. He normally got his mouse. Dad found David's patience useful when a troublesome weasel was killing chickens. It was a very shy creature, but David outwaited it.

Connie comforted Libby when a letter came from Alice in Scotland with the tragic news that David had died. Born in 1872, he had been sixty-two years old. Father Symon had been fifty-three. Libby wished she had been at David's bedside to tell him how much he had meant to her. Her eyes clouded with tears to read that so many of his friends from the railroad and loyal friends of the Symon family had attended the funeral, as well as brother John. "I'll stay here for as long as it takes to settle David's affairs," Alice wrote, "but after that there is nothing to keep me in Scotland."

Nearly a year later Alice wrote from Scotland that she was packing to go to a city in southern California called Long Beach. "I understand the weather is warm there in winter," was her only explanation.

Libby reflected that Alice could have stayed on the farm, or with Marjorie. Both she and Marjorie would have been glad to open their homes to her. But then, she told herself, Idaho and British Columbia were cold in the winter and Alice seemed to have made up her mind.

Still, it didn't seem right that she would go to a city where she didn't know a soul. Or did she know someone?

A second death in 1934 brought the family together in Union. Allie called to say that Mother Lucy Smith had died in her home of a heart attack. She had seemed very healthy until the attack. Grace and Arthur joined Libby, Dad, David and Bob for the long drive to Union. Donald stayed to care for the animals. Libby could see that Dad suffered greatly; he said little on the drive.

—

Besides providing a home for Bobby, David, Donald and Dad, Libby continued her church and local "missionary" work, her reading, and her newspaper writing. In addition to being involved in the lives of many people in Rupert, she carried on a correspondence with her grown children and kept up with the social and intellectual lives of the children who were still at home. She could feel her mind and emotions expanding to include the ever-expanding worlds of her six children. Their joys and achievements were hers too. Lack of information caused her the greatest worry. But unlike some involved mothers, Libby respected the right of her children to make their own mistakes. She made it a point not to interfere directly beyond giving judicious advice, particularly when they asked for it.

For two years Grace kept her marriage to Stanley Jenkins a secret from the school board—a very unsatisfactory arrangement, Libby knew. Grace finally resigned her teaching job and began living on the Jenkins ranch with her husband, but soon faced the fact that being a ranch wife was not for her. She wrote that her husband's mother owned the property and house, causing Grace some consternation—something Libby could well imagine.

Stanley then took a job in Nampa in a service station and Grace tried to find a school in that larger town that would hire a married woman teacher. Libby shook her head in sorrow. Why hadn't Grace married a man with more education?

In the spring of 1935, Arthur wrote that he had qualified for his teaching certificate. He was eighteen years old. Almost immediately he received a phone call from a woman in a rural school district in Jefferson County, north of Pocatello and about two hundred miles from Rupert. Mrs. Miller said her daughter had met him at the college and recommended him as a teacher for Clark School, near Ririe, where several Miller children attended.

Pleased, Arthur caught a ride to the farm and was interviewed. He was hired, and arranged to board with the Millers. Like Libby in Union, he found himself surrounded by a large, close farm family. The pioneering grandfather owned much of the surrounding countryside— dry farms and grazing land for livestock. The old pioneer couple lived a few miles up the road in the little town of Ririe. One son managed the dry farming operations while the other, the father of the girl who had recommended Arthur, ran the livestock. "Both sides of the business are well managed," he wrote. "It is a fine thing to see farmers having a little economic success." He concluded with the fact that he greatly enjoyed the beautiful upper Snake River Valley with its good fishing and mountainous terrain, not far from Yellowstone National Park.

Libby would have preferred to see him pursue a college degree, but he was a very independent-minded person and she knew that he wanted to earn more money than he could working at odd jobs around the college. This way, she reasoned, he could save more money toward furthering his education.

Like her, Arthur celebrated his nineteenth birthday during his first year of teaching, and, like her, very much enjoyed his work, in his case in a one-room school with eight grades. She reflected that he was a natural teacher with a great deal of charisma. Unknown to her, there was another similarity. He was immediately attracted to a young person in the Miller house, the Millers' eldest daughter Alice. In her first quarter at the college in Pocatello Alice had played a part in a school musical and been impressed by Arthur's performance in the lead role.

Her own singing and acting attracted the notice of a group of entertainers who invited her to join them for a long-running gig in Salt
Lake. Thrilled, Alice agreed, hoping that in Salt Lake she would be
"discovered" by someone from Hollywood—her dream. But as she
was packing to leave the dorm, Mrs. Miller arrived and forcibly removed her back to the farm. Someone had notified her that her daughter was about to start on a life of singing and acting, which Mr. Miller
regarded as a low class occupation. Libby would have been in definite
agreement had she known anything about it.

Boarding in the house with the unhappy Alice, who disliked everything about farm life, Arthur fell in love. Alice loved him too, and
they were able to keep it secret during much of Arthur's first year of
teaching. Alice went to Idaho Falls to live with her aunt and uncle and
work in a bank, but she came home on weekends and holidays, and in
due time the romance became obvious. Like Libby, Arthur suffered
coldness and hostility and a sense that he had betrayed the trust of
those who had opened their home to him. In the midst of a winter
blizzard during his second school term, he moved to an unheated
outbuilding on a property closer to the school. Now he walked to
school instead of riding with a sleighload of Miller pupils.

During the Christmas break Libby received a letter from Arthur,
mentioning none of these personal matters. He wrote that Vardis Fisher
had grown up in the upper Snake River Valley, and as a child had been
a classmate of Mr. Miller's. "Fisher writes about the mountain men
and homesteaders of this area. I feel like when I go to Ririe, I see his
characters walking all around me. He is getting excellent national re-
views now, but the locals don't think very highly of him. I fish at Fall
Creek near the deserted log cabin where he lived as a boy."

Libby knew nothing about that writer, but was interested in his
having lived in a log cabin in Idaho. Soon afterward, she was visiting
in the home of Reverend Roseberry, the pastor who followed the cockney
Reverend Phillips in Rupert. By now George Roseberry was a close
personal friend. There was no fire in the living room heating stove

where he disposed of unwanted paper. Libby glanced inside the open stove door and was shocked to see a new book on top of the trash. "George!" she exclaimed, "You should not be burning a book!" She respected the printed word, and associated book-burning with ignorant, repressive regimes. She reached in and retrieved what turned out to be a novel by Vardis Fisher.

"That book should be burned," the pastor said. "It is filthy, not fit to be read."

Over George's objections she took the book home and read it. Upset by the explicit scenes, she agreed completely with her pastor's judgement that it was not fit to read. She talked to Dad. He was not much of a reader of novels, but decided to read this one because Arthur seemed to like the man's work.

Dad completely agreed that the book was unfit to read. "Clearly" he added, "Fisher grew up in poverty and ignorance, to write about it in that detail."

Libby wondered how any child who had lived such a life could have developed such a facility with the English language. "Sometimes I think Arthur is fascinated by the cruel and ugly side of pioneer life," she said.

Dad was silent. Libby realized that he hadn't told her much about his forbearers and their pioneer relatives. The only one she remembered was a one-legged uncle who, as a very young child, had lost his entire leg in a buggy accident. In high school he had set a state high jumping record and was mentioned in *Ripley's Believe It Or Not*. She had met him at a Smith family reunion in Smithville, Utah. Young Arty and Donald had been mesmerized by him.

Libby did not object when Donald, who was a junior in high school and an avid reader, wanted to read the novel by Vardis Fisher. Her feelings were mixed. She deplored the obscenities but judged Donald to be adult enough to draw his own conclusions. Donald would read most of Fisher's books, though on one occasion a librarian was shocked when he asked for one, letting him know that the library did not stock "immoral" books. Donald mentioned to Libby that Fisher saw human nature as nihilistic and despairing. He told her that in his opinion Fisher's *In Tragic Life* (1932) and his latest book, *Passion Spins the Plot* (1934), contained some brilliant writing. "But he is brutally realistic."

"I am not sure," she replied, "whether we need to be shown more of that kind of realism when so much of it abounds in the world and needs to be rectified."

———

In 1935 Libby corresponded with sister Alice in Long Beach, California. Libby briefly wrote about the children and their lives. Alice's letters seemed a little sad, as though she hadn't made friends in the new place. Then one day a letter came from a church member who had found Libby's letters among Alice's effects. Alice had passed away at the age of sixty-one. A service would be held in the Presbyterian church.

Heartsick more than she had imagined she would be, Libby boarded the train with her hastily packed suitcase. Dad and the boys said they could manage. She took a spur line to Elko, Nevada, crossed the desert on the famous transcontinental railroad, chugged over the high Sierra and on to Sacramento. Unable to sleep well despite the familiar swaying and clicking of the rails, she talked occasionally with other passengers but mostly, as the train passed through Oakland, then south through San Luis Obispo, Santa Barbara and Ventura, invited memories of the manse and her early life to unfold before her eyes. She reflected upon the legacy of the Symon family—their closeness and sense of duty to each other, their push to become educated, and their faith and determination to live their Christian ideals—except perhaps for John. David and Alice had been her parents for as long as her actual parents had been, and, like a devoted mother, Alice had come to Libby's aid on many occasions.

Alice had lived only a year after David died. Had she been ill too?

Had she gone to Long Beach because she hadn't wanted to burden Libby by coming to the farm, possibly to die? Could that have been the reason she left John McQueen? No, Libby decided, people who loved each other stayed together to the end. So did people who were disappointed in each other but honored their marriage vows before God. All Libby had been able to learn was that John had lost his restaurant business and seemed to lose himself too—perhaps another casualty of the Depression. He'd had no strong faith to moor him, and his chosen church had rejected him.

Now only Marjorie was left. Libby pondered the fact that neither David nor Alice had had children, neither had John or Nellie. Now past childbearing age, Marjorie had only one child. This meant that if the legacy of the Symon family were to pass to subsequent generations and the larger world, nearly all of it would be through Libby. Or would hedonistic and materialistic values dilute that heritage more each generation until it was unrecognizable? But such speculation was for naught. Her responsibility as a Christian was simply to love God, bear witness to her faith, and encourage the younger generation to raise themseves up through education and morals.

"(She) is like a tree planted by streams of water, that yields its fruit in its season, and its leaf does not wither."

Proverbs 1:3

17 The Fullness of her Life

To Libby's great joy, Donald decided during his senior year in high school to become a Methodist minister. The previous summer he had been chosen as one of five delegates to represent Idaho at a national Methodist youth convention in Berea, Kentucky. Thousands of young people gathered there. To save money on transportation, a minister from Pocatello drove his car. Donald and some of the other Idaho delegates took turns relieving him as the driver so they could travel almost without stopping.

About a week after Donald left for the convention, the postman brought a letter. Donald wrote about the inspirational effect of participating with thousands of like-minded young people in one great meeting, and how he enjoyed sharing ideas about the future of the church with them. Almost as a humorous aside, he said that never in the programs and discussions had he heard communism mentioned, despite what had been written in the paper. Puzzled, she unfolded a newspaper article clipped from a prominent Kentucky newspaper. The headline blared:

COMMUNIST INFILTRATION AND INFLUENCE ON CHURCH YOUTH CAMP

Libby groaned. Clearly the article had been written by an ignorant person. While it was true that many good and sincere people in the church were studying the "Russian experiment," that was far from the intent of the convention. It saddened her that in some instances arguments within the churches had become bitter about the social gospel. She knew that President Roosevelt was often called a communist or a communist sympathizer because of his social programs. And she had heard pacifism lumped together with communism. Why, she wondered, were people so quick to jump to exaggerated and harmful conclusions?

Donald returned from the convention obviously filled with a greater sense of purpose. During his senior year he reported to the Idaho Conference about the youth convention. He also spoke in various Methodist churches about his experience. "I really enjoy doing this, Mom," he told her one evening after supper when they were alone.

She gave it her full attention. "What is it you like most about it?"

"Well, I guess I like being able to talk openly about my beliefs, and it seems to me that people appreciate the way I speak. At least they come up and tell me they do."

"You hail from a line of speakers. Do you think you'd like to be a minister?"

"Yes, I think I would."

She felt ecstatic that one of her sons felt called to the profession of her father, the highest of professions. By the end of his senior year she could tell that he felt committed to continuing his education to become a preacher and pastor. She prayed that he would hold to that commitment through four years of college and three years of graduate school

Libby and Dad were losing "Hank the hired man," and that would bring a big change in their lives. The little college in Gooding that Donald would attend in the fall—only sixty miles from Rupert—was struggling financially and might close. In that case Donald would go to Salem, Oregon, to Willamette University, which meant that they would see much less of him. David lacked Donald's enthusiasm for the farm animals and the haying, so Dad and Libby decided to sell all but one cow, one sow, and two of Dad's work horses. They turned the entire farming operation over to the renter who handled the crops, though the family continued to live in the farmhouse. Dad cared for the remaining animals and quite enjoyed it.

That fall Donald started college in Gooding. He hitchhiked home on weekends and holidays, an activity that frightened Libby. He said he enjoyed the conversations with the men who gave him rides. Then the college gave up the fight and closed its doors. Donald transferred to Willamette University. Salem was much farther from home. To Libby's sorrow he would seldom get back to Rupert again because he worked to support his four years of education. But though he was leaving his close family involvement, his letters always cheered her.

The family at home now consisted of Bobby, who was starting the first grade, and twelve-year-old David, who had become Libby's driver when Dad was not at home. In addition, Connie was now teaching in a Rupert school and living at home—paying Dad for her board. Consolidation having closed Hopewell School, David and Bobby rode the bus to their schools in town. Thus, for the first time since Grace's birth, Libby had the house to herself during school hours. In the evenings Connie worked on correspondence courses and on weekends helped with the cleaning. Libby truly enjoyed having her in the house again, sharing her detailed and often humorous experiences with the little children. Every morning Dad drove Connie to her school, which gave them good opportunities to visit, and if he had to visit a farmer in another direction, she rode the school bus with David and Bobby.

Meanwhile, Arthur seldom wrote letters. Libby hoped he was saving enough money to return to college. But in February of his second year of teaching, her hopes were dashed. While the family was getting ready for church Arthur called to say that he and Alice Miller were getting married. He hoped to introduce her to his family.

Stunned, Libby stood in her corset and slip with the receiver on her ear, the unspoken words on her tongue: Why the big hurry to get married? He had just turned twenty. Was the girl pregnant? In all her upbringing and efforts to raise a respectable and good family, this was something Libby had never imagined would happen. Getting a girl pregnant outside of marriage just couldn't happen in a family related to John Symon. It was a low class phenomenon. But maybe she was jumping to conclusions. Finally she was able to speak. "Is she Mormon?" That part of Idaho was largely Mormon.

"The Millers left the Mormon Church two generations ago. They left Utah to get away from Brigham Young. Now some go to the Presbyterian Church. There's a little one in Ririe. Sometimes Alice goes there with her grandmother and Aunt Marguerite."

Only slightly relieved, Libby asked, "How do her parents feel about your getting married?"

"Well, her father didn't like the idea when I first mentioned it. We had a fight. He was pretty strong but I guess it was a draw in the end. We didn't discuss it again. I borrowed his car. His wife said it was all right."

Still trying to regain her composure after hearing about a physical fight—only a little less disreputable than getting a girl pregnant—Libby didn't completely hear the rest of what he'd said. "Where are you now?"

"In a hotel in Idaho Falls. I was hoping you might prevail on George Roseberry, but that's all right. We can just go to the Justice of the Peace."

Now Libby had the whole picture. "No bring her here. We'll want to meet her. I'll talk to George."

She phoned. George hadn't left for church yet. He agreed to perform a private wedding later that afternoon in the Smith home. He mentioned his fondness for Arthur, whom he remembered from the Methodist Youth Fellowship. After she hung up, Libby went behind the haystack to pray, then prevailed on the boys to help her clean the house before church.

Six hours later Arthur arrived with Alice, a pretty girl with long red hair. For all her disappointment about the circumstances, Libby found herself quite attracted to Alice, who was friendly and cheerful.

Dad, still in his Sunday clothes, seemed very reserved, possibly angry. Also still in their Sunday suits, David and Bobby were clearly pleased to see Arthur.

"Where is Connie?" Arthur asked. Libby explained that yesterday she had gone to Boise on a shopping trip with a teacher friend but was expected back at any moment.

Libby told the operater to connect her to George Roseberry. Twenty minutes later the pastor pulled up in his car, but Connie still wasn't there.

"I'm very close to my sister," Arthur explained, shaking hands with the minister, "and would like her to be here for my wedding, if you wouldn't mind waiting for a little while."

Apparently in no rush, George sat down and waited. To pass the time Arthur talked Alice into playing the piano.

Still struggling with the fact that her young Arthur was getting married, Libby was surprised to hear Alice play a Chopin piece with great skill. Libby told herself that this said something for the way she had been brought up. Smiling to hear such music, David and Bobby sat on the sofa waiting for the wedding. Later Alice played tunes that they all knew and everyone sang, including Libby. Then Arthur and Alice harmonized to *Indian Love Song*, from a popular moving picture. Libby couldn't help but recall the evenings in Lucy and Hyrum Smith's home when she and Dad had harmonized to the accompaniment of his mandolin. Dad had been Arthur's age. The memory helped her cope with the present.

George had to leave soon and Connie still hadn't arrived, so Arthur and Alice stood together before him in the middle of the living room, Libby and Dad behind, David and Bobby on the sofa. Libby felt that George gave a very touching service. It took her back to her own wedding in sister Alice's apartment. No one from Dad's family had been there either. When it was over, George went to his car to get his gift—a print of a Gothic cathedral in France.

"Don't you think you should call your parents?" Libby suggested to Alice when the minister drove away.

"Oh yes. Would you mind?"

"Of course not." Alice went to the phone and gave the operator her parent's number in Ririe. Almost immediately she was speaking in a very low voice.

Giving her privacy, Libby went into the kitchen to fix dinner. She took a venison roast from the icebox.

Arthur came in. "We'll be leaving right away, Mom, so don't cook anything for us."

"Sandwiches then," Libby said, taking bread from the deep drawer and mustard from the icebox.

A minute or two later Alice joined them and reported somewhat shyly, "They called the police but are sending them away. I think everything will be all right if we hurry back. I told them we are married." She gave Libby a little smile.

"Police! I thought you said they knew you were here."

"Mom knew," Alice said. "Daddy didn't. He reported the car stolen."

Dad stood expressionless in the doorway. Libby gave him a covert look of helpless amazement.

"You'll need to eat," Libby insisted, hurriedly arranging cold meat on bread slices. "Have some milk." She nodded at the glasses on the drain board while stirring the cream down into the pitcher of milk.

As Arthur gulped his milk, Libby said, "Alice, please tell your parents that we'd like to meet them as soon as possible. They are welcome here at any time, or we will drive to your home." She sincerely hoped that she and Dad would not be taken for accomplices in this unfortunately rushed wedding.

———

Alice turned out to be a good correspondent, and it pleased Libby to learn a little more about Arthur's activities. But in the summer a well-meaning letter sent a shiver of fear through her. Alice wrote that

Arthur and her father both loved the mountains and were enjoying working together with the sheep. In Libby's view of vocations, herding sheep ranked very near the bottom, along with such work as stable boy or gardener. Would her brilliant son become a sheepherder for his father-in-law?

She didn't know that Arthur was helping his father-in-law care for a flock of sheep in the high open range of Conant Valley, where the Millers were proving up on more land to expand their large holdings. He respected Bob Miller's neatly organized "sheep camp," a small canvas-covered, horsedrawn wagon, a forerunner of a mobile home, with everything needed for living tucked away in its place. It had a tiny stove with a smokestack jutting out the canvas top and a table on hinges that could be pushed up and out of the way when unneeded. Arthur slept on the ground under the stars, which he always liked, while Bob Miller slept on the bunk in the back of the sheep camp. Arthur savored Mr. Miller's well-seasoned mutton stews with light dumplings and his flaky pies made from the berries they picked in that high country. Each began to appreciate the other's brand of humor, and they became friends, both taking pride in their physical strength. Many years later Arthur told his daughter the details of their fight.

It had happened the autumn before his marriage to Alice. Mr. Miller had been gone for weeks gathering his sheep. It had grown dark on a short day near the end of October when Arthur heard the tinkling bells of the lead ewes and knew the sheep were being brought to the barn for the winter. He went outside to talk to Alice's father alone. Walking up to the horse, he explained that he wanted to marry her. Without a word Mr. Miller leapt from his horse and they fell to the ground, wrestling. Arthur was surprised at the older man's strength. Over twenty years younger, Arthur had expected to "take him down." But the fight was a draw, and he gained a measure of respect for Bob Miller. The effect was mutual. Beating the dust off his hat, Mr. Miller removed a flask from his saddlebags and offered Arthur a swig of whisky.

Silently they shared a drink and nothing more was mentioned about Alice. The next February, with the apparent complicity of her mother, the two young people eloped.

Now, at summer's end Arthur returned to his teaching. He and Alice moved out of her parents' house where they had been occupying a room down the hall from Alice's four brothers and younger sister. "We needed our own place," Alice wrote. She also wrote that Arthur was becoming very well respected in the community. Libby was somewhat appalled to learn that in February and March he had arisen night after night to help the ewes give birth, a difficult experience because a break in the fence had allowed the rams of a larger variety to get at the ewes of a smaller variety. Many of them were dying during lambing. Arthur bought some olive oil and saved some of them.

Libby closed her eyes to remove the image of Arthur with sheep and prayed that he would somehow manage to complete his college education despite the fact that Alice was now pregnant.

One Friday evening Arthur phoned to say that he thought he should get divorced.

Thunderstruck, Libby could only ask, "Why?" To her, divorce was as unthinkable, as disreputable and wrong as getting an unmarried girl pregnant—which, by now it was clear, Alice had not been at the time of their marriage.

"She's a very emotional person. I don't think I can live with it." His tone conveyed a very rare plea for help.

Libby stiffened with resolve. "We'll be there tomorrow." She and Dad left early, driving two hundred miles to the tiny apartment in Idaho Falls. Libby seized Arthur by the arm, took him into the bathroom, locked the door and talked to him sternly but in a low voice that wouldn't be heard by Dad or Alice. In no uncertain terms she explained that most women become emotional when they are pregnant, and they need extra love and support at that time, not the threat of divorce. "You *must not* consider divorce." She gave him her firm expression. To her surprise, Arthur listened.

On January 8, 1938, Libby's first grandchild was born, Arthur Roger. Only fourteen months later Alice Corinne "Naida" followed. Libby could only moan to think how the babies would hamper Arthur's education, but at least he was behaving responsibly toward his wife and children. By then they lived in a cramped little trailer behind the log house built by Alice's mother's parents on the bank of the Snake River—that side of Alice's family was less successful than the Millers. Alice wrote that Arthur took his fishing pole to school and caught fish on his way home. For extra income during the summer months, he leased acreage on a nearby farm and grew potatoes. All of it disturbed Libby. This was not what she had in mind for her son.

She prayed constantly that he would somehow rise above his current situation and find a profession more suited to his wonderful mind and reflective of the better opportunities available to men.

—

After four years of teaching in and around Rupert and finishing her B.A. through correspondence, Connie left home with her savings and went to Northern Colorado University in Greely to earn her Master's Degree. She then taught in a school in Colorado, but always maintained her closeness with Libby and Dad through correspondence. In many ways Libby relied on Connie as a sounding board for her joys and concerns. She missed her daughter.

Donald wrote often about his adventures. Now he was supporting his education by trimming and repairing damaged trees. With his good friend from Idaho, Eldon Morse, he had gone into business: Smith & Morse. He wrote that while the minimum wage established under Roosevelt's National Youth Act was thirty-five cents per hour, he was making the princely sum of two dollars an hour, when he got work, which he often did. During the summer he and Eldon pursued a contact and drove to Rochester, Minnesota, where they doctored trees owned by physicians at the Mayo Clinic. But to Libby the important thing remained: he was climbing around in trees to hasten the day when he could become a Methodist minister. He appeared to be staying the course. She thanked God for that.

In the spring and summer of 1940 Libby participated in a series of happy events that made her feel very much like things were right with the world, at least in her corner of it.

Donald was graduating from Willamette University with a B.A. in sociology. He wrote, inviting the family to come to the ceremony and attend his final sermon in a little Methodist church in Falls City, near Salem, where he had been a weekend pastor during his senior year. After the summer he would go to Pennsylvania to attend graduate school. He had met a girl from Washington state. "Mom and Dad, I would very much like you to come to the graduation and meet Betty. I know you'll like her."

That sounded serious and Libby wasn't about to miss it. Dad took a day of vacation time. With Connie, who had just returned home from a year of teaching in Colorado, the four of them got in the car and Dad drove west. David stayed home to take care of the animals and garden. Nine-year-old Bobby, who had just finished the fourth grade, thought it was a great adventure. They stopped for lunch in Boise.

"While you're having desert," Connie said, "I wonder if you'd mind if I went up the street to say hello to Floyd Anderson."

"Of course not," Libby said. "Give him my best."

"Mine too," Dad added. Libby recalled the boy who had attended the Methodist Youth Fellowship and later had taken Connie to the prom in high school. Though Connie had lost touch with him, Libby knew through her Rupert sources that he had worked his way through college and now had a degree in pharmacology. Apparently Connie knew that he worked nearby.

A short time later Connie returned and said Floyd was on vacation from his job. He had driven his mother and aunt to San Francisco to the World's Fair.

Spirits were high as the family continued on toward Salem. Libby always enjoyed such family tours. Speeding past the many fields and farmhouses, Dad and Bobby tried to guess from a distance what crops were growing. But Dad always won that friendly competition.

—

Donald had met Betty Moser while attending classes at Willamette University. He'd had no money for recreation and very little time for dating; he preached in Falls City on weekends and worked long hours in the trees to pay for his books, tuition and room. He and Betty had seen each other at church, in classes at school, and once in a great while they found time to take a walk around Salem. A petite and cheerful girl with a good mind, Betty also worked for her board and room, in her case at the Oregon State School for the Blind. She was a year behind Donald at Willamette. Then, to concentrate on her teaching credential, Betty transferred to a teacher's college for her last two years. Thus, recently Donald had been "dating" her through correspondence.

He became quite sure Betty was the girl he wanted to marry, though she seemed reticent about men and wasn't sure marriage was a good idea. They kept up a correspondence. By the time Donald's graduation arrived in June of 1940, Betty wrote that she did care for him and would come to Salem with her mother for the graduation. They would also attend his last sermon in Falls City. This put Donald in a very fine state of mind. He planned to work during the summer to buy Betty an engagement ring. Deciding that more income would come from steady work in a cannery, he had procured a job at a very respectable fifty-seven cents per hour, starting in two weeks.

With his parents driving from Idaho, Donald saw a chance for a quick visit home. He wrote, asking Betty if she would make the trip with him and his parents to Rupert after the ceremony. "It would give you an opportunity to see the farm where I grew up.

To his joy, Betty accepted the invitation by return mail.

He had been sharing an upstairs apartment in Salem with Eldon

Morse in the home of a very kind couple, the Armstrongs. Like loving parents they had cared for the busy boys and now insisted on providing rooms for the Smiths and Mrs. Moser.

The graduation was on Saturday. Donald felt very proud in his robe and mortar board, walking across the stage to accept his degree. He was very glad that Connie and Bobby had come too.

The next day in Falls City he preached his farewell sermon. Never before had he preached with family members in the congregation. He had worked hard on his sermon and the congregation was attentive. Libby couldn't have felt prouder, seeing her son in the pulpit with such an appreciative congregation.

Donald was constantly aware of Dad and Mom sitting proudly in the pew, and he found it a trying experience, a preaching situation he would long remember. Part way through the sermon, good-natured Connie got the giggles and could not suppress them. She later confessed that, remembering the many silly things they had done together, seeing her little brother standing in the pulpit looking just like a preacher suddenly struck her as being very funny. Mrs. Moser looked at Connie in obvious puzzlement. Betty, feeling that Connie just wasn't being fair to Donald, had a pained look on her face, and Bobby, not knowing what else to do, simply sat and smirked. Donald couldn't figure out what he had said to produce such a bizarre reaction. He had a difficult time keeping his focus on what he was saying.

Finally it was over. The congregation adjourned outside to a wonderful picnic lunch prepared by the women of the congregation. Libby liked Donald's friends and was relieved to like Betty and Mrs. Moser as well as she did—a teacher who had raised four children during some very hard times after their father died. Dad had planned to leave for home right after the picnic, but the Armstrongs suggested they all make a quick trip to the beach.

"Stay with us another night," Mr. Armstrong told Dad, who had never seen an ocean. "We're going to catch crabs and cook them fresh. It's a family custom."

"You cook them right on the beach?" Dad asked.

"We do indeed, and we'd be honored to have you join us. Don has told us a lot about the two of you."

"I'd sure like to go," said Bobby with a grin.

Libby spoke confidentially to Dad, "I'd like very much to see the open sea again." She'd had glimpses of it from the train when she went to Alice's funeral, but hadn't stayed long enough to see much more than a big port with ocean-going vessels.

And so it was that the landlocked Smiths spent a happy evening on the beach in Oregon. The Armstrongs caught crabs in their traps and prepared a fine treat. Bobby ran across the sand. Libby gazed through the cool mist over the pounding ocean, recalling happy times in faraway Carnoustie. Dad took her by the arm and they walked up and down the beach. Connie clearly enjoyed visiting and laughing with Eldon, and Libby could see that Donald felt very proud to be showing off Betty to his parents, and his parents to Betty's mother. They all laughed over the difficulties of pulling off the crab shells, and afterwards, in good form, Libby told the story of her emigration and her first trip "in" to Yost with Dad. Obviously everyone enjoyed the evening as much as she did. It was late when they returned to Salem to spend a second night with the Armstrongs.

The next morning Dad and Libby said good-bye to Connie, who was on her way to Seattle where she would take the ferry to Victoria, British Columbia, to visit her Aunt Marjorie. Libby would have loved to go, but Dad needed to get back to his work. Besides, this was a chance to get to know Betty.

Before leaving Rupert, not knowing that Betty would be returning with them, Libby and Dad had promised friends in Rupert that they would provide a ride home for their daughter, who was also attending the college. When they picked up Margaret and started east, there were six people in the car with all of their luggage. The weather was unpleasantly hot, which never agreed with Libby, so they planned to drive through the night. When night came and Bobby got sleepy, he was tucked in on the floor of the back seat under the feet of the other passengers. Donald and Dad took turns driving, and all went well.

Betty would long remember the cheerful way in which everyone accepted the crowding and inconvenience without complaint. They had a good time with songs, jokes, stories and laughter. Occasionally one might drop off for a short nap.

Somewhere in Oregon, Libby said, "We can't go through Nampa without stopping to visit Grace." Dad agreed.

At that time Grace and Stanley were living in Nampa, Idaho, not far from the Oregon border. Grace was pregnant and no longer taught school. She had written that she was trying to convince Stanley to get a job near a college so he could get a degree that would lead to a rewarding career. Grace thought that because Dad had done that when he had two small children, Stanley could also. But Libby wasn't so sure. Dad had been committed to his education before he met her. With Margaret and a prospective daughter-in-law in the car, Libby kept such thoughts to herself.

It was only about four o'clock in the morning when they found themselves within an hour's drive of Nampa. It would not do to wake Grace so early in the morning. She was feeling nauseated and must have her sleep. So to kill some time they stopped fifty miles west of Nampa. It was a beautiful summer night, chilly but pleasant.

There were no cars on the highway. The air smelled of sagebrush, and a thick canopy of stars sparkled in the desert sky. The travelers walked around to exercise their cramped bodies. They amused themselves reciting poetry. Libby and Dad always enjoyed an opportunity to recite together the many American, English and Scottish poems they knew. Sometimes she could carry on longer, and sometimes he could get through more verses. Betty exclaimed over the length of the poems they had memorized. All of them rested their weary minds by going over the verses they had shared while working on the farm, Bobby joining in. They sang many songs, and just as the light was coming into the eastern sky, nearby coyotes, with that ability of two or three to sound like a large choir, joined in. It was a rare moment. Betty would always cherish that introduction to the family—a family that in the gray dawn of a summer morning walked around in the desert under fading stars. Somehow it perfectly reflected the fanciful, effervescent side of her future mother-in-law's personality.

During Betty's brief visit to the farm she worked with Libby, picked and canned berries and volunteered to do housework. She joined the family for a day of fishing at a nearby mountain lake. She enjoyed visiting with Bobby, who, in his curiosity, reminded her of her own little brother, Dix, when he was that age. This all delighted Libby. She was quite aware that this was the first time she'd had a chance to get acquainted with and share ideas with a prospective spouse of one of her children. Betty had a mental quickness and spontaneous humor, and Libby thought she would be a good life companion for Donald—if only they could refrain from getting married until he was an ordained minister with a church!

Following the visit to Rupert, Donald and Betty returned to the coast—she to her home in Tenino, Washington. Working twelve hour days in Salem, Donald was able to see her only once during the summer but planned a special visit to Tenino before he hitchhiked to Pennsylvania. The thought of the engagement ring he would buy her kept him going.s

In July he received a letter from Connie. To his amazement, she invited him to her wedding on July 21. Yet she had said nothing in June to indicate that she was dating anyone special. Donald, working long hours six days a week, realized he would miss the wedding.

—

Thinking back on it later, Libby agreed with Connie that what happened after their parting in Salem seemed like something from a novel. Connie had a good visit with Aunt Marjorie, Uncle Ernest and Cousin Laurence Hill. Connie particularly liked Laurence, who was just her age and the only cousin on her mother's side. They saw the sights of Victoria—so very British. Connie planned to leave after one day, but Laurence persuaded her to stay and go swimming with him one more day. Connie agreed. As it turned out, that small decision would profoundly change her life.

The next morning Laurence drove Connie to the ferry. As they were saying good-bye, she looked up and saw Floyd Anderson on the high deck of the boat. She thought she must be seeing things. But it actually was the very same tall young man she had tried to visit in Boise.

On the exhilarating ferry ride back to the Seattle side—blue water all around, small green islands dotting the sound—the two good chums became reacquainted. Connie greeted Floyd's mother and aunt, both of whom she had known from the Rupert Church, and while the two women rested on a bench the young people stood at the railing. As the blue water curled back from the prow, they talked about Floyd's experiences at the World's Fair. Then Connie told him about teaching in Colorado.

"Are you married?" he asked with a smile, the wind blowing his hair straight back.

Gesturing toward the birds correcting their wing angles against the blue sky she said, "I'm as free as those sea gulls." She smiled. "I suppose you are married by now."

"No, as a matter of fact I am not." After a moment he asked, "When are you going back to Rupert?"

"I'm getting on a bus as soon as we land."

"Well, that's a coincidence. I'm driving back to Boise. My car's parked at the dock. Why don't you come with us? We'd love to have you."

Connie joined them, and on that drive to Idaho—much of the time on the same road that Libby and the family had traveled only three days earlier—Connie and Floyd began to see each other in a romantic light. After that they dated often, Floyd driving to Rupert from Boise. Soon they set their wedding date. It had happened fast. Libby remarked wryly that romance was in the air, both Donald and Connie being infected at the same time. Connie broke her teaching contract for the coming year and prepared for the wedding.

It was set for the evening of July 21, 1940, at the Methodist Church in Rupert, the reception to be held afterwards on the lawn of the farmhouse. Libby helped Connie rush the invitations into the mail. Grace responded that she was feeling poorly in her pregnancy, not tolerating the heat well, and could not come. It did indeed seem to be a hot summer, Libby thought. Or was she just growing older and feeling it more keenly?

"Dad," Libby said, "I'm so very glad Connie is having a traditional church wedding."

He looked at her with his warm brown eyes, and she couldn't help but remember how difficult the wait had been before their wedding.

The friendly church was Libby's home away from home. Bobby, Arthur, Alice and two-year-old Roger sat in the pew beside her. Alice had left one-year-old Naida with her mother. The church filled up with friends and relatives of the bride and groom, as well as friends of Libby and Dad, neighbors, Connie's teacher friends, acquaintances from the Church, the Grange, and the county offices. A huge display of fresh garden flowers banked the front of the church, most of the bouquets donated by Connie's friends. The predominant color was blue—tall delphiniums and lush blue asters. David wore a blue aster in his lapel. At sixteen he seemed entirely grown up as he escorted Libby to the front pew in her new flower-patterned dress. When the *Wedding March* started, she turned to see Connie coming down the aisle on Dad's arm. He looked very handsome and proud in his dark suit. Connie looked elegant and beautiful in her simple white dress that came just above her ankles. She wore white slippers and a veil over her face. It brought tears to Libby's eyes—her wonderful daughter marrying a Methodist man with a good profession. Now four of her children would be married or engaged, none to Mormons.

Reverend Parrot asked his first question, "Who gives this woman in holy matrimony?"

For a moment Dad struggled with his emotions. A frog in his throat caused an unintentionally loud and gruff, "I do."

Afterwards, as the wedding party left the sanctuary to the jubilant organ music, Connie joked with him, "That was a pretty loud 'I do.' You didn't need to sound that anxious to get rid of me!" She would laugh about that for years to come.

Libby liked to see the buddy-buddy relationship between Connie and Dad. On the drive to the farm she told Dad that she would have liked to have had that kind of closeness with her father. He smiled over at her. Many guests were already there, parking their cars along the road in front of the farmhouse. Dad had strung a festive string of lights across the front lawn from the big popular tree to the top of the fir tree. Before the church service Arthur and Alice had set the table on the lawn and were now, with David and Bobby, setting vases of Dad's beautiful roses on the table, along with the wedding cake, napkins, punch and glasses. People were bringing flowers from the church, setting them around the front step, under the trees, and all over the living room.

Everything went as it ought to at a happy, romantic wedding reception. Libby felt deeply fulfilled to see so many friends walking around with plates of cake and drinking punch—Connie visiting among them with the graciousness of a princess. When they had a moment to talk, Connie reminded Libby that years earlier she had sat with Floyd in the circle of Methodist youth, singing around the campfire in this very place. "Mom," Connie said, taking Libby's hands, "this has been the most wonderful day of my life. Thank you and Dad so very much." Sixty-one years later, still in a "love match" with her husband, Connie vividly recalled the details of her wedding and reception.

The door to the living room was open, the lights from inside providing more illumination as the last of the sunset faded. Overhead,

Dad's string of lights blazed ever brighter. As planned, Alice went to the piano in the living room and Arthur stood on the doorstep. The piano music started. The guests stopped their visiting and listened to Arthur's tender rendition of,

Mexicali Rose don't cry, dear,
I'll come back to you some sunny day—

He ended on a lingering tone: *Mexicali Rose Good-bye..*

Everyone clapped and exclaimed. Then he sang,

Ah, sweet mystery of life at last I've found you. . .
'Tis love and love alone the world is needing—

When it was over the crowd cheered again, Connie and Floyd clapping in the front row. The happy mood continued into the night as Connie stepped up beside Arthur and they sang their favorite duets. The only near mishap was when two-year-old Roger pulled the tablecloth with all the refreshments riding on it, nearly dumping everything on the lawn.

Libby felt as though she had never been so contented. Her stories and witticisms had people laughing wherever she went. She felt deeply happy. Dad added to the festivities by demonstrating that the father of the bride could still lie on his back on the lawn, put one leg of a kitchen chair on his chin, balance it there, then stand up without touching the chair with his hands or allowing it to topple off his chin. Amazed, the crowd exhaled a collective "ah."

Connie changed clothes and, bouyed by the good wishes of the many people, she and Floyd left for Boise. Alice, David and Bobby carried the dishes to the kitchen and joined Libby and Dad in the living room, where they were catching up on Arthur's affairs.

"I'm running for County Superintendent of Schools," Arthur remarked casually.

"But you're so young!" Libby exclaimed, leaning forward in her upholstered chair. "That's the highest position in the school system."

"I think they like my work." He explained that after four years of teaching in the rural schools of Jefferson County he felt the need for an advancement and a better paying job. He had been asked to run for the position.

"Can you win?" Dad asked.

"I'm going about it the same way we did when you ran for Assessor." Arthur smiled. "It should work."

Alice added, "People say he's the most wonderful man they have ever met. When he walks into a room everyone looks at him. And when he speaks to groups they can't get over it, he's so good."

"I guess I got a little practice with all my debating," Arthur added. "Actually I was supposed to be twenty-five to file for the office, but I don't think anyone will notice."

Alarmed that he had falsified his papers, Libby exclaimed, "But Arthur, they will surely find out, won't they?"

"People assume I'm older. I'm a married man with two children. I've taught seventh and eighth grade and been a principal. The teachers support me. Besides, I'll be twenty-four by the swearing in, only one year off. Hey, Alice, why don't you play some more tunes?"

Libby watched her daughter-in-law sit on the piano bench, her long red hair curling against the back of her apple-green dress. She and Arthur spoke a few quiet words, then she played stirring chords with a dramatic rhythm and Arthur sang "*Chloe,*" It sounded better than most singers on the radio. Libby leaned back in her comfortable chair and recalled the rough start to his marriage. Now both of them appeared to be happy, and their two children were thriving.

"*. . .through the dark of night, I've gotta go where you are—*" He looked exuberant. Libby knew he was taking correspondence courses. She sincerely hoped that, despite his age, he would win his election, but did wish he wouldn't take such risks.

Lifting exhausted little Roger to her lap—Dad, David and Bobby joining in the singing—she reflected upon Connie's wedding and reception. It seemed the perfect capstone to the eight years since Dad's election in 1932, as though God were telling her to sit up and take note of her blessings. She wouldn't have uttered such a thing aloud, but knew that she had become ever more respected in Minidoka County and was recognized in the Idaho Conference as an intellectual and spiritual force. People stopped her on the street to ask her advice about personal problems. Even Arthur and Grace seemed more open to her. Perhaps after her baby was born Grace could find a school that would hire a married teacher and Stanley could get some higher education. Donald had completed his college degree and was progressing toward a career as a minister. All of Libby's older children had turned out to be responsible, accomplished adults. David and Bobby were good students and delightful boys to have around the house. Dad was greatly respected and happy in his work. These had been good years, in this place that they had chosen to raise their children. Indeed, . . .*thou annointest my head with oil; my cup runneth over.*

It was the end of a long hot day, but through the open doors a little air began to flow through the house, bringing the scent of freshly cut hay. With deep satisfaction she closed her eyes and welcomed the cooler air as it moved across her damp brow. She would not think about Adolph Hitler or Congress debating whether to declare war against Germany. More important now was this strong sense of gratitude to the Lord of her life for guiding her and her family through difficult times and bestowing upon them so many wonderful gifts.

". . .saying peace, peace when there is no peace."

Jeremiah 6:14 RSV

18   The War Years

Long a vocal supporter of the Peace Movement, Libby watched in despair as the anti-war coalition crumbled around her. It also fell apart across the country. In September, 1940, two months after Connie's wedding, Hitler invaded Poland and Congress passed the Conscription Law requiring all men between the ages of twenty-one and thirty-five to register for the draft on their next birthday. How could this be happening? The Great War had been fought and won—the war to end war—yet once again the trumpet call to war was blaring as news poured in from Europe. This was the first time the United States had ever drafted men in peacetime. Clearly, Libby thought, Congress didn't expect to stay out of the war for long, and every leader in the world would know it. Would her sons be required to bear arms? The thought horrified her so much that when women stopped her in the Square to chat about it, she could think of nothing to say.

Only a few years ago the Peace coalition had been very powerful politically, both in Britain and the United States. In the U.S. it had consisted of isolationists—many Westerners who thought the country should stay out of Europe's affairs—devout Christians everywhere who advocated the peaceful teachings of Jesus, and liberal intellectuals who had unmasked WWI as a for-profit enterprise. Like many Americans, Libby now believed that the Great War had been provoked by capitalists and munitions manufacturers. Historians Morison and Commager noted that in the 1930s:

> America's pacifist mood received official sanc-
> tion from a Senate investigation into bankers
> and munitions makers during WWI. Although
> the findings of this Nye commission failed to
> prove anyone's responsibility for the war, they
> did reveal scandalously high profits, and the
> public concluded that Wall Street wanted the
> war for financial reasons.

Five years earlier Libby would never have anticipated that Congress would risk another world war for mere profiteering. But public opinion was changing dramatically. Now the association with the anti-capitalist sentiment was damaging the Peace Movement. Some politicians lumped pacifists and communists together. Many referred to the supporters of Norman Thomas, among whom Libby was proud to include herself, as communists simply because they voted the socialist ticket—despite the fact that Thomas himself had gone to Russia, studied the system, and returned in disavowal of it as a poor form of government. And now that Germany had defeated France, and Britain was under a vicious bombing attack, both Republicans and Democrats were preparing for war. They didn't seem to care who profited from it or how much. Opponents were seen as unpatriotic. Libby found herself caught in a strange array of emotions.

More than most people she cared what happened to Britain, but she had encouraged many young men of the Methodist faith to be religious conscientious objectors in the event America went to war again. Most people understood that Quakers and Mennonites would fit this classification, but despite her best efforts, the Methodist Church remained divided on the question. That would make it much more difficult for her sons and other Methodists to claim that status. Yet she knew she must remain true to her deeply held beliefs. On the other hand she realized that if the United States refused to fight, England and all of Europe might well find itself occupied by Germany.

Would the United States also be occupied? What would happen then? For years these questions haunted her.

The morning of November 8, 1940, Arthur phoned to say that he had easily won his election and people seemed to believe he had a bright political future.

"Of course they do," she said forcefully. She was elated. "And they are right, you have a brilliant future." She called to Dad, repeating the fact that Arthur had won his election. Dad came to the phone and they listened together, the earpiece between them. His victory delighted Dad too, for he knew that an elected position, however modest, could lead to higher things for so young a man.

"But Arthur, I'm worried for you," Libby said. "Have you heard from your draft board yet?" She could hear the slight whine in her voice. Fear did that to her.

"Don't worry, I'm Class III. That means I am deferred from service for having dependent children."

"Thank heaven for that!"

"I'd say you have me to thank."

She could think of no humorous rejoinder.

——

On November 23, 1940, a call came from Grace. She had given birth to a son and called him Robert. Dad was on his Thanksgiving holiday, so Libby and Art drove with David and Bobby to Nampa to see Grace and her baby. Stanley, who was now only months shy of being thirty-five years old—the top limit of draft age—was pleased to be able to amend his registration to reflect the fact that he now had a dependent child.

Floyd Anderson had registered as a candidate for the medical corps, with his degree in pharmacology, but was informed that he did not qualify. A year later he still hadn't been "called up." Then Connie gave birth to son Laurence, thus qualifying Floyd for a dependent deferment, much to Libby's relief.

In Pennsylvania doing graduate studies and working with refugees from Europe, Donald reflected back on a conversation he'd had with his professor of sociology in Willamette—his respected major professor, the devout Quaker with whom he had worked as an assistant. The man had liked Donald's work. Donald had experienced some disappointment in his relationship with the District Superintendent of the Methodist Church and was feeling uncertain about his commitment to the Methodist Church. He discussed it with his professor.

"I don't want to discourage you in a ministerial career," the professor said, "but I think you would make a good teacher of sociology. I'd be happy to have you back here in Willamette after you get some graduate courses under your belt."

Donald felt tempted.

"Maybe you should take some time to think about it. If you'd like, I can get you a scholarship to a fine little Quaker graduate school near Philadelphia. They have a good work-scholarship program. Right now they are helping refugees from Europe find employment and adjust to this country. You would work with some interesting people. But whatever you decide—sociology or the ministry—graduate work would be an asset."

Donald found the offer appealing. The scholarship was arranged. When the summer was over, he would pack his belongings in a trunk and ship it to Wallingford, Pennsylvania, near the Quaker school. But first he had an important date in Tenino. He hitchhiked north and stayed a couple of days visiting with Betty and her mother. On a quiet evening walk around her home town, he and Betty agreed to write daily. At three cents apiece postage stamps were far cheaper than long distance calls.

Donald reached into his pocket and gave her a ring with a small diamond. He wished it could have been larger, but fortunately Betty wasn't the kind of girl who would hold that against him. They both felt the poignancy of their parting, knowing they might not see each other for years. They agreed to get married as soon as they could work it out, but no date was set. The future was much too uncertain, with Congress passing a peacetime conscription law.

Early the next morning he hitchhiked eastward, stopping to visit his family on the farm. As he prepared to leave again, Libby couldn't help but express her grave concern about his hitchhiking. "How do you know one of those men won't pull a knife on you?"

"The ones I've met are glad to have someone to talk to. I see it as a part of my education."

"Oh Don, I will worry so and pray for your safety. Write as soon as you get there and tell me you're all right."

He promised, but wished she wouldn't worry. Many car owners were interesting people, and this trip didn't disappoint him. He made excellent time. A man who needed a relief driver picked him up part way across Wyoming. They drove straight through to St. Paul, Minnesota. Outside Chicago, the CEO of a large tire manufacturing company took him well across Indiana. Next, an organizer for the Communist Party, working for the Communist candidate for president in the 1940 election, picked him up in Ohio. They drove to Philadelphia, and that man took him a few miles out of the way to deliver him to Wallingford. It was with joy and relief that Mom received his letter.

Now it was late September, 1940. Donald had begun his graduate studies, never having experienced such depth of religious faith as he saw everywhere around him in this Quaker enclave of Pendle Hill. It inspired him to stay in the field of religion.

Meanwhile, England was still being bombed and refugees from Germany's invasions in Europe poured into the country, some of them Donald's responsibility in his work program. They told him about atrocities they had seen. Some of their stories were being printed in the papers. All over the country pacifism was more than criticized, it was being ridiculed. Only the Quakers and Mennonites seemed to escape the scorn, having a well established history of resistance to violence.

Donald's feelings about how he should register for the draft were very confused. He understood, respected and appreciated his mother's beliefs, and had been further influenced by the pacifist teachings of the Quakers, including the professor in Oregon. The Quaker American Friends Service Committee opened several very worthwhile opportunities for alternative service for conscientious objectors, which Donald considered, but on the other hand the refugees with whom he worked provided him with some strong realities. He was pulled between that and his deeply held Christian principles. A group of pacifist Hutterites who had refused to fortify their extensive land holdings in England were asked to leave. Having come on a ship provided by the English government, a small delegation of them visited Pendle Hill to ask the Quakers for advice. They tried to persuade Donald to come with them to Paraguay to start a peaceful farming community. Had it not been for his caring for Betty, he might have gone. His birthday was rapidly approaching, the day of decision.

Leaving the morning of October 16, his twenty-second birthday, he hitchhiked through the colorful autumn countryside. With his mind occupied by spiritual issues and life-altering decisions, for once he did not encourage the driver to converse. By the time he arrived at the county seat near Philadelphia, which throughout the war would remain his "local" draft board, he knew that if his country was invaded, he would fight. He was also convinced that a dictator like Hitler had to be stopped and the only way to stop him was by force. Despite his love and respect for his mother, and his closeness to her, and despite his great respect for his Quaker friends and their sincere faith and pacifism, he reluctantly passed over the opportunity to register as a conscientious objector to military service.

Other important decisions followed. By Christmas, 1940, he faced the fact that he was not a Quaker. He had liked preaching in his "student church" in Oregon and had very much enjoyed his relationship with a congregation. Quakers had no ministers. These factors bolstered his resolve to become an ordained Methodist minister.

He wrote to the Methodist Seminary in Northwestern University in Evanston, Illinois, asking about the possibility of an appointment to a student church in the area. They wrote back that very few appointments were available mid year, but a small struggling church in Winthrop Harbor could use him. They could offer little financial support. He could live in the school dormitory and take advantage of the good rail connection to commute to the church each weekend.

He met a man who needed his car driven to Minneapolis, Minnesota, and was willing to pay the train fare back to Evanston. Donald accepted the offer and was in Evanston to begin the winter quarter at Garrett Evangelican Seminary on the Northwestern campus on January 2, 1941, eleven months before the bombing of Pearl Harbor. That week he began his duties as pastor of the Winthrop Harbor Methodist Church.

In a letter Libby tried to fully express her great pleasure that he had remained on course throughout his student years and would indeed become an ordained minister. "But what of the draft? Will you be forced into the military?"

He had written her that he had not registered as a conscientious objector. "My draft board classified me as a IV," he now wrote in response to her letter. "It means I am deferred to continue my education. It's a deferment given to men who are far enough along in their professional education—certain kinds of professions, including the ministry. I think they reason that it will equip me to serve as a chaplain in the military if they need me after I'm ordained."

Relieved to hear of his deferment, Libby tried to reconcile herself with the idea of his possibly becoming a chaplain in the military. In her next letter she wrote, "Oh, this bombing of England is a fearful thing!" Donald had written that he'd felt torn over his draft registration, and she knew he worried that she would fault him for not registering as a conscientious objector. "Good men differ on what to do about it. I feel that it is up to each man to make his own decision, in his own private way—much like joining a church."

On January 1, 1941, Arthur began his work as Superintendent of Schools. Alice wrote that she and Arthur and their two children had moved into a rented house in Rigby, the Jefferson County seat.

A month later a letter came from Donald, and Libby was glad that she normally sat down to read letters. "Things are going well with my church in Winthrop Harbor," he wrote. "I am living in a dorm at the seminary and commuting by train on weekends. Betty will have enough credits by the end of the winter term to qualify for her teaching certificate. We plan to be married in Seattle on April 26."

Libby lowered the letter, fully absorbing what she had read before continuing. "Betty's mother sent an early wedding present, money for a good used car. I will drive to Seattle and stop in Rupert to pick up you and Dad. The wedding will be in a Seattle church. On our way back to Illinois we'll drive you back to Rupert. Betty and I will proceed to Winthrop Harbor where we will live. She will teach school and I will continue studying at the Seminary, commuting each day to school. With so much war work out here, many people have moved in and there are plenty of teaching jobs."

Well, at least he won't be hitchhiking across the country, Libby thought to herself. She had to admit that the news of a wedding date didn't surprise her much, and that she was glad they would have a church wedding. But now she had to hope they wouldn't have children until he was ordained.

In Chicago Donald bought a good, low mileage 1936 car for $250. He drove west, picking up Libby and continuing to Seattle. Dad had pressing matters at work and didn't feel he could take time away, but he was glad that Libby could go. Alone in the car together on that long drive to Seattle, they visited. It turned out to be the best visit that Libby had had with Donald since his growing up. They talked about the war, the collapse of the Peace Movement, economics, theology,

Donald's school work, and his plans for the future. She learned to her joy that he would return to the West. "I guess it's in my blood," he said.

But there was another matter she had to get off her chest. "I like Betty and look forward to the wedding, but I still feel it is coming too soon. As it is, you are barely eking out an existence." Emphatically she added, "But you *must not* have any children until you finish your education." She and Dad hadn't been the best of models in that regard, but she read widely and knew that now there were ways to prevent pregnancy. Deeply ingrained in her mind was the fact that education was the only way people could rise above their beginnings.

They arrived in Seattle. At the first opportunity Libby discussed this same theme with Betty, who seemed to take it seriously.

Libby was glad for the opportunity to see Eldon Morse again and to meet a number of Donald's other college friends, as well as Betty's younger brother Dix, who was an usher. Donald and Betty had known the minister when they attended Willamette University. He performed a simple, touching wedding in the Seattle church. Betty's older sister Marjorie hosted a nice reception in her home near the church.

Following the reception, Libby watched the young couple leave for what they called a "money-less" honeymoon on Fox Island in the Sound near Tacoma. Betty's mother, Lila Moser, owned a small, rustic cabin there, which had been built by Betty's father long before Betty was born. Lila, who had been a widow since Betty was six years old, had spent many summers in that cabin with her four children. It was a place of happy memories for Betty.

While the newlyweds honeymooned, Libby had a good visit with Lila Moser in the home of Betty's sister. The two mothers agreed that it had been a beautiful wedding, but Lila confided that she felt sorry that Betty had left school with only a teaching certificate when she could have stayed a few months longer and earned a B.A. Hearing this honest concern, Libby shared her fear that children would interfere with Donald's education. With Lila in agreement on that subject, they parted good friends.

The newlyweds drove Libby back to Rupert. This was the second time she had made that long trip by car with Betty, but this time they engaged in more serious visiting, which Libby appreciated. To her joy, she would find in years ahead that Betty was a good correspondent. Much later Libby would reflect upon the fact that the two marriages in the family that ended in divorce, those of Arthur and Grace, were the only two in which she had never met or become acquainted with the intended spouse or their families prior to the marriage. She thought it spoke volumes about family involvement.

After leaving Libby at the farm, Donald and Betty continued eastward and lived there for a few very busy years. Donald was a full time student and part time preacher, Betty a part time teacher and full time preacher's wife.

—

On December 7, 1941, the Japanese bombed Pearl Harbor. Libby could feel the entire country responding with war cries. In horror she listened to the radio the next day and learned that the United States had declared war.

Almost immediately the Draft Law was amended to require the induction of men between the ages of eighteen and forty-five. David would be eighteen in only three months!

Libby pored over the newspaper report, looking for qualifiers or further changes in the law. She concluded that her two older sons would continue to be deferred on the basis of Arthur's dependents and Donald's educational status. However David, a senior in high school, had no obvious deferment possibilities. To her great sorrow, membership in the Methodist Church did not convey the status of conscientious objector. She expected that he would be wanted on the front lines, where in her view Laurence had been sacrificed for the greed of a few men. This sent Libby to the haystack for a session of intense weeping and prayer.

⸺

During the four years of his high school David had been Libby's driver. A quiet, thoughtful boy, he had decided in his junior year that he wanted to become a minister. Greatly pleased, Libby hoped he was old enough to make such a decision. She saw that he helped her in many ways as she visited the shut-ins and people still suffering from the Depression. He was very dependable, being there after school when she needed him to drive. He didn't complain when she took a long time at the various meetings or the homes she was visiting. He read his books and did his homework while he waited, and during their drives together they had talked about pacifism. At a Methodist youth camp the summer after his freshman year, he had signed a pledge, encouraged by the Church and Conference at the time, not to support a war effort in any way. Many youths at the camp had signed it. David assured Libby that he had not taken that vow lightly.

It was a crushing blow when, after the bombing of Pearl Harbor, the Methodist Church did not support the pledges of conscientious objection. Now, throughout the country, military service seemed to be equated with morality itself, even in some quarters of the Methodist Church. Would David fall under the pressures of the constant drumroll for war? How could she expect him to stand up against it when the Church itself had faltered? This was a time of prayer and great soul searching for Libby and Art as well as David. Young Bobby would later speak of the high tension in the household.

During the Christmas holidays Libby could see that David had grown even quieter. He mentioned, however, the terrible complexity of the war issue and the fact that many people were in need of rescue. Donald had written about people who had witnessed atrocities committed by the German military. Jews were being persecuted in every Nazi-occupied country. Turning the other cheek, David knew, meant allowing that to continue. Could a Christian do that in good conscience? Libby could only look at him with pain in her heart.

"Mom," he said at last, "despite everything, I cannot reconcile the clear intent of Jesus, and my own conscious, with taking a machine gun in my hands and killing men. They follow their governments' orders, but I will not kill them because my government wants me to." He and Libby discussed the silent-prayer vigils of Christian pacifists in Europe when they were ordered to provide information about suspected enemies of the German state. Suspected of posing as pacifists, some were tortured and killed, but stories were spreading through a group called the Fellowship of Reconciliation as well as Quaker and Mennonite channels that some had been spared. A few German officers had recognized and acted upon the common Christian bond of faith, which ran deeper than government orders.

Libby knew that this was likely the most important decision David would ever make, and she didn't want to further influence him. "I know the power of prayer," she said. "Whatever you and God decide will be the right thing, even if it is different from your pledge. I do not hold you to that. You were very young."

On his birthday, March 14, 1942, David drove to town, walked into the draft board office, and registered as a conscientious objector. Libby was very proud of her son, as was Dad. At school, some of the senior boys talked about what they were going to do to the "Japs" and Nazis when they got "over there." David avoided such conversations, but because the draft board was comprised of local citizens who had known the Smiths for years, word of his registration spread. Slurs about his supposed lack of courage began to be spoken within his hearing. Libby felt the sting as though these things had been said to her. Indeed, she sensed that even some of the people who had supported Dad's reelections were turning cold.

It seemed that all American life now revolved around the war and the Smiths were viewed as not being "on the team." On posters everywhere a stern Uncle Sam pointed his bony finger and said, "Uncle Sam wants YOU!" Hollywood enthusiastically promoted patriotic and military themes in its movies. Popular songs on the radio included such examples as *Praise the Lord and Pass the Ammunition*. Cartoonists turned out vicious caricatures of German and Japanese people. Hatred seemed to be presented as patriotic, a situation that incensed and saddened Libby.

She concluded that the best way to counter the hatred was to continue to show Christian love and compassion for those who were hated, and to have faith that the madness would stop. The Project area was home to many loyal people of Japanese descent, a number of whom attended Rupert High School—generally outstanding students. The student body president was Japanese, but to Libby's consternation the unreasoning suspicion and agitation by a vocal minority in town caused him to resign.

While the local Japanese were allowed to remain in their homes and businesses, those from the West Coast suffered a great deal of undeserved mistreatment. They were "relocated" to internment camps, one of which was in Hunt, very near Rupert. Since the previous summer, 1942, with David as her driver and assistant, Libby had spent many hours visiting the Japanese whose lives had been so rudely interrupted, helping in any way she could. Every Sunday she and David conducted Sunday Bible study classes in the barracks of the camp.

Meanwhile Dad, with his many contacts, found David a job on a farm. Hoping this would make him eligible for an agricultural deferment, David amended his registration to request that deferment. Dad spoke to some of the people on the draft board about it, knowing that other senior boys were being deferred because they planned to continue working on their family farms. Each morning after graduation Dad drove David to the farm, and in great suspense the family waited to see what the draft board would do.

Hearing nothing by the end of summer, David amended his registration to include an educational deferment, then boarded a bus to Salem, Oregon, where he enrolled in Willamette University with the stated intent to become a Methodist minister. During the semester he was assigned to a small "student church." Now, Libby thought, he had what Donald had—involvement in higher education aimed at the ministry, and a church. She prayed that he would be deferred from military service and be allowed to continue his education.

Plans were made for David to take the young people from his church to the Methodist camp at Wallowa Lake the next summer, in the Blue Mountains in Northeast Oregon. Still no word came from the draft board. Worried, he wrote the Board, further amending his registration to request a medical corps deferment as a stretcher carrier—dangerous work on the front lines of the battle zones. If nothing else, Libby hoped, this would tell the board that he was motivated by religious conviction, not fear or lack of patriotism. Meanwhile, she and Dad were proud that he made an excellent showing on the college debate team and was selected to compete out of state the following semester.

Near the end of the semester a card finally arrived in David's mailbox at school. It was from the Rupert Draft Board: Educational deferment denied, medical corps deferment denied.

Dad assured Libby that he was doing everything he could with the board, but worried that David's enrollment in college might be a detriment to getting an agricultural deferment. Libby wrote to David of her worry. Instead of signing up for a second semester, he returned to Rupert, pulled on his old boots and went to do the winter work for the farmer. All spring Libby, Dad and Bobby waited anxiously to see what the draft board would do.

Summer arrived. David took a break from his farm work to fulfill his obligation to serve as a counselor to his Salem youth group at the Wallawa Lake Methodist Camp in Oregon. There he met another counselor from Idaho— vivacious nineteen-year-old Alice Brown, a teacher whose father was the pastor in Wilder, Idaho. Her mother was a delegate to the Idaho Conference. Libby responded to David's letter that she did indeed know Mrs. Brown from Conference, and liked her.

Later Libby would learn that David and Alice were attracted to each other from the start, though Alice had been engaged to someone else. They had much in common. She too had signed the pledge not to support the war effort, and she admired David for the stand he had taken.

Just after David notified his draft board of his return to Rupert, another card arrived. It instructed him to report to a particular U.S. Forest Service office the following Monday and bring anything he needed in the way of personal supplies. He would be transported to the site of his Civilian Public Service (CPS).

That meant that he would work in the Forest Service until the war ended. In the meantime, Libby sadly realized, he could neither further his education nor be paid for his work. The Quakers and Mennonites who oversaw the conscientious objectors (COs) would require money for his food, because the Methodist Church provided no support. Libby and Art must send money. Each time Dad wrote a check he would feel again the sting that the citizen draft board had denied David three possible deferments. Rupert was a very small town. He and Libby heard rumors that some of the people on the board thought they might be criticized for granting a deferment to the son of a county official who had taken steps on his behalf.

Along with other COs, including many Mennonites and Quakers, David was bused to a camp in Terry, Montana, to work on a team that was digging ditches for a survey team to provide irrigation on the properties of returning veterans. During this time of hard physical labor he appreciated the encouraging letters from Libby and Alice Brown. Twice Alice traveled to Terry to visit him, having broken her engagement to the other young man. For Libby's birthday David wrote her a letter she would treasure. It was found in her effects after her death (see Epilogue).

When the Forest Service announced that a new smokejumping unit was being formed—experimental and dangerous work—David volunteered. When Libby heard of it she moaned to think of the great danger. She suspected that he hoped to show that, despite the unkind rumors of ignorant people, conscientious objectors could be brave.

The smokejumpers fought forest fires in roadless areas of the Northwest by parachuting down to them. Military leaders were studying this new program. From it they would later develop the procedures to be used for quickly dropping paratroopers into combat.

Libby prayed that David's faith would keep him well and that he would survive despite repeatedly "hurling himself out of airplanes," sometimes barely missing raging firestorms. The very thought terrified her. David jumped to thirteen fires, Libby continuing to write him encouraging letters.

As part of her local "missionary work" she proudly explained to friends and acquaintances the valuable work performed by the smokejumpers. She also told them of her Sunday visits to the Japanese internment camp to conduct Bible study classes, which she continued to do with Bobby, her new driver, as she had done with David. In the spring of 1945, after Germany and Italy had surrendered but the war in the Pacific continued, she made efforts to send a care package to the bombed out family of a German prisoner of war who was incarcerated in a camp in nearby Paul. Under guard, these prisoners worked the sugar beet fields, including the field owned by the Smiths.

"Care packages to Germans!" people exclaimed. "Why not to the British, the Dutch and other victims of the Nazis?"

This gave Libby an opportunity to make her point—very rare in those days—that victims of war existed on both sides of the conflict. Every time the German prisoners were trucked to the farm to work, she sent Bobby out to the field with lemonade and cookies for them, and in the summer of 1945 would coax five-year-old Naida to do the same, though her granddaughter feared both the Germans and the gun-bearing guards. Thus Libby constantly used the local situation as an opportunity to teach her Christian beliefs to everyone around her. She felt that most of the local people, like people everywhere, were fundamentally good but needed reminders of the Christian perspective. It seemed to her that most people in Rupert were fairly tolerant, but the vocal minority who marched to the hateful propaganda seen in cartoons and movies continued to upset her. Sometimes she thought it upset her excessively. Attuned to every whisper, she grieved that her dear, kind David would be the object of any suspicion and hatred, any at all.

She continued her local "missionary work," did Conference work, and taught the women's Sunday School class, but these were not happy years for Libby.

—

Meanwhile Arthur continued administering the Jefferson County School District. Alice wrote that her brothers had joined various branches of the service. One of them was a bombardier stationed in England, making regular drops on Germany. She wrote that she and Arthur were enjoying their house. Roger and Naida had a swing in back, and they rode their tricycles up and down the sidewalk with other children. Arthur often fished after work and returned with trout for dinner. She mentioned that she and Arthur liked to dance on Saturday nights at the Rigby dance hall. They also entertained other young couples in the evenings and liked to sing duets. Then Alice wrote that she was pregnant again.

In the spring of 1943 the news came first over the radio. Congress had amended the Draft Law again, this time requiring that all men with "dependent deferments" be notified that in order to maintain their deferment they must change to a job deemed essential to the war effort, if they were not already in one. The criterion was whether the job could be performed by a woman or a man too old to fight in the war. The broadcaster went on to list some serious Allied setbacks. "We need more manpower," he asserted. "Otherwise we will lose this war and our sons and brothers will have died in vain. You able-bodied men out there, wherever you are, drop what you are doing and join now. You are desperately needed for the defense of this country. You mothers, sweethearts and wives of men who are not listening to this broadcast because your men are working in jobs that you or other women could do, tell them to sign up now."

Libby turned off the radio. Similar pleas could be heard almost daily and all deferments were in jeopardy. She knew that many male teachers with dependent children were volunteering for military service, some to avoid "the embarrassment of being drafted." She also knew that men who enlisted voluntarily could choose their branch of service and perhaps avoid being sent to the front lines—a big incentive to enlist. There were other incentives. Draftees departed in ignominy whereas volunteers received the farewells of heroes. Lately she had read reports in the paper about proposals to grant veterans educational and financial benefits. Arthur, Libby knew, would be under pressure to enlist, as well as Stanley and Floyd.

In the early morning of December 1, 1943, Dad had just gotten up and was about to shave when the five short rings pulled him to the telephone. It was Arthur on the line, announcing the birth of his third child, Marguerite Dewar. Mother and baby were doing well.

Libby called from the bedroom, "Is that Arthur?"

"Yes," Dad called back. "Alice had a baby girl this morning. She has your middle name. Both are doing well."

"Give them my love and congratulations."

"I heard that," Arthur said, "give her my love too." He hesitated, then said, "Dad, for three years now I've been working at the top of the educational system in this little district and I don't feel particularly challenged by it any more. There isn't any money in it either, and everyone knows my job could be done nicely by an older man. After all, most superintendents are fifty—"

"You're not thinking of—"

"Maybe just getting tired of waiting for the ax to fall. What's going on there in Rupert?"

"Not much. People don't seem to give much credence to David's statement of conscientious objection as a religious position. They don't really know him."

"Do they know about my deferral, and Don's?"

"Oh sure. People around here know all about everybody else's business. I wouldn't be surprised if there were ten people listening on this line. You know how it is. A few people around here have said some pretty nasty things about the Smith family."

There was a profound silence on the line, then Arthur said, "Well, most people are pretty caught up in the war. Not so very long ago I'll bet some of those same people were what we in the Southern Branch used to call 'fellow travelers.' It is simply amazing how this country has turned around, politically."

Dad had once talked with Arthur about the fact many young people at the college in Pocatello were active socialists. Arthur too had leaned in that direction, but judging by his use of the disparaging term "fellow travelers," Dad knew Arthur was also turning around politically.

—

Alice was hurt to hear that Arthur wanted to volunteer. "What am I supposed to do with all these kids?" she cried, newborn in her arms.

He waited until the baby was six months old. On May 4, 1944, a year before the war would end, Arthur enlisted in the Navy and resigned as Superintendent of Schools. Alice was devastated. The Millers felt that he had abandoned their beloved daughter. They couldn't understand it. Bob Miller still believed the U.S. should stay out of the affairs of other countries—he had refused to enlist during the Great War.

Libby was terribly saddened. She despised war, and now felt increasingly alone in her stand. Her brother Laurence had died fighting in the "war to end all war." She had believed that promise, but now her eldest son, who bore Laurence's name, had volunteered. While her neighbors and friends spoke proudly of their sons in uniform, she could not come to terms with nor be proud of having a son in the Navy. She empathized with one well known Methodist leader of the

Peace Movement who upon receiving the news of Pearl Harbor simply collapsed, physically and mentally. And Bobby! If the war lasted long enough it could involve him too. She knew he admired Arthur and was fascinated by military airplanes. He studied books about those planes and built wooden models of them. They hung from the ceiling over his bed. Would he follow Arthur's example and enlist?

⎯

The 1943 change in the law meant that Stanley Jenkins either had to find a job essential to the war effort or be drafted. He knew that an older man could run a service station and that, having left ranch work, he was ineligible for an agricultural deferment. However many "war effort" jobs could be found on the west coast. He and Grace discussed moving to Portland to find work in the booming shipbuilding industry. Grace wrote that though she was happy with her "nice little house in Nampa," she preferred relocating to Portland rather than having Stanley killed in the war, leaving her with two-year-old Robert. Besides, Portland had pleasant weather and more than one institution of higher education. Perhaps she and Stanley could both further their educations.

They packed their belongings and with their meager savings bought an old but serviceable trailer to pull behind the car. They could camp on the way and, if housing was scarce in Portland, have a place to live on a temporary basis. Grace's first letter from Portland mentioned a crush of "immigrants" from all parts of the country, people who hoped to find jobs in the shipbuilding industry. Few jobs were left and absolutely no affordable housing could be found. Finally Stanley found work in a shipyard and they parked their very substandard trailer in a crowded trailer court, the only one anywhere near his work. The place was badly maintained. Grace wrote that the sewer pipes from many trailers leaked, forming little open ditches. Fearful that Robert would contract some terrible disease, she made sure Stanley removed his shoes and outer clothes at the end of each work day because he had walked across those "ditches."

Libby lowered the letter, recalling how her own father had removed his outer garments upon arriving home after visiting the sick and dying. She felt Grace's pain, knowing how poorly suited her daughter was to such conditions. Tears filled her eyes to think of her brilliant daughter leading that kind of life when she could have been teaching in a school and making money to better her circumstances. But Grace was determined to stay home with Robert and not leave him with a babysitter, even though she might have been eligible to teach in Portland.

In faraway Fairbanks, Alaska, where Connie and Floyd had moved to see if they liked it, Floyd hadn't heard from his draft board. Connie wrote that she was required to pull heavy draperies over their windows every night because people anywhere near the west coast feared that the Japanese might make a military landing. By mid 1943, Floyd still hadn't heard from his draft board, though his job could be performed by an older man. He and Connie were moving to Ogden, Utah. That put them within visiting range. Libby was very anxious to be near Connie again and to see baby Laurence, who was already up and running around.

Despite her disappointment about Arthur's enlistment, Libby was proud to hear that he had ranked in the top five percent of all the military men on an I.Q. test. For that reason he was sent to a "think tank" in Chicago, where he found himself in group discussions with some of the brightest men in the country. Arthur wrote that it broadened his horizons. The group considered hypothetical questions such as what the country should do in the event of defeat by Germany, a question Libby had lain awake nights worrying about. She knew that the Quakers would be her own model of behavior if that came to pass. A month later Arthur was sent to a Naval Training base in Monterey, California. Alice left the three children with her parents and joined him, and they spent three happy months together in that beautiful coastal setting.

Later Arthur wrote from Corpus Christi, Texas. With his good scores in math and science he had been sent to the training station there, where qualified instructors were needed for teaching the operation of the developing devices such as radar and sonar. He checked out math and physics books and spent many hours of intensive review and study. Having had only two years of college and a few correspondence courses, he was pleased to win a high test score. He was therefore retained state side as a radar and sonar instructor.

Months later Libby received a letter from Alice postmarked Corpus Christi, lamenting the moldy unit of a former "motor court" in which she and Arthur and the children were living. Their "cardboard shack" had no bedrooms. "Roger and Naida sleep outside in a 'pup tent.' The trains run just outside the back door and make the dishes rattle on the shelves. The whistle wakes us up several times every night."

Arthur's work in the Navy intensified Libby's soul searching. On one hand she felt very proud that his academic ability put him in the position of an instructor where he would not actually kill other men. But on a rational and moral basis, she saw no difference between dropping bombs on people and teaching naval pilots the skills to do it effectively. Yet on another level of thinking, she didn't want Hitler to win the war. She also found it impossible to feel pride in what Arthur saw as a great personal achievement: he was the All Navy champion wrestler in his weight class. She couldn't bear the thought of her son removing his clothes and fighting like an animal.

In February of 1944, just a few months before Donald would receive his graduate degree from the seminary, Betty and Donald became parents. They had written Libby asking if she would come and spend some time with them, and help with the new baby. She responded. "Of course I will come." Glad to be out of Rupert, she took the train to Illinois, during which she relived her trip of 1905, but from the opposite direction.

To Libby's delight, the baby girl was named Heather for the flower of Scotland. On that visit Libby showed Betty more of her Scottish humor. It was normal medical practice at the time for new mothers to spend a week or two in the hospital—Betty paid $14 per day. Libby went to the room that Betty shared with another young mother. The three got to talking, Libby telling a story about her children growing up on the farm. Betty and the other young mother were obviously delighted.

She told of a more recent event. Feeling a little unwell, she had not gone to church with Dad and Bob. They had been gone for only a short while when she heard piercing squeals. In her robe and slippers she hurried outside, looked around the farmyard, and figured out what had happened. The sow had broken out of her pen and run across the cover of the septic tank, which had collapsed beneath her great weight. The struggling "beastie" looked up at Libby from the sewage and squealed piteously for help. Libby didn't know how she would save it from drowning. It thrashed desperately in the muck a couple of feet below ground level.

Mentioning that Dad always handled farm emergencies, Libby said she finally located a long, sturdy board. She dragged it to the "sess pool," where the smell was "fearful," and worked for some time trying to get the end of it under the pig. Succeeding at last, she pushed down on her end and raised the sow's front quarters above water. By now Betty and her friend were laughing out loud. With a slight gesture of her hands Libby showed how when she pushed down, the pig would rise up, and when she released the pressure, the pig would sink.

She allowed herself a tiny smile to see the young women howl in their hospital beds at the thought of her playing see-saw with a pig. She told them she sat down on the end of the plank to wait for Dad. When he finally arrived and answered her call, this was the last thing he expected to see, "although he knew I had been feeling somewhat unwell."

Gasping for breath and with tears running down her cheeks, the roommate pleaded, "Mrs. Smith! Please! I'll have to ask you to leave. I can't stop laughing and my stitches are killing me."

For the rest of the hospital stay the roommate constantly reminded Betty how fortunate she was to have such a delightful mother-in-law.

—

In May, 1945, Germany conceded defeat and it seemed that Japan would soon follow. Arthur wrote from Texas that he thought the war would soon be over, and that Alice and the children had returned to Idaho. "The feeling around here is that there isn't much need to teach radar to more men. My guess is that we teachers will be allowed to go home before we are officially mustered out. Besides that, I've accumulated a little leave. From what I hear, our radar was a decisive factor in the Allied victory—we were ahead of the Axis countries the whole time." He ended by describing a hurricane that had done damage to the barracks despite all the men pushing hard against one side of every building. "I'm glad Alice and the kids got out of here when they did. I went over to where we lived. None of the houses were left, only the concrete pads. Every stick of wood was gone. The trees behind us were still there. I saw a couple of rattlesnakes hanging from the branches."

Released from service in early summer, Arthur took a job in the Rogers Seed Company in Idaho Falls to support his family while waiting for his mustering out papers. Meanwhile, David continued jumping into fires for the Forest Service. In August, to Libby's horror, devastating atom bombs were dropped on the cities of Hiroshima and Nagasaki, but at last the Japanese surrendered. Still David was not released. By that time Libby's place behind the haystack felt to her like a "slough of despond." On the matter of peace, Dad had stood beside her throughout the war years, but Rupert no longer seemed like a large family pulling together through hard times.

She continued to have many friends in town, and to her embarrassment some of the women who attended her Sunday School classes acted like they worshiped her as a spiritual leader, but for six years her faith had led her down a somewhat different path from most other people. This feeling of separation affected her theology. Her dedication to the social gospel never ceased, but a small pietistic group of women also captivated her interest and helped her through that difficult time.

The Two by Two Women believed that devout Christians should have no interest in worldly affairs. With very little organization they went about, two by two, doing missionary work. Like the disciples that Jesus sent out two by two (Mark 6:13), they took no money, no extra provisions and depended entirely on the hospitality of those to whom they ministered. Visiting and praying with these devout women, Libby felt herself reliving her own conversion experience at age seventeen. But in the social and family situation in which she was then living, this aspect of her religious faith was difficult to share with anyone, including Dad. Sometimes she stayed at home praying with these women instead of going to church. The sincere personal faith of the Two by Two women filled a need in her, and she furnished them a place to stay when they worked in the Rupert area.

—

For the analytically minded Smith family, the aftermath of WWII never ceased. For the rest of their lives Libby's children would debate and discuss the facts and interpretations leading to the varied paths the three sons had taken: deferment, enlistment, and conscientious objection. David would always remember the scars left by the slings and arrows of people who couldn't understand how anyone could have refused to fight during WWII. As he grew older Arthur emphasized the patriotic reason for his enlistment. Donald expressed his position in poetry:

A SOLDIER'S PRAYER
O God, I'm a soldier by trade,
It's an honorable business.
I help to keep the peace;
I protect innocent men from evildoers,
And make an honest living for my family.
The wife and kids, they're proud of me you know.

O God, I'm a soldier by trade.
I carry out the orders given me
by my superior officer.
I guess he knew what's right;
It's not my place to ask.

Today we have a man to crucify.
I like the man!
I hardly see how he could be so bad
deserving death.

O God, this seems a silly thing to ask
but help me drive these nasty, brutal nails
as gently as I can.

And when we set this cross into the ground,
into the hole we dug to hold it upright,
Lord, keep me calm, so I can let it slip
into the hole without that ghastly jolt
it gives a man when careless soldiers
just drop it in and let it bump the bottom.

Why this man must die, I'll never know.
But let me help him go
As gently as I can.
　　　Ranchland Poems by Don Ian Smith, 1990

Nineteen years younger than Grace, Bobby would not have his life plans changed by WWII. However, his feelings about government would be influenced by the disturbing sight of soldiers with machine guns standing over German prisoners of war as they thinned sugar beets in the fields behind the house, the barb wired "concentration camp" filled with American citizens of Japanese descent where he accompanied his mother on Sundays, and the government's apparent capriciousness with regard to David.

Libby thanked God it was over.

"The tumult and the shouting dies—The captains and the kings depart."

From *Recessional* by Rudyard Kipling

19   After the War

Libby had only Bobby at home now—a cheerful and very active young teen. Like all her children, he was a good student and a leader in the Methodist Youth Fellowship. He played the trumpet a little and looked forward to going out for the high school football team. Dark-haired, he was handsome like his father but had her blue eyes. Libby and Dad had raised all their children to be independent, and after so much mothering, she relaxed even more with Bobby. He rewarded her with good behavior, although his fondness for adventure sometime caused her and Dad some concern.

When school was out in May, 1945, Bobby and a friend decided to ride their bicycles from Rupert to Salmon to visit Donald, who was beginning his long service in the church in Salmon, an isolated small town in central Idaho over three-hundred miles north of Rupert. The two boys, who would be entering high school in September, wanted to see the spectacular mountain scenery of the Sawtooth National Forest and the Salmon River country.

Libby and Dad reluctantly gave their permission. But it was with deep concern that they watched the two not-quite-fourteen-year-old boys pedal away on a trip that would take them through vast uninhabited areas. They planned to spend several days on route, camping each night near the road. Libby explained this undertaking to six-year-old Naida, who was visiting on the farm while her father, who had been released from the Navy but not yet officially discharged, settled with her mother in Idaho Falls.

A week later five short rings brought Libby, as always, swiftly to the telephone. With great relief she heard Bobby's voice and learned that the boys had arrived in good health and high spirits. They had cycled over the Galena summit, elevation 8,700 feet, and through two hundred miles of forested country with only an occasional ranch and two very small towns. After a week in Salmon, the boys pedaled back to Rupert, arriving three weeks after they left.

That trip was a preview of things to come with Bobby. Later he would scale the highest peaks, fly a small plane many times over the jungles of Mexico, and find himself threatened by a political uprising in a remote area of Malaysia.

In August, soon after the news of the Japanese surrender and the official end of the war, the postman brought a letter from David. Libby hurried to her chair and tore it open, expecting news of his release from civilian service. Instead he invited the family to his wedding in September. He had worked overtime, earning two weeks of "compensatory time," during which he and Alice Brown would honeymoon.

Libby didn't know whether to laugh or cry. Her son would marry before he had any higher education to speak of. He had only one semester of college to his credit. And unlike the hordes of returning veterans, he would be ineligible for the educational benefits of the G.I. Bill. Yet he had suffered, worked hard for no pay, and been segregated from the world. Surely, she decided, he deserved a little happiness with this pretty young woman from a good Christian home, a teacher who could help with the financial support while he attended college. Alice Brown, she knew, had helped him throughout the years of his difficult service. Libby wouldn't try to talk him into waiting. If Donald and Betty were any example, she reasoned, David and Alice could succeed in their dreams too. It would, however, become one more daily prayer for Libby.

On September 19, the family gathered in the little town of Wilder, not far from Boise, where Alice Brown's father was the pastor. Donald and Betty came from Salmon, Donald to serve as best man. Now an ordained minister with two churches in that mountainous region of eastern Idaho—Salmon and Challis—Donald had made the vacant parsonage in Challis available as the honeymoon retreat, which David and Alice had gladly accepted.

Libby and Dad sat in the pew with Bobby, Betty, Arthur, his wife, and their three children. Only Connie and Grace couldn't come, Connie pregnant and feeling ill in Ogden, Utah, and Grace with an ill child in Portland. The Wilder church filled with friends and relatives of the Browns. Alice's father performed a thoughtful ceremony, David standing tall and looking too thin.

Afterwards, a reception was held at the church, arranged by Mrs. Brown. Over punch, Libby quietly shared her hopes for David's education with Mrs. Brown, mentioning that the newlyweds ought not to have children until he completed seminary and was settled in the ministry. Mrs. Brown expressed complete agreement. "But of course," Libby added with a smile, "we couldn't be more pleased that he has married into a family of dedicated church people."

She conversed with many of the Brown family. Among her own family, she joked about the need to henceforth distinguish between "David's Alice" and "Arthur's Alice." Since Arthur's daughter Alice Corinne would always be called "Naida," further confusion was avoided.

David and his bride left for Challis in her car, which was in serious need of two new tires. What followed would be added to Libby's repertoire of humorous stories. Wartime rationing was still in effect although the war had officially ended a month earlier. With her savings as a teacher, Alice had the money to buy new tires but no stamps to authorize the purchase—government stamps being required for the purchase of many items. Fortunately, David knew all about fixing flats because in that one day he experienced ten or eleven of them, each time lurching to a difficult stop. He had to jack up the car, remove the tire and innertube, locate the hole by pouring on water, dry

and patch the tube—already patched and repatched many times—
stuff the tube back into the outer-tire, pump up the tube with the
little handpump, and they would continue up the road. By nightfall
they were still a long way from Challis and the towns were farther and
farther apart. Knowing he couldn't see to patch another tire, David
stopped at the next town hoping to find a room to rent. The only
motor court was fully occupied, so David went around town asking
people if they knew of a room where he and his bride might spend the
night. Finally someone told him of a woman who might have some
space in the back of the State Liquor Store. Neither of them had imagined sleeping such a place, but they gladly accepted it. During the
night a drunk drove into Alice's car, which was parked in front of the
store, and pushed it up on the sidewalk. In the morning they found
the damage to be light and the proprietress to be very kind. She gave
them a much needed wedding gift: two tire stamps. Soon they were
happily on their way.

To Libby, the larger context of the story of the ministerial student
and his bride sleeping in the State Liquor Store was part of the tragedy of war and the unfair treatment of conscientious objectors, but
she hid that beneath her very humorous presentation. After the honeymoon, David returned to his camp in Downey, Idaho, where he
continued to work overtime to garner leave.

In celebration of Thanksgiving, 1945, Libby invited all her busy
children to join them in Rupert. All were able to come. For her this
was a meaningful Thanksgiving. The war was over. Bob and Dad helped
her prepare the house and the food. Connie, who was pregnant but
feeling better, arrived with Floyd and little Laurence "Larry." Floyd
had not been drafted despite the change of law in 1943, and was now
working for a large drug store with branches in many western cities.
Grace was able to bring her Robert on the train from Portland. Donald,
Betty and little Heather came from Salmon. Arthur and Alice and
their three children came from Idaho Falls. David's Alice, who now
taught school in Downey, drove David from his camp.

Front row: Robert Jenkins, "Larry" Anderson, Marguerite (Libby's arms), Libby, "Dad," Naida (Dad's lap), Roger. Second row: Bob, Grace, "David's Alice," Connie, "Arthur's Alice," Heather (her mother's arms), Betty, Donald. Back row: David, Floyd Anderson, Arthur. Thanksgiving, 1945.

With all six of Libby's children present and the daughters-in-law helping, a large meal was served and afterwards everyone visited with their usual Smith intensity. At the spur of the moment it was decided that they should have a photograph taken. Libby called a photographer whom she knew to be home for the holiday. By now it was rather late in the evening, but the kind man agreed to return to his studio. Everyone piled into cars and met him there. The children were over-tired, but after many retakes, an acceptable picture was finally taken.

Afterwards the children and grandchildren got in their cars and waved good-bye. At home, Bob turned out the yard light and went to his room.

Across the dark gulf between their twin beds, Libby shared with Dad her deep sense of betrayal by the government. "Donald was deferred based on his pursuit of higher education and choice of career, but not David. Men everywhere received agricultural deferments, but not David. Arthur was released last summer, but David must continue in the CPS camp without the slightest idea of a release date. They are holding him at their whim! This is supposed to be a free country. Yet not even the slaves were required to ask people back home to send money for food so they wouldn't starve to death. Oh, Art, I'm so very upset about David continuing in that camp! He should be progressing in his education."

Dad didn't point out that Donald had been further along in his studies. "I agree with you," he said, "that if men in the military are released, those doing alternative service should be treated the same way. Alternative service was not supposed to be punishment"

"They are punishing him for his religious beliefs!"

"It is wrong."

"Yes, very wrong." But this was Thanksgiving and Libby didn't want to end the day on this note. She thought about some of the things she had learned today. "I think Arthur will make a good lawyer." He was now teaching science at O.E. Bell Jr. High School in Idaho Falls. His mustering out papers had finally arrived in October, and he had decided not to continue in the field of education despite Jefferson County's request that he run for Superintendent again. He would teach for a year and save money, then enter the University of Idaho as a law student. The G.I. Bill would pay his family's housing and his school expenses while he got his degree. "And to think the *military* will make it possible!" She couldn't help but color that word with bit of invective.

Dad lay in silence, then his voice warmed the gap between them. "He'll make a fine lawyer. And Lib, this was a fine Thanksgiving."

"Yes, it was." She had much to be thankful for—the end of the war and the health of every one of her family.

In January David was transferred to the Cascade Locks Camp near Portland, where he was assigned to work in a logging project. Alice taught school in Portland and rented a room there, and David visited her on weekends. That winter, doing the unfamiliar work of logging, he sustained a serious wound to his foot. The doctor assigned to the conscientious objectors sewed the blood vessels incorrectly, which nearly killed David before the source of the trouble was understood. He was hospitalized for weeks. On her small teacher's salary Alice paid the medical expenses. After his release from the hospital he was returned to the logging camp, where he worked until his release from service in June of 1946—nearly a year after the war ended.

During David's long "incarceration," as she called it, Libby could hardly contain her disparagement for the "incompetent" doctor who nearly killed him, nor her resentment of the government. In 1936, 1940 and 1944 she had voted for Norman Thomas on the Socialist ticket, and would continue to do so in 1948 and 1952—the last time Thomas would run for office. Dad quietly supported her political opinions.

Soon after David's release from CPS he was appointed at the Idaho Conference to be pastor of a church on Southside Boulevard in Nampa.

It was a substantial church that would provide an income and make it possible for him to attend the College of Idaho in nearby Caldwell. After a happy summer with Alice, "free of bondage," he gave much of his attention to a full load of studies. Like Donald before him, David was a part-time pastor while his wife worked as a full time minister's wife—administrator, secretary and jill of all trades. Before that first year was over she gave birth to baby Colleen. After his second year at the college David was transferred to the Wilder Church, where he continued his work toward his B.A. degree at the College of Idaho. During that time, baby Davina was added to the family. Though Libby had hoped family responsibilities could have been avoided, she felt extremely pleased to see David and Alice's determination that he would finish college and go to seminary. Steadfastly, they stayed on course, pursuing his dream of ordination to the ministry. Every step of the way, letters kept Libby apprised of David's progress. She delighted as well in all the little advances of David's girls, such as new teeth and first steps.

—

In 1946 two additional grandsons were born. Connie gave birth to David Anderson in Ogden, and Betty to Rockwell in Salmon. Connie kept in close touch through telephone calls and letters. Betty wrote informative letters about the Salmon church, its growth and building projects.

Arthur's Alice told about Arthur's activities at the University of Idaho in Moscow. They lived on campus in a "Vets Village" apartment. In addition to his heavy load of classes, Arthur worked on Saturdays at a service station. He built his older children bicycles from abandoned parts and taught them to ride. Now they rode across town each day to their school, lunches in hand. In the evenings Alice worked in a restaurant and he cared for the three children, putting them to bed and studying late into the night.

With great determination Arthur continued this program of work and study and came out with a law degree in only two and a half years. Libby gladly helped by caring for Roger and Naida the first summer, and Naida the second summer, seeing to it that they went to Vacation Bible School.

In the spring of 1948, in private celebration of his degree in jurisprudence, Arthur walked across Idaho's Primitive Area. Later Libby marveled to hear some details of this journey through that wilderness—the home of rattlesnakes and grizzly bears. Believing his Rupert friends would be interested, she wrote an article about it for the *Minidoka County News.* "The Primitive Area is a trackless wilderness extending about a hundred and twenty miles as the crow flies," she wrote. "Not being a crow, he walked up and down the mountains of the Idaho panhandle with nothing but a rifle, fishing pole and a backpack containing beans and a little bacon. He is now studying for the bar examination and clerking for a law firm in Idaho Falls, where he plans to reside with his family."

In the fall of 1949, Arthur passed the Idaho bar and accepted an invitation to join a prestigious law firm in Idaho Falls. Libby now rejoiced that at last he had a profession worthy of him.

—

Not long after Grace and Stanley began their life in Portland the war ended and the shipbuilding industry collapsed. Grace wrote that Stanley had found a job in a slaughterhouse. On several occasions over the next few years she took son Robert on the train to Nampa to visit her former neighbors and old teaching chums. Then she would take the spur line to Rupert and visit the family. "Mom," she said on one of these visits, "I don't know whether Stanley and I will ever be able to buy a house as nice as the one we left in Nampa. He doesn't make enough money. I often wish we had never moved to Portland."

"But he could have been drafted."

"Mom, the war was practically over when we moved there. And maybe it would have been good if he *had* been drafted. Then he could have gone to school on the G.I. Bill, like Arthur. We could have bought a house with no downpayment. Many people all over the country are doing that." Her voice went into the same sort of whine that Libby sometimes heard in her own voice when she talked of her sorrows. "He could have pulled himself up out of the slaughterhouse." Grace looked like she might cry. "I have so many friends in Nampa. I wish we could move back there."

"Why don't you?"

"Stanley doesn't want to!" In years to come Grace would revisit that theme with her son.

Libby couldn't help but notice history repeating itself—Grace wanting to go back to where she had lived before. She had wanted city life, yet married a rancher. Libby had done that—married a farmer. And there had come a time during the Depression when she felt very sorry to have left her house in Union. But not for long. Things had worked out. Sometimes it seemed that the lessons in humility that she was learning were somehow being repeated in Grace's life. Practiced in comforting distressed people, she wanted to tell Grace that *"God's ways are not always our ways,"* but suspected that Grace might not believe that God played that great a role in her life.

Four years later Grace wrote that Portland was bursting at the seams. People who came for the shipbuilding had stayed, returning veterans had settled there, and the Baby Boom was on, creating a strong demand for elementary schoolteachers. With Robert entering the fourth grade, Grace returned to the classroom. Soon Libby would read with relief that the two incomes had enabled Grace and Stanley to buy a nice house in a good neighborhood. It had a room where Libby could sleep when she came to visit. The train connections to Portland were simple.

Knowing that Dad and Bob could take care of themselves, Libby went to visit Grace. The house was indeed neat and pretty. And Grace was happy again. She felt like the mistress of her life again. Much like Libby, she was deeply involved in the political affairs surrounding her, especially those affecting the schools. Like Libby, she was an articulate leader of every group in which she participated.

On her visits to the farm over the years, normally traveling by train, Grace talked passionately about her involvement in the effort to stop the "P.E. lobby" from advancing undeserving boys and giving coaches professional benefits based solely on the performance of sports teams, at a cost to more deserving teachers. Characteristic of Grace, though this involved some risk to her own career, she fought on and stood firmly on her principles. Libby felt very proud of her.

Libby also visited Connie and their two children, now in Richland, Washington. Dad took time off in the fall to visit Donald in Salmon, very much enjoying their hunting trips together in the mountains around Salmon, which Donald loved so much. For many years to come Donald would work closely with his congregation and community in Salmon.

—

A great change came to Libby's life at the end of 1948. After sixteen years as County Assessor, Dad was offered a position with the Idaho State Tax Commission. That meant being a resource person for all the assessors in the forty-four counties—helping them with difficult problems—as well as equalizing the assessment standards in all the counties. His office would be in Boise, the state Capitol. The offer included an attractive salary increase. The job would begin almost immediately.

Libby quickly agreed with Dad that it was time to move. Bob had just started his senior year in Rupert High School and was the star running back on the varsity football team. However he was a sociable boy who made friends easily. He said he didn't mind moving—after football season. He saw it as a new adventure. Dad accepted the offer and resigned as Minidoka County Assessor.

Libby left Rupert with him on a Saturday to search for a house. They checked into the Idanha Hotel in Boise, then drove the twenty miles to Caldwell. With the exception of Donald, all of Bob's siblings had attended the College of Idaho in Caldwell, not far from Boise, and Bob also thought it would be a good choice. At that time there was no four year college in Boise, and since Dad would spend as much or more time on the road as in his Boise office, they might just as well live in Caldwell where Bob could live at home and walk to school. A realtor took Libby and Dad to a good house on Cleveland Avenue, directly across the street from the main entrance to the college.

"I think this is the house," Libby told Dad. They signed the papers. Dad remained at the hotel where he would live and walk to his work until the family was ready to move into the house in Caldwell.

Returning to Rupert by train, Libby set about renting the house to the same man who for a number of years had been renting the fields. She closed down her responsibilities with the church and newspaper, and began to box up or give away many belongings the family had collected over the nearly quarter century since they had moved to Rupert. The process of packing and saying her good-byes brought some cherished memories to the fore, but no tears. Libby felt quite ready to go. With Dad's increased salary and the growing landlord's share from the crops, they could readily make the payments on the house in Caldwell.

Dad came home for his last Christmas in Rupert, then drove Libby and Bob to Caldwell, traveling behind the many goods they had shipped ahead. The family settled in their new home, Bob enrolling in Caldwell High School on January 2 and Dad beginning his commuting to Boise.

Libby liked her new house, and noticed that Dad came home enlivened from his work. He had a nice office in the State House, but he also enjoyed traveling about the state in his state car.

Dad, Bob and Libby transferred their church membership to the Caldwell Methodist Church—a larger church than Rupert to match the much larger population of the town, and Bob continued to be Libby's driver. She enjoyed her new life in Caldwell, but found herself a little more reserved than she had been in the early days in Rupert, where so many young people had moved, sharing common interests in farming. Nevertheless, she and Dad were soon quite active in their new church, though never as prominent in the life of the church as they had been in Rupert.

Libby continued to read voluminously, healing some from the war years. Her thirst for knowledge led her to a wide range of books and journals. She read novels that sounded interesting and was particularly enchanted by *How Green Was My Valley* by Llewellan, the story of a Welsh mining community. She also liked A.B. Guthrie's *The Way West,* the story of a wagon train. She was attracted to writers like E. Stanley Jones, with his fresh new ideas about missionary work among the poor people in India. Having been through the Great Depression, she was interested in the writings of many idealists who were looking for solutions to economic problems in several socialist concepts of government, including the Presbyterian minister Norman Thomas, whom she continued to support when he ran for President on the Socialist ticket. These writers stressed the failure of capitalism and free enterprise. She liked Thomas' comment that "capitalism is a gamblers' economy." She was attracted to the writings of liberal religious leaders like Harry Emerson Fosdick and the dynamic Methodist bishop, Francis J. McConnell, who led his denomination in ecumenical affairs and social action programs. She was influenced by the work of Charles Clayton Morrison, who in 1908 founded the journal *Christian Century,* named for the popular belief that enlightened Christians would, through social action and political wisdom, bring about a Christian society in the 20th century.

Though Libby continued to act upon a social gospel side of Christianity, programs to make the world a better place, she also continued to be interested in pietistic groups, such as the Quakers and the Two by Two women.

With Dad away from home much of the time, Bob drove her to the church, where many of her social activities took place, about a mile and a half from the house. The neighbor woman, who was in her late thirties, became extremely fond of Libby—coming in to see if she needed anything at the grocery store or if she would like to be driven somewhere. With great emphasis this generous woman told all the family members that "Mrs. Smith" was the "most wonderful person" she had ever met. This always came back to Libby, and she loved the woman for her unstinting generosity and openness.

In the fall of 1949, Bob entered the College of Idaho. He was a gifted public speaker, active in the International Relations Club and the church youth program. The following year the Korean War erupted. Young men all over the country were being drafted and shipped to Korea, much to Libby's dismay, but Bob received an educational deferment. Libby felt elated when he told her that he intended to pursue a career in the ministry. Looking back over her life, her disappointment in not having a career as a teacher or missionary, she nevertheless knew that God had given her the assignment of providing the world with three ministers. She realized that they would have more Christian influence in the world than she could have accomplished in any other career than motherhood.

In addition, Arthur was building a distinguished career in law. Knowing that the world needed good lawyers, Libby felt very proud of him. The Law was a respected vocation. He had not become a sheepherder or hobo as she had once feared. In January, 1950, he and his family moved into a newly built two-bedroom house. With a veterans 30-year loan they paid nothing down and signed a 4.5% loan on $8,400. A month later Arthur bought a late model Pontiac. "He is like a boy with a new toy," Alice wrote, causing Libby to reflect that at thirty-three years of age this was the first car he had ever owned.

"We have lived in such awful places," Alice continued, "but now we feel like up and coming people. I have been buying new furniture."

Libby sank into her chair with a satisfied sigh, placing the letter back in its envelope. She thought of Connie, also able to furnish her house the way she wanted it, now that Floyd owned his own store. And what wonderful daughters—both excellent teachers with the same dedication to learning and the same loving concern for their students as she had had.

Grace was developing deep professional roots in the Portland area, but fairly frequently visited Caldwell. She had returned to college during the summers and earned a master's degree, and was rapidly earning a reputation as an outstanding teacher and activist who involved herself in courageous causes inside and out of the educational sphere. Like Libby, she felt passionate about issues on the liberal side of the political spectrum.

One day in the spring of 1951, the telephone rang—a "desk style" phone with a revolving dialing mechanism that required no operator to connect to local numbers. This call was long distance, Arthur's Alice.

"You helped us so much right after we were married," Alice said quietly. "Remember when you came and explained to Arthur how it is with pregnant women?"

"That they become emotional."

"Yes." Alice hesitated. "This is hard to say, but I was hoping you could come here and, well, straighten him out again, if you wouldn't mind."

Mystified, Libby asked, "What is the trouble?"

"He drinks too much." Alice paused, during which Libby's insides went weak. She had hoped that his drinking had been only a school boy's foolishness. "The partners like to go out for a drink after work," Alice was saying. "Sometimes they do it to celebrate Arthur's victories in court—fifteen straight wins in a row so far. They are all so proud of him. I wouldn't mind that, but he likes to stay in the bar after the others leave. Sometimes he doesn't come home until closing time, after 2 a.m. I'm worried about him, Mom. He's gotten into a couple of fights. He likes to fight when he's been drinking. I've done everything I can think of. I tried having parties here at the house, so at least we'd be together and he wouldn't need to drive the car, but he doesn't want to drink at home. I'm afraid one of those drunks will pull a knife and kill him. I hate to tell you that. But I'm so worried! I also worry that if he doesn't stop drinking he could lose his job with the firm."

Nearly sick to her stomach, Libby closed her eyes. *What is it in Arthur that makes him do this?* She'd had the same feeling when he left the College of Idaho to ride the rails. Her influence over him had been nil then, or so it seemed. What influence could she possibly have now? He was a very strong minded person.

"He respects you a lot," Alice was saying. "I think you might make a difference, if you could come and talk to him."

Libby reflected on the many other troubled people she had counseled over the years, including young women whose husbands were drinking. But this time she must speak to her son, not the troubled wife. "I'll talk to Dad. We can probably come on Friday. I'm sure Dad would want to help." And Libby had a lot of praying to do.

"Oh, thank you so very much, Mom. I'll have dinner for you at 6:30. Arthur won't know anything about our conversation, just that you're coming. I'm sure you'll want to talk to him alone. You can go to the basement."

In the spring twilight the little white house on 24th Street looked like something out of a *Good Homes and Gardens* magazine, with spring flowers flanking the walkway to the door. Inside, the new maroon and gray furniture and gray wall-to-wall carpeting furthered the modern image, as did the "blond" wood of the spinet piano and coffee tables. Alice always kept her house extremely neat and clean. Libby hugged her and the children one by one, giving Marguerite a small doll she had found in the dimestore. Then she and Dad sat on the sofa with Bob, who always enjoyed seeing Arthur and knew nothing about the purpose of the visit.

"He'll be here any minute," Alice assured them, sitting on a chair. The three children sat on a smaller sofa that matched the bigger one. Libby asked each of them to tell her what they were learning in school and what new thing they had learned today. Each time she heard the approach of a car she expected it would be Arthur, but the engine sound would fade down the street and she would focus again on what was being said.

After a considerable time, Alice asked them to come to the kitchen table. "We might as well eat," she said, "before everything dries up. There's no sense in starving you."

Afterwards they returned to their places in the living room. Arthur had not come home, nor had he called with an explanation. There wasn't much more to say. Quietly Alice said, "I think we could find him in one of the bars, if you wouldn't mind driving me downtown. You could wait in front and I'll go in."

Libby disguised a horrified glance at Dad—to think of going from bar to bar in search of her son! In a flash of memory she saw again the drunk in the doorway when she was a girl. Dad returned her look with an almost imperceptible shake of his head. Bob was staring at the ceiling.

"I doubt that would do any good" Libby said. "I think we'd probably better just go."

Tears filled Alice's eyes as she hugged Libby good-bye. "I can't believe he didn't come home when he knew you'd be here. I'm so embarrassed. And sorry I asked you to come such a terribly long way."

Libby's sorrow had nothing to do with the two hundred and eighty mile drive. Engulfed by the import of what had happened, she sat in the front seat looking at the twin cones of the headlights as they penetrated the darkness of the deserted highway. Her son was under the sway of a great enemy of the civilized world—liquor. If only Prohibition had not been repealed! But now everywhere she looked fashionable people were depicted with a glass of liquor in one hand and a cigarette in the other. Arthur too had smoked for many years. Somehow her teaching had missed him. In that she had failed. All the good feelings she'd had of late vanished and no joke or funny story came to mind to diffuse the tension in the car.

After many silent miles, Libby allowed herself to say to Dad, "Sometimes I feel like the things I have always stood for have become old-fashioned."

Dad looked over and said, "He's a grown man now. I doubt there's a thing we can do about it." After a few minutes he added, "Lib, I believe he must have forgotten we were coming, maybe had a couple of drinks with his friends then realized we were at the house. I think he stayed away out of respect—not wanting us to see him like that."

"Oh, poor, poor Arthur!"

Bob leaned forward from the back seat. "He'll be all right. And Mom, your faith and standards are not old fashioned. The world needs people like you, now more than ever. Dad, why don't you let me drive, and you two try to get some rest."

―

Libby's happy, adventuresome Bob was a source of immense satisfaction, though his adventures continued to cause her some concern. As he had done his last summer in Rupert, he continued working for two more summers as a tourist guide in Jackson Hole, Wyoming. Libby was glad that he told her of his climbing Mt. Moran and the Grand Teton after he had made the climbs, instead of before. A close family friend had fallen to his death on the Grand Teton (El.13,770). The photograph of Bob standing victorious in his Lindsay kilt on the uppermost tip of the Grand Teton with blue sky around his knees would hang on Libby's walls for many years. Visitors were treated to her story about that climb and her worry afterwards, though he came through it unscathed.

In his senior year of college Bob was appointed pastor of a small church near Caldwell, where his sermons would be remembered for years. But now, just before his senior year, he and Libby were planning his wedding. The previous year he had become enamored of a local Caldwell girl, the daughter of friends in the Methodist Church. Libby was fond of the girl, and the romance and engagement progressed to a church wedding on August 17, 1952.

The entire family gathered on the eve of the wedding. David came the farthest—from Evanston, Illinois—with five-year old Colleen, who would be the flower girl, and four-year-old Davina. Alice, having recently given birth to baby Elizabeth, had stayed in Illinois to rest in a quiet house. David was on a short summer break before finishing his graduate work in the Methodist Seminary on the Northwestern campus. Libby hugged him and told him the truth, that he looked well and she was very proud of him. She knew that he and Alice had been working extremely hard, serving two churches while he completed his course work. Libby hugged Colleen and Davina, though Davina was uneasy about giving herself to a "fearful old woman," Libby quipped in an aside to David.

Arthur and his Alice arrived from Idaho Falls with Marguerite. Alice immediately went to the spare bedroom and didn't come out. Some time later Donald and Betty arrived with their Heather and Rockwell as well as Roger and Naida, who had been living with Donald's family during the summer. Libby hugged them all, then went to the bedroom where she learned, to her horror, that Alice had divorced Arthur the previous December, hoping to shock him out of drinking. Libby felt herself staring at Alice, who had deliberately broken the vows taken in the Rupert living room. That seemed absolutely wrong to Libby, even though Alice hastened to add that it had seemed to be working. He was drinking much less and had given her a new engagement ring. As Libby glanced at the ring, Alice said she was very upset with him over something she had learned on the trip to Caldwell. About that, she would say no more, adding that she needed to rest after the "nerve-wracking trip."

The doorbell rang again. It was Grace, Stanley and Robert from Albany, Oregon—Robert looking very tall for twelve years old. Connie, Floyd, Larry and six-year-old David came in a little later from Walla Walla, Washington, all looking robust and happy.

The intense Smith visiting was underway, dominated by political discussions. As the focus of attention, Bob held forth in his slightly amused manner, asking David questions about the campus at Northwestern, where he planned to do his graduate work. Connie and Arthur left together to go for a walk. About an hour later they returned, Alice still in the bedroom. When Libby went to the kitchen to prepare another pitcher of ice water, Connie joined her, quietly telling her that Arthur and Alice were having a new round of serious fighting. Back in the living room Libby noticed the pall of Arthur's difficulties spreading. She made up her mind. This was Bob's happy time. She would ignore all discord and unhappiness. The rest of the family followed her lead.

Late the next morning, after two big frying pans of scrambled eggs and a loaf and a half of toasted bread had been consumed, Libby went to her room, put on her corset and got ready for the wedding, which was scheduled to start at 1 p.m. Dad dressed in his Sunday suit. In every room of the house, mothers were helping their children into their good clothes. When they were finished, Libby herded the children outside near the front step so a photograph could be taken. Her grandchildren were now a sizeable group. Bob came from the back porch, dressed in a new suit. He smiled at his nieces and nephews as Betty snapped the picture. Libby saw that Bob could hardly stop smiling, even when he got in the car with her and Dad to drive to the church. He was truly happy. She had once thought that he might pick a more outgoing girl, but now reflected that the quiet, sweet, and efficient Eraleen "Lee" was probably just the right wife to be a great help and support in Bob's ministry.

The chancel of the sanctuary was luxurious with baskets of summer flowers. While the organ played, the pews of the large Caldwell Church were rapidly filling. Libby noticed with satisfaction the many people on the groom's side. Earleen's family also had many friends and relatives. In addition, scores of well-wishers from the college and the congregation had come to see the popular young couple say their vows. It reminded Libby of Connie's wedding, held in the home church

Grandchildren in Caldwell just before Bob's wedding, August, 1952. Unless otherwise noted, the last name is Smith. Front row l-r: David Anderson, Rockwell, Colleen, Heather, Davina. Back row: Roger, Naida, Robert Jenkins, Larry Anderson, Marguerite.

of both the bride and groom.

The usher escorted Libby and Dad to the front row. To the strains of the familiar *Wedding March*, she turned to watch the four brides-maids in their pale blue gowns halt-step slowly down the aisle, one at a time. All the earlier weddings of her children paraded through her mind, and she felt very pleased that this last one was everything a wedding ought to be, with all of her children present. The last of the bridesmaids, thirteen-year-old Naida, looked very grown up. How fast time flew when one grew old! Bob and the groom's men filed in from the side along the railing. In her frothy pink gown, little Colleen came timidly down the aisle scattering rose petals from a basket. Ob-viously feeling the stares of hundreds of strangers, she lurched a time or two toward the pews as though to dive for cover, but a gesture from her father's hand restored her courage and she resumed her work, ul-timately arriving safely at the chancel. Libby stood up to the signal of the organ music and turned with the congregation to see Eraleen, veiled and in full traditional splendor, starting down the aisle on her father's arm.

Libby was far from sad, though she blinked tears to see Bob stand-ing beside his bride. At his birth she had wondered if she would be able to "totter" down the aisle at his high school graduation. Now she silently thanked God that she had been healthy and vigorous for his junior year of college and his wedding. Next month he would be-gin preaching at the Fruitland church—a married man with a fine mind and a determination to go to the seminary at Northwest-ern. Despite Arthur's problems, Libby knew she had done well as a mother, and knew she had finished her most important work.

After a sumptuous reception in the church, and before they dis-persed again, the six children and Libby and Dad posed for a group photo. David took his girls to visit his wife's relatives. Arthur and his Alice left together, too upset to deal with their children. Two months later Libby would hear that Arthur had married Sharon Johnson, a new graduate of Idaho Falls High School. But now she turned her

Bob's Wedding, August 1952. Front: Grace, Libby, Dad, Connie. Back: Bob, Arthur, David, Donald

attention to the problem of Arthur's children. The family came to the rescue.

Grace agreed to take Marguerite with her and Libby. They would spend a couple of weeks with Grace and Stanley in Albany, where Grace now taught school. It was not far from Portland. Donald and Betty agreed to take Roger and Naida back to Salmon until school started.

In Stanley's car, Grace sat in the front. Twelve-year-old Robert, Libby and Marguerite shared the back seat. As the car hummed across the sagebrush desert of eastern Oregon, they talked about many things, including the fact that Albany was located near the coast.

"I have never seen the ocean," Marguerite said, turning to Libby, "Have you?"

"Yes. I lived quite near the sea when I was your age." Knowing that this was a good opportunity to get to know eight-year-old Marguerite, with whom she had spent little time, she continued, "Every summer my family spent several weeks there."

"Did you swim in the ocean?"

"Yes, we all did."

"Oh, I want to do that! When we get to Albany, would you go swimming with me?"

Grace turned to look over the seat-back. Covertly exchanging an amused glance with her, Libby said to Marguerite, "Well, I suppose we could wait for a dark, moonless night. Then I could put on my swimming suit and we could go tripping lightly into the waves." She illustrated that with a fluttering of fingers, and gave Marguerite a big smile to let her know that she had not been serious.

"Well done, thou good and faithful servant...enter thou into the joy of thy lord."

Mathew 25:21 KJV

20   Retirement

Bob's wedding marked the start of Libby's retirement. Her mothering responsibilities had been diminishing for many years, but now for the first time since the move to Union the choice of where she would live was not in any way dictated by the consideration of where it would be best for her children to live. After their honeymoon Bob and Eraleen moved into the parsonage provided by the little Methodist church in Fruitland, Bob's "student church." They would both commute to Caldwell to finish their last year at the College of Idaho.

Dad had tired of the drive to Boise, so he and Libby rented the Caldwell house to an art professor and, like honeymooners themselves, shopped in Boise for a rental house that suited their needs. They picked out a small, nicely kept house in an older neighborhood of green lawns and spreading shade trees on the north side of the city. It was a short walk from a Methodist Church, a neighborhood grocery store, and a bus line. Libby would need no driver while Dad traveled about the state. For two and a half peaceful years they lived in that house, Libby often taking the train to visit her children.

Bob and Lee graduated from college in June, 1953, then to Libby's joy, Bob followed his two older brothers to the seminary at Northwestern to do his graduate work. He also served a "student church" there. In the summer of 1954 Bob and Lee came home to show off their newborn Susan. By now Libby worried less when her sons added the responsibility of fatherhood to their lives. In all cases they had received professional degrees while supporting families. Bob proved to be no exception. After ordination, he was rewarded by an appointment as associate pastor in a large suburban church in Milwaukee, Wisconsin, where he would share in the preaching and have an opportunity to address very large congregations.

A letter from Bob announced the birth of a second daughter, Patricia, in 1955. Libby found in the letter no hint that he planned to return to the West after his ordination. Indeed, she had heard no such hints in her conversations with him, but she hoped he would return some day. She missed him.

———

Dad retired in 1955. He had turned sixty-five and Libby was sixty-seven. Moving back to Caldwell, they settled down to a quiet life in their own house. Ecstatic to have Libby back, the neighbor woman came in daily at 10 a.m. to talk and laugh with her friend and see if she could use any help. Every week she washed and set Libby's hair. Through correspondence, Dad kept up his connection with the Rupert farming community and the Hopewell Grange. Libby enjoyed discussing with him what was happening in the families of old friends. It comforted them that the Rupert farm was in good hands with a responsible renter. With the regular income from the house and crops, they could have afforded to travel more extensively, but limited themselves to visits to their children: Connie in Washington, Arthur and Donald in Idaho, and Grace and David in Oregon. David and Alice now served a church in Tillamook and were the parents of four daughters, including Deborah born in 1953.

Libby had never seen Scotland since leaving it, and people continually asked why she didn't go. She answered that she had no living relatives there—not mentioning that older brother John had never corresponded during all the intervening years. If people probed further, she told them that her knee gave her trouble. It did, the same leg that had been infected when she was a child. Sometimes she said with a wry twist that she couldn't go abroad in the bracelet she was required to wear which was engraved with the words, "I am not drunk; I am in a diabetic coma." In the United States that was recognized by all medical professionals, but, she said, "who knows what they might think in a foreign country? I could be inadvertently thrown in a drunk tank!" That generally produced a good deal of laughter. Actually, she felt vulnerable traveling for long periods of time far from her doctors, and she refused to entertain the thought of flying—a form of travel now standard for long journeys, one that Bob and David both urged her to try. Dad never tried to influence her in that, for which she was grateful.

Marjorie still lived on the west coast of Canada with her husband, but she too had become less interested in travel than in her youth. It pleased Libby to hear that Connie visited occasionally with Marjorie, but Libby's energy for travel was limited. In addition to that, reading and church work absorbed her time.

Wryly she would tell Dad when entering the house after the neighbor delivered her home from visiting a housebound person, "I talked to that *old man* again." Quite often she was older than the "old people" she counseled. Her inflection conveyed a complex array of meanings to those who understood her well. Among other things it was a backhanded comment on her own deteriorating health.

Letters from her children and daughters-in-law kept Libby emotionally involved with six very different, very busy lives. In 1958 Bob phoned to say that he and Lee had a son, Arthur, his third child. They called him Arty. Later he wrote that he had bought an old, broken down airplane and was repairing it. "When I finish, I'll fly out west to see you."

"Oh, Dad," moaned Libby, handing him the letter. "He'll kill himself yet! She could see by Dad's warm expression that he understood precisely her mix of worry and humor.

Absent the concerns of earlier years, their life now had a genteel quality about it. She enjoyed reading quietly near Dad. She also liked the way he kept the lawn and the flowers, the large irises, gladiolus, roses and peonies that he nurtured in the beds alongside the house. "Old Duff," she called him. In the summer when they held meetings at their home, which they did at least once a month, a vase of fresh flowers always brightened the coffee table in the living room. In the back of the back yard, between the alley and Libby's clothesline, Dad grew fine vegetables, a couple of vines of Concord grapes along a wire trellis, and rhubarb—a small garden reminiscent of Union and Rupert. She made grape jelly and rhubarb pie for him. Though she wasn't supposed to eat sugar, she couldn't help but sample her treats.

When they drove west, they sometimes visited Grace, Connie, and David on the same trip. Floyd was now well established in his own pharmacy and Connie was back in the classroom, teaching school in Walla Walla. Her David, her younger boy, had started the first grade. Grace continued to be a dynamic force in the Portland area school system. In 1956, after twenty-two years of marriage, Grace and Stanley recognized their differences and divorced. But through it all, a much improved relationship had developed between Grace and Libby, a source of comfort for all concerned. The focal point in Grace's life was Robert, now in high school, who was showing very promising achievements in technical and mathematical areas. Connie's Laurence and David also excelled in school.

When Dad and Libby traveled eastward they visited Donald in the mountains of Salmon and Arthur in Idaho Falls—now doing legal work for the City of Idaho Falls. Both of these sons shared Dad's interest in hunting and fishing, and they both lived in proximity to excellent hunting and trout fishing. While Dad enjoyed these outings, Libby became better acquainted with her grandchildren, such as Heidi, born to Donald and Betty in 1955, and Arthur's Christine (1954) and Kathleen (1956), though sometimes Arthur's marital upsets interfered. Very soon after he married Sharon, Alice had taken the three older children to live on the California coast near where she and Arthur had spent three happy months during the war. By now Libby had learned not to dwell on Arthur's problems, other than to pray for him. She recognized that she had done her best and God was in charge. This gave her a great deal of peace.

Dad stayed physically active and never lost his excited demeanor as he packed the car to go on a hunting or fishing trip with one of his sons. His hair remained dark and full, his physique that of a much younger man. Able to exert himself for hours without becoming winded, he was, however, bothered by indigestion, sometimes rather severe, but nothing that kept him from enjoying his years of retirement or hiking up a mountain after a deer.

In the summer of 1958, Naida wrote that she had returned from Germany after a disappointing year and wanted to come and live with them while she attended the College of Idaho. She wrote, "I feel I need to be with you, Grandma."

Libby discussed it with Dad, and they agreed to accept her in their home. Libby had told Connie and Grace that Naida seemed like another of her children because she had spent so much time on the farm. Besides, having an extra driver in the house seemed like a good idea.

At about the same time a startling letter arrived from Bob. After two years of serving the big church in suburban Milwaukee, he had applied for missionary work in China—China, where so many missionaries had been beheaded by the Communists! And where Communists still controlled the country, by all reports becoming ever more intolerant. But then she reminded herself of ministers she had criticized who seemed intent upon nothing more than being transferred to bigger and more prosperous churches. Some, like the minister in Glasgow long ago, seemed disappointed to be given work among the poor. But Bob was leaving a prosperous church to work among the very downtrodden. She couldn't help but feel proud of him. He wrote that the training provided by the Board of Missions called for a year of immersion in the Chinese language. He and Lee had decided to do the studying at Yale University in Connecticut. They were preparing to move in time for the start of the fall semester.

Over the next year Libby would feel conflicting emotions—great joy that one of her sons felt called to missionary work and sadness to know that after his language course, Bob would be gone for at least four more years. During the year Bob wrote that he could not get clearance from the Mission Board to go to China. Instead they would go to Malaysia—a politically unsettled, poverty ridden peninsula where Chinese was spoken, south of Viet Nam. The water might be tainted and revolution could threaten. Once again Bob was embarking on a dangerous adventure, this time with a wife and three children. But even if he came through it unscathed, Libby knew that with her very high blood pressure, she might not live to see him again.

Lately it seemed that she and Dad were attending an increasing number of funerals—people she had worked with in the church while Bob was in college. Whereas in earlier years they had hardly glanced at the obituaries in the newspaper, now they read them first, making quiet comments back and forth regarding the circumstances of those deaths. The *Minidoka County News,* to which they also subscribed, often contained death notices of old friends. One day in late summer Dad drove Libby to the cemetery just outside Caldwell to find a plot where they would be buried. Together they selected a peaceful place on a hill beneath mature, spreading trees. The following spring Allie and Clarence would come to visit from Utah and Dad would drive them to the cemetery to see where he and Libby would be buried. Dad would turn off the engine and these two couples who had shared so much of their young lives would sit for a quiet time in the car.

Naida arrived in late August and signed up for a full load of studies. When classes started the household fell into a routine. She left before eight o'clock in the morning, dashed back for lunch, then left again for more classes. During the pleasant late autumn afternoons Libby and Dad would be reading in the screened front porch when Naida returned from school to join them. Always interested in intellectual matters, Libby would ask about the content of lectures and the professors' opinions, some of whom she remembered from Bob's time at the college. Naida seemed eager to share her experiences. The conversation would continue while they fixed dinner and ate their meal, Dad joining the discussion. After the dishes were washed, Naida retreated to her "room" on the screened back porch—Bob's old room—where she did homework until late.

As it turned out, with Dad at home and the friendly neighbor woman popping in to inquire about what might be needed from the store, Naida was never called upon to drive the car. Dad drove Libby to church meetings, Fellowship of Reconciliation meetings in homes of other dedicated pacifists, and to the store to shop. Being together every day and night had brought them very close together again, and they had settled into a peaceful sharing of all their thoughts without hesitation, whether about theological matters, Conference, newspaper items, or letters from their interesting children.

Bob and Lee were enjoying their crash course in Chinese. For six hours a day they immersed themselves in the language. Five-year old Susan and three-year-old Patricia were learning it right along with them, because the family was expected to speak Chinese at home. Libby smiled to think that baby Arty might learn Chinese before he learned English. In addition, Bob and Lee were assigned work with Christian students on the Yale campus.

"Dad," Libby asked, "Do you think Bob and Eraleen can become completely fluent in only one year? Enough to counsel people and deeply understand their problems?"

Dad lowered the Grange Newsletter. "They are both good students. I think the mission board must have expected they could, or they wouldn't be paying for this language course."

"I suppose so. But I can't help but recall that no matter how hard I tried, I didn't do as well with French as some of my classmates. A person needs an ear for foreign language."

Dad raised his eyebrows. "We'll just have to see. He might be brilliant at it. You said your sister Marjorie picked up that African language quite readily."

That was true. Maybe Bob took after Marjorie. Libby found her-self anxious to see him and his family again. She felt the need for a thorough visit about how he viewed his forthcoming mission work. She wrote him that she very much hoped he could come west to visit before he left for the distant shores of Kuala Lumpur.

—

On a Saturday in late October Arthur arrived with a buck deer to contribute to Naida's board. Dad went to the locker with him. That night, looking cheerful and healthy, Arthur escorted his daughter to the college homecoming dance. When they returned, Dad switched off the TV and all visited for a time. Naida went to bed, then Dad. When Libby pushed out of her chair to follow, Arthur walked up to her and quietly said, "Mom, my life has changed." They looked each other in the eye, Libby wondering what that meant. In an offhand manner he added, "You know, I think that group called AA might have the right idea about a few things."

Libby had always assumed people could quit drinking if they wanted to badly enough and allowed God to help. But she said, "I suppose so."

"Good night, Mom." Something in his voice told her he hoped to close some of the old distance between them.

"Good night, Lamb." Her old pet name for her babies came readily to her tongue.

Through the door of her room she heard Arthur switch off the hall light and close the door of the spare room. Normally he insisted on staying at a motel. She could tell that Dad lay awake in his bed. "I think he joined Alcoholics Anonymous," she told him. Later she would learn that Arthur had indeed joined AA and embarked upon an active program of counseling others who were addicted to alcohol. He would never take another drink. Within the next five months Libby, Dad and Naida would learn that he had divorced Sharon, married LuRee, whom he had met at an AA meeting, and with her became the father of Lisa—April, 29, 1959.

One January evening as Libby was stepping out of the bathtub, she realized her nose was bleeding alarmingly. She couldn't stop it with tissue. She used the bath towel. The blood didn't slow down. "Dad," she called, "something's not right here."

He sprang out of his chair, took one look at the towel and called an ambulance. Profuse amounts of blood had soaked several large towels before the ambulance arrived. He stayed by her side as the men put her on the gurney and wheeled her out. In the car he followed the ambulance to the emergency room of the hospital, and listened carefully to what the doctor said about such large breaks in blood vessels of the head. "You're lucky," the doctor said as he cauterized the blood vessel. "This might have occurred in the brain."

Numb in the face from the anesthesia and still smelling the burned flesh in her nose, Libby joked on the way home, "Now that I have a relief valve, I'll live to be a hundred." Dad's concern about her diabetes and very high blood pressure triggered her urge to make light of it, but his concern also made her feel more secure. They had reached an unspoken balance. He never questioned her about the box of ginger snaps that she hid behind the cereal, and she never hid them where he couldn't find them quite readily. He did a good job of pretending not to know of their existence.

Every Thursday night at eight Dad turned on the TV to watch the Perry Mason show. The actor who played the role of an outstanding lawyer reminded them both of Arthur—his burly frame, large thoughtful eyes, and forceful manner. Lured by the theme music, Naida would leave her homework and join them to watch Perry Mason prove his clients' innocence by uncovering the identities of the true guilty parties, always on the witness stand. Arthur had said that in reality such revelations hardly ever occurred on the witness stand, but that didn't stop Libby from greatly enjoying the show. She felt that she was vicariously participating in her son's world. Arthur was becoming one of Idaho's finest defense attorneys.

Often during the TV commercials Libby would see Dad get up and go to the kitchen. She would hear the cupboard being opened and a bottle of Milk of Magnesia being removed. A line of those dark blue bottles, many with long white drips caked down their sides, stood on a shelf too high for her to reach. Identical bottles had stood in the top cupboard shelf in Rupert. One night as he returned to his chair she gave him a look, silently telling him that she knew his heartburn was acting up more than usual and it worried her. He gave her a confirming glance. Realizing that Naida had seen it, Libby made light of it "As long as they make that stuff, Dad'll live."

"What stuff?"

"Milk of Magnesia, for indigestion."

Sometimes during the week Dad donned his suit and hat and drove to Boise to lunch with friends who worked in the State House. Usually he had been asked for his advice on a tax problem. As Libby watched him go out the back door, she could see beneath his professional manner a boyish delight to know that he was needed in his retirement. She felt happy for him, and proud. She saw that he still walked in the measured manner that had attracted her when they first met. He had all his teeth, though a number were gold filled. His square-jawed face was only a little craggier, his dark wavy hair salted with only a little white. His body remained strong but slim. Libby, on the other hand, had been snowy white and a wearer of a full set of dentures for over thirty years. When she walked her old knee hurt.

Dad was gone to Boise on a Wednesday during the college Easter vacation. Having just hung up the phone after a consoling a grieving woman, Libby was still sitting at the dining room table when Naida sat across the corner from her. They got to talking, and Libby guided the subject to her granddaughter's future. "Have you given more thought to your major?"

"I still haven't decided. I can declare it sometime next year. It's a hard decision."

"What subjects do you like the most? Which ones come the easiest to you?"

"Language, anthropology—the way Dr. Dadabay teaches it. Sometimes I think I'd really like to be an archeologist. But I can't imagine doing that and having a family too. I'd have to travel far away on digs, so I guess I'll forget about anthropology."

For the moment Libby ignored the impediment of family and went to the more fundamental matter. "How does archeology make the world a better place?"

"Well, it improves our understanding of where we came from."

Libby spoke carefully. "Is that as important as alleviating the suffering of those who are on the earth today? Wouldn't you prefer to help the many, many sick and starving people? People in poverty stricken countries who have no money, no hope? Dying children who could be saved?" She smiled her kindly smile.

"Yes, I would like that, but I'm not sure how to get myself into such a career. What should I major in?"

"Medicine. You could work with the United Nations. They always need doctors who do well in language. You could work with UNICEF, for example, a group of people affiliated with the United Nations dedicated to helping save the children of the world. UNICEF has very high ideals."

Her granddaughter sat thinking. "My high school biology teacher said I should go into medicine. But when I looked into it, I found that the standards for girls are quite a bit higher. Boys can get a couple of B's in college and still get into medical school. Girls must have all A's. And all the scholarships go to boys. None are open to girls, no matter what their grades. At least not in California when I checked, and I imagine that would be true everywhere. I couldn't possibly afford medical school without scholarships, and I don't think my dad would want to pay for it—it takes eight years. And even if I could afford medical school, I'd probably get a couple of B's along the way and ruin it."

"You could get all A's if you dedicated yourself to it. You've done well here."

Naida looked at her. "It's more than that. I've heard that women in medical school have no time to do anything else. They don't have time to date, much less get married and have children. I'm already nineteen. In eight years I'll be twenty-seven."

"That seems old too you?"

"Yes. A number of my high school friends are married and starting families."

Libby had heard enough. She leaned forward. "Nah-ee-da," she said enunciating every syllable and tapping the words with her forefinger. "A woman need not get married. Remember that. A women need not be married." She paused to let that hang between them. "Many women have lived noble and fulfilling lives without *men*." She gave it the low pitched, slightly unpleasant tone that her mother had used to convey the lower motivations of most men when it came to dating and marriage.

Naida thought for a while before responding. "I don't think I could be single all my life. I'd feel left out. Even eight years it seems too long."

Libby knew she'd said enough. In some ways little had changed since she was young—so many girls plunging headlong into procreation! Nowadays more careers were opening to women, but where were the morally high toned young women? Girls like some of Libby's friends in Scotland? Optimistic girls who eagerly responded to the speeches of the Suffragettes? Sadly, it seemed that the deeper meaning of the Woman's Movement had died with its leaders, or died when women got the vote. But she cared about this granddaughter and realized that if Naida was determined to get married, she'd better give that some thought too.

"What is the most important trait you would look for in a husband?" Libby asked.

"One single trait? That's hard. I don't know. Maybe intelligence."

Libby was ready for that. "A man might be very intelligent but cruel and cold. In fact, a very intelligent man can be crueler than one who is less intelligent."

"I don't know. What do you think is the most important trait for a husband to have?"

"Sparkle."

"Sparkle?" She looked astonished. "What do you mean? How do you know if a man has sparkle?"

"There is a spark between people. You can feel it, and see it in his eyes."

"Did Grandpa have it?"

Caught a little off guard, Libby said, "Yes," then wryly and very much under her breath added, "Some might say he still does."

Naida looked at her as though wondering if people that old could know the first thing about love. She finally said, "What was Grandpa like when he was young?"

The conversation had taken a personal turn, so Libby steered it to a lighter plane. "We sang together. He liked learning the songs from Scotland."

"Would you sing me some of those songs?"

For the next hour Libby sang songs in English and Gaelic, which she translated. Some had many verses and most told of romances. When she sang *Loch Lomond*, Naida asked if she had ever seen that lake. By now quite deep into her past, Libby described the beautiful woods and trails around it and told her about Maggie and how they had hiked and picnicked on the shores of Loch Lomond along with many other people.

In May, 1959, Naida packed to leave. She had decided to transfer to the University of California in Berkeley. Libby hugged her.

Hugging back, Naida said, "You healed me, Grandma, just like I knew you would." Then she climbed into the car of a student who was on his way to California.

Libby and Dad settled down to an even quieter retirement. The neighbor woman came in daily and the postman brought letters from the children. In addition Connie, Grace and Donald came to visit. In the fall Libby and Dad boarded the train for New Haven, Connecticut, to visit Bob and his family.

While they were in New Haven Connie phoned. "Mom, Laurence Hill called last night. I tried to call, but no one answered."

"We were out. What has happened?" With a sinking feeling, she knew before she heard the words."

"Marjorie passed away. She had a stroke. The service will be tomorrow."

Libby wouldn't be able to attend the funeral, but that couldn't be helped. Marjorie would have understood. *I am the last of the seven*, Libby realized.

—

Five months later, on Friday night, March 18, 1960, Dad was suddenly stuck by a sharp pain in his chest. He called out to Libby. Seeing his excruciating pain, she at once called for an ambulance and set about trying to make him comfortable. He was treated for a heart attack, though a recent examination had shown his heart to be very healthy. Libby tried to express her doubts to the doctor, but soon his pain was relieved and he seemed to be resting quite well.

Still very worried, she called all six of her children early on Saturday morning, telling them of Dad's attack. Connie and Floyd had a free weekend. They drove at once from Walla Walla to see Dad and be with her. Arthur, in Idaho Falls phoned Donald. They decided that Arthur would drive to Salmon, and after Donald's church service on Sunday, they would drive together to Caldwell. With Dad improving, Libby thought that would be all right.

Bob and Lee were nearing the end of their course in Chinese, having become very fluent. When they received the phone call, Dad seemed stabilized. Libby said she would keep them advised of any change. She called David in Tillamook and told him the same thing, and Grace, in Portland.

On Sunday morning Dad continued to rest well and was served the usual hospital breakfast. Almost immediately after his breakfast he suffered more severe chest pain. Nothing seemed to relieve him and his condition became critical. Emergency tests revealed that his problem had not been with his heart. His esophagus had ruptured. He was dying of the same thing that had killed his father. Connie and Libby sat at his bedside, neither of them able to believe this was happening. Floyd set about calling the other children but with mixed results in getting through to them. Donald and all of his family had left home for church. He was getting ready to begin the church service when the word came that Dad's condition was critical.

He and Arthur left for Caldwell right after the church service, before 1:00 p.m. They drove fast hoping that even if Dad couldn't be saved they would be able to be with him for a last visit and be there to comfort Mom. Bob and Lee arrived on a flight from New Haven, Connecticut, on Monday. They had planned a trip west in another month, before leaving for Kuala Lumpur. They had never expected the visit west would be to attend a funeral.

Dad did not live long after the lethal breakfast. He was pronounced dead just after 2:00 p.m, March 20. It was Libby's birthday. In Tillamook and Portland it was only 1:00 p.m. By the time Floyd was able to reach David and Grace, he could tell them only that Dad had died. Of all the children, only Connie was there to close her beloved father's eyes and be with her mother when she faced the hard fact that her companion of fifty years had left her.

The family had all been looking forward to a joyous gathering at Christmas to celebrate the fiftieth anniversary of that quiet little wedding in the McQueen apartment in Salt Lake City in 1910. The death had been so sudden that it was difficult to grasp the reality of it. Instead of a Christmas-Anniversary party, they were all gathering on

March 20 to plan for the funeral.

Dad had established himself as a cherished grandfather. His grand-children loved him. With his expertise, he helped several of them gain an appreciation of, and some ability in, the sport of trout fishing. One of Connie's boys who had often helped him catch grasshoppers, a favorite fishing bait, affectionately called him Grandhopper. One of the subdued conversations among the several family members was the discussion of summer plans that had been made with him, and now would never come to pass.

Libby spoke little. Practiced in grieving with Scottish stoicism over a lifetime of many disappointments and hardships, she kept her weeping private. For once she was unable to find any humor in the situation, so she limited her comments to practical matters that needed to be attended to. In pleasant times she had always been a happy, sociable and outspoken person. In times of grief she kept her feelings a private matter between herself and God. While family members spent some time sharing memories of times past, Libby, who normally would have joined in the discussions, listened. Perhaps her mind was far away, walking with her handsome young man on a beautiful autumn day in the Salt Lake Valley. Perhaps she was simply numb with grief and loss.

She drew comfort from the willingness of her children to take over the mundane funeral arrangements. The usual legal matters that needed to be cared for she left in the hands of Arthur, the attorney. Three sons who were Methodist ministers and two daughters who were school teachers could certainly plan a funeral.

The large Caldwell Methodist Church was filled for the service. Dad had been popular and widely known in his state-wide work. He still had friends at the State House in Boise, and was very well liked by fellow members of the church. Mom's long involvement as a member of the Methodist Annual Conference had produced many friends among the clergy. In addition to her sons, there were twelve other ministers present at the service. Flower arrangements came from many areas of the state and beyond.

She sat in the front of the church surrounded by all of her six children, their husbands and wives and a number of the older grandchildren. She wore her favorite black dress, the same one that she had worn at a number of weddings. Through the years she had often said: "The Scotch do not show their emotions." She was true to her heritage. Grandchildren wept quietly, sons and daughters dabbed at their eyes with their handkerchiefs. Libby sat solemn and tearless.

The minister spoke highly of Dad. Fine music was furnished by church members who had known him. He was buried in the plot he and Libby had selected in the Canyon Hill Cemetery, on a rise of ground with a sweeping view of the Boise River on one side, and, appropriately, a fine well tended field on the other, a field that late in March was being prepared for the planting of sugar beets. It seemed right that he should be laid to rest between two sights that had always brought joy to his heart—a trout stream and a field of sugar beets that promised a good harvest.

Soon after the funeral the six sons and daughters had to return to their homes and their work. Dad's work had taken him away from home for days at a time, and spending time alone was not a new experience for Libby. But now she seemed somewhat dazed by the sudden change in her life. Strong willed, she had always made the decisions and Art had agreed with them, but now, without him to discuss things with or give his approval, she seemed at a loss concerning the future. Her life had emptied. The spark had gone out. Without him she found that she was much less interested in various church and political activities. She had no children living near Caldwell, and felt no desire to remain in Caldwell where she had a host of friends and could have been involved in numerous activities. This might have been the best therapy for her loneliness, but she chose to leave.

As a memorial to Dad, Libby arranged for a large painting—disciples on the road to Emmaus on the first Easter morning—to be placed in the narthex of the Caldwell Church. Then she found a renter for her house and accepted an invitation from Connie and Floyd to live with them. Moving to Walla Walla, she lived in an apartment very near Connie's family.

She had some good years there, reading, writing poetry and attending the Methodist Church with Connie and Floyd, but she felt limited in her involvement. She had always been a leader in any group in which she participated. Now she couldn't seem to get up enough interest to become a leader, and she had never enjoyed being a passive member. She missed having Dad to share things with her. Connie was good company and did her best to make life interesting, but the spark never returned.

For almost fifty years Libby had been the mistress of her life. Or so it had seemed. Now she fully realized the extent to which her life had been a partnership. None of her audiences had been more appreciative than Dad. And when she looked at her life and saw how dependent she was on other people and how drained she was of the humor to alleviate it for them, she felt very ill at ease and discontented. Then Floyd took a new job in Tacoma, Washington, and she didn't want to move there.

She decided she should live with David, who was now serving a church in Oregon City. His fifth daughter, Roberta, born in 1961, was a delightful four-year old and the four older granddaughters were interesting, Colleen preparing to go to college to become a teacher. Perhaps so many granddaughters and a church where her son was the pastor would rekindle some of the dead feeling in her life. But after several years she recognized that the role of the pastor's mother was an awkward one for her. She had always been free to criticize the sermons—one of her favorite intellectual activities—and this would not do where her son was pastor. Furthermore, she felt less comfortable imposing upon a daughter-in-law than a daughter.

Then David was appointed to serve the Caldwell Church, and she made the move with them back to Caldwell. She was immensely proud of having a son serving the large church where she and Dad had been

1966, Salmon, Idaho. Libby at the wedding of Granddaughter
Heather Smith and Lynn Thomas

members. But her health had failed considerably and she felt keenly that she was a burden in the home of David and Alice. She tried living for awhile with a woman in Nampa who maintained an assisted living facility for several older people, but her independent spirit found this too confining. She spent some time with Arthur in Idaho Falls, where she got along with LuRee but felt that she was in the home of a stranger. She felt extremely restless. She was needing the kind of care that it was difficult for any of her children to give her.

Donald, after twenty years in Salmon, had been appointed to a church in Boise. She decided to move to a care center in Boise, with him living nearby where he and Betty and their children could visit often. She lived there discontentedly for two years. Her life had been so full, she had been so independent, that in any well regulated convalescent facility she felt a prisoner. They wouldn't let her leave and they wouldn't allow her to eat anything with sugar. When in charge of herself, she had dealt with her diabetes by self testing and medication.

Her short-term memory began to fail. There were times when small pinpoint strokes robbed her of rational facilities, and she was painfully aware of it. At other times she had all her faculties. On one occasion, returning to the center from a visit with Donald and Betty, she looked at the sign on the front lawn and asked, "Why do they call it a convalescent center? The word convalescent implies that one is recovering. No one ever convalesces here."

On Tuesday morning, May 14, 1974, the director of Boise Convalescent Center called Donald. Mom had gotten up, dressed, eaten breakfast in the dining room, and gone back to her room to rest. Shortly after breakfast a nurse had gone to the room to give her some medication. She was lying peacefully on her bed, taking a nap from which she would never awaken.

The death certificate listed congestive heart failure as the cause of death. The tired old heart that had served her so well for eighty-seven years, including over fifty years of very high blood pressure, had given up and rested. There was no sign of suffering or a struggle.

Donald had very mixed feelings as he drove to the Convalescent Center. He would miss his mother. The center was near his home and he had tried to stop by to see her almost every day, even when she forgot the visits and asked why he never came to see her. He enjoyed sharing family news with her; he cherished being able to ask her questions about the past and having the benefit of her memory for things that had happened long ago. He had tried to encourage her to write the story of her life. She had managed to write a number of disconnected but interesting bits that were found scattered in her room. One such piece of paper held this message:

> Six wonderful children—God in his infinite wisdom, through all my trials, fears, and struggles, has guided me in the right paths.

That was a truth she knew deep in her heart. She had spent a great deal of time asking herself the question that, two years earlier, visiting Naida had asked: What would you do differently if you had your life to live over?

"Have more children," she had answered without hesitation. To Naida's incredulous "Really?" and her mention of the problems caused by overpopulation, Libby explained that her children did not contribute to the problems of the world. On the contrary, they were in the business of finding solutions. She knew she had been a good mother.

But at the same time she felt so miserable and found her life to be such a burden that Donald rejoiced that morning, knowing that she was being set free from all that she had found so unbearable.

A year earlier doctors had told him that she would die without a surgery that would mean her constantly wearing a catheter and collection bag. It would be attached to her bed at night and to her leg in the daytime when she moved about, which she did quite often. She hated "the thing" and constantly worried that it was overflowing. By her insistent requests to have it checked when it didn't need to be, she annoyed the nurses and created poor relations with many of them. Her enjoyment of life had deteriorated so much that Donald had often felt guilty for having allowed the doctors to do the surgery.

Heidi, a senior in high school would miss her grandmother. She had visited the home often. For a grandchild or stranger, Mom was always able to put on a pleasant face and tell fascinating and funny stories about her past. Heidi had shared with her grandmother her plans to become a veterinarian and would later enjoy telling people about her grandmother's reply:

"You could be a real doctor. Why would you want to work with filthy beasts?"

So emotions were mixed—the sadness of loss and the gladness of knowing her troubled spirit was no longer captive.

Phone calls went out and the family gathered, all of her six children, their spouses, numerous grandchildren and several of Dad's relatives from Utah. On Libby's side her nephew Laurence Hill came from Vancouver, British Columbia, a barrister and Marjorie's only child.

The funeral was held on Friday in the Caldwell Methodist Church. A retired minister who had been their pastor in Rupert when Mom and Dad and some of the children had been active came to conduct the service. Six other ministers served as pall bearers.

A great number of friends in the Caldwell Church made the service almost a duplicate of Dad's funeral fourteen years earlier. All six of her children, with spouses and many of her grandchildren, sat together in the front of the church, joined by Laurence Hill. It was a large family group.

Libby's parents, John and Elizabeth Symon, had raised seven children. All of these seven combined had raised only seven children, of which Libby, their seventh child, had raised six. At the service all of those six would "rise up and call her blessed" (Proverbs 31:28).

In mid May the well kept Canyon Hill Cemetery is beautiful. The abundant shade trees have their full compliment of summer leaves.

From its elevation above the Boise River one can see for miles. In this peaceful setting Libby was laid to rest beside the companion with whom she had shared so many hard times and good times, harmonious duets and occasional discords, defeats and triumphs.

In many ways they were a most unlikely couple. In every respect Perth, Scotland, is a very long way from Union, Utah. But the mysterious power that had brought them together had so tuned them, that like two very different strings on Art's mandolin, they had blended together to make a wistful and haunting harmony that would not soon be forgotten by any who had heard it played.

EPILOGUE

Terry, Mont.
March 18, 1943

Dearest Mom,

Tonight I walked up to the drugstore to see if I could buy some gift for your birthday. The store was closed for the first time in many weeks so my gift shall have to be in the form of this letter.

I know that you do not think highly of your birthday, but even though you may not, it is a significant date for six of us. It is significant because it is your day and a day in which we turn our thoughts to you. It is a wonderful thing, as I grow a little older, to be able to view you and what you stand for more objectively. I know that you have been far more than just a parent to me. You have been a teacher, an example, and a courageous mother. Above all else, though, you have been an uncompromising Christian. I know that I am in no position to appreciate the hardships you must have gone through. There must have been many, many trying and heartbreaking experiences that you suffered through for your ideals. I stand in awe when I think of you as a girl of eighteen venturing to this country alone, seeking your fortune out in the West. The courage it took then and later after you were married and had a family to watch over. The early days of the farm — the courage it took to come through all these things, I deeply admire. This isn't meant to be sentimental flattery, Mom, because I mean it and there are five others who do too. We all deeply admire you as an individual as well as being a most wonderful mother. If it were not for you and your uncompromising attitudes for those things which are right, I would not be witnessing for a Christian cause in

C.P.S. Your influence upon our lives has been profound and shall be until we die: Don is a minister. Art certainly has high ideals and is gifted with a wonderful mind. Grace is interested in those causes you have been championing. Connie shall be a good and a Christian mother because of you. Bob has every advantage and from all reports, is making use of them. As for me, I sincerely hope that I can capture for myself that spirit which has made you so good and strong through the years. So to a wonderful mother it's "Happy Birthday."

All my love,
David

After-words

GRACE ELIZABETH, 1912-1999, married Paul Szigethy in 1963. In 1977 she retired from a distinguished teaching career, but continued to take leadership roles in social and political causes in Portland, ultimately working to better conditions for the elderly. Grace died November 6, 1999, of breast cancer and other problems, and was entombed at Fir Lawn Cemetery in Hillsboro, Oregon.

Grace's son Robert Jenkins, an engineer, has long worked with a company that produces highly technical medical devices. He lives with his wife in Beaverton, Oregon.

Grace has three grandchildren.

CONSTANCE ALICE, b. 1914, lives with Floyd Anderson, her husband of sixty-one years, in Tacoma, Washington. Multiple Sclerosis forced her to terminate her teaching career. Their two sons live in Washington state:

Laurence, "Larry," retired from a long teaching career, and now enjoys repairing the diesel engines of school busses;

David retired as regional director of wildlife for the Alaska Department of Fish and Game and now teaches mathmatics in a college near his parents.

"Connie" has five grandchildren and one great-grandchild.

ARTHUR LAURENCE, 1916-1988, served for thirty-nine years as City Attorney of Idaho Falls, Idaho. Two months before his death from colon cancer he flew to Washington state to represent his city at the wrap-up of the notable Washington Power case. He died July 24, 1988, and was buried in Rose Hill Cemetery in Idaho Falls. His three children in California:

(Arthur) Roger is an artist and singer;

(Alice) Naida West retired from college teaching and consulting, and now writes and publishes full-time;

Marguerite Flower recently retired from a teaching career.

Together they have six children and five grandchildren.

Arthur's three children in Idaho Falls:

Christine Southwick is an active real estate agent with three children and two grandchildren;

Kathleen Smith works in property management;

Lisa Smith has had careers in a medical clinic and in insurance.

Additionally Arthur had four stepdaughters.

Arthur has nine grandchildren and seven great-grandchildren.

DON IAN, b. 1918, retired as a Methodist minister and, while pastoring at Salmon, Idaho, owner and operator of a small cattle ranch. He is now a full-time author who lives with his wife Betty of sixty years. They recently left Boise, where he had his last church, and moved back to Salmon. He is the author of six books. Their three children:

Heather Thomas is an active rancher in Salmon, a magazine journalist, and author of twelve books;

Rockwell is a radio engineer in Boise;

Heidi Smith is a veterinarian who raises endurance horses in Tendoy, Idaho, near Salmon.

Don has six grandchildren and five great-grandchildren.

DAVID SYMON, 1924-2001, retired from the Methodist ministry in 1986. Known for his independent thinking and work with troubled young people, he lived in Nampa, Idaho, with Alice, his wife of fifty-five years, until he died on April 21, 2001, of complications of surgery and other problems. Services were held in the Nampa Southside Church in Nampa, where he began his ministry fifty-five years earlier. Their five daughters:

Colleen Smith and Davina Hartley have active careers as teachers and administrators in Washington state;

Elizabeth "Liz" Boerl is a Methodist minister in Boise, Idaho;

Deborah "Debbie" Meyer is an excutive secretary, living in Milwaukie, Oregon;

Roberta Cason is raising a family in North Bend, WA, and woking for Microsoft.

David has twelve grandchildren and one great-grandchild.

ROBERT LINDSAY, b. 1931, returned from his mission in Kuala Lumpur, Malaysia, studied law at the University of Idaho and practiced law in Nampa, Idaho, until he nearly won an election for U.S. Senator against a popular incumbent. He moved his family to Washington D.C., where he worked for a congressman. Later he moved his family to Florida, where he developed property and resumed preaching. Now he lives near Pulaski, Tennessee, with his wife Eraleen "Lee" in an alternative community of his design and construction. Their three children:

Susan is a musician presently living in Illinois;

Patricia is an artist working in Tennessee;

Arthur works in landscape design in Florida.

"Bob" has six grandchildren.

THE TWENTY GRANDCHILDREN of Elizabeth and Arthur, some of whom are now retired, include eight teachers and professors; four workers in numbers, medicine, science and mathematics; several workers in literature and words; and at least ten noted public speakers, entertainers, and singers. These categories are nonexclusive. A number of the grandchildren are multi-talented. Many of the forty-one great-grandchildren are following the lead of their forbearers.